English Language and Literature

for the IB Diploma

Brad Philpot

Cambridge University Press's mission is to advance learning, knowledge and research worldwide.

Our IB Diploma resources aim to:
- encourage learners to explore concepts, ideas and topics that have local and global significance
- help students develop a positive attitude to learning in preparation for higher education
- assist students in approaching complex questions, applying critical-thinking skills and forming reasoned answers.

CAMBRIDGE
UNIVERSITY PRESS

CAMBRIDGE
UNIVERSITY PRESS

University Printing House, Cambridge CB2 8BS, United Kingdom

Cambridge University Press is part of the University of Cambridge.

It furthers the University's mission by disseminating knowledge in the pursuit of education, learning and research at the highest international levels of excellence.

www.cambridge.org
Information on this title: www.cambridge.org/9781107400344

First published 2011
7th printing 2014

Printed in the United Kingdom by Cambrian Printers Ltd

A catalogue record for this publication is available from the British Library

ISBN 978-1-107-40034-4 Paperback

Cambridge University Press has no responsibility for the persistence or accuracy of URLs for external or third-party internet websites referred to in this publication, and does not guarantee that any content on such websites is, or will remain, accurate or appropriate.

This material has been developed independently by the publisher and the content is in no way connected with nor endorsed by the International Baccalaureate.

Contents

Contents

Introduction

Who is this coursebook for?

This coursebook is for students of the English language and literature course that forms part of the International Baccalaureate (IB) Diploma Programme. It has been written specifically to provide support for students who are following the new IB Language A: language and literature course. This is one of three courses that can be taken to meet the Group 1 requirement of the IB; the others are the Language A: literature course and the Language A: literature and performance course.

Teachers and students following other courses or syllabuses may also find this coursebook useful as a pre-university course on English language and literature.

As a student following the IB language and literature course you are likely to be a native or near-native speaker of English. Both the course and coursebook differentiate between higher level (HL) and standard level (SL). Before you take the course at HL or SL, you will need to know what is expected of you and what you can expect from the course, depending on the level you are taking.

Standard level

At SL you must have an effective level of proficiency, meaning you can understand demanding texts with implicit meaning. You are able to speak English fluently and effectively for social, academic and professional purposes.

You will be required to commit at least 150 hours to your studies over a period of two academic years, if you are to grasp the core principles of this course and achieve successful exam results at SL. This coursebook offers an introduction to these core principles and concepts, which you and your teacher will want to add to, using other literary and non-literary texts.

Higher level

At HL you should be able to express ideas fluently and precisely. You should be able to construct coherent arguments in English if you are to take this course at higher level. Although you may have been placed in HL for reasons besides proficiency, keep in mind that examiners have higher expectations of HL students. The criteria and grade boundaries also distinguish between HL and SL.

In addition to starting out with the right level of proficiency, you will have to commit time to your studies. In order to fully grasp the concepts of the course and achieve good marks, you will need to spend at least 240 hours working on the course at HL. You will need to cover all of the core principles of SL and beyond.

What is the English language and literature course about?

In order to understand the fundamental principles of this course, try the following 'thought experiment'. Imagine for a moment that you are a Martian who comes to planet Earth. You happen to be an apt learner of languages and you quickly decipher the code known as English. You want to learn all that you can about the people who speak and write different varieties of English, so you study Anglophone cultures: those cultures and regions where English is spoken and written. You travel to places like the UK, Ireland, the USA, Jamaica, West Africa, Australia, Singapore, India and many more. You pick up scraps of evidence, or 'texts', that tell you about the life of the Anglophone world. This collection of texts consists of poems, speeches, propaganda posters, short stories, personal letters and news articles. Through your studies of these texts you begin to piece together a rough picture of what is called 'culture', which is to say the common values of a society and what it regards as literary arts.

The Martian perspective helps you approach various texts with objectivity and curiosity. More traditional perspectives on the subject matter of this course will also prove useful; concepts from the fields of linguistics, journalism, advertising and literary studies are relevant to the content of this course. Generally speaking the course is designed to increase your literacy skills, so that you can offer critical responses to a broad range of texts.

The coursebook is divided into four parts, which correspond to the four distinct parts of the course.

Part 1 Language in cultural context

In this first part of the course you will ask yourself questions such as *Why are there different varieties of English? What do people wish to achieve through learning and speaking English?* and *What is intended in a particular text?* These questions cover a range of topics, from language and power to dialects and social values. In this part of the course there is a strong emphasis on close reading as you develop textual analysis skills. By examining a number of non-fiction texts, you will come to understand how concepts such as audience, purpose, theme, content, tone, mood, stylistic devices and structure help us construct meaning.

Part 2 Language and mass communication

In part 2 you will continue your study of texts and begin to understand how they are disseminated through various media. *What constitutes good journalism? How are digital media changing the ways in which we interact?* These are just a couple of questions you will answer in this part of the course. By looking at the mechanics of different texts, exploring rhetorical devices and studying advertising techniques, you will begin to understand how language is used to persuade, inform and entertain.

Part 3 Literature: texts and contexts

In part 3 you will study the contexts in which literary texts are written and received. You will establish a greater awareness of the relationship between writer, reader, culture and text. This will be valuable as you begin to research the contexts in which your part 3 literary texts were written, and you explore the different ways in which these texts can be read. Many of the texts in Part 3 of the coursebook have been taken from the prescribed list of authors (PLA). Others have been taken from the list of prescribed literature in translation (PLT). Reading texts in translation will help you broaden your scope on literature and culture.

Part 4 Literature: critical study

The word *culture* means both the shared values of a society and the arts which that society holds in high esteem. In part 4 you will ask *What makes English poetic?* In this part of the course you are expected to gain a greater understanding of the mechanics of literature, exploring various literary devices, such as imagery, irony and narrative voice. Through a study of these devices you will gain a greater understanding and appreciation of the texts you are studying in part 4. Since your part 4 texts have to come from the PLA, this coursebook has many examples of texts from this list.

How is the course assessed?

	Part 1	Part 2	Part 3		Part 4	
Title	Language in cultural context	Language and mass communication	Literature: texts and contexts		Literature: critical study	
Focus	The English language, culture, identity, language and power, textual analysis, close reading skills	The media, journalism, propaganda, rhetoric, advertising techniques, bias, sensationalism	Genre, movement, approaches to literature, traditions of literary criticism		Literary devices (e.g. imagery, plot, conflict, characterisation, setting, symbolism, irony)	
Texts	miscellaneous non-fiction	miscellaneous non-fiction	**SL** 1 × PLT 1 × free choice	**HL** 1 × PLA 1 × PLT 1 × free choice	**SL** 2 × PLA	**HL** 3 × PLA
Assessment	Written tasks 1 (SL / HL) and 2 (HL only)					
	Further oral activities Paper 1		Paper 2		Individual oral commentary	

PLA   prescribed list of authors

PLT   prescribed literature in translation list

free choice   at SL your school's free choice of text must have been written originally in English; at HL the school's free text may be a text in translation

In the table above, you will notice that each of the four parts is assessed in a different way. Your work will be assessed both internally and externally. External assessment includes the written tasks, Paper 1 and Paper 2, which are sent to an official examiner for assessment. Internal assessment includes the oral exams, which are assessed in school by your teacher. In the end you will receive a grade from 7 to 1, where 7 is excellent and 1 is a failing grade.

This coursebook offers several examples of student responses to exam questions, transcriptions of oral presentations and examples of good practice. In order to learn from these, you should look at them in light of the requirements and criteria for each type of assessment. The outlines of course content, assessment requirements and criteria that follow are based on the specifications in the official IB Language A: language and literature guide. While these outlines are intended for quick and easy reference, the official document should be consulted for a more detailed understanding of the course.

Weight of assessment

External assessment	Paper 1: Textual analysis / comparative textual analysis	25%	
	Paper 2: Essay	25%	**70%**
	Written task(s)	20%	
Internal assessment	Individual oral commentary	15%	**30%**
	Further oral activity	15%	

Paper 1: Textual analysis / comparative textual analysis

The Paper 1 exam is different for SL and HL students. At SL Paper 1 consists of a textual analysis and lasts 1 hour and 30 minutes. At HL it consists of a comparative textual analysis and lasts for 2 hours. The exam will account for 25% of your final grade.

At SL you will be asked to analyse one of two unseen texts. These texts will be non-literary texts and may include images, such as advertisements or brochures. Your analysis will comment on the intended audience and purpose of your chosen text, as well as an exploration of other aspects, such as stylistic devices. There is a guiding question for each of the two texts, which will help you focus on a relevant aspect of analysis.

At HL you will be asked to analyse one pair from two pairs of unseen texts. These texts may be either literary or non-literary, though you will never be asked to compare two literary texts. One of the texts may include images, such as press photos or cartoons. Each pair of texts is thematically linked and invites comparative commentary. In your analysis you will comment on different aspects of the texts, such as their intended audiences and purposes. You will also be expected to identify and explain the significance of stylistic devices in the texts.

There is no word count, though you are expected to explore all aspects of the text, or texts, in depth. Although the exam is based on unseen texts, it is a good idea to prepare for this exam by practising writing textual analyses in class, with and without time constraints. (See Chapter 2, pages 56–66, for further guidance on Paper 1.)

Criteria

	Summary of descriptors	**Marks available**
Criterion A	*Understanding of the text(s)* For maximum marks, your understanding of the text(s) is very perceptive and you place the text(s) in its context. Your analysis is supported with examples from the text.	5
Criterion B	*Understanding of the use and effects of stylistic features* For maximum marks, you can identify many stylistic devices and understand the effects they have on the reader.	5
Criterion C	*Organisation and development* For maximum marks, your analysis is well organised and structured. You integrate examples well into your commentary and use signposts to indicate the relation between ideas. Your arguments are well developed.	5

Criterion D	*Language* For maximum marks, your writing style is clear and exact. You demonstrate an effective range of vocabulary and your use of grammar is appropriate and accurate.	5
Total		**20**

Paper 2: Essay

In part 3 you explore literary texts in context, two at standard level and three at higher level. Paper 2 consists of six unseen questions, of which you have to answer one. At SL Paper 2 lasts 1 hour and 30 minutes. At HL it lasts for 2 hours. It is marked by an external examiner and accounts for 25% of your final grade.

While the six essay questions are the same at SL and HL, the responses from HL students are expected to have more complexity and depth. At both SL and HL you are expected to refer to at least two of the literary texts that you have read for part 3. You are not allowed to take the texts you have studied into the exam with you.

The questions may be on the relationship between the texts you have studied, their authors, the periods in which they were written or the styles they employ. Your essay must be structured and coherent and it must answer the question you have chosen. (See Chapter 6, pages 148–159, for further guidance on Paper 2.)

Criteria

	Summary of descriptors	Marks available
Criterion A	*Knowledge and understanding* For maximum marks, you demonstrate a perceptive understanding of the texts and show how contextual knowledge influences the ways the texts are read and interpreted.	5
Criterion B	*Response to the question* For maximum marks, you show that you have understood all of the implications of the question. Your essay answers the question with much focus and insight.	5
Criterion C	*Understanding the use and effects of stylistic features* For maximum marks, you are very aware of the effects of the stylistic devices on the reader. You support your understanding of the literary texts with good examples.	5
Criterion D	*Organisation and development* Your essay is structured coherently and illustrations are well integrated. Your arguments are developed and the essay follows a logical sequence.	5
Criterion E	*Language* For maximum marks, your use of English is effective and appropriate. Your use of grammar and spelling is accurate and your use of vocabulary is varied.	5
Total		**25**

Written tasks

You will be asked to keep a portfolio of assignments, known as written tasks. There are two kinds of written task, referred to as written task 1 and written task 2.

Written task 1

Written task 1 pertains to students at both levels. It is a creative writing assignment of 800–1000 words in which you demonstrate an understanding of both the course content as a whole and a particular text type. You can write different types of texts, ranging from news articles to brochures. Notice that written task 1 is not an essay or a polemic piece that expresses your opinion. Examples in this course book of written task 1 responses include a letter to a government organisation (pages 24–25) and a tabloid newspaper feature (page 134) reporting on the events in a Shakespeare play.

Although there is room for your own creativity and expression in written task 1, make sure you meet the requirements (see below) and make your work relevant to your course material. You must also write a rationale of 200–300 words for each written task 1, explaining to the examiner the thought process behind your composition.

Written task 2

For written task 2 at higher level you have to write a critical response of 800–1000 words to a text, either literary or non-literary, that you have studied in class. Your response must answer one of six prescribed questions. These questions, which you will find in the IB guide for Language A: language and literature (see pages 45–46), are very general and relate to three areas of study.

- In the first area of study (reader, culture and text) you explore the contexts in which your text was written and read:
  1. How could the text be read and interpreted differently by two different readers?
  2. If the text had been written in a different time or place or language or for a different audience, how and why might it differ?
- In the second area of study (power and priviledge) you examine the representation of social groups, genders and/or minorities in particular texts:
  1. How and why is a social group represented in a particular way?
  2. Which social groups are marginalised, excluded or silenced within the text?
- In the third area of study (text and genre) you write about the significance of form, structure or genre to a particular text:
  1. How does the text conform to, or deviate from, the conventions of a particular genre, and for what purpose?
  2. How has the text borrowed from other texts, and with what effects?

Your critical response should be in the style of an academic essay with well developed arguments, an introduction and a conclusion. You also have to fill in a form that outlines your critical response, including the prescribed question, the title of the text or texts that you have analysed and a few key points that state the focus of your response. This outline will be part of the assessment (see below).

The written task or tasks that you send for external assessment will account for 20% of your final grade.

Throughout your studies you will keep a portfolio of written tasks. At SL you must include a minimum of three tasks in this portfolio. One should reflect your understanding of part 1 and another should relate to part 2. For the literary parts of the syllabus you must have written at least one written task. Two months before the exams you will select, together with your teacher, which one you will send to the examiner.

HL students must include at least four tasks in their portfolio, one corresponding to each part of the syllabus. Two months prior to the exams, HL students submit two written tasks. One must relate to the non-literary parts of the syllabus. The other must relate to the literary parts of the syllabus. One of these final tasks for submission must be a written task 1. The other must be a written task 2.

Requirements

		Part 1	Part 2	Part 3	Part 4
SL	Minimum number of tasks in portfolio	1	1	1	
	To submit			1	
HL	Minimum number of tasks in portfolio	1	1	1	1
	To submit		1		1

- All written tasks must be 800–1000 words. For written task 1, this word count excludes the rationale, which must be 200–300 words.
- Although the written tasks are externally assessed, your teacher can give you general feedback with an indication of a grade.
- At HL, one of the two tasks submitted must be a written task 2. It can be from either the language or the literature parts of the syllabus.

Criteria

	Written task 1 (SL and HL)	Written task 2 (HL)	Marks available
Criterion A	*Rationale* For maximum marks, your rationale clearly explains the relation between what you have studied as part of the course and your written task.	*Outline* For maximum marks, your outline offers a clear overview of your response.	2
Criterion B	*Task and content* For maximum marks, your task demonstrates an excellent understanding of the course. The type of text lends itself well to its content. Your task is a good example of a particular text type.	*Response to the question* For maximum marks, your analysis of your text, or texts, is insightful and very relevant to the prescribed question. You illustrate your arguments with relevant examples.	8
Criterion C	*Organisation* For maximum marks, your task should be a coherent piece with an effective structure.	*Organisation and argument* For maximum marks, you develop your ideas effectively with coherent structure.	5

Criterion D	*Language and style* For maximum marks, your style should be appropriate for the task that you have chosen. Your command of the English language is convincing.	*Language and style* For maximum marks, your use of English is very accurate, using a register that is appropriate and effective. You use a range of vocabulary and sentence structures.	5
Total			**20**

Individual oral commentary

In the individual oral commentary, you receive a passage of text of no longer than 40 lines from a work that you have studied for part 4 of Language A: language and literature. You also have two guiding questions that relate to both the language and the content of the passage. You must comment on the the theme of the passage, the stylistic devices employed and the use of language. Your approach must be well structured and coherent. Your teacher, or teachers, will assess your commentary, but a recording may be sent to an external moderator. The marks count towards 15% of your final grade. (See Chapter 8, pages 211–222, for further guidance on the individual oral commentary.)

Requirements

- You are not allowed to know in advance which passage you will have in the exam.
- Once you have been given your passage, you have 20 minutes to prepare your commentary. You cannot take any other notes in with you.
- You must speak for at least 10 minutes on the passage without interruption.
- After the 10th minute your teacher may engage in a discussion with you to clarify any points you made earlier.
- The moderator will not listen to anything after the 15th minute.
- Your commentary is recorded.

Criteria

	Summary of descriptors	**Marks available**
Criterion A	*Knowledge and understanding of the text or extract* For maximum marks, you show an in-depth understanding of the text. Your interpretation of the text shows evidence of critical thinking and insight. The examples you choose support your arguments well.	10
Criterion B	*Understanding of the use and effect of literary features* For maximum marks, you can identify the literary devices used in the text and understand their importance. Your commentary explores the effects of various devices on the text's audience.	10
Criterion C	*Organisation* For maximum marks, your commentary is well structured and coherent. Your examples are well integrated into the commentary.	5

Criterion D	*Language* For maximum marks, your use of English is fluent and appropriate. Your use of vocabulary is varied and effective. You speak in complete sentences in an academic register.	5
Total		**30**

Further oral activities

To test your understanding of parts 1 and 2 of the course, you will be asked to do at least two further oral activities. Each further oral activity should demonstrate your understanding of the course content. Your teacher helps you decide on the type of oral performance you will give. You may want to conduct a traditional presentation, have a debate with another student or take on a role of a participant in a discussion. Each student's performance is assessed individually by the teacher or teachers, who will be looking for a clear connection between the oral activity and what you have studied in the course. After you have finished your performance you have to write a reflective statement in which you comment on your efforts and your aims. The marks from your best performance will be sent to the IB and will account for 15% of your final grade.

Criteria

	Summary of descriptors	**Marks available**
Criterion A	*Knowledge and understanding of text(s) and subject matter or extract* For maximum marks, you are knowledgeable on the topics you explore and understand the significance of the text(s) within the context of these topics.	10
Criterion B	*Understanding of how language is used* For maximum marks, you show how language is used in the text(s) to create a certain effect on the reader. You can appreciate the use of various styles and structures for the purposes of the text(s).	10
Criterion C	*Organisation* For maximum marks, the structure of the activity is clear. If there are roles, they are clearly defined. Supporting examples are well integrated into the activity. It is organised coherently.	5
Criterion D	*Language* For maximum marks, your use of English is appropriate to the task. Your vocabulary is effective and varied.	5
Total		**30**

The IB learner profile

The International Baccalaureate (IB) has a learner profile outlining skills which are desirable in a student and which you should keep in mind throughout your course (and beyond!). This profile is integrated into the texts, sample student work and activities you will find in this coursebook. There are ten learning outcomes in the profile.

Inquirers

You will learn several approaches to studying texts, that turn you into an inquirer. Part 1 covers questions you should ask of texts, such as *Who is the target audience of this text? Why did the writer write this text?* and *What can be gathered from this text?* You will be encouraged to approach texts like a detective approaching a crime scene or an anthropologist approaching a foreign culture. In part 3 you research the contexts in which literary texts were written, learning more about different periods and places.

Knowledgeable

You must demonstrate understanding of the course content, moving from being inquiring to being knowledgeable. For the sample student responses in the coursebook the students carried out their own further research. For example, in the further oral activity on pages 211–222, in which two students discuss the English language, they refer to various texts, writers and organisations.

Thinkers

Throughout the coursebook you are asked to consider the effects of language. Since good thinkers look at the logic behind arguments, you will explore several persuasive texts, studying famous speeches such as Martin Luther King's 'I have a dream' (pages 41–42) and by deconstructing advertisements (pages 100–107). Thinkers explore possibilities and interpretations of texts, which is exactly what you will do with literary texts in parts 3 and 4 of the coursebook.

Communicators

This coursebook stresses the importance of literacy skills, which include not only the ability to identify various stylistic devices in a range of texts, but also the ability to actively use them. The sample written tasks are perhaps the best examples of students applying communication tools. Other assessments, such as the further oral activities, also show students as communicators.

Principled

The coursebook raises many discussion points and calls on you to give your opinion. Rather than prescribing a set of values, this book encourages you to explore your own. As you discuss various texts you will be asking yourself: *What is my opinion? What are my principles?*

Open-minded

Besides being principled, you will need to keep an open mind when exploring different texts. The coursebook contains texts in different varieties of English from all over the world and from many different periods. For example, you will read call centre information from India (pages 4–5) and an extract from a novel about the effects of apartheid in South Africa (pages 186–87), and you will analyse an advert for cigarettes, looking at the power of persuasive language.

Caring

An IB learner cares about human rights. Several texts in this coursebook draw your attention to injustices in the world, both past and present. You will glimpse the life of a prisoner in the infamous former gulag system of the USSR in *One Day in the Life of Ivan Denisovich* (pages 141–42) and the inequalities of the caste system in India in *Untouchable* (pages 169–70). Another text, a manifesto for a campaign against AIDS in Africa (page 106), shows a constructive solution to an urgent problem. The selection of texts in the coursebook will raise awareness of wider issues and social inequalities in the world.

Risk-takers

The sample student responses are good examples of students taking risks, be they in the analysis of a poem during an individual oral commentary or through a written task that criticises Ireland's language policies. In the sample Paper 1 answers (pages 58–67), students analyse texts out of context, and in one further oral activity (pages 30–32), some students take on the roles of influential people in media and politics in the USA. Throughout these assessments, you need not be concerned about giving the 'wrong' answer. Rather, focus on giving well-educated responses, backing up your arguments with coherent explanations and examples. Dare to make your own interpretations and express your own ideas.

Balanced

Just as you explore both sides of every argument in Theory of Knowledge (TOK), you will also have to show balance and consideration throughout this course. In the sample further oral commentaries, you will notice that the students show respect for each other and demonstrate a fair balance of opinion. Sometimes in an activity you may find that you are even asked to voice opinions that are not your own, for the purposes of the debate.

Reflective

The one who should be most involved in your learning experience is you. Use the assessment criteria to assess your own performances and discuss your progress with your teacher. In this coursebook you will see how the criteria are applied to students' work in the sample responses. If you compare your assessment of their work with the examiner's, you will become better at reflecting on your own work.

Academic honesty

As you will have understood by now, there is an emphasis in this course on originality and expressiveness. Because being original is challenging, especially in an age when so many ideas have been expressed and posted on the Internet, it can be tempting to cut corners. Besides the IB learner profile, you are asked to adhere to one more principle: academic honesty. Here are some tips on how to avoid plagiarism, stimulate originality and give your work more depth.

- Before you look on the Internet or at other students' work for help, ask yourself how you would respond to the task at hand. This will help stimulate creative and original thought.
- After you have consulted various sources, use critical judgement to assess their quality and usefulness. Just because something is on the Internet or in a book does not automatically give it validity or authority.
- If you use any ideas or statements from other people, be sure to reference your sources through footnotes or a bibliography. There are tools, both on-and offline, to help you reference your work efficiently and consistently. Spending time learning how to cite your sources is very worthwhile, as you will be rewarded with higher marks.

You should not, however, be discouraged from exploring the Internet for primary or secondary sources. There is a wealth of resources that you can learn from. Your teacher will help guide you through this forest of information. Remember that the task of research, far from being daunting, should be enjoyable and enlightening.

How to use this coursebook

The purpose of this coursebook is to supplement your school curriculum and complement the texts that have been chosen for more detailed study. The terms and concepts outlined in this book will help you explore both the literary and non-literary texts you are working on in class.

The coursebook is divided into four parts, which correspond to the four parts of the English language and literature course. Each part consists of two chapters, which each explore the course content from a different perspective. The chapters are divided into units, covering different topics within each chapter. Each unit is built around carefully chosen texts and activities, so that you can apply what you have learned. There are more activities which invite you to apply the theory you have learned to your own work. The final unit in most of the chapters concentrates on the appropriate form of assessment for that part of the course. The assessment-linked units include sample student responses, for both written and oral assessments, examiner's or teacher's comments and tips for maximising your success.

The coursebook also contains several special features, which are designed to add to your learning experience. These are outlined below.

Activities

The numbered activities in the coursebook provide a bridge between theory and practice. They aim to engage you both with the texts used in this book and with the texts you are studying throughout your course. The activities range from matching exercises and drawing Venn diagrams to comparing different texts, from individual work to whole-class discussions. You have plenty of opportunity to improve your skills and give your opinion. While many activities test your understanding of the content of this coursebook, you should approach them as starting points for further discussion and exploration of what you have covered in the course as a whole.

Figures

The pictures and diagrams in this coursebook aim to provide more than just a means of making the pages look attractive. They form the basis for discussion, help illustrate course content, give context to texts and create memorable learning experiences.

Key terms

Key terms are highlighted when they are first used (in bold green type or bold white in boxes). They are used in context and supported with illustrative examples. Nearby, on the same page or spread, you will find a clear definition of the key terms. In addition, a glossary of all the key terms can be found at the back of the book, so that you can refer back to a term and remind yourself of the definition.

Quotes

Quotes are useful for generating classroom discussion. You will find numerous short, thought-provoking quotes in the margin of this coursebook, offering further insight into the content of the main text. You may want to use some of them in your oral presentations and written work.

Discussion

Most texts are accompanied by discussion boxes. These quotes are designed to engage you with the text and stimulate critical analysis. While there are no right or wrong answers to these questions, you are encouraged to come up with informal answers. Classroom discussions provide good preparation for the internal oral assessment.

Further resources

These boxes will suggest where to go for a deeper understanding of a particular theory. Because different resources suit different students, you will find suggestions for a wide range of media, including books, websites, anthologies and documentaries.

Tips

The tip boxes are there to guide you with advice and effective learning strategies. They help you prepare for your exam and focus on the core content of the course.

Higher level (HL) activities

Higher level students are expected to go *deeper* into the course material than at standard level, exploring the same concepts with more examples, and *beyond* the SL course material – adding new concepts and theory to your repertoire. The higher level boxes give you suggestions for extensions to the core studies of the course, including challenging activities and engaging ideas. They encourage HL students to become owners of the course material by creating a library of texts, researching texts further and preparing work for other students in the class.

Extended essays

As part of the core curriculum of the IB Diploma, you have to write an extended essay of up to 4000 words. The extended essay boxes in this coursebook give you plenty of ideas and sample titles to help you narrow your focus and explore relevant topics in depth. If you choose not to write your extended essay on English language and literature, you will nevertheless find the ideas here useful for instigating classroom discussion.

Theory of knowledge (TOK) boxes

How do you know what you know? This question captures the essence of TOK, an essential part of the core curriculum of the IB Diploma. As you read through this coursebook, you will come across TOK boxes with many 'knowledge issues' – deeper, epistemological problems such as *Can we avoid cultural bias when analysing texts? What constitutes the 'literary arts'?* or *Do the media reflect or determine reality?* These questions and others you will meet in this coursebook serve as starting points for your TOK essay or presentation. You can explore these questions during your TOK or English language and literature lessons.

Now over to you!

You are about to embark on a rigorous and stimulating course, which will require many hours of study. To acquire the skills you need, you must practise working with texts and language regularly. This book will help you to refine those skills and point you in the right direction.

There will be rewards for your hard work. As well as achieving a good result in your exam, you will also develop an appreciation of the literary arts; an ability to identify different stylistic devices and structural elements in a wide range of texts; and a greater awareness of the world around you and how language is used for many different purposes.

1 Language in cultural context

Chapter 1 The English language

Objectives

By the end of this chapter you will be able to

- understand why the English language became a global language
- understand why there are so many varieties of English
- plan and write a part 1 written task 1
- plan and conduct a part 1 further oral activity.

In this book you will approach the English language as anthropologists. You may think of anthropologists as people who study little-known cultures, deep in the jungle, writing observations in a journal or making recordings of an obscure language; but anthropology is the study of all human cultures, including English-speaking cultures. As students of the English language, you should consider yourselves students of the Anglophone world, a vast network of diverse cultures of English speakers which is alive and buzzing around us today, from the street corners of Singapore to the cornfields of Iowa.

You will not have to look hard to find evidence to learn about these cultures. All you have to do is look at film posters, text messages, advertisements or websites. These are all carriers of cultural information, and for the sake of our study we will call these pieces of evidence 'texts'. You may think of texts as books, but you will be using a much broader definition of the term. Texts are the covers of magazines, the graffiti found on billboards, the poetry read in cafés, or the speeches of politicians. They are manuals, private letters and even Tweets. Texts are little mirrors that reflect cultural values. You should approach them with the same care and scrutiny that an anthropologist would use.

Your study of Anglophone cultures is going to take you around the world. While you may often think of English-speaking countries as places such as the United Kingdom (UK), the United States of America (USA) or Australia, you will also explore countries like Nigeria, South Africa and the Caribbean. You will have to learn more about these places in order to understand the meaning of the texts in this coursebook. Your goal will not be to make generalisations about Anglophone cultures (such as how the British are good at hiding their emotions – the famous British 'stiff upper lip') but to learn to appreciate how culture and context help shape the meaning of texts.

In this chapter you will find out how culture and context help shape the meaning of texts and tell us more about the Anglophone world. In Unit 1.1 you will explore the reasons why English has become the language of global communication. You will also see, in Unit 1.2, how different varieties of English reflect people's social, regional and historical background. At the end of the chapter you will find two assessment sections, with a sample part 1 written task and a sample part 1 further oral activity.

Anglophone world refers to the places in the world where English is spoken.

Text is any written work or transcribed piece of speech. For the sake of our studies, we will think of texts as clues that lead to a better understanding of one of the many Anglophone cultures, and these clues can range from e-mails to poems and from advertisements and posters to books.

Culture can have two different meanings:
1. It describes the values, goals, convictions and attitudes that people share in a society. Parts 1 and 2 of the IB English language and literature course are particularly interested in this aspect of culture.
2. It refers to the fine arts and a society's appreciation of the arts. Parts 3 and 4 of the course are particularly concerned with this, through a study of literature.

Context refers to the circumstances that surround the writing and the reading of a text. Trying to understand why a text was written (the purpose) and whom it was written for (the audience) are good starting points for understanding context.

Quick Quiz

1 **How many people speak English as a native language?**
   a 200 million   c 600 million
   b 400 million   d 1 billion

2 **How many people speak English as an additional language?**
   a 300 million   c 600 million
   b 400 million   d 1 billion

3 **How many people are learning English today as a foreign language?**
   a 300 million   c 600 million
   b 400 million   d 2 billion

'There is no retreat from English as the world language; no retreat from an English-speaking world.'
Sir Shridath Ramphal (1928–)

Answers
1 c. According to the Wolfram Alpha database 600 million people speak English as a native language.
2 c and d. Between 600 million and 1 billion people speak English as an additional language, depending on the source of the information and the definition of 'additional language'.
3 d. Over 2 billion people are learning English, according to Jay Walker (see the further resources suggestion on page 6).

Unit 1.1 English as a global language

The number of English language users in the world is expanding as rapidly today as it has for the past 400 years. Between 1602, when Elizabeth was queen, and 1952, when Elizabeth II became queen, the number of native speakers of English increased 50-fold, from 7 to 250 million speakers. At the height of its power it was claimed that the sun never set on the British Empire. In fact, the sun still does not set on the English-speaking world. Today there are more people who speak English as an additional language than there are native speakers of English, and English is the only language for which that is true. It is the world's number one **lingua franca**, which is to say that it is spoken by many people who do not share a native language.

Marshall McLuhan, the Canadian philosopher and writer, once said that the world is becoming a 'global village'. He was referring to the way in which people with similar interests are reaching out and making contact with each other, forming networks through various media and a common language. English has become the common language that facilitates this process of **convergence**. In linguistics, the term *convergence* refers to the phenomenon of people coming together, making connections and accommodating for each other through their use of language.

Of all the languages in the world, why has the English language become the world's number one lingua franca? Why is English the language of the global village? We will explore three answers to these questions, focusing on the British Empire, economics and fashion.

The British Empire

Let us begin our study of the global nature of English by reading an extract (Text 1.1) from a communication phrase book from the International Maritime Organization (IMO). It demonstrates the interconnected nature of McLuhan's global village and the need for English as a lingua franca.

Text 1.1 *IMO Standard Marine Communication Phrases*, International Maritime Organization, 2001

In order to prevent miscommunication and accidents in harbours and seas around the world, the IMO has been developing standard methods for communication since 1973. According to the International Convention on Standards of Training, Certification and Watchkeeping, officers of ships over a certain size are required to speak and understand Standard Marine Communication Phrases (SMCP) in English. The SMCP was designed for native and non-native speakers of English in such a way that it reduces the risk of any miscommunication. Text 1.1 is from a book used by Dutch seafarers containing many Dutch-to-English translations of maritime vocabulary and expressions, all of which have been approved by the IMO.

MAYDAY
– THIS IS TWO-ONE-ONE-TWO-THREE-NINE-SIX-EIGHT-ZERO MOTOR VESSEL "BIRTE" CALL SIGN DELTA ALPHA MIKE KILO
– POSITION SIX TWO DEGREES ONE ONE DECIMAL EIGHT MINUTES NORTH
– ZERO ZERO SEVEN DEGREES FOUR FOUR MINUTES EAST
– I AM ON FIRE AFTER EXPLOSION
– I REQUIRE FIRE FIGHTING ASSISTANCE
– SMOKE NOT TOXIC OVER

Figure 1.1 Marshall McLuhan (1911–80) popularised the term *global village*.

Figure 1.2 The Port of Hong Kong is a modern-day example of the influence of the British Empire on the language of seafaring.

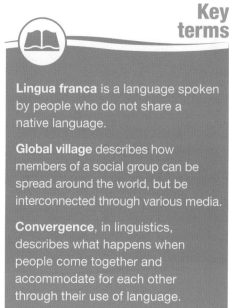

Key terms

Lingua franca is a language spoken by people who do not share a native language.

Global village describes how members of a social group can be spread around the world, but be interconnected through various media.

Convergence, in linguistics, describes what happens when people come together and accommodate for each other through their use of language.

Text 1.1 could be spoken anywhere on the open seas or in any port around the world. How did English become the language of the seas? If you look at Figure 1.3, a map of the English-speaking world, you can see that many ports, from Hong Kong to Kingston, are historically connected to the UK through the British Empire. In your studies of the Anglophone world, it is important to recognise the historical significance of the British Empire. It is not difficult to see why English became the language of the shipping industry.

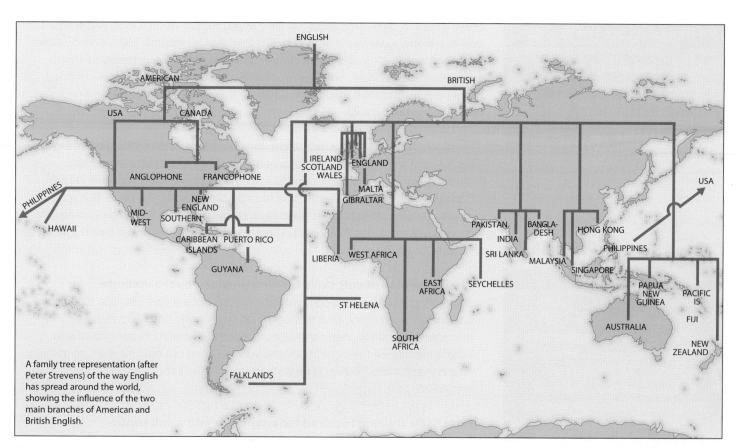

A family tree representation (after Peter Strevens) of the way English has spread around the world, showing the influence of the two main branches of American and British English.

Figure 1.3 English speaking countries around the world.

discussion

1 How does Text 1.1 define its speaker? Where do you see evidence that this is the language of ocean-going vessels?
2 Although it is said that English is the language of the seas because of the British Empire, you can see that the IMO uses American English. 'International Maritime Organization' is spelled with a 'z'. Why do you think this is?

This map helps you imagine the powerful presence of the British Empire and the linguistic footprint it left on the world. You may wonder why people around the world continued to speak English even after British troops went home. In order to answer this, we must look to the economic ties of people in former British colonies such as India.

Economic factors

Economic factors have also determined the success of the English language around the world. This can be seen best within the borders of India where over a hundred dialects are spoken. The English language, however, is one of the few languages that connect people from all corners of this vast country. In India today there are many economic advantages of learning English. Not only have Indians learned English to overcome linguistic barriers within their own country, but economically India has become very outward looking and many Indians have learned English to compete in the world market. Figure 1.4 shows the line of work taken up by many Indians in call centres. Text 1.2 shows how many Indians are looking for training to improve their accents and increase their employment opportunities in these offices that communicate with the USA and the UK regularly. Keep in mind that this text was written 63 years after the British left India.

Further resources

The Story of English is a TV series from 1986 that documents the rise of the English language from its Anglo-Saxon origins to its global dominance today. It covers a range of topics, including Shakespeare's influence on the language and interesting accents from all over the world.

Text 1.2 Call centre training

The text can best be understood in the context of Business Process Outsourcing (BPO), a phenomenon that has taken hold around the world for several decades. Large companies from the West have outsourced their customer care and telesales departments to India. Consequently, many Indians have shown an aptitude for learning the required communication skills. As Indians handle complaints, run credit checks and sell products over the phone, a command of the English language is essential. Many agencies offer 'accent neutralising' or 'accent reduction' training, so that Indian employees sound authentic and even 'local'. Some even specialise in Scottish or Welsh accents. Text 1.2 is based on many websites which offer advice to Indian call centre employees who seek to refine their speaking skills.

Have you decided to join a call centre, but you are thinking of joining a training institute first to hone your skills for a better pay package? With call centres mushrooming in all major cities in India, the call centre training institutes in Delhi, Bangalore, Chennai, Hyderabad and Mumbai are following the pace. But you have to be ultra careful before selecting an institute. This article throws some light on what are the things that you can analyse before selecting a call centre training institute for yourself.

Check the kind of soft skills training provided by the institute

Soft skills primarily include communication skills, accent-neutralisation training, customer management, time management, team work, crisis and stress management and telephone etiquette. Out of these, communication skills and accent training are the most important; you must find out how the institute trains on these soft skills. Do they have a structured course to help you learn these skills with ease?

Hard skills training required for easy entry into a call centre

To support your soft skills, you need to learn some other things like working on the computer and applications like MS Word, MS Excel and MS PowerPoint.

discussion

1 What do you know about the target audience for Text 1.2? Where do you find evidence in this text that indicates this?
2 How does the text indicate that there are direct economic benefits for call centre workers who speak English fluently without an Indian accent?

You would need to learn how to use all the basic tools that are used in the call centre such as VoIP telephone equipment, the desktop computer and customer care management, applications, etc. If you want to get into a technical call centre, then preliminary training on that product or service must be given. You must also learn the terminology used in a call centre.

Find out if the instructors are experienced and qualified

Insist on meeting a few trainers and instructors in the call centre training institute to get an idea about their teaching style. Don't hesitate to ask about the qualifications and experience of the trainers. You may also ask for one trial session, wherein you can attend an actual class at the institute.

Supporting infrastructure and equipment of the call centre training institute

Visit the institute and see if it has the required space, seating capacity, computer systems and other resources to accommodate each student comfortably. Also, find out about the level of personal attention given to each student.

Formal certification for your successful course completion

Find out if the institute provides a formal certification of training or not. This will help you while presenting your qualifications and documents in the interview.

100% quality placement – Is it the truth or just a gimmick?

Does the institute offer guaranteed, reputable placements, as it claims? With the never-ending demand of trained call centre agents, these institutes have become like training/recruitment providers for call centres. Ask the institute about all the call centres where they have placed their candidates in the past and check if they are reputed companies.

Conduct a background check to be absolutely sure

Ask for references. If they are unable to give you any good references, visit the training institute and chat with the students and trainers about the institute. Also, do a quick search on the web to get reviews about that institute if any.

It is good to join a training institute before getting a call centre job to learn all the tricks of the trade. It will make you a trained candidate and you would be able to negotiate a better salary as compared to an un-trained person. The salary for beginners in call centres ranges from Rs. 8 000 to Rs.12 000 per month. After getting appropriate training, you would be able to demand the upper salary level.

Text 1.2 raises the issue of **language currency**. There are many reasons why people learn languages. Mastering English can bring rewards and at one end of the spectrum of reasons is **instrumental motivation**. This means that people who have learned English can accomplish something through it, such as preventing an accident (Text 1.1) or providing customer service (Text 1.2). What is more, a candidate who can speak and understand English well may have a better chance in a job interview than someone whose English is not as good. It may mean a contract is awarded to one company rather than another. In short, English opens doors.

'If you want to take full advantage
of the Internet there is only one
way to do it: learn English.'
Michael Specter (1955–)

Figure 1.4 Many Indians learn English in order to work in call centres. They deal with phone calls from all over the Anglophone world, regarding everything from insurance queries to customer service.

At the other end of the spectrum of why people learn languages is **integrative motivation**, which refers to learning a language in order to integrate and become a member of a society. Compare the possible reasons for learning English as opposed to Finnish. If you are learning Finnish, most likely your interests lie in living among the 5 million Finnish speakers in Finland and Sweden. Perhaps you are married to a Finnish person and you want to communicate with your in-laws or colleagues about local events and culture. The language is very bound to its culture. English, on the other hand, especially in a global context, is becoming less bound to one particular culture, which is the result of its high currency and status as a lingua franca.

In India, proficiency in the English language can indicate how 'upwardly mobile' a person is. There is a varying degree of **bilingualism** in India, meaning that people regularly use multiple languages, including English, for different purposes. There is also evidence that Indian people are making the English language their own. Studies by V.S. Dubey and David Crystal show that English words used in Indian matrimonial adverts (where people advertise for a prospective partner), for example, can have their own special meaning. In the context of the adverts, a phrase such as *clean-shaven* actually means 'Punjabi, but not bearded' and *respectable* means 'wealthy'. In short, Indians have given new meanings to English words.

In this discussion on why Indians learn English you will have discovered that language is an expression of identity. Why people learn English says a lot about who they are. In order to understand why English has become the cross-cultural language of the world, we need to recognise how people identify with Anglophone cultures. There is something fashionable about these cultures which attracts people to learn the language.

Fashion

Anglophone culture is spread around the world today through influential media such as MTV and the BBC. For many people, the English language has become associated with blue jeans, MP3 players and celebrities like David Beckham. Text 1.3 shows how the English language has seeped into the Dutch language. Both teenagers and adults find it fashionable to use English words in their daily speech. This is testimony to the influence of popular Anglophone cultures.

Text 1.3 *Cosmo Girl* (Dutch edition), August 2009

'There is no more reason for language to change than there is for automobiles to add fins one year and remove them the next, for jackets to have three buttons one year and two the next.'
Paul Postal (1936–)

discussion

1 With reference to Text 1.3, can you see how the English language has been integrated into the Dutch language?
2 A word like *hotste* contains the Dutch suffix *-ste*, which is a superlative, attached to the English root *hot*. The Dutch word *hotste* can be translated into English by the word *hottest*. Can you find more examples?
3 Why do you think teenage girls borrow English words to express themselves in Dutch?
4 Do you think, from this example, that the English language is invading or corrupting the Dutch language?

Text 1.3 draws our attention to a phenomenon known as **language borrowing**, where one culture imports words from another language. The Dutch are not the first to import English words into their language. The Japanese say *karisamas* (Christmas), and the French say *le weekend* (the weekend). We call these words **loanwords**, and they are the result of different cultures coming into contact with each other. In fact, as the British came into contact with many cultures during the expansion of the British Empire, they too borrowed words from other languages. The word *jazz* came from West African languages while *sofa* is from Arabic and *boomerang* from the Aboriginal people of Australia. These are just a few of the great many words that English has picked up as it has come into contact with other cultures.

Why do people borrow words from other languages? There are several reasons. A language may prove insufficient to describe certain ideas or sentiments. A concept may be foreign by nature, such as Christmas for the Japanese. Last but not least, words are borrowed from other languages for reasons of fashion. Although the Dutch have many sufficient words to describe the latest trends, English proves more fashionable. We see this to such an extent in Text 1.3 that a native speaker of English can read almost the entire cover.

In this unit, you have so far explored several reasons why English has become the world's number one lingua franca. The growth of the British Empire around the world accounted for the initial spread of the English language. After the decline of the British Empire, however, English remained an important world language for reasons of economics and fashion. You explored one case of English in India in Text 1.2, but there

Key terms

Language borrowing describes the act of importing words into one language from another culture's language.

Loanwords are the words that one culture borrows and incorporates from another language.

are many similar situations of English still being used in former British colonies such as Hong Kong and South Africa. Through trade and commerce English has connected people with no common language. To this day, economic and financial reasons motivate people to learn English. A fashionable language, English has become associated with successful trends and the cultures that create them.

Having been so closely associated with the British Empire, English could have suffered as a result of the decline of the Empire and the growth of nationalism in its former colonies. Yet in spite of the connection with the British Empire and the spread of Anglophone culture, the English language has become a powerful tool. Using English, Mahatma Ghandi once united the people of India against the British. Today, Chinese businesses hire Belgian consultants to teach them English. The world has become a global village thanks to English.

Activity 1.1
Study Figures 1.5, 1.6 and 1.7. Why is English used in these three situations? Explain their contexts with reference to the reasons for using English explored in this unit.

Figure 1.5 English is often used to make a point in demonstrations and protests.

Figure 1.6 Bilingual signs like these can be found in major airports all over the world.

Figure 1.7 Kaká often displays his religious convictions on his football shirt.

Unit 1.2 Varieties of English

As you read the language of seafarers in Text 1.1, you may have questioned whether it was really English at all. In fact, it was a good example of **jargon**, a kind of language that reflects a particular profession or field of expertise. While the phrases in that text were intended to convey a message from one ship to another, they also told us something about the nature of seafaring. Ships' captains must be clear and concise in their communications.

We all speak a variety of English that tells the world something about who we are. We call this our **idiolect**. Our idiolect is like our linguistic fingerprint, which reveals where we come from, whom we socialise with and what we aspire to become.

As you continue your study of the English language in its various cultural contexts, you will begin to see how people display their identity through their unique use of language. This unit will focus on the three main reasons that account for why people speak English differently:

1 social reasons
2 historical reasons
3 regional reasons.

Whereas in Unit 1.1 you saw the result of cultures converging, here the focus will be on the process of **divergence**. As you will see, the spread of English around the world has resulted in new varieties or 'brands' of English. People have taken the English language and made it their own, creating more linguistic diversity in the Anglophone world and forging new Englishes.

The term *new Englishes* raises an important question which we must address before exploring a range of texts. Are new Englishes, such as Caribbean English, Singapore English or South African English, **languages**, **accents** or **dialects**? A language is a system of communication that everyone in a society can understand and use for communication with each other. The term *accent* technically refers to the way in which someone pronounces a language. A dialect is a variety of a language that is unique in pronunciation, grammar and vocabulary. Linguists sometimes joke by saying a language is simply a dialect with an army and a navy. In other words, a dialect that goes on to become the standard language of a people is usually the dialect originally spoken by the people who are rich and powerful.

Although we do not think of British and American English as dialects, in fact that is what they are. They are standardised dialects to which others are often compared. The more the other dialects deviate from this 'norm', the lower the status we tend to attach to them. When studying the English-speaking world it is important to put aside such prejudices and to recognise new Englishes as dialects that express individual identity.

An underlying question runs through much of this chapter: who *owns* English? By 'own' we mean the right to say which forms of English are correct or incorrect, or whose English is standard and whose English is non-standard. There tend to be two opposing views on this topic. Some say the British own English since the language originated in the British Isles. The opposite view imagines English speakers as shareholders, with the bulk of the stocks found in the USA. There is also, however, a third view: because there are more non-native speakers than native speakers of English, both no one and everyone can be said to 'own' English.

Social influences on English

The judgements we often make of people's dialects are actually judgements we make about social differences. Whether we admit to it or not, we all have opinions about what constitutes 'correct' and 'incorrect' English. Take for example the kind of English used by travellers, or gypsies. In the Guy Ritchie film *Snatch* we can see how speakers of standardised British English look down upon this dialect. When one traveller pronounces the word *dogs* as 'dags' he is curtly corrected. Such situations happen not only in works of fiction, but also in everyday life.

Some people consider 'deviations' from the standard dialect as signs of a degenerating language and culture. Other people see these deviations as a celebration of diversity and an expression of identity. Besides judgements on the correctness or incorrectness of a particular English, people respond to language use in many other different ways, labelling it *ugly* or *beautiful*, or perhaps *crass* or *elegant*. The problem with such terms is that they are judgemental and fail to recognise the diversity of Englishes.

As you read Text 1.4 taken from *Pygmalion* by George Bernard Shaw, ask yourself how the Note Taker's attitude towards the Flower Girl's dialect reflects his attitudes towards her social class.

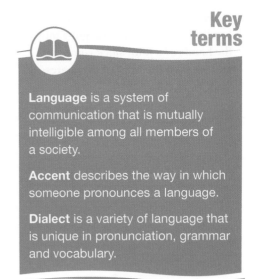

Key terms

Language is a system of communication that is mutually intelligible among all members of a society.

Accent describes the way in which someone pronounces a language.

Dialect is a variety of language that is unique in pronunciation, grammar and vocabulary.

'It is impossible for an Englishman to open his mouth without making some other Englishman despise him.'
George Bernard Shaw (1856–1950)

Extended essay

The Kenyan writer Ngugi wa Thiong'o makes the case for a broader understanding of literature written in the English language in his essay 'On the Abolition of the English Department'. Discuss.

An extended essay with this title presents a good opportunity to discuss issues of ownership within the English-speaking world. It is best to focus on one particular country or culture (e.g. Kenya and the East African perspective of English). Write an extended essay discussing issues of language ownership using the title above or one of your own. If you write about Ngugi wa Thiong'o, be sure to respond to his ideas and explore the East African perspective of English.

'There is no such thing as the Queen's English. The property has gone into the hands of a joint stock company and we own the bulk of the shares.'
Mark Twain (1835–1910)

Figure 1.8 Rex Harrison as Henry Higgins (the Note Taker) and Audrey Hepburn as Eliza Doolittle (the Flower Girl) in *My Fair Lady*, the classic 1964 film rendition of George Bernard Shaw's play *Pygmalion*.

discussion

1 Do you agree with the Note Taker's statements about the Flower Girl's use of English? Will her 'kerbstone English' keep her in the 'gutter'? Or are there other factors that determine her position in society?
2 What do you think of the Note Taker's proposition? Is it possible to transform a Cockney girl into a duchess by teaching her to speak differently? Does such a plan ignore her sense of identity and dignity, or is it a generous offer?

Text 1.4 *Pygmalion*, George Bernard Shaw, 1914

Pygmalion by George Bernard Shaw was produced in 1914 for a 'highbrow' upper-class audience in London. At the time it was considered quite scandalous and improper to present in London theatres a Cockney dialect, which was associated with the lower classes of East London. In the following scene, Liza Doolittle, a Cockney-speaking flower girl, comes into contact with Henry Higgins (the Note Taker), who is a linguist and member of the upper class. The scene takes place in Covent Garden, where both the Opera House and the bustling fruit and vegetable market were situated, bringing the wealthy and the poor into close proximity. By setting the scene in Covent Garden, Shaw confronts his audience with the stark class differences in London.

The Note Taker	Simply phonetics. The science of speech. That's my profession; also my hobby. Happy is the man who can make a living by his hobby! You can spot an Irishman or a Yorkshireman by his brogue. I can place any man within six miles. I can place him within two miles in London. Sometimes within two streets.
The Flower Girl	Ought to be ashamed of himself, unmanly coward!
The Gentleman	But is there a living in that?
The Note Taker	Oh yes. Quite a fat one. This is an age of upstarts. Men begin in Kentish Town with 80 pounds a year, and end in Park Lane with a hundred thousand. They want to drop Kentish Town;

	but they give themselves away every time they open their mouths. Now I can teach them –
The Flower Girl	Let him mind his own business and leave a poor girl –
The Note Taker	[*explosively*] Woman: cease this detestable boohooing instantly; or else seek the shelter of some other place of worship.
The Flower Girl	[*with feeble defiance*] I've a right to be here if I like, same as you.
The Note Taker	A woman who utters such depressing and disgusting sounds has no right to be anywhere – no right to live. Remember that you are a human being with a soul and the divine gift of articulate speech: that your native language is the language of Shakespeare and Milton and The Bible; and don't sit there crooning like a bilious pigeon.
The Flower Girl	[*quite overwhelmed, and looking up at him in mingled wonder and deprecation without daring to raise her head*] Ah–ah–ah–ow–ow–oo!
The Note Taker	[*whipping out his book*] Heavens! what a sound! [*He writes; then holds out the book and reads, reproducing her vowels exactly*] Ah–ah–ah–ow–ow–ow–oo!
The Flower Girl	[*tickled by the performance, and laughing in spite of herself*] Garn!
The Note Taker	You see this creature with her kerbstone English: the English that will keep her in the gutter to the end of her days. Well, sir, in three months I could pass that girl off as a duchess at an ambassador's garden party. I could even get her a place as lady's maid or shop assistant, which requires better English. That's the sort of thing I do for commercial millionaires. And on the profits of it I do genuine scientific work in phonetics, and a little as a poet on Miltonic lines.

When studying the use of English in context, it is important to understand the concept of **register**. Register is the level of formality or informality of the language. The 'detestable' sound that the Flower Girl makes, the 'Ah–ah–ah–ow–ow–oo!' sound, is not as formal as the language the Note Taker would use. He condemns her use of English because of the register she employs with him. Throughout the play, the Flower Girl seems to use a register that is less formal than the circumstances demand. When the linguistic features are normally used in informal situations, we call them **colloquialisms**. The word *garn* is an example of a colloquialism. The Note Taker is not accustomed to this level of informality the first time he meets someone.

Certain Englishes, such as Jamaican Patois, Cockney or African American English, tend to be looked down on, and this attitude is linked to other attitudes to do with formality and what is suitable or customary. We all have different cultural understandings of what linguistic behaviour is felt to be appropriate in which circumstance. When one person finds someone else's use of language 'snobby' or 'crass', there is often a clash of cultural norms and expectations. The cartoon in Figure 1.9 draws our attention to such a clash of cultures.

Key terms

Register is the level of formality or informality expressed through one's use of language.

Colloquialisms are linguistic features that are associated with informal situations.

Linguistic determinism is the concept that language determines what we are able to think.

Sapir–Whorf hypothesis suggests that people of different cultures think and behave differently because their languages dictate how they think and behave.

'A different language is a different vision of life.'
Federico Fellini (1894–1956)

TOK

Both in his fictional work and his essays, George Orwell explores a very fundamental question: does language determine thought? The notion that you cannot think a thought without the language to express it is also known as **linguistic determinism**. Orwell's fascination with this notion took root in the work of two linguists, Benjamin Whorf and Edward Sapir, who studied the languages and cultures of Native Americans. Whorf's research suggested that the Inuit people have more words for 'snow' because they live in it. To this day, many people still cite the famous 'Eskimo' argument in support of the **Sapir–Whorf hypothesis**, which can best be explained in the words of Edward Sapir:

The 'real world' is to a large extent unconsciously built upon the language habits of the group. No two languages are ever sufficiently similar to be considered as representing the same social reality. The worlds in which different societies live are distinct worlds, not merely the same world with different labels attached … We see and hear and otherwise experience very largely as we do because the language habits of our community predispose certain choices of interpretation.

Source: 'The status of linguistics as a science', in *Culture, Language and Personality*, edited by D.G. Mandelbaum, University of California Press,1958.

Do you believe in the Sapir–Whorf hypothesis? Is it a matter of belief? Have you ever been struck by a phrase, perhaps from another language, that made you see the world differently? Is this proof of the Sapir–Whorf hypothesis?

"I lost the spelling bee on the word 'gangsta.'"

Figure 1.9 How does this cartoon expose a clash of cultures? (Spelling bees are spelling competitions that take place regularly in American schools.)

One text that addresses such attitudes towards language and register is an essay written by George Orwell in 1946 called *Politics and the English Language*. In the following extract from the essay (Text 1.5), Orwell takes up the fight against vague writing and sloppy English, which, according to Orwell, contaminate our thoughts. The notion that language can determine thought is a topic that you will want to explore further in your TOK class.

Text 1.5 *Politics and the English Language*, George Orwell, 1946

George Orwell, the pen name of Eric Arthur Blair, is most famous for his novel *Nineteen Eighty-Four* and novella *Animal Farm*. In these works, just as in others about his travels in Burma and Spain, there is a common theme of anti-totalitarianism. Through various essays and novels, Orwell explored the notion of language as a political tool that can be used to manipulate the minds of the masses. As you can see from the following extract, he was an advocate of using clear and unambiguous language.

Most people who bother with the matter at all would admit that the English language is in a bad way, but it is generally assumed that we cannot by conscious action do anything about it. Our civilization is decadent and our language – so the argument runs – must inevitably share in the general collapse. It follows that any struggle against the abuse of language is a sentimental archaism, like preferring candles to electric light or hansom cabs to aeroplanes. Underneath this lies the half-conscious belief that language is a natural growth and not an instrument which we shape for our own purposes.

Now, it is clear that the decline of a language must ultimately have political and economic causes: it is not due simply to the bad influence of this or that individual writer. But an effect can become a cause, reinforcing the original cause and producing the same effect in an intensified form, and so on indefinitely. A man may take to drink because he feels himself to be a failure, and then fail all the more completely because he drinks. It is rather the same thing that is happening to the English language. It becomes ugly and inaccurate because our thoughts are foolish, but the slovenliness of our language makes it easier for us to have foolish thoughts. The point is that the process is reversible. Modern English, especially written English, is full of bad habits which spread by imitation and which can be avoided if one is willing to take the necessary trouble. If one gets rid of these habits one can think more clearly, and to think clearly is a necessary first step toward political regeneration: so that the fight against bad English is not frivolous and is not the exclusive concern of professional writers.

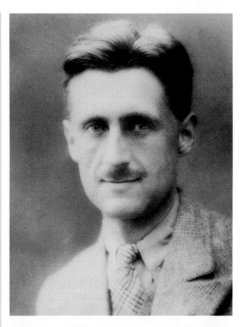

Figure 1.10 Eric Arthur Blair (1903–1950), more famously known as George Orwell.

Historical influences on English

People speak differently because people move around, and they have done so for hundreds of years. Take for example the use of English in the areas of the USA known as the South. By the early 1860s almost a million people had emigrated from the British Isles to the USA and settled in this region. To this day, the accents and dialects of the people of the South both reflect their British roots *and* express a unique identity that is different from their British ancestry. As you read Text 1.6 (from a letter by an American), notice how linguistic features such as the silent 'r' at the end of words reflect the language's British ancestry. Notice also how other features distinguish it from the standardised British English of today.

'Tongues, like governments, have a natural tendency to degeneration.'
Samuel Johnson (1709–84)

discussion

1 What do you think of Orwell's argument that poor language leads to a corruption of thought? Is there, as Samuel Johnson once said, a natural tendency for languages to degenerate?
2 The greater context of Text 1.5 is a political one. Orwell's purpose in his essay is to warn us about the effects of the inaccurate and ambiguous language used by politicians to manipulate the public and gain power. Do you find this idea relevant today?

Text 1.6 Letter from Artemus Ward to the Prince of Wales, early 1860s

The USA was in civil war between 1861 and 1865. The North wanted democracy and the abolition of slavery. The South, on the other hand, was partial to a system of aristocracy and the enslavement of African Americans. America's foreign relations with Britain during this time were difficult. Britain was sympathetic to the Confederates in the South, who were initially winning the war. Many Confederates wanted Britain to formally aid the efforts of the South, and there were reasons to believe they would. For example, the British had built a steamship and converted it into the Confederates' first warship, commanded by Captain Semmes.

The following extract is taken from a satirical letter presented by Artemus Ward to the Prince of Wales (the future King Edward VII) in the early 1860s. Artemus Ward was a fictional persona of the stand-up comedian Charles Farrar Browne, who performed Ward's 'lectures' in the South and in Britain. He gained fame for his performances and sympathy for his ideas.

'Time changes all things: there is no reason why language should escape this universal law.'
Ferdinand de Saussure (1857–1913)

Figure 1.11 Charles Farrar Browne (1834–67), also known as Artemus Ward.

discussion

1 How does Charles Farrar Browne use language to create the character of Artemus Ward? How would you describe his character based on the language of this text?

2 How does Artemus Ward use language to create humour?

3 What is your opinion of Artemus Ward's Southern accent? Do you think this variety of English is only appropriate for stand-up comedy? Could someone with such an accent seriously conduct business, run for public office or educate children? How might our attitudes towards his accent be different if the Confederates had won the American civil war?

Figure 1.12 Chinua Achebe (1930–).

Friend Wales,

You remember me. I saw you in Canady a few years ago. I remember you too. I seldim forget a person.

I hearn of your marriage to the Printcis Alexandry, & ment ter writ you a congratoolatory letter at the time, but I've bin bildin a barn this summer, & hain't had no time to write letters to folks. Excoose me.

Numeris changes has tooken place since we met in the body politic. The body politic, in fack, is sick. I sometimes think it has got biles, friend Wales.

In my country, we've got a war, while your country, in conjunktion with Cap'n Sems of the 'Alobarmy' manetanes a nootrol position!

… Yes, Sir, we've got a war, and the troo Patrit has to make sacrifisses, you bet.

I have alreddy given two cousins to the war, & I stand reddy to sacrifiss my wife's brother ruther'n not see the rebelyin krusht. And if wuss cums to wuss I'll shed ev'ry drop of blud my able-bodid relations has got to prosekoot the war. I think sumbody oughter be prosekooted, & it may as well be the war as any body else. When I git a goakin [joking] fit onto me it's no use to try ter stop me.

You hearn about the draft, friend Wales, no doubt. It caus'd sum squirmin', but it was fairly conducted, I think, for it hit all classes …

We hain't got any daily paper in our town, but we've got a female sewin' circle, which ansers the same purpuss, and we wasn't long in supents as to who was drafted …

Respects to St. George & the Dragon.

Ever be 'appy.

A. Ward.

Regional influences on English

It is difficult to discuss historical differences in language without discussing regional differences. As the British Empire expanded to all corners of the world, unique varieties of English came into existence – new Englishes that were characteristic of their region. As people forged new Englishes, they had two identities to consider: on the one hand they needed a language that was mutually intelligible and which connected them to the wealth of the British Empire; on the other hand they needed to express their independence and a new regional identity. Although the language of Artemus Ward (Text 1.6) may contain traces of his British ancestry, it also reflects his Southern identity. The Nigerian author Chinua Achebe explains what it means to find a balance between these two interests in *Morning Yet on Creation Day* (1975).

The African writer should aim to use English in a way that brings out his message best without altering the language to the extent that its value as a medium of international exchange will be lost. He should aim at fashioning out an English which is at once universal and able to carry his peculiar experience. But it will have to be a new English, still in full communion with its ancestral home but altered to suit its new African surroundings.

We will turn to another Nigerian artist, Fela Kuti, to see a different brand of English from the same country. As you read his song lyrics in Text 1.7, ask yourself why he speaks so differently from Chinua Achebe, even though they are both from Nigeria.

Text 1.7 *Coffin for head of state*, Fela Kuti, 1979

Fela Kuti was a musician and political activist in Nigeria in the 1970s and 1980s. His mother was a well-known anti-colonialism activist and his father was head of a teachers' union. After having studied music in England, Kuti travelled and performed in the USA. He returned to Nigeria and laid the foundation for a style of music that became known as Afrobeat.

Kuti's lyrics often spoke out against the colonial mentality that was entrenched in his country's people and government. On his album *Zombie*, which appeared in 1977, he had accused the Nigerian government of using child soldiers. As a result, Nigerian soldiers stormed the compound where Kuti and his family lived. His mother died of injuries from this incident. In response, Kuti, together with hundreds of his 'Movement of the People' followers, carried his mother's coffin to the Dodan Barrack in Lagos, where he demanded that General Olusegun Obasanjo and Lieutenant Y'arada of the Nigerian military help carry the coffin. Eventually they did. Kuti also wrote the song 'Coffin for head of state'.

> Amen, Amen, Amen …
> Amen, Amen, Amen …
> Amen, Amen, Amen …
> Amen, Amen, Amen …
> Through Jesus Christ our Lord
> By the grace of Almighty Lord
> Through Jesus Christ our Lord
> By the grace of Almighty Lord
> 'In Spiritus Christus …'
> 'Allah Wakubar Mohammed Salamalekum …'
>
> So I waka waka waka[1]
> I go many places
> I see my people
> Dem dey[2] cry cry
> Amen, Amen, Amen
> Amen, Amen, Amen, …
> Amen, Amen, Amen, …
> Amen, Amen, Amen, …
> I say I waka waka waka …
> I waka many village anywhere in Africa
> I waka many village anywhere in Africa
> Pastor's house na him dey fine pass
> My people them dey stay for poor surroundings
> Pastor's dress na him dey clean pass
> E hard for my people for them to buy soap
> Pastor na him them give respect pass
> And them do bad bad bad bad bad bad things
>
> Through Jesus Christ our Lord
> By the grace of Almighty Lord
> Through Jesus Christ our Lord

discussion

1 How is the language of Fela Kuti different from the language of Chinua Achebe?

2 How do you think Achebe would respond to Kuti's use of English? Is Kuti's English *still in full communion with its ancestral home but altered to suit its new African surroundings*?

3 How does the context in which the song was written (the attack on Kuti's compound and death of his mother) determine the kind of language used by Fela Kuti?

Figure 1.13 Fela Kuti (1938–97).

By the grace of Almighty Lord
'In Spiritus Christus ...'
'Allah Wakubar Mohammed Salamalekum ...'

So I waka waka waka
I go many places
I go business places
I see see see
All the bad bad bad things
Them dey do do do

Call corruption
Them dey call nepotism
Inside the promotions
And inside all business
I say I waka waka waka
I see see see
So I waka waka waka ...

I waka many business anywhere in Africa
I waka many business anywhere in Africa
North and South dem get dem policies
One Christian and the other one Muslim
Anywhere the Muslims dem dey reign
Na[3] Senior Allaha-ji na 'im be Director
Anywhere the Christians dem dey reign
Na the best friend to Bishop na 'im be Director
It is a known fact that for many thousand years
We Africans, we had our own traditions
These money making organisations
Them come put we Africans in total confusion

Through Jesus Christ our Lord
By the grace of Almighty Lord
Through Jesus Christ our Lord
By the grace of Almighty Lord
'In Spiritus Christus ...'
'Allah Wakubar Mohammed Salamalekum ...'

So I waka waka waka
I go many places
I go government places
I see see see
All the bad bad bad things
Den[4] dey do do do

Look Obasanjo!
Before anything at all, him go dey shout:
'Oh Lord, oh Lord, oh Lord, Almighty Lord!'

'Oh Lord, oh God!'
And dem do bad bad bad bad bad bad things

Through Jesus Christ our Lord
(Amen, Amen, Amen!)
By the grace of Almighty Lord
(Amen, Amen, Amen!)

I say, look Yar'Adua!
I say, look Yar'Adua!
Before anything at all, him go dey shout:
'Habba Allah, habba Allah, habba Allah!'
'Habba Allah, habba Allah!"
And dem do, yes yes
And dem do bad bad bad bad bad bad things

Through Mohammed our Lord
(Amen, Amen, Amen!)
By the grace of Almighty Allah
(Amen, Amen, Amen!)

Waka, waka, waka!

So I waka waka waka
I go many places
I go government places
I see see see
All the bad bad bad things
Dem they do do do

Den steal all the money
Dem kill many students
Dem burn many houses
Dem burn my house too
Them kill my mama

So I carry the coffin
I waka waka waka
Movement of the People
Dem waka waka waka
Young African Pioneers
I waka waka waka

We go Obalende
We go Dodan barracks
We reach dem gate o
We put the coffin down
Obasanjo dey there
With den big fat stomach
Yar'Adua dey there

With den neck like ostrich
We put the coffin down

But them take am!

Dem no wan[5] take am[6]
Dem no want take am
Who go want take coffin?
Them must take am
Na the bad bad bad things
Wey they don[7] do
Them no want take am
Obasanjo grab am
Yar'Adua carry am
Yes, them no want take am
Obasanjo carry am
Yar'Adua tow am
Them no want take am
Them no want take am

E dey for them office
E dey there now now now now now
E dey there now now now now now
E dey there now now now now now
E dey there now now now now now ...

But them take am!

[1] **waka**   walk
[2] **Dem dey**   Them, they
[3] **Na**   That
[4] **Den**   Then
[5] **wan**   want to
[6] **am**   it (from 'him')
[7] **don**   don't

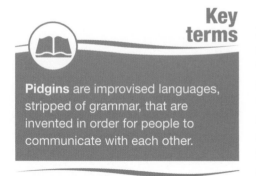

Key terms

Pidgins are improvised languages, stripped of grammar, that are invented in order for people to communicate with each other.

In order to account for Fela Kuti's use of English, we must discuss British colonialism and the slave trade to the West Indies. Why do people in both Jamaica and Nigeria say 'Dem no wan take am' ('They don't want to take them')? This grammatical structure reflects the nature of the Yoruba language, spoken throughout West Africa, from where the slaves were taken. British and Portuguese trade with West Africa required a common language, a lingua franca. Where there is a demand to communicate, a supply of language must be invented. Such inventions are called **pidgins** – improvised languages, stripped of grammar, for shopping at the market, loading ships and bartering. When newer generations then adapt this improvised language and develop it into a complete language that covers all speech situations, we call it a **creole**. Fela Kuti sang in a language known as Nigerian Pidgin, which is actually a creole. The lyrics of Text 1.6 contain the cultural DNA of Nigeria and offer a small window into its history.

People who speak creoles are able to adapt the way they speak to accommodate the needs of their audiences. In Nigeria people can choose to speak with more Yoruba-based vocabulary or more English-based vocabulary, depending on whom they are talking to. We call this **code-switching**. That is to say, Nigerians can go back and forth between several varieties of language as the situation requires.

Speakers consciously decide to speak one variety over another as a kind of statement about where their loyalties lie. Fela Kuti sang in Nigerian Pidgin in order to express his affiliation to the local culture. In contrast, Chinua Achebe writes in a variety of English that is accessible for the greater Anglophone world. Nigerians can therefore choose to express their identity along a continuum, showing at the one end their local pride and at the other end their allegiance to a more global community.

There is one final concept to help us understand regional influence on language. We have stated that there is a kind of lingua franca, or world English, which is highly accessible to all (such as the language used in this coursebook). The opposite of a lingua franca is called a **vernacular**, where linguistic features are used to distinguish local identity. The language of Artemus Ward is a good example (Text 1.6). We can see evidence throughout the text that he belongs to a rural community, as he builds barns and receives his news through the local sewing circle. Furthermore, he expresses his membership to this culture by referring to people as 'folks' and Alabama as 'Alobarmy'. Through language, he proves his loyalty to the South and the cause of the Confederates in the civil war.

At one end of the language continuum, speakers of English can express through language the degree to which they identify with their *local* region. At the opposite end, speakers make their language accessible to the *global* community by reducing their use of vernacular language. Code-switching is, however, a common phenomenon, and some people can choose from a broader range of language than others because of regional and historical influences.

Convergence and divergence

In the previous unit you explored how the English language facilitates the formation of a global community (convergence). In this unit you have looked at how individuals can express unique identities by creating new varieties of English (divergence). As communities come together or split apart, there are always linguistic consequences. You have seen some of the consequences by looking at the linguistic features of the various texts you have studied – loanwords and colloquialisms, vernaculars and creoles. As you will see in the coming units, the convergence and divergence of cultures do not go unnoticed. Some people are worried that English poses a threat to other languages. Others see opportunities to reshape the English language to meet new needs.

Key terms

Code-switching can be done by speakers who speak two dialects of a language or two entirely different languages, switching from one to the other depending on whom they are talking to or what they wish to accomplish.

Vernacular is the opposite of a lingua franca. It is language that is characteristic of a region.

Extended essay

African American English (AAE) and Ebonics: how should we recognise these varieties of English?

There is a movement in the USA to officially recognise AAE as an official language. In 1996 a school board in Oakland presented the idea that students should be taught in *Ebonics*. *Ebonics* is a more contentious term than AAE, as it is characterised more by its colloquialisms than its status as a vernacular. In 2010 the US Drug Enforcement Agency created a media stir when it employed nine translators of Ebonics.

Write an extended essay discussing the issues of varieties of English and using the title above or one of your own. Be sure to include examples of varieties, reporting from various media, as well as a discussion of relevant linguistic terms.

discussion

1 In what ways is the English these mothers speak in Text 1.8 different from the kind of English you are accustomed to speaking and hearing?

2 How is their use of English an example of both cultural convergence *and* cultural divergence?

Figure 1.14 Arthur Yap (1943–2006).

Text 1.8 *2 mothers in a hdb[1] playground*, Arthur Yap, 1981

Arthur Yap is a revered poet in Singapore. After receiving a scholarship to study English in Britain, he returned to the National University of Singapore where he taught creative writing. His poetry usually plays with the varieties of English found in everyday Singapore. He is known for not using capital letters and for playing with punctuation.

ah beng is so smart
already he can watch tv & know the whole story.
your kim cheong is also quite smart,
what boy is he[2] in the exam?
this playground is not too bad, but i'm always
so worried, car here, care there.

    at exam time, it's worse

because you know why?

    kim cheong eats so little.

give him some complan.[3] my ah beng was like that,
now he's different. if you give him anything
he's sure to finish it all up.

    sure, sure. cheong's father buys him
    vitamins but he keeps it inside his mouth
    & later gives it to the cat.
    i scold like mad but what for?
    if i don't see it, how can i scold?

on saturday, tv showed a new type,
special for children. why don't you call
his father[4] buy some?[5] maybe they are better.

[1] **hdb** the Housing and Development Board
[2] **what boy is he …?** What place did he get …?
[3] **complan** a proprietary vitamin supplement
[4] **his father** your husband
[5] **why don't you call his father buy some?** Why don't you ask his father to buy some?

Activity 1.2

Do some research on Singapore English (Text 1.8).

- Find out about how it came into existence and present your findings to the class.
- Try to make predictions about the future of this dialect.
- As the youth of Singapore come into contact with the global community, is Singapore English dying out?
- Alternatively, as it is taught in schools and spoken in people's homes, is it gaining recognition and becoming more standardised?

Assessment: Part 1 written task 1

Part of your external assessment for the course consists of writing a portfolio of written tasks. There are two kinds of written tasks. Written task 2 only pertains to higher level students and will be discussed in Chapter 7. Written task 1, for both higher and standard level students, is a creative writing assignment in which you

- imitate a certain form of writing *and*
- demonstrate your understanding of the topics covered in class.

You may want to write a letter to an organisation, a brochure for an advertising campaign, or a transcribed interview for a magazine. Although there are many possibilities, much of your success will rest on selecting the right type of text for the right purpose. Here are some examples of students' written tasks, both good and poor, to help you gain a sense of what is expected.

Good written tasks	Poor written tasks
After studying the role of Ebonics in education and law enforcement (see page 19), a student adopted the role of editor-in-chief of *Ebony* magazine and commented on her magazine's coverage of the news events in an editorial (letter from the editor). (Part 1 of the course)	After studying the Information Technology (IT) revolution and how IT is changing the way we communicate, a student wrote a poem entitled 'Ode to my computer'. This type of text did not lend itself well to the purpose of demonstrating an understanding of the cultural implications of IT. (Part 2)
After reading *Disgrace* by J.M. Coetzee, a student wrote a letter from one character to another. In the context of the novel, it was appropriate for the character to put his ideas into a letter as he had difficulty expressing his apology in person. This idea is very much in the spirit of the author's intentions. (Part 3)	After reading *Pygmalion*, a student wrote an obituary of Eliza Doolittle containing a bullet-pointed list of events that happened to her after the play. The problem with this text was that it was too hypothetical and did not reflect a good understanding of the play. The student would have been more successful if she had produced a sample of an autobiography, as written by Eliza, about her time with Henry Higgins during the period of the play. (Part 4)

If you have not already done so, you will want to become familiar with the requirements and the assessment criteria for the written tasks, which can be found in the official Language A: language and literature guide. A summary of the requirements and assessment criteria can also be found in the Introduction to this coursebook, on pages vi–ix.

Throughout this coursebook you will find several tips, examples and instructions to help you with written tasks 1 and 2. For now, we will focus on a sample written task 1 that meets the IB Diploma requirements and demonstrates a clear understanding of what the student has learned in part 1 of the course.

The sample part 1 written task 1 on pages 23–25 took its inspiration from a study of the preservation of the Irish language, which some people believe is threatened by the English language. In class, the students had discussed notions such as **language death, language planning** and **linguistic imperialism**. The spread of English as a lingua franca does not always have positive implications. Take the Maori language, for example. Many Maori speak English at home with their children because they know it will help their children advance in New Zealand society. Yet many are concerned that the Maori language could die if it is not promoted more among younger generations. The government of New Zealand has actively committed itself to preserving the Maori language, subsidising institutions that spread the use of the Maori language.

TOK

In your study of ethics, you may have come across the notion of cultural imperialism, the spread of a system of values and beliefs around the world. This phenomenon is often associated with the spread of the English language. In your TOK class, as you discuss both benefits and drawbacks of globalisation, be sure to discuss the role of English.

English, as one side of the argument goes, is threatening other languages with extinction; this is the case with Maori. At the same time, the spread of English has also given rise to new varieties of English, such as Nigerian English. Is the world becoming linguistically richer or poorer because of this spread of English? Do we have an ethical duty to prevent the spread of English? Should we use language planning to prevent languages from dying out? These are good questions for a TOK presentation. Edward Said's book *Culture and Imperialism* could provide guidance on this discussion.

Key terms

Language death occurs when the last native speakers of a language have died and no new generations speak their ancestors' language fluently.

Language planning is a term for the efforts made to prevent language death.

Linguistic imperialism is the dominance of one language over others. Many people see English as a threat to other languages.

It can be argued that Ireland was the first colony of the British Empire and it is fair to say that the English language is far more dominant in Ireland today than Gaelic or, as we will refer to it here, Irish. Because the Irish do not want to lose touch with their cultural heritage, great efforts have been made to give Irish a special status in society. You can see this in Texts 1.9 and 1.10 below.

You will also see from the student's work that there is a clear understanding of both form and content. The writer sounds well informed, and the case for Hiberno-English is convincing. What's more, the letter adheres to the conventions of formal letter writing.

Text 1.9 Article 8 from the Irish Constitution

- The Irish language as the national language is the first official language.
- The English language is recognised as a second official language.
- Provision may, however, be made by law for the exclusive use of either of the said languages for any one or more official purposes, either throughout the State or in any part thereof.

Figure 1.15 Place names in Irish and English on road signs in Ireland.

Text 1.10 About the Official Language Act, Office of An Coimisinéir Teanga, 2008

Irish used to be a compulsory requirement for employment in the public sector until this system came to an end in 1974. The government of the day decided that Irish and English would be put on an equal footing in the entrance examinations for the civil service, i.e. that candidates would be able to use Irish or English, or both languages, in competitions and that recognition would be given to candidates who were competent in both languages.

In the years following that arrangement, the ability of the civil service to provide an effective service for those wishing to conduct their business through Irish decreased.

Towards the end of the 1970s, the Irish language movement, particularly Conradh na Gaeilge, began a campaign for a Language Rights Bill or a Language Act and the debate on the issue continued for more than twenty years …

In 2002 the government published the first draft of a bill aimed at providing more services of a higher quality through Irish in the public sector. The bill was debated and various amendments were made to it until it was passed unanimously by both the Dáil and the Seanad in summer 2003.

On 14 July 2003, the President signed the Official Languages Act 2003 into law and the provisions of the Act were gradually brought into force over a three-year period. This was the first time the provision of services in general through Irish by the state system was placed on a statutory footing.

The aim of the Official Languages Act 2003 is to increase and improve in an organised manner over a period of time the quantity and quality of services provided for the public through Irish by public bodies. The legislation intends to create a space for the language in public affairs in Ireland.

The Office of An Coimisinéir Teanga was established under the Official Languages Act as an independent statutory office operating as an ombudsman's[1] service and as a compliance agency.

[1] **ombudsman** an independent and trusted person who mediates between an individual and an organisation.

Sample written task (HL)

Rationale

Even though my class did not really go to Dublin, we studied the languages of Ireland in class. We had a classroom discussion about how Standard British English is threatening Gaelic (or Irish), and we explored language planning in Ireland. We studied the website of the Office of An Coimisinéir Teanga and read various documents, including the Official Languages Act from 2003. Furthermore, I talked to a teacher at school who comes from Ireland. All in all, I was surprised that Ireland was so successful in preserving Irish and preventing it from language death. But I was also alarmed to learn that the Office of An Coimisinéir Teanga did not write anything about the distinct variety of English that many people actually speak in Ireland known as Irish English or Hiberno-English. I think this is because Hiberno-English is seen as a lesser English than British English. In fact, there is no reference even to British English, just simply 'English'. I found it concerning that such an organisation does not distinguish different kinds of Englishes more carefully.

I thought that writing a letter to the Office of An Coimisinéir Teanga would be a good written task, because it would give me the opportunity to express my opinion directly to an influential organisation in Ireland. I tried to make the letter as real as possible, including a greeting and a closing phrase. I stated my intention clearly, included an enlightening anecdote and presented many persuasive arguments. The letter has a clear purpose, in which I suggest a new role for Hiberno-English and ask for a response.

The letter shows my understanding of the coursework, as I address Irish stereotypes in film and the language associated with them. Furthermore, I present a strong case for Hiberno-English by referring to its cultural importance.

Jan Student   Office of An Coimisinéir Teanga
Fictitious Lane 1   An Spidéal,
Amsterdam   Galway Ireland
The Netherlands

29 September, 2011

Dear An Coimisinéir Teanga,

I study English in Holland. Our class went on a trip to Dublin recently, and I came back with some interesting ideas on language planning. I have read the Official Languages Act that you published, and I have a few suggestions. Perhaps an outsider's perspective will be useful.

I understand that your organisation helps preserve the Irish language, or Gaelic as it is known, which is threatened by the English language. I can see that you look into legal cases that are related to Article 8 of the Irish Constitution. In all of the texts I have read from your organisation, and the Irish Constitution, I see no mention of Hiberno-English. I would like to suggest that Hiberno-English also be given a role in the Official Languages Act.

During my studies of languages, I have learned that there are unique varieties of English all around the world. They are getting more official recognition. Hiberno-English, widely spoken in Ireland, is also different from British English in grammar, pronunciation and vocabulary. But I do not have to tell you about it, because it is the variety of language you hear most often in Ireland. It is the language of the people. Hiberno-English is used by great Irish writers such as J.M. Synge, James Joyce and Roddy Doyle. It is the language of the much loved rugby commentator Mícheál Ó Muircheartaigh (Michael Moriarty) and politicians such as Jackie Healy Rae.

There is a kind of Hiberno-English British English continuum, meaning that speakers from the Pale to the West Coast can express themselves to different extremes using these varieties of English, depending on who they are talking to. Linguists refer to this phenomenon as code switching, which is common in creole languages and places with a colonial past. During my visit to Ireland, I noticed that the English that people spoke to me was different from the English they spoke with each other. After an evening at a local pub with my host family, I learned many new words and phrases, such as *craic* for joke and *How's tricks?* for 'How are you?' I came to understand that many patterns in Hiberno-English reflect the influences of Gaelic, such as the use of the word *after* in phrases like *I was after getting some bread*, meaning 'I was on my way to get some bread'. Similarly my host mother said she was *after losing weight* meaning she was trying to lose weight. When I looked confused, she realised instantly where the differences lay between standard and Hiberno-English. She accommodated for me accordingly.

Such differences between Hiberno-English and British English have been documented by linguists. In fact there is a Hiberno-English–English dictionary. I realise that British English is seen as 'correct' English in your country, but I think this is wrong. This idea is old-fashioned. Basically, it means that anyone in Ireland who can cover up his Irish identity and act British can get a better job. This discrimination stems from a PR problem concerning Ireland. Often Irish speakers are portrayed badly in films, swearing and drinking heavily. Take for example Tom Cruise's brutish character from *Far and Away*, or Brad Pitt's performance in *Snatch*. Tom Reeve's film *Holy Water* takes place in Ireland and is full of swearing. This portrayal of the Irish people is not fair, as it suggests they all speak slang rather than a highly developed and documented language, Hiberno-English.

Something must be done to stop this stigmatisation of the Irish people, who speak a very unique and beautiful variety of English. The best place to start is from within the government. Because your organisation is very influential with the Irish government, I turn my request to you. The languages act of 2003 is already quite old. If you write a new one, maybe you can say that Hiberno-English is good enough for working in a government office or that public notifications can be in Hiberno-English. I realise that this may be radical, but it would also give the language of the people more status. And it would be a boost for the Irish identity. The language of the people needs to be recognised or children will grow up thinking the language they speak is inferior to that of their British counterparts.

I realise that your organisation takes language-related matters seriously. I hope that I have persuaded you to take up the cause of Hiberno-English and lobby for its official recognition. Could you please write back to me and tell me what you think of my ideas? I would appreciate that very much.

Yours sincerely,

Jan Student

Examiner's comments

Generally speaking, the letter to the Office of An Coimisinéir Teanga is the kind of work that is expected at HL. It is a very plausible letter that could be sent off to Ireland, although, as explained below, the style and register are not always appropriate. The following marks and comments could be expected from an IB examiner for this written task.

Criterion A: Rationale – 2 out of 2

In the rationale the student explains his position well. For example, he states that he will address the problem of Irish stereotypes and present the cultural importance of Hiberno-English. Three references to films are made and the names of many Irish writers are mentioned. The rationale meets the word count.

Criterion B: Task and content – 7 out of 8

The letter is very appropriate to the coursework, just as the content was appropriate to the task. The student has found an effective way to express opinions on language planning, language status and the varieties of English. Nevertheless, there is not much reference to the specific source of study, the Official Language Act of 2003 and Article 8 from the Irish Constitution. Furthermore, suggesting that Hiberno-English is officially recognised is a little implausible because of the social connotations that come along with this variety of English. Nevertheless, these social connotations were addressed and explored. The points of the letter are clear, though they are not always nuanced. The conventions of letter writing are adhered to, as the written task opens with a clear purpose and finishes with a request. The anecdotal stories about the pub, school field trip and host family are very plausible and work well. There is ample explanation of Hiberno-English, as the student uses examples of linguistic features, titles of films and names of writers.

Criterion C: Organisation and development – 5 out of 5

The task is well organised and coherently structured. Each paragraph has its own purpose which is clearly announced with topic sentences such as *Something must be done to stop this stigmatisation of the Irish people*. One paragraph starts and ends by stating that Hiberno-English is well documented, which adds to the coherence of the task.

Criterion D: Language – 4 out of 5

The register was appropriate for the most part, though it slipped in some places, most notably in lines such as *I think this is wrong* and *This idea is old-fashioned*. Instead of stating an opinion, the student should have offered persuasive arguments.

Writing in a more persuasive and nuanced style is also related to the vocabulary that is used. The following four suggestions for improving your writing deal with word choice and style.

Four ways to invigorate your writing

1 The verb *to get*

The verb *to get* is too ambiguous and is characteristic of spoken English. It can be replaced by other verbs that convey meaning more accurately.

Instead of

> They are **getting** more official recognition.
> It means that anyone in Ireland who can cover up his Irish identity and act British can **get** a better job.

use

> They are **receiving** more official recognition.
> It means that anyone ... who can cover up his Irish identity ... **is eligible for better employment opportunities**.

2 Linking words

In persuasive writing you should write sentences that flow well. To avoid short or 'choppy' sentences, use adverbial phrases, *-ing* verbs and conjunctions. In the following improved sentences, there is an example of an adverbial phrase (*As a student of English*), an *-ing* verb (*Viewing British English*) and a conjunction (*Dublin, where I learned about language planning*).

Instead of

> I study English in Holland. Our class went on a trip to Dublin recently, and I came back with some interesting ideas on language planning.

use

> **As** a student of English, I recently travelled to Dublin, **where** I learned about language planning.

Or instead of

> I realise that British English is seen as 'correct' English in your country, but I think this is wrong. This idea is old-fashioned. Basically, it means that anyone in Ireland, who can cover up his Irish identity and act British, can get a better job. This is discrimination.

use

> **Viewing** British English as the only correct variety of English is rather old-fashioned **and** could lead to discrimination against those who sound overly Irish.

3 Active sentences

Active forms of verbs are often more persuasive than passive forms. We will return to this important tip in later chapters.

> I built the house. = **active**
>
> The house was built by me. = **passive**

Instead of

> Hiberno-English is **used by** great Irish writers like J.M. Synge, James Joyce and Roddy Doyle.

use

> Great Irish writers like J.M. Synge, James Joyce and Roddy Doyle have **written** in Hiberno-English.

4 Subject, verb and object

As far as grammar is concerned, the student's letter is almost flawless. There is one instance, however, when it slips into the language of spoken English, which allows for phrases which do not always have a subject and a verb, and often an object, as with written sentences. These three parts of speech, subject + verb + object, are the essential building blocks of proper sentences, which you will need for your essay and for your written tasks. Notice how the second sentence below begins with the word *or* and lacks a subject.

Instead of

> If you write a new one, maybe you can say that Hiberno-English is also good enough for working in a government office. **Or** that public notifications can be in Hiberno-English.

use

> As efforts are made to draft a new Language Act, one may accept Hiberno-English as a valid form of communication within government bodies and for the publication of official notices.

Further resources

Language Magazine is a popular monthly publication with an online edition that covers a wide range of topics relating to part 1 of the course. You could use articles from the magazine as the basis of interesting classroom discussions.

tip

Your written task should be between 800 and 1000 words, *excluding* a rationale of between 200 and 300 words. This means that you may not be able to choose a shorter type of text, such as a poem or an advertisement. There are exceptions, as infomercials or epic poems could be long enough. If you want to make your written task seem plausible, however, remember to take the word count into consideration.

Key terms

Speech act is a broad term that refers to any situation in which spoken language is used.

Ideas for part 1 written tasks

1 Language is often in the news as people regularly defend the status of their language. For example, the English Academy of Southern Africa, the only academy of its kind in the Anglophone world, is devoted to preserving, standardising and developing their variety of English. Another, more controversial, variety of English is Ebonics, which has often appeared in the news. West African Vernacular English (WAVE) has gained recognition over the years, which has both upset and delighted many people. In brief, people care about the fate of their English. An opinion column or editorial about these Englishes would be very appropriate for a part 1 written task. Be sure to include examples of language in practice from texts that you have studied in class.

2 Research a singer or writer from a country where a non-standardised English or dialect is spoken. Examples include Bob Marley, Fela Kuti or Chinua Achebe. Pretend you have interviewed this person about their attitude towards English, creoles and pidgins, and linguistic imperialism. How does their use of language express their identity? Write a transcribed interview for a magazine or newspaper.

3 Like the student who wrote the sample written task in this unit, you can look at how certain minorities or social groups are portrayed in popular film and how language is used to stereotype them. Many popular children's films such as *Shrek* or *Dumbo* contain a range of linguistic features that typify people from certain regions and classes. You can write an article about this phenomenon for *Language Magazine* or another plausible context. Be sure to include multiple examples of language from multiple sources in order to make your case strong.

4 Write an official document on language planning. You can imitate Text 1.9, from the Irish constitution, or Text 1.10, on the Official Language Act of Ireland. Research a multilingual country where an official document like this may be necessary, such as India, New Zealand, Trinidad and Tobago, or South Africa. Focus on the threat of English, linguistic imperialism and language death. Be sure to include a very good rationale.

Written task proposal

Before you start your written task 1, it is a good idea to write a written task proposal for your teacher. By answering the following four questions you will be better able to formulate your ideas and you will make your writing more successful.

1 What type of text do you plan to write?
2 What topic do you plan to write about?
3 How does this type of text lend itself to this topic?
4 How do you think your written task will show the examiner that you have understood the coursework?

The four questions could also form a starting point for the rationale.

Assessment: Part 1 further oral activity

You will be asked to conduct at least two further oral activities, one for part 1 and another for part 2 of your course. For each of these oral activities you will have to:

• demonstrate your understanding of the coursework *and*
• perform a **speech act** alone or together with classmates.

You may decide to perform a sketch or have a conversation on the topics discussed in class. Presentations, debates and interviews are also common further oral activities. Whichever type of speech act you prepare, it is essential that you demonstrate your knowledge of the coursework. Talk to your teacher and consult the official course guide for further possible forms of performances. An overview of the requirements and criteria can also be found in the Introduction. Before you begin, be sure you are familiar with the assessment criteria and listen to as many sample activities from former students as possible.

The sample further oral activity below takes its inspiration from Text 1.11. It is the inaugural speech of Nelson Mandela, who became the president of South Africa in 1994, after years of being imprisoned by apartheid governments. The student pretends to be Antjie Krog, a prominent journalist and poet from South Africa, who most likely witnessed the speech first-hand in 1994. In the oral activity, the year is 2014 and she is speaking at an event of the African National Congress (ANC), the ruling political party of South Africa, upon the 20th anniversary of Mandela's speech

---

Text 1.11 Inaugural Address, Nelson Mandela, 10 May 1994

Your Majesties, Your Highnesses, Distinguished Guests, Comrades and Friends.

Today, all of us do, by our presence here, and by our celebrations in other parts of our country and the world, confer glory and hope to newborn liberty. Out of the experience of an extraordinary human disaster that lasted too long, must be born a society of which all humanity will be proud. Our daily deeds as ordinary South Africans must produce an actual South African reality that will reinforce humanity's belief in justice, strengthen its confidence in the nobility of the human soul and sustain all our hopes for a glorious life for all. All this we owe both to ourselves and to the peoples of the world who are so well represented here today.

To my compatriots, I have no hesitation in saying that each one of us is as intimately attached to the soil of this beautiful country as are the famous jacaranda trees of Pretoria and the mimosa trees of the bushveld. Each time one of us touches the soil of this land, we feel a sense of personal renewal. The national mood changes as the seasons change. We are moved by a sense of joy and exhilaration when the grass turns green and the flowers bloom.

That spiritual and physical oneness we all share with this common homeland explains the depth of the pain we all carried in our hearts as we saw our country tear itself apart in a terrible conflict, and as we saw it spurned, outlawed and isolated by the peoples of the world, precisely because it has become the universal base of the pernicious ideology and practice of racism and racial oppression.

We, the people of South Africa, feel fulfilled that humanity has taken us back into its bosom, that we, who were outlaws not so long ago, have today been given the rare privilege to be host to the nations of the world on our own soil. We thank all our distinguished international guests for having come to take possession with the people of our country of what is, after all, a common victory for justice, for peace, for human dignity. We trust that you will continue to stand by us as we tackle the challenges of building peace, prosperity, non-sexism, non-racialism and democracy.

We deeply appreciate the role that the masses of our people and their political mass democratic, religious, women, youth, business, traditional and other leaders have played to bring about this conclusion. Not least among them is my Second Deputy President, the Honorable F.W. de Klerk.

We would also like to pay tribute to our security forces, in all their ranks, for the distinguished role they have played in securing our first democratic elections and the transition to democracy, from blood-thirsty forces which still refuse to see the light.

The time for the healing of the wounds has come. The moment to bridge the chasms that divide us has come. The time to build is upon us. We have, at last, achieved our political emancipation. We pledge ourselves to liberate all our people from the continuing bondage of poverty, deprivation, suffering, gender and other discrimination. We succeeded to take our last steps to freedom in conditions of relative peace. We commit ourselves to the construction of a complete, just and lasting peace.

We have triumphed in the effort to implant hope in the breasts of the millions of our people. We enter into a covenant that we shall build the society in which all South Africans, both black and white, will be able to walk tall, without any fear in their hearts, assured of their inalienable right to human dignity – a rainbow nation at peace with itself and the world.

As a token of its commitment to the renewal of our country, the new Interim Government of National Unity will, as a matter of urgency, address the issue of amnesty for various categories of our people who are currently serving terms of imprisonment.

We dedicate this day to all the heroes and heroines in this country and the rest of the world who sacrificed in many ways and surrendered their lives so that we could be free. Their dreams have become reality. Freedom is their reward.

We are both humbled and elevated by the honor and privilege that you, the people of South Africa, have bestowed on us, as the first President of a united, democratic, non-racial and non-sexist South Africa, to lead our country out of the valley of darkness.

We understand it still that there is no easy road to freedom. We know it well that none of us acting alone can achieve success. We must therefore act together as a united people, for national reconciliation, for nation building, for the birth of a new world. Let there be justice for all. Let there be peace for all. Let there be work, bread, water and salt for all.

Let each know that for each the body, the mind and the soul have been freed to fulfill themselves. Never, never and never again shall it be that this beautiful land will again experience the oppression of one by another and suffer the indignity of being the skunk of the world.

Let freedom reign. The sun shall never set on so glorious a human achievement!

God bless Africa!

Thank you.

Sample further oral activity (SL)

Thank you, members of the ANC for inviting me here today to speak to you on this 20th anniversary of Nelson Mandela's inauguration. Many of you know me and my work. You know me as a reporter from the Truth and Reconciliation Commission in the 1990s. Many of you know my works of poetry, written in both Afrikaans and English. And for those of you who know my works intimately, you know that the words and ideas of Nelson Mandela are dear to me. They have influenced my writing and shaped me. They have shaped us all. I stand before you today to tell you why I think Madiba's words still ring true today, 20 years later.

I was only one of hundreds of thousands of people who came to Pretoria on 10 May, 1994. People of all races, from all corners of the world, queens, presidents, and local citizens came to hear his words on that day. It is therefore no wonder that of all the words he used in his speech, the word 'people' was used most frequently. In combination with this word, he spoke of 'humanity'. He appealed to our sense of national and global citizenship when he stated so clearly:

'Our daily deeds as ordinary South Africans must produce an actual South African reality that will reinforce humanity's belief in justice, strengthen its confidence in the nobility of the human soul and sustain all our hopes for a glorious life for all.'

He let us know that in our corner of the world, something great had happened to restore faith in all of humanity. On the very steps of the Union buildings in Pretoria, where the concept of apartheid had been conceived, he invited the world to gather to celebrate diversity. Where we had devised a shameful state of disgrace, he drew a colossal crowd of hope. Where we had unjustly accused the innocent, he promised reconciliation. He captured this sharp juxtaposition of our country and times best in the final lines of his speech, where he said that we had suffered the 'indignity of being the skunk of the world', and then immediately stated that 'the sun shall never set on so glorious a human achievement!' This was Madiba at his best. How symbolic that was. How moving and how noble it was to see Madiba make that day – a day that should have been about his personal achievement – a day for the people of South Africa and a day for all of the oppressed people in the world.

As a writer I always want to know how one makes an audience feel a certain way. How did Madiba make us feel as one? How did he unite us? As I re-read his words from that day in 1994, I see much reference to the land and nature. He spoke of the soil of this country that we all share, the rich earth, the grass and blossoms. He reminded us of how we are interconnected through the seasons that affect our moods. He pointed out that 'that spiritual and physical oneness we all share with this common homeland explains the depth of the pain we all carried in our hearts as we saw our country tear itself apart in a terrible conflict'. I, as a farmer's daughter, Madiba, as the son of a tribal leader, and all of us, as children of Africa, knew the pain of seeing our homeland torn apart for decade after decade. He united us by tapping into that emotion. He united us by saying that 'the time for the healing of the wounds has come'.

My questions, as a writer, continue. It is one thing to unify us, speak of healing and draw the world's attention to our suffering, but how did he make us believe in a future that is brighter and full of more opportunity than today? I believe he did this by celebrating the achievements of others. In a style that was characteristic of our great leader, he quite humbly appointed F.W. de Klerk Deputy President, giving credit to the man who began our country's great transition. He saluted the security forces for organizing free and fair elections. Remember, many of these forces had a history of hunting down members of the ANC. He dedicated his day to the prisoners and freedom fighters, who for centuries tried to bring democracy and justice to Africa.

And this brings me to my final point. Just as Madiba led by example, by honouring his predecessors, by showing humility and forgiving his enemies, we too must continue in this spirit. The dream of freedom is not yet entirely fulfilled in the townships of Johannesburg. There is not yet 'peace for all' on farms where owners are chased off their land. The ideal of non-racial violence is not a reality where xenophobia exists between South Africans and Zimbabweans and Malawians. Nelson Mandela and the ANC received a mandate on 10 May 1994 to 'lead our country out of the valley of darkness', as he said in his words. He warned us that there would be 'no easy road to freedom' and that 'none of us acting alone [could] achieve success'. The world's eyes are still watching South Africa. They do not only watch us when we host the World Cup for football or rugby. Oppressed peoples all over the world look to us as leaders, as pioneers in this field of democracy, diversity and human rights. Madiba has given us big shoes to fill, and we must fill them. We must deliver on his promise that:

'South Africans, both black and white, will be able to walk tall, without any fear in their hearts, assured of their inalienable right to human dignity – a rainbow nation at peace with itself and the world.'

Thank you ANC for inviting me here today on 10 May 2014. The words of our great leader are as relevant today as they were in 1994. And when we meet on this day for decades to come, I hope that we can say that that this rainbow nation is at peace with itself and the world.

Reflective statement

I think my further oral activity went rather well. In class we studied an entire unit on South Africa, including this inaugural speech by Nelson Mandela. I wanted to show that I understood the deeper meaning of the text in its context. This means that I had to learn about life after apartheid in South Africa, even though I have never even been there. As Mandela predicted, rebuilding this nation would be difficult. Today there are problems with crime and poverty that cannot be ignored. This is why I wanted Antjie Krog to address this in her speech. She is highly respected among many people in South Africa. It made sense for her, of all people, to comment on Mandela's words. I learned a lot from this activity and enjoyed preparing it as well.

tip

In further oral activities you should focus on one or two learning outcomes and specific topics from the IB Language A: language and literature guide. The more relevant your performance is to these outcomes and topics, the greater your chances are of scoring well.

Furthermore, your further oral activities should be based on one, or more, texts from the coursework. This ensures focus and coherence.

Teacher's comments

The following assessment and comments are based on the oral presentation. On the whole, the student's performance is focused on the Nelson Mandela's inaugural address, which gave it a strong sense of purpose and coherence. It commented well on a text in its context.

Criterion A: Knowledge and understanding of the text(s) and subject matter or extract – 9 out of 10

The student explores the ramifications of Mandela's speech in South Africa both in 1994 and 2014. The student explains the effects of Mandela's words on Antjie Krog and the rest of South Africans. The student explores several themes, such as humanity and unification. Mandela's words are also looked at in light of the current problems of South Africa, such as crime and poverty. The student is knowledgeable on the text, as there is reference to and explanation of the original speech.

Criterion B: Understanding of how language is used – 9 out of 10

The student demonstrates an awareness of the meaning of Mandela's words and their effect on his audience then, in 1994, and now in 2014. Certain phrases, such as *the skunk of the world* and *so glorious a human achievement* are singled out and explored further in depth. The whole organizing principle of this speech – a call to remember Mandela's words – narrows the focus of this further oral activity down to the use of language in context. This is commended.

Criterion C: Organisation – 5 out of 5

There is strong coherence in this student's speech, as it continually returns to a guiding question: *Why do Mandela's words still ring true today?* The student offers several explanations which are illustrated well with supporting quotations from Mandela's speech. There are signposts and markers for the audience, such as questions and topic sentences that keep the piece coherent and effective.

Criterion D: Language – 5 out of 5

The student's use of English is effective and appropriate. The student uses parallel constructions and strong phrases such as *where the concept of apartheid had been conceived, he invited the world to gather to celebrate diversity. Where we had devised a shameful state of disgrace, he drew a colossal crowd of hope. Where we had unjustly accused the innocent, he promised reconciliation.* The speech contains many of the main elements of good speech writing, as it appeals to the audience's emotions and sense of logic. What is more, the speech contains a good level and use of vocabulary with words such as *mandate* and *xenophobia*. This shows a command of the English language.

Ideas for part 1 further oral activities

1. Find a speech that you find intriguing or moving. Working with another student, take on the roles of interviewer and speaker (or speech writer) respectively. Ask about the choice of language in the speech and explain the effects that the speech has had on you and others. Make sure the dialogue allows both of you an equal chance to speak so that both of you can be assessed fairly.

2. Explore a text that is closely related to a particular culture. For example, many young Australians travel to Turkey every year on Anzac Day to honour Australian soldiers who fought at Gallipoli in the First World War. You could analyse a brochure from a travel agent that sells trips to Turkey to young Australians. If you

Further resources

The World in Words is a Public Broadcasting Service (PBS) podcast about many language issues that are relevant to part 1 of the course. As a source of inspiration for your further oral activity, listen to an episode to hear people discussing language issues.

are studying a different Anglophone culture, you may want to explore a different holiday or tradition with another suitable text.

3 You have seen how important the British Empire was in the spread of English around the world. Find one or more texts that were written during this period of expansion and exploitation, such as the poem 'White man's burden' by Rudyard Kipling. Explain how a post-colonial reading of this text is different from original interpretations of it would have been.

4 Take two texts, such as lyrics from two rap stars, and in pairs discuss how they express two different identities. Do they instigate racial inclusion or exclusion? Explain how contextual information helped you better understand the identities and the culture of the authors.

5 In groups, discuss how the use of the Internet has changed the English language and will continue to change it in the coming decades. Do some research on the topic and make several predictions about how people will speak and write in 50 years. The *Gr8 Db8* by David Crystal would serve as a good point of reference.

Chapter 1 summary

We started this chapter by establishing an anthropological approach to language. Since language and culture are inseparable, it is impossible *not* to study the contexts in which texts were written and received.

In this chapter you have studied two linguistic effects: convergence, or the processes by which cultures come together, and divergence, or the process by which they display independence. Globalisation has brought people together, creating situations that are facilitated through the English language. Communications on ocean-going vessels is one such situation. You have seen how the British Empire helped establish the role of English as the world's number one lingua franca and how economic factors have continued to increase bilingualism in former colonies such as India. Cultural trends play an important role in increasing the currency of the English language around the world.

You have also explored how cultures have adopted English but have used it to express their unique identity. In the case of Cockney English, for example, social differences are reflected through language. The history of each English-speaking culture, such as the American South, also accounts for the linguistic differences between English speakers. Finally, you have seen that the ways in which people identify with the region in which they live are often reflected in the ways in which they speak.

In the sample assessment materials, you saw how students demonstrate their understanding of the multi-faceted issues of language in the Anglophone world. The part 1 written task, a creative assignment, allows you to explore a range of different text types and language-related topics. Similarly the part 1 further oral activity allows room for creativity and the opportunity to express ideas about language and culture.

As you continue to explore the cultures of the Anglophone world through a study of various texts, you will require certain tools to analyse them more closely and interpret them more accurately. The next chapter will introduce you to these tools, so that you will be better able to appreciate not only the diversity but also the global nature of the English language.

Chapter 2 Close reading

In the last chapter you discovered that texts can be seen as pieces of evidence to help us better understand a culture. To unlock this evidence, various tools are necessary to analyse texts more carefully. Just as detectives need forensic tools to understand crime scenes, you too will require tools to help you reconstruct the contexts in which the texts were written. Having acquired these tools, you will be able to read more carefully and understand how context influences our interpretation of texts.

In this chapter, therefore, you will learn to develop skills that enable you to engage in **close reading**. Close reading is the skill of analysing and interpreting texts. You are faced with a multitude of texts every day in many different forms and contexts, from websites to airports. Practising the skill of close reading will help you understand your own environment and the cultures of the Anglophone world better.

If you are to approach a text in the same way a detective approaches a crime scene, you will have to ask questions. It makes it easier if we group the questions into five main categories in which you can organise your analysis. In each of the following five units of this chapter, you will explore one of these five areas: audience and purpose; content and theme; tone and mood; stylistic devices; and structure. You can refer to these five categories or analytical tools as the 'Big 5'.

The table below gives you a list of questions you can ask about any text. Each question relates to the five analytical tools – the 'Big 5' – that you will be exploring in this chapter.

Analytical tools – the Big 5	Questions
Audience and purpose	Who wrote the text? Who was it written for? Why did the writer write it?
Content and theme	What is the text about?
Tone and mood	What is the writer's tone? How does the text make the reader feel?
Stylistic devices	What stylistic devices does the writer use?
Structure	What kind of text is it? What structural conventions are used?

Key term

Close reading refers to the practice of analysing and interpreting texts.

tip

The Big 5

Use the Big 5 model to help you analyse texts. You will find it useful when preparing for Paper 1, the written tasks or the individual oral commentary. Think of each aspect of the Big 5 as a lens through which you can look at texts, each revealing new levels of understanding.
1 Audience and purpose
2 Content and theme
3 Tone and mood
4 Stylistic devices
5 Structure

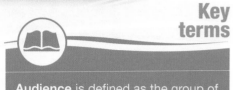

Audience is defined as the group of listeners or readers for whom a text or message is intended.

Purpose describes the writer's intentions in writing a text, be they to entertain, enlighten, persuade, inform, evaluate, define, instruct or explain. Writers and speakers want to instigate a response from their audience.

Context of interpretation refers to the factors that can influence a reader of a text, such as time, place and personal experience.

Unit 2.1 **Audience and purpose**

In order to study the relationship between a text and the context in which it was written, you need to know and understand the concepts of **audience** and **purpose**. If you have ever eavesdropped on a conversation, or accidentally overheard something that was not intended for you to hear, then you will already know the importance of these concepts. If you eavesdrop, you have to create a context by 'filling in the gaps' or looking for what is implied. In this unit you are going to look at a text out of context in order to understand the importance of both its audience and its purpose.

Audience

Texts are neither written nor read in a vacuum. It is important to understand that both time and place can influence how and why a text is written and how it is interpreted by the reader. Have you ever read something that you did not particularly enjoy but could nonetheless appreciate? The next time you are in a newsagent's browsing for magazines, look through a magazine that targets people with completely different interests from your own. What does this tell you about who you are?

In Chapter 1 you read and analysed various texts and, while you were doing this, you may have experienced some distance between yourself and the intended audience. The jargon of Text 1.1, for example, placed an imaginary boundary around the people that it targeted, namely seafarers. Similarly, unless you work in a call centre in India, you probably did not closely identify with the target audience of Text 1.2.

As you explore a wider range of texts, keep in mind these two important questions:
• Who was the text written for?
• How are you part of or different from the target audience?

"I want to read something directly targeted at me."

Figure 2.1 Can you explain the humour of this cartoon? Is every one of us unique or does each of us fit into a neatly defined 'target audience'?

Context of interpretation

Has your interpretation of a text ever been different from someone else's? This is perfectly plausible as language can be very ambiguous. What's more, readers are often influenced by the contexts in which they read. That is to say, readers are affected by their particular circumstances and environment, and their personal history. This is known as the **context of interpretation**. You should keep in mind that you may interpret a text differently from the way the author intended it to be interpreted.

Purpose

Every writer wants to instigate a response from their audience. Every text therefore has a purpose. Keep in mind these two important questions when seeking the purpose of a text:
• What is the writer's intention?
• Why did the writer write the text?

Context of composition

Writers are people who, like everyone else, are affected by their environment and their personal experiences. Time, race, gender, nationality and family history are a few factors that influence writers and their work. These factors comprise what is known as the **context of composition**. As you have seen, you have to be like a detective when you read texts, looking for pieces of evidence that reflect the context of composition. These pieces of evidence are called contextual clues.

Figure 2.2 (page 38) shows the relationship between the context of composition, the context of interpretation and human communication.

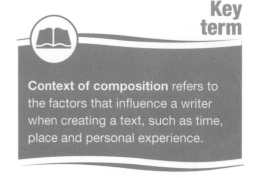

Key term

Context of composition refers to the factors that influence a writer when creating a text, such as time, place and personal experience.

'**What is written without effort is in general read without pleasure.**'
Samuel Johnson (1709–84)

Activity 2.1

This activity will help you understand the importance of context and improve your close reading.

1 Each student in the class finds a text that implicitly reflects cultural values. Text 2.1 is a good example.
2 Using a word processing program, remove the main contextual clues from your text, such as the formatting, the title, the name of the author and year of publication. This has been done to Text 2.1.
3 Working in groups, ask the other students to hunt for the remaining contextual clues in the text. These may be words or phrases that make implications about the context of composition and the target audience. Organise this discussion in a table similar to the one below. For practice, add to the table below with reference to Text 2.1.
4 Compare and contrast as readers the students in your group with the intended target audience. Are the students part of the target audience?
5 Reveal the missing contextual information on the text. How well did the students understand the text through the remaining contextual clues? How accurate were their descriptions of the context of composition and the intended target audience? (For the missing contextual information on Text 2.1, see answers below.)

	Context of composition	Target audience
Time	Author refers to the aristocracy of Europe, which indicates writing was in a different period from ours.	Text targets an audience who understand loanwords from French (e.g. *en famille*, *d'oyley* and *tente-en-pié*) – possibly upper class Britons.
Place	Author seems to be writing from an English perspective as there are multiple references to English customs at the beginning of each paragraph.	Author writes about the growing popularity of afternoon tea in Europe and the Americas, so target audience may be in these regions. Author instructs on how to consume English tea properly.

Answers: Activity 2.1
Text 2.1 is from The Whole Art of Dining by Jean Rey. The book was published in 1921, in an era when an English-speaking upper class was growing around the world and people were being encouraged to consume more material goods. According to the introduction to Rey's book, the style of a picnic or banquet reveals the position in society of its host. Rey teaches the growing wealthy class about the dining habits of the decadent. Elsewhere in the book, he explains when to wear white gloves, how to present objects on a sideboard and where to order delicacies.

Context of composition

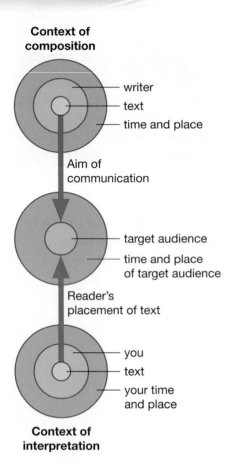

writer
text
time and place

Aim of communication

target audience
time and place of target audience

Reader's placement of text

you
text
your time and place

Context of interpretation

Figure 2.2 Three important concepts that help us understand how meaning is conveyed through texts: the context of composition, the target audience and the context of interpretation.

Text 2.1

The Tea, or 'Afternoon Tea' of England, is also becoming every day more in vogue among the aristocracy of all the countries of Europe, and in both Americas.

As is well known, tea is served in England in various ways, according to where and to whom served.

In most private houses in England when tea is taken *en famille*,[1] that is, without special visitors or ceremony, it is served in the dining-room at the same table where the other meals are taken.

According to the number of persons present at this meal, one or more plates of cut bread and butter, on paper d'oyley,[2] are placed on the table; also, some plates of cut cake, various kinds of pastry specially for tea, plates of water-cress, celery, etc., and jam or marmalade.

To the left of the lady of the house are placed as many cups and saucers as persons present at table; and to the right a tray holding a large tea-pot with the tea ready prepared and a jug of boiling water or a silver kettle on a spirit-stand, a jug of cold milk and another (smaller) with cream.

The sugar-basin should be placed on the cloth to the right and a slop-basin on the tray.

The lady of the house generally pours out the tea, and when pouring it she usually asks each person to be served (if she does not already know) 'Do you take sugar?' 'Do you like your tea sweet?'

It is generally the custom to take two cups of tea, and each person helps himself to the things on the table.

Buttered toast, toasted tea cake, muffins, crumpets, etc., are also served at tea.

Tea is not considered as a meal in the proper sense of the word; but only a collation or 'tente-en-pié,[3] between luncheon and dinner.

Formerly, tea in private houses was always served on the point of five o'clock; hence the origin of the phrase 'five o'clock tea' used abroad.

The tea of the English working-class is the most eccentric[4] of meals, and one of the greatest injuries a gourmet could possibly conceive (according to the ideas of Brillat-Savarin); for with the tea they partake of various kinds of salted meat and dried fish, such as 'corned-beef', kippers, bloaters, red herrings, winkles, shrimps, pickles, watercresses, cucumber, lettuce, jam or marmalade, bread and butter, and cake. This incongruous[5] kind of food may, no doubt, be quite nice and tasty for this class of people, but it must shock any one endowed with refined epicurean[6] instinct.

In a family where there is a nursery of small children, tea for them takes the place of dinner or supper. In addition to bread and butter, etc., boiled eggs, some fish, or light meat and fruit are served. This is also called 'High tea' or 'Meat tea.'

[1] *en famille*   French for 'with the family'
[2] **d'oyley**   is a decorative piece of lace to protect the wood of tables or sideboards; here made of cut paper
[3] **tente-en-pié**   (modern-day Spanish *tentempié*) means a snack or something to eat to keep you going between meals
[4] **eccentric**   strange, different from the ordinary
[5] **incongruous**   out of place, not consistent or harmonious
[6] **epicurean**   fond of good tastes or luxuries

Figure 2.3 A Victorian afternoon tea in the 1860s.

As you prepare for Paper 1 you will explore a range of texts. You have seen in this unit that, for a good analysis of their audience and purpose, you must comment on the context of composition and context of interpretation. It is important to question *why* the writer has written the text you are studying. You may find that you do not belong to the target audience that the writer had in mind for the text and you have seen how to explore the differences between your context of interpretation and that of the target audience. Practise writing about the audience and purpose of a range of texts to improve your skills of close reading.

Besides asking yourself who the text was written for, and who wrote it and why, another key question you should always ask about a text is *What is it about?* In the next unit you are going to explore two ways to approach this question.

Unit 2.2 **Content and theme**

There are two ways to answer the question *What is the text about?* At one level, you can summarise the literal **content** of the text, referring to the events, people and topics in the text. At another level, you can look for a deeper meaning by making inferences and reading 'between the lines'. This second approach leads to a discussion of **theme**, which is the message or main idea of the text. When you write about a text, you will need to be able to distinguish between these two concepts.

The terms *content* and *theme* will become very familiar to you when you discuss fiction texts. When analysing non-fiction texts too, however, you will find these terms equally useful.

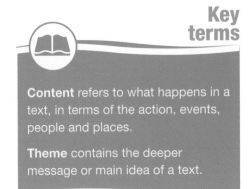

tip

*This **is** a congratulatory letter from Artemus Ward to the Prince of Wales.* Notice that all the statements in the activity are in the present tense. Even though the author may have written the text long ago, we write a textual analysis in the present tense because the text continues to be read and still generates discussion today.

Activity 2.2

The following statements relate to Text 1.6, the letter you read in Chapter 1 from Artemus Ward to the Prince of Wales (see pages 13–14). For each of the statements, decide whether it is about content or theme, giving reasons for your answer.

1 This is a congratulatory letter from Artemus Ward to the Prince of Wales.
2 Artemus Ward thinks England has a duty to support the Confederates of the South in their war against the North.
3 War is not something that can be won in a courtroom: it costs lives on the battlefield.
4 There is a war in America, and people are being drafted from all social classes.
5 The text is about England's neutral position in the American Civil War.
6 The text is about England's hypocrisy in funding the Confederate navy while claiming to remain 'neutral'.
7 Artemus Ward lives in a rural place in the South where people build barns and there are no newspapers.
8 Artemus Ward thinks the South would win the war if England contributed more to the Confederates.

Content

As you engage in the close reading of a text, always ask the 'obvious' questions about its content:

• Who are the people involved in the text and what are their roles?
• Does the text make reference to a particular time or event?
• What happens in the text? What kind of action takes place?

While these questions may seem simple, they serve as a starting point for a more complex understanding of the text. Try asking the questions about some of the texts you are studying for part 1 of the course and you will see their importance. Some questions may be more applicable to some texts than others.

Theme

All writers and speakers have a message they want to convey (see Figure 2.2, page 38). The message of a text is closely related to but different from the writer's purpose. A sign in a factory, for example, may tell you to wear head protection (message) in an effort to promote safety (purpose). You need to read 'between the lines' of the message about head protection to discover its purpose.

When you read a text, ask the following questions in order to read between the lines and discover the text's deeper themes:

• What is the author's message?
• What is the significance of the text to its audience?
• What is the text actually saying?

"I'm not trying to say anything—I'm just talking."

Figure 2.4 Why do we find this cartoon funny? How does it comment on the importance of content and theme in communication?

Activity 2.3

We will continue to explore content and theme by looking at a piece of non-fiction. Text 2.2 is from a famous speech by Martin Luther King. As you read the speech, find statements or key words that tell you something about its content and theme. Copy the table below and write the statements and words under the appropriate heading.

Content	Theme
demonstration the Emancipation Proclamation	freedom injustice

Text 2.2 'I have a dream', Martin Luther King, 1963

Dr Martin Luther King Jr was a Baptist minister from the South of the USA. He made his famous speech, 'I have a dream', in 1963 when people were campaigning for civil rights to be accorded to black people in the USA. Together with 300 000 people, King marched from the Washington Monument to the Lincoln Memorial in Washington DC to give this speech, demand racial equality and lobby for better rights for workers. His efforts were successful: the Civil Rights Act was passed in 1964. His televised speech established his place as one of America's greatest orators.

I am happy to join with you today in what will go down in history as the greatest demonstration for freedom in the history of our nation.

   Five score years ago, a great American, in whose symbolic shadow we stand signed the Emancipation Proclamation. This momentous decree came as a great beacon light of hope to millions of Negro slaves who had been seared in the flames of withering injustice. It came as a joyous daybreak to end the long night of captivity.

Figure 2.5 Martin Luther King (1929–68).

41

discussion

1 After reading the text, discuss your initial impressions. Then watch a video recording of King's speech online. How does the video add to your understanding of the text? How does the video provide a context for the text?

2 Look at the use of concrete and abstract nouns in the text. Concrete nouns are words such as *shadow*, *heat* and *lips*. Abstract nouns are words such as *struggle*, *segregation* and *justice*. How does the difference between concrete and abstract nouns help you distinguish the content from the themes of the text?

But one hundred years later, we must face the tragic fact that the Negro still is not free. One hundred years later, the life of the Negro is still sadly crippled by the manacles of segregation and the chains of discrimination. One hundred years later, the Negro lives on a lonely island of poverty in the midst of a vast ocean of material prosperity. One hundred years later, the Negro is still languishing in the corners of American society and finds himself in exile in his own land. So we have come here today to dramatize an appalling condition.

… We must forever conduct our struggle on the high plane of dignity and discipline. We must not allow our creative protest to degenerate into physical violence. Again and again we must rise to the majestic heights of meeting physical force with soul force. The marvellous new militancy which has engulfed the Negro community must not lead us to distrust of all white people, for many of our white brothers, as evidenced by their presence here today, have come to realise that their destiny is tied up with our destiny and their freedom is inextricably bound to our freedom. We cannot walk alone.

… I have a dream that one day this nation will rise up and live out the true meaning of its creed: 'We hold these truths to be self-evident: that all men are created equal.'

I have a dream that one day on the red hills of Georgia the sons of former slaves and the sons of former slave owners will be able to sit down together at a table of brotherhood.

I have a dream that one day even the state of Mississippi, a desert state, sweltering with the heat of injustice and oppression, will be transformed into an oasis of freedom and justice.

I have a dream that my four children will one day live in a nation where they will not be judged by the colour of their skin, but by the content of their character.

I have a dream today.

I have a dream that one day the state of Alabama, whose governor's lips are presently dripping with the words of interposition[1] and nullification;[2] will be transformed into a situation where little black boys and black girls will be able to join hands with little white boys and white girls and walk together as sisters and brothers.

I have a dream today.

[1] **interposition** a political position that claims that individual states in the USA have the right to protect their interests from federal violation; interposition is not constitutional

[2] **nullification** a state's right to nullify or ignore federal laws that are deemed to be unconstitutional by the state; like interposition, nullification is not constitutional

Analysing content and theme in the exam

To prepare for Paper 1, it is important to practise commenting on the content and themes of various texts. Here is a brief paragraph that one student wrote on the content and theme of the 'I have a dream' speech in Text 2.2.

'I have a dream' is a call to Americans to fight peacefully for Civil Rights. King asks America to deliver on a promise made by Abraham Lincoln and the founding fathers of America that all people should be treated as equals. In fact he quotes the Declaration of Independence by saying 'We hold these truths to be self-evident: that all men are created equal.' He is literally standing in front of the Lincoln Memorial to remind Americans of Lincoln's Emancipation Declaration, a document that freed slaves in the USA over a hundred years before King's speech. Americans of all races are gathered in this peaceful demonstration to show that they are concerned about the lack of equality and Civil Rights in America. King tells them that black and white children should be allowed to hold hands in places like Alabama. He tells them that former slave owners should be able to sit at the same table and eat with former slaves. He tells them that politicians and states do not have the right to ignore federal laws that prevent discrimination. In brief his words 'I have a dream' refer to the vision of equality that he has for the country.

By reading the student's response to Text 2.2 you gain a sense of how to comment on the content and themes of texts. Good close reading skills include this ability to identify and explore the content and themes of different types of texts.

Activity 2.4

In the table below you can see how one student has used both deductive and inductive reasoning to come to conclusions about the 'I have a dream' speech by Martin Luther King.

Type of reasoning	Premise 1	Premise 2	Conclusion
Deductive	Both the Emancipation Proclamation and the Bill of Rights state that all people are equal in the USA. (general)	Alabama is in the USA. (general)	Therefore girls and boys of all races should be able to hold hands in Alabama. (specific)
Inductive	People of all races are gathered at this protest. (specific)	This protest is non-violent. (specific)	All races can (and must) work together peacefully to achieve Civil Rights. (general)

Copy the table outline and make two conclusions about the theme of a text that you are studying for part 1. Use both deductive and inductive reasoning, as in the example above.

Unit 2.3 **Tone and mood**

You have looked at the *who* and the *what* of texts by studying the concepts of audience, purpose, content and theme. Now you are going to learn *how* a writer uses language to instigate a response from the readers. We will also look at how readers feel in response to the language of various texts. A writer uses a particular **tone**, which puts the reader in a particular **mood**. You can think of it as a cause and effect relationship.

TOK

The analysis of texts requires logic. In order to come to a conclusion about the theme of a text you have to establish several arguments. In other words, we have to be able to use both **deductive reasoning** and **inductive reasoning**. Deductive reasoning comes to a specific conclusion by drawing on general **premises**. Inductive reasoning comes to a general conclusion by drawing on specific cases.

Key terms

Deductive reasoning refers to an argument that comes to a specific conclusion by drawing on *general* rules.

Inductive reasoning refers to an argument that comes to a general conclusion by drawing on *specific* cases.

Premises are statements or propositions that arguments rely on to come to conclusions.

Tone refers to the language used by a speaker or writer to instigate an emotional effect on the listener or reader.

Mood refers to the atmosphere that is created for an audience through the tone of a text.

Key term

Diction is the choice of vocabulary that a writer uses in order to create a tone.

Tone

Tone is very much related to the context of composition. If we think of the author of a piece of writing being in a certain state of mind – perhaps frustrated, troubled or hurt – then we can imagine what kind of vocabulary they might use to convey the message. We refer to this choice of vocabulary as the writer's **diction**. Writers create their tone through their diction.

When you read a text, ask the following questions in order to gain a deeper awareness of the use of tone:

- How does the author sound?
- What is the writer's tone?
- What kind of diction does the writer use?

The following table lists some of Martin Luther King's diction from Text 2.2 alongside the tone that the diction creates. Notice the difference between the choice of words and the tone they create: despite the use of words like *sadly* and *lonely*, the writer sounds neither sad nor lonely. Instead the tone created is empathetic and disenfranchised.

Diction		Tone	
sadly	languishing	empathetic	frustrated
lonely	shameful	disenfranchised	accusing

'The most important things are the hardest to say, because words diminish them.'
Stephen King (1947–)

How do we make this jump from *sadly* to *empathetic*? We imagine how the writer must have felt to select that particular word in that context. We imagine how it must have felt for Martin Luther King to represent all African Americans on that particular day in August 1963. We imagine what it must have felt like to speak in the shadow of the Lincoln Memorial. The jump from diction to tone is a mental exercise that relies heavily on the context of composition.

Mood

When commenting on a text, especially in an academic setting, students often forget to write about how the text makes them *feel*. Textual analysis, however, should include comments on the reader's feelings in response to the text. A writer's diction affects readers. Language has the power to put us in a certain mood.

In order to discover how this process works, you have to ask two more key questions when studying a text:

- How does the text make the reader feel?
- How does the writer use diction to put the reader in a certain mood?

The following table gives some examples of the diction of Martin Luther King in Text 2.2 alongside the reader's corresponding mood. The list of mood words is not prescriptive, however, as everyone is entitled to feel something different and every reader will have a personal response on reading the text.

Diction		Mood	
crippled	poverty	sorry	ashamed
manacles	exile	guilty	abandoned
chains		oppressive	

We make the jump from the diction to the mood by imagining how the target audience must have received those words in 1963. We also feel their resonance in our context of interpretation today.

In order to understand how language can put us in a particular mood, we need to understand that words operate at two levels. At one level, words stand for something in a literal sense. Their literal meaning is what we call **denotation**. At a deeper level, words are surrounded by an aura of emotional meaning, which we call **connotation**. A word like *crippled* literally means 'not physically able', but its connotation calls on sentiments of sympathy or feeling sorry for someone.

In textual analysis, writing about sentiments in an appropriate way requires a very sophisticated vocabulary. Instead of stating that a text is *light* or *scary*, for example, you should use more meaningful language such as *whimsical* or *threatening*. In fact many teachers would say that a good variety of descriptive vocabulary is what distinguishes a top-level textual analysis from the rest. You will therefore need to build up a good vocabulary of useful adjectives and adverbs for when you talk or write about tone and mood.

Activity 2.5

There are many adjectives that can be used to accurately describe the tone and mood of a text. You are going to complete a table with adjectives from the boxes below about two texts. First, read Texts 2.3 and 2.4 on page 46.

Now copy the table below and complete it with the tone and mood adjectives in the boxes. Write each word in the appropriate column.

Tone words

adventuresome	anxious	celebratory	confident	determined	dignified
disappointed	encouraging	euphoric	fatalistic	hopeful	hopeless
hyperbolic	ominous	passionate	reassuring	resigned	severe
solemn	tragic	wise	zealous		

Mood words

apprehensive	desolate	disappointed	disheartened	empathetic	empowered
engaged	fascinated	frustrated	intrigued	mournful	optimistic
sentimental	solemn	suspicious	tough	uplifted	

	Relevant to Text 2.3 only	**Relevant to Texts 2.3 and 2.4**	**Relevant to Text 2.4 only**
Tone words	encouraging	confident	determined
Mood words	zealous	intrigued	disappointed

As a class, discuss your tables, referring to the language as used in Texts 2.3 and 2.4. Does everyone's table look the same, or have you put a word in a different column from some of the other students?

Key terms

Denotation refers to what a word stands for in its most literal sense.

Connotation refers to the aura of emotional meaning that we associate with a word.

tip

Describing the tone and mood of a text is a skill that takes time to develop. There is no single list of vocabulary to learn and use to describe the tone or mood of a particular text. In order to build on your vocabulary, you could try creating a spider diagram or mind map around the diction of a particular text. As a class you could brainstorm vocabulary for how a text or word made you feel. Get into the habit of reading book and film reviews, discussing texts in class and doing vocabulary-building exercises, such as the activity on this page.

Higher level

In Chapter 1 you were invited to create a 'library' of texts for classroom discussion (see page 2). The texts in your library will require some contextual descriptions, such as the ones that have been written for many texts in this coursebook. Writing contextual descriptions means doing research on the context of composition and the original target audience of the texts that you are studying in class.

Start by researching Texts 2.3 and 2.4. Find out more about Captain A.J.N. Tremearne's book on West Africa and Captain Scott's expedition to the South Pole. Why were these texts written? Who were they written for?

Further resources

The British Library has an excellent website with a wealth of resource material and categories that reflect the content of this course. The 'Language and Literature' page at www.bl.uk/learning/langlit/index.html is a good place to start for information about Texts 2.3 and 2.4. The site has many interesting primary sources, that is to say original documents, such as travel logs and cookbooks from the 18th century. If you are interested in the dialects of England, you can find an interactive map with recordings of ordinary people speaking in their vernacular.

Text 2.3 *The Niger and the West Sudan*, Captain A.J.N. Tremearne, 1910

What a wonderful fascination there is in the name of West Africa, the most mysterious part of that very mysterious continent! What visions of cannibals, 'jujus' and sacrifices it conjures up; what thoughts of conquests of new countries and new peoples; what desires of travel and exploration! There are other things – fever, for instance – which will come later and tend to shatter some of the virgin illusions, but in spite of everything there will always remain some attraction about this land which one will never shake off. It is said that when once a man has the call of the bush in his blood he will continue to answer to it until he leaves his bones there – unless by some lucky chance he be invalided in time to die at home.

Figure 2.6 Captain Scott and his team on their expedition to the South Pole in 1912.

Text 2.4 From the diary of Captain Robert Falcon Scott, 1912

Thursday March 29

Since the 21st we have had a continuous gale from W.S.W. and S.W. We had fuel to make two cups of tea apiece and bare food for two days on the 20th. Every day we have been ready to start for our depot 11 miles away, but outside the door of the tent it remains a scene of whirling drift. I do not think we can hope for any better things now. We shall stick it out to the end, but we are getting weaker; of course, and the end cannot be far.

It seems a pity, but I do not think I can write more. – R. Scott

Last entry. For God's sake look after our people.

Message to the Public

… Had we lived, I should have had a tale to tell of the hardihood, endurance, and courage of my companions which would have stirred the heart of every Englishman. These rough notes and our dead bodies must tell the tale, but surely, surely, a great rich country like ours will see that those who are dependent on us are properly provided for. – R. Scott

Unit 2.4 **Stylistic devices**

As you look at the diction used by writers, you will probably come across **stylistic devices** that you recognise. In your exploration of how writers convey a message, you will see that they rely on various 'tricks of the trade'. The English language has, after all, been used for writing all sorts of texts, from brochures, posters and reviews to literary novels, plays and poems, for many years. If we consider all types of writing as craft or forms of art that have evolved, then it makes sense to ask what kinds of language tools writers have at their disposal.

As you approach different types of texts, ask yourself the following key questions:
- How does the writer instigate a particular response?
- What stylistic devices does the writer use?
- Is there a difference between what the writer says and what the writer means?
- What stylistic devices does the writer use to make comparisons?

Writers use stylistic devices as tools of communication. Just as builders use hammers and wrenches to construct a house, writers use irony and analogy to convey a message. As you become more familiar with these tools, you will begin to understand texts at a deeper level. Learning to identify stylistic devices is another skill of close reading that you will develop throughout the English language and literature course through your analysis of a wide variety of texts.

This unit provides the starting point for your exploration of stylistic devices. In the coming chapters you will be exploring persuasive language, advertising techniques and rhetorical devices, and in part 4 you will look at devices such as metaphor, personification and alliteration. For now though, in this unit, we will discuss two broad categories of stylistic devices that are used in many forms of communication: irony and figurative language. Understanding how writers apply these two devices will help you analyse texts better.

Irony

Look at Figure 2.7 and ask yourself why you might ask a question you already know the answer to. With Figure 2.4 on page 41 we established a very important rule of communication: we speak because we have something to say. When we say one thing but mean something else, this does not mean that the rules of communication have broken down. It is instead what happens when we use **verbal irony**.

"Do I know how fast I was going? Isn't that your job?"

Figure 2.7 Why do traffic police officers always ask speeding motorists this question? What are they *really* saying?

'Language is the armoury of the human mind, and at once contains the trophies of its past and the weapons of its future conquests.'
Samuel Taylor Coleridge (1772–1834)

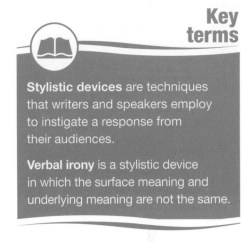

Key terms

Stylistic devices are techniques that writers and speakers employ to instigate a response from their audiences.

Verbal irony is a stylistic device in which the surface meaning and underlying meaning are not the same.

'Any definition of irony – though hundreds might be given, and very few of them would be accepted – must include this, that the surface meaning and the underlying meaning of what is said are not the same.'
Henry Watson Fowler (1858–1933)

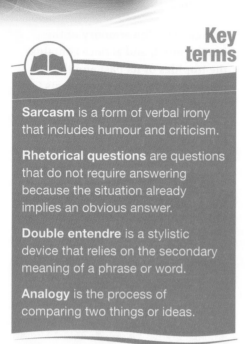

While there are many kinds of verbal irony, one characteristic is true of all: there is a discrepancy between the surface meaning and the underlying meaning. Since irony relies on these two levels of meaning, it can only be effective in context. You are going to look at three kinds of verbal irony: sarcasm, rhetorical questions and double entendre.

Sarcasm

Verbal irony is often confused with sarcasm. Sarcasm, however, is a form of verbal irony that includes humour and criticism. We usually hear sarcasm in the tone of the speaker, such as when a player says 'Thanks for dropping the ball, again!' In the context of a sports match, if one player said this to another, it would not sound very friendly (and the player would not really mean he was grateful)!

Rhetorical question

Sarcasm often takes the form of rhetorical questions. Such questions do not require an answer, as the answer is usually implied. In Figure 2.7 we see a driver being approached by a traffic police officer. Such situations are common and we know the script. The police officer usually already has evidence of the speeding violation and does not need to consult the motorist. Why then do they always ask the perpetrator 'Do you know how fast you were going?' The motorist responds to this rhetorical question with another rhetorical question: 'Isn't that your job?'

Double entendre

There are some words that lend themselves better to irony than others, since some words, such as homonyms, look and sound the same but have two different meanings. Notice the use of the word *dressing* in the following joke:

'Why did the tomato blush?' 'Because he saw the salad dressing!'

A joke like this one, also called a pun, relies on ambiguous language that has secondary meaning. The word *dressing* is both a noun, as in 'sauce', and a verb noun, as in 'putting one's clothes on'. This type of verbal irony is also known as double entendre.

All in all, people do not always say what they mean or mean what they say. There is, however, always meaning in what is said and irony is a common stylistic device that demonstrates this rule.

Figurative speech

If we do not always literally mean what we say, then there must be a figurative layer of speech. In Text 2.2 Martin Luther King expresses ideas that have no literal sense. For example, in the line *The Negro lives on a lonely island of poverty in the midst of a vast ocean of material prosperity*, we have an example of figurative speech. There is no such physical thing as 'a vast ocean of material prosperity', but we can imagine it in a figurative sense. In essence the writer is painting an image in our minds by putting intangible notions, such as poverty and prosperity, onto tangible places, such as an island and an ocean. Our mind can follow the writer as he does this because we understand the concept of figurative speech.

Analogy and metaphor

Analogy is the process of comparing one thing or idea to another. Every day we hear expressions such as *She's got her head in the clouds* or *I don't know where you're coming from with that.* Expressions like these shed light on how we think. These two expressions compare, respectively, absent-mindedness to air and difference to foreignness. Both these expressions make use of a stylistic device known as **metaphor**, which you will study further in Chapter 8. For now, it is important to establish that we all hear and read metaphors in everyday situations – they are not used just by great poets such as Shakespeare.

The cognitive linguists George Lakoff and Mark Johnson believe that we structure a lot of our thought around metaphor. In their book *Metaphors We Live By*, they present as an example the statement *ARGUMENT IS WAR*. Below are some of the examples from everyday speech that Lakoff and Johnson cite to show that metaphor is an important factor in how we think and communicate:

- Your claims are indefensible.
- He attacked every weak point in my argument.
- His criticisms were right on target.
- I demolished his argument.
- I've never won an argument with him.

Key term

Metaphor is the use of language to make a comparison between two things or ideas by applying a word or phrase to something that does not *literally* mean that.

Activity 2.6

Below is a list of stylistic devices (1–6) you have learned about in this unit and a list of phrases (a–f) taken from the poem 'Half-caste' by John Agard (Text 2.5). Read the poem, then match the devices to the phrases.

1 Verbal irony
2 Sarcasm
3 Rhetorical question
4 Double entendre
5 Metaphor
6 Figurative speech

a Excuse me / standing on one leg / I'm half-caste (lines 1–3)
b wha yu mean / when yu say half-caste (5–6)
c yu mean tchaikovsky / sit down at dah piano / an mix a black key / wid a white key / is a half-caste symphony? / (26–30)
d I'm sure you'll understand / why I offer yu half-a-hand (38–9)
e I dream half-a-dream (43)
f I half-caste human being / cast half-a-shadow (45–6)

Text 2.5 *Half-caste*, John Agard

John Agard is a popular contemporary poet of mixed race. He grew up in British Guiana (now Guyana) in the 1950s and immigrated to Britain in 1977. He has spread awareness of Caribbean culture as a travelling lecturer around the world. His poetry has won several awards and has often appeared in British secondary school exams.

```
1      Excuse me
       standing on one leg
       I'm half-caste

       Explain yuself
5      wha yu mean
       when yu say half-caste
```

Answers: Activity 2.6

1 a. *The irony of being half-caste is understood through the situation where the narrator is literally standing on one leg. His other leg may be in a plaster cast, which is a homophone of caste.*

2 d. *Offering someone a hand is a sign of respect. Offering someone half a hand implies there is only half as much respect. The statement is sarcastic because there is humour involved and the narrator is critical of the 'you' character for calling him a half-caste. (Later he accuses the 'you' character of using only half his mind.)*

3 b. *The narrator asks what is meant by half-caste, but does not really expect an answer. This makes it a rhetorical question. Furthermore, every question mark in this poem indicates a rhetorical question.*

4 e. *The word dream can also be used to refer to people's ambitions and aspirations. The poet is implying that he has half as much ability to fulfil his aspirations because he is half-caste.*

5 c. *The Tchaikovsky example is given as metaphor. Beautiful music is created with both black and white keys, just as beautiful people are created from mixed race.*

6 f. *People of mixed race, who are sometimes called half-caste, cannot literally cast half a shadow. This is a figure of speech with implications.*

Figure 2.8 The British poet John Agard (1949–).

```
        yu mean when picasso
        mix red an green
        is a half-caste canvas?
10      explain yuself
        wha u mean
        when yu say half-caste
        yu mean when light an shadow
        mix in de sky
15      is a half-caste weather?
        well in dat case
        england weather
        nearly always half-caste
        in fact some o dem cloud
20      half-caste till dem overcast
        so spiteful dem don't want de sun pass
        ah rass?
        explain yuself
        wha yu mean
25      when yu say half-caste
        yu mean tchaikovsky
        sit down at dah piano
        an mix a black key
        wid a white key
30      is a half-caste symphony?

        Explain yuself
        wha yu mean
        Ah listening to yu wid de keen
        half of mih ear
35      Ah looking at u wid de keen
        half of mih eye
        an when I'm introduced to yu
        I'm sure you'll understand
        why I offer yu half-a-hand
40      an when I sleep at night
        I close half-a-eye
        consequently when I dream
        I dream half-a-dream
        an when moon begin to glow
45      I half-caste human being
        cast half-a-shadow
        but yu must come back tomorrow
        wid de whole of yu eye
        an de whole of yu ear
50      an de whole of yu mind

        an I will tell yu
        de other half
        of my story
```

Unit 2.5 **Structure**

As you continue to explore how writers convey a message, it is important to consider the structure of the text and the different structural conventions that writers use. When engaging in close reading of a text the key questions to ask are:

• What kind of text is it?
• What structural conventions are used in the text?

Although these questions may seem elementary, they are fundamental to a good textual analysis. We can often identify different types of text quickly and easily: a news article is often presented in columns, with a headline, images and newsworthy information; a brochure is often folded once or twice, printed on glossy paper and with clear bullet-pointed information; a poster for a film (Figure 2.9, for example) has certain structural conventions that we easily recognise, such as image placement, title and the starring actors' and producer's names.

Figure 2.9 How does this film poster adhere to the structural conventions of film posters? This poster is from 1942. How does it compare with film posters we see today?

Why is it important to study the structural conventions of certain text types? Recognising different types of text is a skill of media literacy that is becoming ever more important in this digital age, where the differences between an opinion column and a blog, a letter and an e-mail, or an advertisement and a search engine are becoming blurred. Understanding the conventions for writing different types of text is also a useful skill for producing your written tasks.

Throughout this book are examples of how to 'deconstruct' different texts. That is to say, the elements that define a certain type of text are broken down. In the case of letters, for example, you will look at headings and greetings, for poems rhythm and rhyming schemes, for advertisements copy and image placement. By defining the structural elements of these different types of text you can create models on which to base your own written tasks.

There is another purpose to this deconstructing of texts, besides raising awareness of different structural conventions. In your analysis of a text, you will need to ask why the writer chose to write that particular type of text. How does the type of text suit the purpose of the writer? The answer to this question reveals a lot about the context in which a text is written and read.

Figure 2.10 Ahmed Kathrada (1929–).

discussion

1   Of all of the texts that Kathrada could have written in prison to support his cause, why do you think he chose to write a personal letter to his girlfriend? How might these personal letters be of historical significance for South Africa?

2   Comment on the tone of the writer. How does he use diction to establish a tone?

3   How might you read this letter differently from its intended audience, Sylvia Neame?

In this unit, we will look at two very different types of letters, a personal letter and a letter to a newspaper editor. For each letter, ask yourself why the writer chose that particular type of text.

A deconstructed personal letter

The first text we will look at is a letter from Ahmed Kathrada to his girlfriend, Sylvia Neame. As you read Text 2.6 and its context, ask yourself why, of all the types of text he could have written and had smuggled out of prison to support his cause, Kathrada chose to write in the form of letters.

Text 2.6 *Letters from Robben Island*, Ahmed Kathrada, 1999

Ahmed Kathrada, also known as Kathy, is a South African of Indian origin. He had been a non-violent, anti-apartheid activist for more than two decades when, in 1964, he was arrested and unjustly accused of trying to overthrow the South African government. He spent 25 years in prisons before the apartheid rule came to an end in South Africa and he was released, together with his fellow prisoners, including Nelson Mandela. After his release, he became very active in the African National Congress, which won South Africa's first fully democratic elections in 1994.

The following letter was written during Kathy's time at the Robben Island prison in 1964. It was smuggled out of prison by his lawyer and delivered to his girlfriend, Sylvia Neame. Because Sylvia was a white South African, their relationship would have been considered illegal. She was also a political activist. The collection of his letters was published in 1999.

To Sylvia Neame,[1] (February or March, 1964)[2]

I don't know what the outcome of our case is going to be eventually. I am prepared mentally for a heavy sentence. As long as they don't hang us, we are confident we won't have to remain in jail for a very long time. It is almost a year since I broke my house arrest. Strange what laws I actually and wittingly broke and what I get charged with. The fact remains that I expected to be arrested sooner or later, so what difference does it really make if I am serving under the Suppression of Communism Act, the Group Areas Act or the Sabotage Act. In the end we will be saboteurs or communists or both, and in the South African context it is nothing to be ashamed of. There are lots of things concerning the period of my underground days which I am tempted to write about but which it is inadvisable to broach at this stage. They are things best left for history. That is one of the reasons why[3] I ask you again to give serious thought to the diary, collection of material, etc. The problem about keeping them safely can be overcome by sending everything out to England to be kept there. I am getting more and more keen that one day these must be written up and feel that, with my assistance, you will be the best person to write it …

In the years to come there will be different versions of the history of the past 20 to 30 years – and I just must see at least one version influenced by the way I have lived through these years and the way I look at them …

A few days ago one of the nicer warders got talking to me and said he wondered why I got 'mixed up' in all this business, meaning politics generally. How does one explain to a chap like him that to live a life of humiliation and without dignity is not worth living? He seems to have gathered over the months

from supervising the visits that I was not down-and-out and poor and was having a comfortable life outside. To him that is enough. He is so sincere in his interest. The tragedy is there must be thousands and thousands of whites who think like him. When will they ever emerge from the mental *backveld* in which they are living[4]?

The letter by Ahmed Kathrada contains some of the key characteristics of letter writing, as listed below. The numbers correspond to the superscript numbers noted in Text 2.6.

1 Greeting

In an informal letter it is usual to begin with *Dear* followed by the first name of the person who is addressed. In a formal letter titles such as *Dr*, *Mr*, *Miss*, *Ms* or *Mrs* are used with the person's family name. (For a woman, use *Ms* if you do not know whether she is married or not.)

2 Date

In the age of e-mail, we are not accustomed to writing dates in our correspondence, because they are automatically included. A date can be important for understanding the context of a letter. It serves as a reference if we look back on the letter later in life. The date usually comes before the greeting. In the UK, the date is usually written as follows:

- 26 October 2012
- 26th October 2012

  In the USA, it is usually written:

- October 26th, 2012
- October 26, 2012
- 26th of October 2012

3 Opening purpose

Usually in the opening few lines of a letter, even a personal letter, the writer gives a reason for writing. In the letter from Robben Island, the purpose is not made clear until a little later on. This indicates that the reader to whom the letter is addressed is probably patient and willing to sit through some preliminary lines. Do not be afraid to be direct in stating your purpose. It is quite customary to write, *I am writing to you because …* This flags up an important bit of information for the reader, and many readers like letters that are to the point.

4 Anecdote

An **anecdote** is not necessarily characteristic of all letter writing, but we see one here in Ahmed Kathrada's letter which has shared characteristics with journal or diary writing. The second paragraph of this letter could be seen as an anecdote. Anecdotes or examples often illustrate the point you are trying to persuade your reader about, and help them understand your meaning.

Conclusion

Text 2.6 is an extract from a longer letter and does not include the conclusion. However, letters usually conclude with a reiteratation of the purpose of writing and a request for the reader to undertake some kind of action. A closing phrase such as *Yours truly*, *Yours sincerely* or *Regards* are personal ways of concluding your letter. Usually this is followed by a simple signature. In a formal letter you normally type out your full name below your signature.

Extended essay

Racial discrimination on three continents: how three writers, Martin Luther King, John Agard and Ahmed Kathrada, use language as a tool for their cause; a study of texts in context.

You have now read texts by Martin Luther King, John Agard and Ahmed Kathrada, all of which deal with themes of civil rights, oppression and emancipation on three different continents. For your extended essay you could focus on these texts, or others, as expressions of how ethnic minorities have experienced segregation and discrimination. The title above would make a suitable extended essay question.

Key term

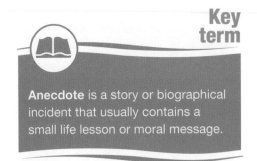

Anecdote is a story or biographical incident that usually contains a small life lesson or moral message.

A deconstructed letter to the editor

A letter written to the editor of a newspaper is different from a personal letter, such as Ahmed Kathrada's letter in Text 2.6. You could think of letters as desserts. Just as there are many different types of dessert, so too there are many different types of letter. However different one is from another, desserts all share common attributes: they tend to be sweet and involve a combination of similar ingredients. In the same way, a letter to a newspaper editor is very different from a personal letter but some of the characteristics of personal letters you read about above can still apply.

Letters to the editor are often sent to a magazine or newspaper in response to an article or feature. They reflect the opinions of the publication's readers. Editors decide which letters to publish and which letters to discard. Text 2.7 is a letter from a reader to the editor of a newspaper in Australia.

"Dear Editor: How are you? I am fine. Having a wonderful time. Wish you were here. Love, Sally."

Figure 2.11 How does this cartoon highlight the different conventions used in different types of letter?

discussion

1   Does the author of this text like or dislike the article by Caroline Overington? Where do you see evidence of Jerry Mayer's opinion?

2   What kind of stylistic device is used in the last line of the text?

3   How is this letter similar to the letter in Text 2.6? How are the two letters different?

4   How typical do you think Texts 2.6 and 2.7 are of personal letters and letters to the editor?

Text 2.7 Letter to the editor of *The Australian*, 2009

This letter was written in response to an article entitled 'Family's fifth generation in care of state' which appeared in *The Australian* newspaper in 2009. (You can read the article in the sample Paper 1 higher level exam on pages 61–62). The 'Stolen Generation' mentioned in the article and letter refers to the government's practice of removing Australian Aboriginals from their families between 1870 and 1970 approximately.

To The Australian,[1]
The arguments for separating Aboriginal children from their parents as presented in Caroline Overington's excellent article ('Family's fifth generation in care of state', 20/2/09[2]) are remarkably similar to those used some 60 or 70 years ago for what

subsequently became known as the Stolen Generation. Basically, the reasons proposed then as now were and are to break the vicious cycle of unemployed, uneducated parents having uneducated children who were unemployable ad infinitum.[3] What name shall we give the current practice of separating the children?[4]

Jerry Mayer
Northbridge, NSW[5]

The letter contains further examples of the key characteristics of letter writing as listed below. The numbers correspond to the numbers noted in Text 2.7.

1   Greeting
Notice how the greeting in this letter to the editor is different from the greeting in Text 2.6. This letter addresses the newspaper, *The Australian*. Other common greetings in letters to the editor are *Sir, Dear Sir, Dear Editor* or *To whom it may concern.*

2   Reference
Letters to the editor are often in response to a previously published article. It is essential to include the title, date and author's name of the original piece that you are responding to.

3   Point
Letters to the editor are brief. They state their point immediately and succinctly. Correspondents often criticise the original article, but commending the author and reiterating the points the author makes are also very common in letters to the editor.

4   Call to answer
Finishing a letter to the editor with a rhetorical question is quite common. It is not only a challenge to the editor but also to the readers of the magazine or newspaper. If you decide to write a letter to the editor for a written task, you will need to be careful here as there is a fine line between instigating further discussion and sounding cynical.

5   Signature
Notice that either Jerry Mayer or the editor of *The Australian* has included the place from which the letter was written. This is common practice in letters to the editor, as readers will want to know more about the context in which these ideas have been produced.

Activity 2.7
As a class, draw a Venn diagram like the one in Figure 2.12 (page 56).
1   List the features that Texts 2.6 and 2.7 have in common in the overlapping section in the middle.
2   List unique features of each of the texts in the parts of the circles that do not overlap.
3   There are more types of letter, such as letters of complaint or cover letters. Introduce a third circle that relates to a new type of letter that you have found.
4   Repeat the activity with different text types, such as speeches (graduation, memorial or opening speeches), opinion pieces (essays, blogs or columns) or advertisements (billboards, pop-ups or magazine ads). What are the common structures of these other types of text?

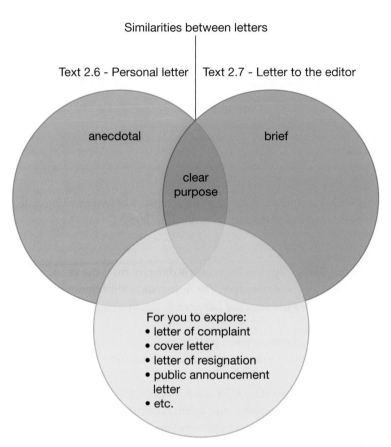

Figure 2.12 Venn diagrams, such as this one, help to analyse the similarities and differences of texts.

Activity 2.8

In this unit we have deconstructed two letters. For this activity, try deconstructing a text type of your choice, defining its key structural elements. Each student could focus on a different type of text and present their deconstructed text to the class.

Choose from the text types below.

advertisement	autobiography	biography	brochure
cartoon	diary	drama script	editorial
feature article	guide	instructions	letter of application
letter of complaint	letter to the editor	manifesto	news article
novel	op-ed	opinion column	poster
press release	report	review	short story
song lyrics	speech	transcribed interview	travel writing

Assessment: Paper 1

For standard level students, Paper 1 tests your ability to analyse one of two unseen texts. For higher level students, it tests your ability to compare one of two *pairs* of unseen texts. The paper (1½ hours for standard level; 2 hours for higher level) represents 25% of your final grade.

To prepare for the exam, study the sample Paper 1 exam and sample student responses below. Look at the marks that the sample responses were awarded to help you assess how to give the best answer possible.

After you have become familiar with the assessment criteria, you can try to take the sample Paper 1 exam. You will notice that the students have chosen Section A of the exam. You could use Section B as a mock exam, under exam conditions, or you may want to approach these texts without time restrictions, carefully applying all that you have learned in part 1 of the course, as a homework assignment or work in class. Keep in mind that you must demonstrate an understanding of stylistic devices, structure and language, in a well-structured analysis, and you will perform well in the Paper 1 exam.

tip

Although the sample exams in this coursebook are not real past IB Diploma exam papers, they offer a good indication of what you can expect during the real exam. For further exam preparation you can order past exam papers or teacher support material from the International Baccalaureate on its website www.ibo.org

Sample exam Paper 1 (SL): Textual analysis

*Write an analysis on **one** of the following texts. Include comments on the significance of context, audience, purpose, and formal and stylistic features.*

Text 1

Cleaning Products 101

1   As you walk down the aisles of your grocery store, you may have a hard
     time imagining that people once cared for their floors, windows, and
     clothes without the aid of commercial products. They made soap from
     tallow and ashes, and cleaners from lemon juice, borax, vinegar, and
5   baking soda. Before the advent of the myriad products we take for granted
     today, a homemaker had to have a basic understanding of the chemistry of
     cleaning in order to keep a tidy house. She would have been familiar with
     the bleaching properties of lemon juice, the disinfecting power of vinegar,
     and the grease-cutting abilities of baking soda. She would have known that
10   a tablecloth stained with blueberries would require very different treatment
     than one marred by gravy. Homekeeping generations ago was as much a
     science as an art.
        Because of the convenience offered by many new products, much of
     that knowledge has faded. But it's just as important today as it was a century
15   ago to understand how cleaning products work. Because there are so many
     products to choose from, cupboards can quickly become cluttered, and
     confusion about which products to use can abound. A little knowledge
     about ingredients and their individual properties can help remedy that.
     Armed with a few facts, you can confidently choose the cleansers,
20   polishes, and detergents that will allow you to clean more effectively
     and efficiently.

     From *Martha Stewart's Homekeeping Handbook* by Martha Stewart (2006).

Guiding questions:
* *What kind of audience is targeted by this text?*
* *How does the text create a particular effect on the reader?*

Text 2

Preparing Makes Sense

1 The likelihood that you and your family will survive a house fire depends as much on having a working smoke detector and an exit strategy, as on a well-trained fire department. The same is true for surviving a terrorist attack or other emergency. We must have the tools and plans in place to make
5 it on our own, at least for a period of time, no matter where we are when disaster strikes. Just like having a working smoke detector, preparing for the unexpected makes sense. **Get ready now.**

Get a Kit of Emergency Supplies

Be prepared to improvise and use what you have on hand to make it on your own for **at least three days**, maybe longer. While there are many things that
10 might make you more comfortable, think first about fresh water, food and clean air.

    Consider two kits. In one, put everything you will need to stay where you are and make it on your own. The other should be a lightweight, smaller version you can take with you if you have to get away.
15   You'll need a gallon of **water** per person per day for drinking and sanitation. Include in the kits a three day supply of non-perishable foods that are easy to store and prepare such as protein bars, dried fruit or canned foods. If you live in a cold weather climate, include **warm clothes** and a sleeping bag for each member of the family.

From *Preparing Makes Sense*, US Department of Homeland Security (2002).

Guiding questions:
- *What kind of audience is targeted by this text?*
- *How does the text create a particular effect on the reader?*

Sample student response (SL)

Text 1 appears in a handbook on homekeeping and deals with cleaning products specifically. The text introduces homekeepers to a brief history of cleaning products and educates them in current cleaning products.

    It is fair to say that this text is targeting women who are interested in housekeeping. We know women are the target audience, because the text refers to how women used to clean their homes. *She would have been familiar with the bleaching properties of lemon juice* (lines 7–8). This indicates that women are interested in the history of cleaning. These are not women who casually grab a cleaning product in the grocery store on the way home from work. These are women who have time to read an introduction to cleaning products, study labels on cleaning products and carefully select the right products for the right jobs. In fact they don't just clean their floors, windows and clothes, they *cared* for them (line 2).

    The purpose of this text is to enlighten women on the history of cleaning products and to inform them about current products. It is a kind of call to return to one's roots. In lines 13–15 we see evidence of this, *Because of the convenience offered by many new products, much of that knowledge has faded. But it's just as important today as it was a century ago.* If the author can convince the reader of the importance of this subject, then she can get them to read on through this section on cleaning products. We see this especially in lines 19–21, *Armed with a few facts, you can confidently choose the cleansers, polishes, and detergents that will allow you to clean more effectively and efficiently.* We assume the reader wants to clean more effectively and efficiently, after learning about the theoretical side of cleaning.

The style of the text activates the reader. This is primarily due to the grammar and vocabulary. The text is written in the second person, or 'you' form. *As you walk down the aisles of your grocery store you may have a hard time* (lines 1–2). This makes the reader feel involved in the story. Furthermore the style is very explanatory. Two sentences in the second paragraph begin with the word *because* (lines 13 and 15). The reader gets the impression that this historical explanation will help her make sense of the 'myriad' of products available today (line 5). Words like *chemistry* (line 6) and *science* (line 12) indicate that there is some sensible way of understanding soap from tallow and ashes, and cleaners from lemon juice, borax, vinegar, and baking soda (lines 3–5). It is almost as if the author walks the reader through a forest before showing her the clearing up ahead.

The author also uses a lot of imagery and parallel structures to convey her message. Lines like *bleaching properties of lemon juice, the disinfecting power of vinegar, and the grease-cutting abilities of baking soda* (lines 8–9) serve as visualisations of a tidy house (line 7). Grammatically speaking these are parallel structures that read smoothly for the reader. We see them again in line 10, *tablecloth stained with blueberries and one marred by gravy* (line 11), and again in lines 16–17, *cupboards can quickly become cluttered, and confusion about which products to use can abound.* Again these images remind us what kinds of challenges the homekeeper must face. The author may have presented the reader with these images in order to scare her into reading the rest of the text about cleaning solutions.

Structurally speaking we can also see that this text is meant to activate homekeepers. There is a large clue that this is an introduction to cleaning products. Besides the title *Cleaning Products 101* we see a few lines that indicate a new section of factual information on products will follow: *A little knowledge about ingredients and their individual properties can help remedy that. Armed with a few facts, you can confidently choose the cleansers* (lines 17–19). This indicates a structural shift in the text and a lot of the reader's expectations hinge on these lines.

All in all the text suits its purpose in introducing the reader to the importance of cleaning products for homekeeping. Martha Stewart makes an effort to convince her readers to read on and learn more about the science of these cleaning products. She promises to prepare her readers with the essential knowledge to keep a proper home.

Examiner's comments

The following comments offer an indication of how an examiner might assess this student's response, which on the whole met the top descriptors of the grading criteria.

tip

You may have noticed that the sample student response is structured using some of the Big 5 (see page 35). As a default method of analysing a text, you could focus on one aspect of the Big 5 per paragraph. If you come across a text that does not lend itself well to all five aspects, then you are free to deviate from this method. Think of the Big 5 as a support to guide you when outlining your Paper 1 answer rather than a list that has to be worked through at all costs.

Criterion A: Understanding of the text – 4 out of 5

The analysis of the text is very insightful. The student understands correctly that the text introduces a chapter on cleaning products in a larger work on homekeeping. There is good awareness of the target audience, as the student notices how homekeepers 'care' for their homes. This example also demonstrates critical thinking.

Criterion B: Understanding of the use and effects of stylistic features – 4 out of 5

The student understands the use of stylistic devices, citing the words *science* and *chemistry*, which are meant to mystify the reader. Furthermore, the student identifies the use of imagery and integrates relevant examples of it. Generally speaking, the illustrations are very well chosen, as they support the main ideas. Well done.

Criterion C: Organisation and development – 5 out of 5

The student includes excellent signposts for the reader. The paragraphs are organised around several textual aspects, such as audience, purpose, style, imagery and structure. Everything in each paragraph is relevant to the topic sentence of the paragraph, including the examples. The quotes are well integrated into response, so that the points are backed up and explained properly. The introduction and conclusion are concise and effective. The main arguments are developed coherently.

Criterion D: Language – 4 out of 5

The use of vocabulary is appropriate to the task, though there could have been more sophisticated use of linking words. Generally speaking, the text is fluent, which is due to proper use of grammar and punctuation.

Activity 2.9

If we were to categorise every sentence as a particular sentence type, you would need several easily recognisable standard types, such as questions, statements, opinions, anecdotes, proposals and explanations, just to name a few. For the sake of this activity we will pretend that there are only *three* types of sentences and all sentences must fit into these three categories: Points, Illustrations and Explanations, or PIE.

1   Look at the table below, which presents the PIE method for structuring ideas and paragraphs using examples from the sample student response to the Paper 1 question which you read above.

2   Find more examples of the PIE structure in the student's commentary to complete the table.

The PIE method	Examples from sample student response	More examples from sample student response
Points Statements or convictions; may be opinions or facts, but they are presented as the subject matter. May be bold or frivolous. There are usually stated at start of an argument or paragraph.	*It is fair to say that this text is targeting women who are interested in housekeeping.*	

Illustrations Examples, quotes, anecdotes or figures that show what an abstract point looks like in concrete terms. They need line numbers, references and quotation marks with them.	*We know women are the target audience, because the text refers to how women used to clean their homes. 'She would have been familiar with the bleaching properties of lemon juice'* (lines 7–8).	
Explanations These link illustrations to points and make ideas logical. They often include the words *because* or *due to*. They usually come at the end of an argument.	*This indicates that the subject is a 'she' and is someone who is interested in the history of cleaning.*	

Sample exam Paper 1 (HL): Comparative textual analysis

Choose either Section A or Section B

SECTION A

Analyse, compare and contrast the following two texts. Include comments on the similarities and differences between the texts and the significance of context, audience, purpose, and formal and stylistic features

Text 1

1 Family's fifth generation in care of state
   The Australian, February 20, 2009
   Caroline Overington

5 State welfare workers have begun removing the fifth generation of
   Aboriginal children from their parents, meaning some indigenous families
   have an 80-year history with child protection services.
       There are few signs the cycle will be broken, as more Aboriginal
   children are being separated from their parents than at any time in
   Australian history.
10   *The Australian* spoke yesterday to an Aboriginal woman whose daughter
   became the family's fifth generation to be raised by the state, when she was
   taken from her home in June 2007 and placed with white foster parents on
   the NSW central coast.
       Her mother was a state ward; so too were her grandparents, her
15 great-grandmother and her great-great-grandmother.
       The NSW Department of Community Services removed the girl after an
   older sister, aged 14, tried to hang herself.
       The girls' mother told *The Australian*: 'After the Stolen Generation report, they
   said it would never happen again but it's happening. You don't want to tell child
20 welfare that you need help, because they will come and take your children.'

61

'My daughter was seven years old when they came for her. My husband fell down on his knees on the lawn. She was screaming. The last memory I have is of her hand against the glass, (and her) saying, "Please let me stay."'

25 The mother, who was born in 1967, was left on a railway line when she was three days old. She was sent to live with white foster parents until she ran away at the age of 12. When caught, she went to a Brisbane institution known as Wilson, where she stayed until she was 18. Her mother was raised at the Parramatta Girls' Home in Sydney in the 1950s.

30 Her father was born in 1940 on the Woorabinda mission, which was established inland of Rockhampton, in central Queensland, in 1927. At the age of eight, he was taken by Children's Services, Queensland (now the Department of Child Safety) to live at the Nudgee orphanage in Brisbane's north.

35 His mother was also a state ward, taken into servitude on Palm Island at 15. His grandmother was raised at Woorabinda, under the care of the Aboriginal Commissioner.

The Australian revealed last year there were between six and 10 times as many Aboriginal children in state care today than at the height of the
40 Stolen Generations era. The most recent data, from the Australian Institute of Health and Welfare, shows 9074 Aboriginal and Torres Strait Islander children in out-of-home care.

Text 2

1 Then all eyes turned to the cause of the commotion. A tall, rugged white man stood on the bank above them. He could easily have been mistaken for a pastoralist or a grazier with his tanned complexion except that he was wearing khaki clothing. Fear and anxiety swept over them when they
5 realized that the fateful day they had been dreading had come at last. They always knew that it would only be a matter of time before the government would track them down. When Constable Riggs, Protector of Aborigines, finally spoke his voice was full of authority and purpose. They knew without a doubt that he was the one who took their children in broad daylight – not
10 like the evil spirits who came into their camps in the night.

'I've come to take Molly, Gracie and Daisy, the three half-caste girls, with me to go to school at the Moore River Native Settlement,' he informed the family.

The old man nodded to show that he understood what Riggs was saying.
15 The rest of the family just hung their heads refusing to face the man who was taking their daughters away from them. Silent tears welled in their eyes and trickled down their cheeks.

'Come on, you girls,' he ordered. 'Don't worry about taking anything. We'll pick up what you need later.'
20 When the two girls stood up, he noticed that the third girl was missing. 'Where's the other one, Daisy?' he asked anxiously.

'She's with her mummy and daddy at Murra Munda Station,' the old man informed him.

'She's not at Murra Munda or at Jimbalbar goldfields. I called into those
25 places before I came here,' said the Constable. 'Hurry up then, I want to get started. We've got a long way to go yet. You girls can ride this horse back to the depot,' he said, handing the reins over to Molly. Riggs was annoyed that he had to go miles out of his way to find these girls.

30 Molly and Gracie sat silently on the horse, tears streaming down their cheeks as Constable Riggs turned the big bay stallion and led the way back to the depot. A high pitched wail broke out. The cries of agonised mothers and the women, and the deep sobs of grandfathers, uncles and cousins filled the air. Molly and Gracie looked back just once before they disappeared through the river gums. Behind them, those remaining in 35 the camp found strong sharp objects and gashed themselves and inflicted wounds to their heads and bodies as an expression of their sorrow.

From *Rabbit Proof Fence* by Doris Pilkington (1996).

SECTION B

Analyse, compare and contrast the following two texts. Include comments on the similarities and differences between the texts and the significance of context, audience, purpose, and formal and stylistic features

Text 3

1 At the end of the summer of 1975 Moira and I headed back to our home in New Orleans from our cabin in northern Wisconsin. We stopped for a night with Aunt Lois Ambrose in Normal, Illinois. She had a handsome set of the Biddle edition of the journals of Lewis and Clark. We admired them; 5 then I confessed that I had never read them. Aunt Lois gave the set to us.

I read the journals that fall and was entranced.

On Christmas Day 1975, we got to talking about where we wanted to go to celebrate our country's two hundredth birthday. I suggested Lemhi Pass, where Meriwether Lewis was the first American to cross the 10 Continental Divide. Moira immediately agreed. When we told the kids, Stephenie, Barry, Andy, Grace and Hugh, they loved the idea. Our friend Michael C. Fluitt agreed to accompany us for the journey.

It grew into a fairly big project. We decided to leave from Wood River, Illinois, on May 14, the 172nd anniversary of the departure of the expedition, 15 and follow Lewis and Clark to the Pacific. We had two Chevy pickups, two canoes riding on top, and plenty of camping gear. I invited my students at the University of New Orleans to join us for any or all of the trip. Twenty-five came along, by car or plane, to meet in Missoula, Montana.

Through the late spring of 1976, we made our way up the Missouri River, 20 camping at Lewis and Clark campsites in Missouri, Kansas, Iowa, Nebraska, and the Dakotas. We canoed the river at every stop. Each night, around the campfire, we would read aloud from the journals. In late June, we made a five-day, 165-mile canoe trip through the Missouri River Breaks in northern Montana. On July 1 we canoed through the Gates of the Mountains, just 25 north of Helena.

On July 4, we were at Lemhi Pass, with all the students and some friends. It was the most glorious night of our lives. You could reach out and touch the stars. Except for a logging road, the place was unchanged since Lewis was there. Around the campfire we took turns enumerating the reasons we 30 loved our country (not so easy to do with young people in 1976, in the wake of Richard Nixon's resignation and the fall of Saigon, but we did it with great success). We sang patriotic songs. We indulged ourselves in an outpouring of patriotism.

In the HL comparative textual analysis on Paper 1, a common pitfall for students is to write one long paragraph on the first text, followed by another paragraph on the second text, and then a concluding paragraph with a comparison of the two texts. This structure, however, does not always allow the student to demonstrate insight into the texts. Instead, try comparing and contrasting one aspect of writing (e.g. structure, tone, narration) with reference to both texts within each of your paragraphs.

From *Undaunted Courage: Meriwether Lewis, Thomas Jefferson, and the Opening of the American West* by Stephen Ambrose (1997).

Text 4

LEWIS AND CLARK TRAIL FEATURED TOUR
7 - Day Lewis and Clark: In Their Footsteps
Horseback Adventure along the Lolo Trail in Idaho

Fill out the form on the bottom of the page and you will receive addtional information.
This tour is escorted by one of the Lewis and Clark and trail affiliates.
READ TRAVEL BLOG >>

Horseback along the Lolo Trail in Idaho in the footsteps of Lewis and Clark

Date: August
Length: 7 days / 6 Nights
Trip Rating: Moderate

DESCRIPTION: You will travel by horse along the last remaining section of the **Lewis and Clark Trail** preserved in its primitive natural state. Experience the identical terrain, campsites, weather, and exhilaration that Lewis and Clark recorded in their expedition journals. Horseback riding experience is not required and several stops are made during the day to stretch the legs and view the country. Price includes all meals and camping. Other than sleeping bags, bring your personal belongings for the trip. All horses, vehicles, camping and cooking supplies are provided from arrival location.

Ken Burns, *Producer of PBS Lewis and Clark: In Their Footsteps,* "the greatest service I can imagine along the exquisitely beautiful Lolo Trail."

Arrivals: Lewiston, Idaho
Departures: Lewiston, Idaho
Airfare not included

Sample student response (HL)

Texts 1 and 2 are two different kinds of texts on the same topic, the Stolen Generation. The Stolen Generation refers to the Aboriginal 'half-castes' that were taken from their families and put into foster homes or boarding schools. Text 2 offers us a dramatic representation of what this practice once looked like in the days when they used to use horses (line 26). Text 1 on the other hand is a news article about how this practice is still happening through the Department of Child Safety. Whereas Text 1 is found in **The Australian**, a newspaper presumably, Text 2 is an extract from a novel called **Rabbit Proof Fence**. Both pieces share a common stance on this issue, and they both condemn the practice.

Even though these texts share a common interest, the audiences of these two texts differ. When people read newspapers, they often scan for articles that catch their interest. Text 1 may be one of several articles the reader reads. Moreover, like all articles, it must also be newsworthy. Lines 7–9 present such a newsworthy piece of information, as *more Aboriginal children are being separated from their parents than at any time in Australian history.* That is a big piece of news that Australians should care about, and therefore the text has an informative purpose. Whereas Text 1 tells us about the problem, Text 2 shows us the problem. The audience of Text 2 has more time to devote to learning about this problem, as the text is an extract from a novel. Usually novel readers expect to be enlightened on a matter by reading a dramatisation of events, characters and story lines. We see a dramatisation of events in lines 11–13, *'I've come to take Molly, Gracie and Daisy, the three half-caste girls, with me to go to school at the Moore River Native Settlement,' he informed the family.* This scene serves both to entertain the reader, by transporting the reader to another place, and to inform the reader about this place that he or she may not know enough about. Readers of the novel want to see what the Stolen Generation looked like and feel the suffering of these people, whereas readers of the newspaper article want to know the facts, numbers and stories of reality, today.

Because the audience and purpose of the texts are so different, they are structurally different as well. Text 2 seeks to tell a narrative story, where the reader is told a story from beginning to end. We see the greater Aboriginal family before the constable arrives. We watch him arrive through their eyes, and we watch him go through their eyes. While Text 2 focuses on one tragic event, Text 1 retells multiple stories of aboriginals being removed from their families for generations. We as readers can almost see an interviewer sitting down with an interviewee, recording the stories that go backwards in time. The mother talks first about her daughter, then herself, her parents, her father's mother and her father's grandmother. The writer most likely goes back in time with a lot of place names, years and ancestral ties, in order to reinforce the idea that this problem is endemic to Australia. While Overington may have chosen this structure to stress her point, the reader may become bogged down by the details and put the article away. Pilkington on the other hand carries the reader through the single event with enough action and dialogue that the reader will want to find out how it ends. These structural differences lie in the fact that they are different forms of communication.

Although the texts are different forms of communication, both authors share a similar narrative technique to convince their readers that removing Aboriginals from their families is a bad practice. News articles, like Text 1, always have a responsibility to be objective, and thus we see facts and statistics: *The Australian revealed last year there were between six and 10 times as many Aboriginal children in state care today than at the height of the Stolen Generations era* (lines 38–40). But the bulk of the article tells the story of one family that has been extremely affected by the removal policies of child protection services. Although the story is told without embellishment, it is a selection from a greater story. What's more, Overington has her interviewee supply the emotions and drama, such as in lines 22–24, *She was screaming. The last memory I have is of her hand against the glass, (and her) saying, 'Please let me stay.'* Similarly, Text 2 seems to be a sober retelling of events, without the narrator's emotional involvement. Lines like 34–36 show a very objective method of storytelling: *those remaining in the camp found strong sharp objects and gashed themselves and inflicted wounds to their heads and bodies as an expression of their sorrow.* Despite this objective, anthropological tone, the reader is meant to have an emotional response. There are also examples of narration that are more direct, where the narrator does not

Higher level

HL

In Activity 2.9 on pages 60–61, the PIE method was presented as a method for structuring paragraphs and ideas. Fill in a table similar to the one in the activity for the HL sample student response.

Alternatively, make a photocopy of the student's work. Highlight all the points, illustrations and examples with three different-coloured highlighter pens (one for each aspect: structure, tone and narration). If you do this in groups you can compare each group's results within the class.

simply show us action but tells us about the characters' emotional state of being, such as in lines 4–5, *Fear and anxiety swept over them when they realized that the fateful day they had been dreading had come at last.* Both authors try to keep an emotional distance from the events, while trying to create empathy in the reader. They may have chosen this style because they want readers to condemn these practices for what they are, and not because an emotional narrative begged them to care.

In summary, we see that both texts tell the stories of Aboriginal children being removed from their families. They offer accounts of events, images of tears, and a portrayal of emotions. In both texts, the reader is presented with these images and stories and may decide what to make of them. Although these practices are not condemned outright, the reader is meant to be shocked.

Examiner's comments

The following assessment of the student's response, which received high marks, offers insight into what examiners expect from students at HL

Criterion A: Understanding of the text – 5 out of 5

The student seems to understand the limitations and opportunities of novels and news articles very well. The student compares and contrasts the different expectations that the readers of these texts have, writing that *readers of the novel want to see what the Stolen Generation looked like and feel the suffering of these people, whereas readers of the newspaper article want to know the facts, numbers and stories of reality, today.*
This shows excellent understanding of the contexts and purposes of the texts.

Criterion B: Understanding of the use and effects of stylistic features – 5 out of 5

The student demonstrates critical thinking by making an interpretation about the writers' choices of narrative technique: *Both authors try to keep an emotional distance from the events, while trying to create empathy in the reader. They may have chosen this style because they want readers to condemn these practices for what they are, and not because an emotional narrative begged them to care.* This shows an awareness of the effects of the stylistic devices on the reader. This point and others are supported with appropriate examples from the texts.

Criterion C: Organisation and development – 4 out of 5

The comparative textual analysis is truly comparative. The paragraphs are structured in such a way that there is a balanced discussion of both texts, looking at audience, purpose, narrative technique and tone. Because the examples are well integrated, the text flows well.

Criterion D: Language – 5 out of 5

The register of the commentary is academic and the writing is free of grammatical errors and spelling mistakes. The choice of vocabulary is varied and appropriate to the task. The student took risks when writing longer sentences with parallel structures and complex clauses, which is highly commended here.

Activity 2.10

The comparative textual analysis is very much about seeing relationships between two texts. In order to express the relationships between two texts or multiple ideas, you need a good vocabulary of suitable linking words. This will help you score well on structuring ideas and integrating quotes. It is the glue that sticks good ideas together!

1 Re-read the sample responses and find the linking words.
2 Look at the table below and the linking words in each category.
3 Copy and complete the table with any other linking words you have found.
4 Repeat the activity with other texts, such as newspaper and magazine articles.

Category	Examples of linking words
Compare	similarly, in comparison, like, just as in
Contrast	whereas, while, on the other hand, nevertheless, despite, however, but
Summarise	all in all, to summarise, in brief, in conclusion, to conclude
Add information	what is more, furthermore, in addition, besides, as well as
Set up quotes	such as in line …, we see an example, for instance, namely
Give a reason	due to, in order to, therefore, on account of
Sequence ideas	first, secondly …, the former, the latter, consequently, lastly

Chapter 2 summary

In this chapter you have focused on the set of skills you need in order to engage in close reading of different types of text. You were given five lenses through which you can look at any type of text. For each aspect of the Big 5, you learned to ask several questions of any text you have to analyse.

By studying the contexts of composition and interpretation of various texts, you have addressed the notions of audience and purpose. You have learned to differentiate between the content and theme of texts. You have also seen how writers establish a tone through the use of diction, which in turn creates a mood for readers and listeners. Irony and figurative speech are two devices that writers use to convey their message. Furthermore, you have looked at the structural elements that define both personal letters and letters to the editor.

In Part 1 of this coursebook you have focused on three topics: the English language, close reading skills and the forms of assessment used to test your knowledge – the part 1 written task and further oral activity, and the textual analysis questions in Paper 1. You have studied English in its cultural contexts, looking at language from the bottom up, as a human need to communicate, be it through letters, personal ads or journals.

In part 2 of the coursebook you will be looking at language as a top-down process, focusing on how institutions, organisations and broadcasting networks use language to persuade, inform and entertain the general public. You will continue to explore language as a human endeavour and communication as an art.

Chapter 3 The media

Key terms

Public opinion is the collection of opinions and beliefs held by the adult population of a nation.

Media literacy is the skill of analysing various texts in relation to the media in which they are published.

Objectives

By the end of this chapter you will be able to
- identify sensationalism, bias and newsworthiness
- understand how the Internet facilitates communication
- plan and write a part 2 written task 1.

In Part 1 you explored communication as a bottom-up process, looking at how ordinary people interact on a daily basis, socially and professionally, through personal letters and classified ads. In Part 2 you will be looking at language as a top-down process, focusing on how ideas and messages are disseminated to 'the masses' through various distribution channels. You will discover how **public opinion** is shaped through language.

Public opinion is like the pulse of a nation. It is the general consensus on issues such as who should be elected, which brands are trendy and how children should be educated. In this chapter you will be asking yourself how public opinion is managed through channels of mass communication, also known as the media. Understanding how language in the media is used as a tool to shape public opinion is part of **media literacy**.

The word *media* refers to the physical carriers of information, such as radios, televisions, T-shirts or posters. We frequently make an interesting 'mistake' when referring to the media. Have you ever heard someone say, 'The media *thinks* this' or 'The media *does* that'? Strictly speaking, this is grammatically incorrect, as the word *media* is the plural form of *medium*. It can be argued, therefore, that it should take the plural verbs *think* or *do*. However, *media* has come to be seen as a collective noun and it is therefore now acceptable in standard English to treat it as a singular noun, taking a singular verb.

When people refer to the media, especially to the concept of it as a single entity, they mean broadcasting networks (such as the BBC), publishing houses and syndications (such as *The Times*), or even well-known and influential television shows such as *The Oprah Winfrey Show*. As we develop a sense of media literacy, we should make a distinction between, on the one hand, the *devices* that carry the messages and, on the other, the *people* – i.e. networks, stations and syndications – responsible for bringing us them.

The Canadian philosopher and writer Marshall McLuhan once said, 'The medium is the message.' He was referring to how an actual medium or device, such as a radio, television or computer, can determine the nature of the message that it carries. Think of mass communication as a spectrum: at one end is the

Figure 3.1 The storyline of the film *Wag the Dog* suggests that the media have the power to shape public opinion (see page 70).

notion of the media consisting of corporate business people who sit around boardroom tables deciding what the public will watch, read or listen to; at the other end is the view of the media being something increasingly controlled by ordinary people who have access to distribution channels such as websites, podcasts and radio frequencies.

In this chapter you will develop media literacy skills by exploring both ends of this spectrum. In Unit 3.1 you will be focusing on journalism and the linguistic devices used by networks, stations and syndications in their attempts to consciously shape public opinion. In Unit 3.2 you will explore how a very powerful medium, the Internet, is changing the way in which we interact and disseminate messages. At the end of the chapter you will have the chance to look at a sample written task which demonstrates a student's understanding of many of the ideas discussed in this chapter.

Unit 3.1 **Journalism**

Having access to millions of viewers and listeners gives the media considerable power. Producers of television and radio programmes have a great responsibility, since their media can be highly influential on public opinion. In this unit you are going to explore several concepts, such as bias, newsworthiness and sensationalism, to help you understand the responsibility that news networks have.

Bias

Television producers, journalists and columnists have the ability to 'manufacture consent'. This term, coined by the political scientist and linguist Noam Chomsky, is used to refer to the media's ability to create the impression that everyone agrees with a particular ideological position. The concept of manufactured consent can be understood in the context of the war in Iraq, which started in early 2003. Critics, such as Robert Greenwald, have argued that some American news networks actively helped shape opinion of Iraq in the USA in the build-up to the war. In Greenwald's documentary, *Outfoxed*, he claims that in late 2002 and early 2003 viewers of one particular network, Fox News, had a different view of the world from viewers of other American news networks. For example, 67% of Fox viewers felt there was a link between Osama bin Laden and Saddam Hussein, compared to only 16% of people who watched and listened to the Public Broadcasting Station (PBS) and National Public Radio (NPR). How do we account for this difference of opinion between the consumers of these different media? The figures suggest **bias** on the part of the Fox News network.

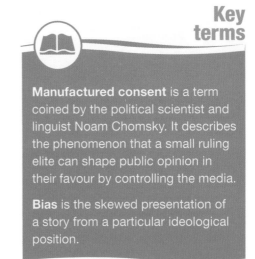

Key terms

Manufactured consent is a term coined by the political scientist and linguist Noam Chomsky. It describes the phenomenon that a small ruling elite can shape public opinion in their favour by controlling the media.

Bias is the skewed presentation of a story from a particular ideological position.

Figure 3.2 Noam Chomsky (1928–), often revered as one of the founders of modern linguistics, has published many books on the role of the media in shaping public opinion, including *Manufacturing Consent*.

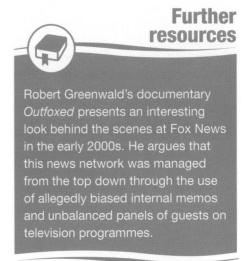

Further resources

Robert Greenwald's documentary *Outfoxed* presents an interesting look behind the scenes at Fox News in the early 2000s. He argues that this news network was managed from the top down through the use of allegedly biased internal memos and unbalanced panels of guests on television programmes.

Activity 3.1

Defining *bias* can be challenging. As a class, create a spider diagram of all the synonyms that you associate with the word *bias*. Then discuss the diagram and the issues raised. This should help you to understand this abstract concept.

Some people refer to the media as the 'fourth estate'. This view draws on the traditional way of dividing power in countries into three main groups – the church and religious groups (the first estate), the nobility (the second estate) and the rest of the population (the third estate). When the term fourth estate is applied to the media, it usually means the press (i.e. newspapers).

The film *Wag the Dog* draws our attention to this phenomenon. In this film, the US president wants to distract the nation's attention away from his personal affairs so that he can win an election. To do this, he invents a war in a Balkan country and hires a studio to stage the war, film it and broadcast it. The title of the film alludes to the expression *the tail wagging the dog*. Normally it is the dog that uses its tail to reflect a feeling, or state, of contentment (by wagging its tail). Similarly, a nation normally uses the media to reflect the state of that nation. But what happens when the media become an entity that does not *reflect* the state of a nation but *determines* it, as in the film? If the tail is wagging the dog, then the roles have been reversed and the dog is being controlled by the situation. Do you think that the media can both reflect and determine public opinion? Can the media shape the future of a nation?

No journalist likes to be accused of being biased: a journalist's job is to present the news in the most objective and unbiased way possible. There are reasons, however, why this can be difficult to achieve.

- First of all, journalists are under pressure to be the first to break a story.
- Secondly, journalists are under pressure to write stories that sell.
- Finally, it can be tempting to tell the public what it is thought they want to hear instead of telling them just the facts, or what they need to hear.

Activity 3.2

In October 2010, two candidates from the state of Delaware for the American Senate, Chris Coons and Christine O'Donnell, held a debate. As the candidates discussed the role of religion in state education, O'Donnell questioned whether the US Constitution separates church and state, an issue which is addressed by the First Amendment of the US Constitution.

Below are five headlines (a–e) from newspapers and news networks that reported the debate.

   a   Christine O'Donnell stumbles on First Amendment, *San Francisco Chronicle.*
   b   In debate, O'Donnell gets a lesson on First Amendment, *The Seattle Times.*
   c   ABC News exclusive: Christine O'Donnell stands her ground on First Amendment statement, blames media for distortions, ABC News.
   d   O'Donnell questions separation of Church, State in Senate debate, Fox News.
   e   Christine O'Donnell blanks on First Amendment, CNN.

1   Rate each headline for bias from 1 to 5, where 1 = 'hardly biased' and 5 = 'extremely biased'.
2   Explain your ratings to the rest of your class by referring to specific use of language from the headlines.
3   You could then view the debate online in order to see the difference between reality and the portrayal of reality through the headlines.

Newsworthiness

As you study the issue of journalism you will discover how difficult it can be to report on events without putting someone in a good or bad light. The problem of bias does not always lie in the language used to report an event; it can also lie in the initial decision of whether to report the event at all. How do journalists and editors select the news?

There are three criteria for determining whether a story or event is newsworthy, or worthy of being covered in the media. For a story to be newsworthy, it has to be sensational, it has to be relevant, or it has to be extraordinary, or a combination of all three. We will apply all three criteria to several stories released by the WikiLeaks organisation in 2010.

In 2006, several journalists, dissidents and technologists launched the WikiLeaks website, offering diplomats, soldiers or anyone else a place to submit sensitive and secret documents anonymously. While the website's fame grew over the years, exposing corporate scandals and US military plans, it was not until the website published the US diplomatic cables leak in November 2010 that it really made headlines round the world. Among the documents released was evidence that the US government had allegedly spied on the Secretary General of the United Nations, and there were other stories too that caused embarrassment, anger and damage to governments in many countries. What was the value of telling these secrets to the world? What made them newsworthy?

Sensationalism

First of all, sensationalism sells. There is an expression in the media world, *If it bleeds it leads*. This is to say, if there is murder, blood or controversy in a particular news story, then that story is put on the front page of the newspaper, the most prominent place for a story to attract attention. Bad news is good for circulation, as many readers tend to enjoy a story full of intrigue, plot and sensation (a 'juicy story', in other words).

Advertisers want a high circulation of the newspapers that they advertise in and advertising space in the most popular papers comes at a high price. Similarly, in television, if a programme is popular and has high ratings, the adjacent advertisement slots are very expensive. Advertisers provide much of the income for newspapers and other media networks, so journalists have to do a balancing act between reporting the truth on the one hand and considering both advertisers and sales on the other. In fact, many newspapers and broadcasting networks receive government subsidies in order to help them maintain high standards of fair and balanced journalism.

WikiLeaks, however, is not a conventional news provider, as its website is free of ads. It is run by volunteers, supported by sponsors and protected by fans. The website claims to be built on the ideals of freedom of speech and transparency and its supporters believe that US citizens have a right to know how their taxes are spent. If the leaks have embarrassed US officials, then the supporters claim it was not done with a profit motive in mind but in the interest of upholding ideals.

Nevertheless, the negative news of these leaks generated income for commercial newspapers and magazines around the world. Viewers, readers and listeners were intrigued by the US government's secrets and how they were leaked. The stories were as sensational as a James Bond film.

Relevance

Whenever we open a newspaper, watch the daily television news or browse news-providing websites, one question we often end up asking ourselves is *Why should I care?* In other words, what makes a particular story relevant to us and, from there, why is it newsworthy?

For example, not every plane crash will be reported in your national newspapers. Usually the story has to be relevant to a particular country, perhaps involving citizens of that country, for it to be reported there. If you browse through the documents on WikiLeaks, not all of them turn out to be sensational or relevant. This is not to say, however, that they are irrelevant for everyone. For a parent whose soldier son is killed in a war, details of the fighting in that war would be relevant.

Extraordinariness

Some stories simply lend themselves to sensational coverage because they are extraordinary. The story of a dog biting a man is rarely deemed newsworthy. However if a man were to bite a dog, you would read about it. This common phrase in the world of journalism, *Man bites dog*, explains how the extraordinary is newsworthy. In the case of WikiLeaks, little was disclosed that was not already suspected but what made it extraordinary was how it gave everyone with an Internet connection access to top-secret documents.

'Early in life I had noticed that no event is ever correctly reported in a newspaper.'
George Orwell (1903–50)

'In journalism, there has always been a tension between getting it first and getting it right'
Ellen Goodman (1941–)

Figure 3.3 Julian Assange, the co-founder of the WikiLeaks website.

'It's all storytelling, you know. That's what journalism is all about.'
Tom Brokaw (1940–)

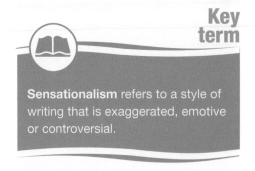

Key term

Sensationalism refers to a style of writing that is exaggerated, emotive or controversial.

'The news media are, for the most part, the bringers of bad news … and it's not entirely the media's fault, bad news gets higher ratings and sells more papers than good news.'
Peter McWilliams (1950–2000)

Part 2 – Language and mass communication

'I have always been firmly persuaded that our newspapers cannot be edited in the interests of the general public from the counting room.'

Franklin D. Roosevelt (1882–1945)

TOK

Testing the authenticity of a primary source means exploring the four 'ways of knowing' (WOKs) of the TOK syllabus.

- *Perception* – if seeing is believing, you may want to go straight to the primary source. Looking at the original documents on the WikiLeaks website or a 'mirror site' may convince you of their authenticity.
- *Language* – what makes the WikiLeaks leaks so convincing is both the language of the original documents and the language of the reporting on them. We must be careful, nonetheless, especially of secondary sources, as they offer interpretations of the original.
- *Emotion* – many people do not bother with primary sources because they blindly trust secondary sources or have a 'gut feeling' that they are correct. Be wary of such intuitions, as they are not founded on fact. Some people's first response to the WikiLeaks affair was to say that the leaks had been 'planted' by the US government. Why might some people have such a gut feeling?
- *Reason* – before the leaked diplomatic cables were made public on the world's media, several major newspapers from around the world were asked to verify their authenticity. Many newspapers knew the WikiLeaks informants. Furthermore, the US government did not deny the authenticity of the documents. Nevertheless, you should ask yourself what this proves.

Figure 3.4 This cartoon raises some basic, but important, questions about the nature of good journalism. What is the difference between rumours and news? Why might a news story contain lies? What does innuendo mean? Why does innuendo not belong in good investigative journalism?

Journalism and linguistic devices

You have seen how journalism can be biased and sensational because of the constant pressure to provide newsworthy stories. Now let us turn to the linguistic devices that characterise sensationalism and bias.

Emotive language

The hallmark of sensationalism is **emotive language**. The headlines in the activity about the Christine O'Donnell story (Activity 3.2, page 70) included words and phrases such as *stumbles*, *gets a lesson* and *blanks*. These all contain emotive language: they have connotations which sound more extreme than blander, more basic vocabulary. They appeal to our emotions. The journalist could have said, for example, that O'Donnell *did not know* the First Amendment instead of *stumbles* or *blanks*; the straightforward *did not know* would have been less emotive, less 'loaded'.

Euphemisms

Some people refer to the media as 'the filter'. This is an interesting image that suggests our version of reality is really someone else's selection of reality. In more extreme terms, one could argue that our news is censored. While we may think of **censorship** as a device allowing governments to intervene and remove news stories, burn books or block radio frequencies, there is also the notion of censorship through language, which can be seen as a more devious sort of censorship.

Newspapers can filter the truth by the use of **euphemisms**. Euphemisms are words that make unpleasant things or ideas sound milder and less offensive. We use them to be less direct when talking about taboos or ideas that may be difficult to accept or embarrassing. Instead of saying that someone has *died*, for example, we say they have *passed away*. We often find euphemisms being used in reports about wars. Below are some examples of euphemistic words and phrases used in reports about modern wars. Next to them is a more direct way of saying what they mean. The examples reveal how language can be used as a tool by governments and journalists to manufacture consent and, in this case, justify wars.

Euphemism	Meaning
collateral damage	death of civilians
to neutralise	to kill
friendly fire	accidental killing of soldiers on the same side
enhanced interrogation	torture
air campaign	bombing

Figure 3.5 While Sparky the republican penguin seems comical, do you think he presents a case for censorship that many people subscribe to?

Vague language

Some words in the English language have very clear meanings, such as *chair* or *bachelor*. Others words, especially quantifiers, such as *a lot*, *frequently* or *far away*, are vaguer and may mean something different to one reader or another. Part of becoming more media literate is learning to spot vague language. Writers may use such devices to avoid honest reporting while readers can make false presumptions if they do not spot vague language.

In Text 3.3 you will be looking at the front page of a tabloid newspaper, *The Sun*. In one of the articles, we see vague language about a 'stunning model', who was the 'passion flower' of Jean Collin's husband. This husband planned to 'ditch' his soap-star wife, after stealing 'half her fortune' and running away with his lover. As critical readers we have to ask ourselves several questions about this vague language: How one can quantify this lover's good looks? What is a 'passion flower'? Was he 'ditching' his wife or was she divorcing him? How much exactly is 'half her fortune'? There is room for several interpretations to this text, which is why we should be wary of vague language.

'Political language ... is designed to make lies sound truthful and murder respectable, and to give an appearance of solidity to pure wind.'
George Orwell (1903–50)

Higher level

HL

Complete a comparative textual analysis of Texts 3.1 and 3.2 as if they are texts in the Paper 1 exam. Use the tools that you have developed in Chapters 1 and 2, looking at audience, purpose, theme, content, tone, mood, stylistic devices and structure.

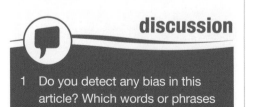

discussion

1 Do you detect any bias in this article? Which words or phrases indicate possible bias?
2 What light does the text shed on Ugandan culture and politics?

Activity 3.3

Texts 3.1 and 3.2 are two newspaper articles which both report on political campaigns.
1 Read the two articles and find examples of emotive language, euphemisms and vague language in each article. Add to the examples that have been provided in the table below.
2 Copy and complete a table like the one below with the examples you have found.
3 Compare and contrast the linguistic devices used in the two texts. Look out for further examples in other texts you read.

	Emotive language	Euphemisms	Vague language
Text 3.1	The man was forced to take off his shirt.	People's president	... about 100 posters
Text 3.2	We deplore action of this kind in or out of politics.	The bugging incident	... the mystery deepens.

Text 3.1 'Inside Bitama's camp', *The New Vision*, 29th October 2010

The New Vision is a pro-government publication in Uganda. The president of Uganda, Yoweri Museveni, faced a presidential election in 2011. In the run-up to the election this article reported on an opposition candidate, Paddy Bitama, and how he arrived at the official nomination as an election candidate.

Comedian Paddy Bitama of Amarula Family got off the list of presidential candidates in a dust of light moments. Having set off from Chez Johnson, Nakulabye, Bitama got a suit, a C Class Mercedes Benz and a convoy of vehicles but forgot the campaign posters. When roadside cheerers reminded him, he sent DJ Messe to Nasser Road to print about 100 posters.

Among the supporters in the convoy was his colleague, Kapere, who was wearing an NRM[1] T-shirt. However, Kapere was forced to take off his shirt after colleagues noticed it.

On reaching Kisekka market, the convoy met a man who was having lunch by the roadside. Bitama grabbed an Irish potato from his plate saying as a people's president, he had to eat with them. The man just shook his head.

At Spear Motors, when the Police asked why his car had no sticker,[2] he claimed to have lost it adding that he was too busy to pick another one from the Electoral Commission.

Bitama also had sh2m[3] in cash but no one bothered to count it because he was supposed to have banked sh8m before going for nomination.

Meanwhile he had assured bodaboda[4] riders that he had a deal with a filling station in Lugogo to refund their fuel. However, when they reached Lugogo and the bodabodas demanded for their fuel, he told them they would get it after he has been sworn in as president.

[1] **NRM** the National Resistance Movement of President Yoweri Museveni

[2] **sticker** a licence granted by the police that must be displayed on a candidate's vehicle to show it is part of an election convoy

[3] **sh2m** 2 million Ugandan shillings

[4] **bodaboda** bicycle taxi

Text 3.2 'GOP security aide among 5 arrested in bugging affair', Bob Woodward and Carl Bernstein, *The Washington Post*, 19th June 1972

In 1972 five men were caught breaking into the Watergate Hotel in Washington DC, where the Democratic Party were organising their presidential campaign. Investigative journalists Bob Woodward and Carl Bernstein discovered a link between the five burglars and the Republican President, Richard Nixon. Text 3.2 is the article that broke the story of Nixon's involvement in the bugging scandal which eventually led to his resignation.

Figure 3.6 Carl Bernstein and Bob Woodward at *The Washington Post* in 1972.

One of the five men arrested early Saturday in the attempt to bug the Democratic National Committee headquarters is the salaried security coordinator for President Nixon's reelection committee.

The suspect, former CIA employee James W. McCord Jr., 53, also holds a separate contract to provide security services to the Republican National Committee, GOP[1] national chairman Bob Dole said yesterday.

Former Attorney General John N. Mitchell, head of the Committee for the Re-Election of the President, said yesterday McCord was employed to help install that committee's own security system.

In a statement issued in Los Angeles, Mitchell said McCord and the other four men arrested at Democratic headquarters Saturday 'were not operating either in our behalf or with our consent' in the alleged bugging attempt.

Dole issued a similar statement, adding that 'we deplore action of this kind in or out of politics.' An aide to Dole said he was unsure at this time exactly what security services McCord was hired to perform by the National Committee.

Police sources said last night that they were seeking a sixth man in connection with the attempted bugging. The sources would give no other details.

Other sources close to the investigation said yesterday that there still was no explanation as to why the five suspects might have attempted to bug Democratic headquarters in the Watergate at 2600 Virginia Ave., NW, or if they were working for other individuals or organizations.

'We're baffled at this point ... the mystery deepens,' a high Democratic Party source said.

Democratic National Committee Chairman Lawrence F. O'Brien said the 'bugging incident ... raised the ugliest questions about the integrity of the political process that I have encountered in a quarter century.

'No mere statement of innocence by Mr. Nixon's campaign manager will dispel these questions.'

The Democratic presidential candidates were not available for comment yesterday.

O'Brien, in his statement, called on Attorney General Richard G. Kleindienst to order an immediate, 'searching professional investigation' of the entire matter by the FBI.

A spokesman for Kleindienst said yesterday, 'The FBI is already investigating. ... Their investigative report will be turned over to the criminal division for appropriate action.'

The White House did not comment.

[1] **GOP** the Grand Old Party, or GOP, is a nickname for the Republican Party

discussion

1 After learning that this text eventually led to President Nixon's resignation, did you expect a more sensational story? How does the use of language in this report serve its purpose well?

2 Notice that Text 3.2 quotes a lot of people. Does the use of quotes make the reporting more or less biased? Compare the use of quotes in Text 3.2 with their use in Text 3.1.

Key terms

Tabloid in its literal sense refers to a newspaper that is smaller than a broadsheet; it is also used to refer to sensational or biased newspapers.

Broadsheet is a newspaper that is larger than a tabloid; the format is often associated with in-depth reporting and a balanced presentation of opinions.

A deconstructed tabloid news article

As you learn to become more media literate, it is important to recognise the structure of sensationalism. The format and layout of a newspaper can do a lot to determine the message that is conveyed. Over the years, a newspaper format known as the **tabloid** has come to be associated with sensationalism and emotive language. Tabloids are physically smaller than **broadsheets**, which have the reputation of more objective reporting and a more balanced presentation of opinions.

As you study Text 3.3, notice all the features of sensationalism it displays. The British newspaper the *Sun* is a good example of tabloid journalism and renowned for its sensationalist approach to news reporting.

Text 3.3 'Werewolf seized in Southend', *The Sun*, 24th July, 1987

discussion

1 Do you see evidence of emotive or vague language? What is the effect of the language of this text on the reader?
2 How does this text make use of the structural conventions of tabloid newspapers?

Masthead

Tabloid newspapers are often referred to as 'red tops' because of the red masthead background. In the masthead you often find the name of the newspaper, the date of publication and the price. White letters on a red background scream for attention.

Ears

In the upper corners of most newspapers, both tabloids and broadsheets, are little stories, also known as 'teasers', that make you want to open the newspaper and read on. Teasers in the top corners of the newspaper are known as 'ears'.

Copy

The main text of an article is called the 'copy'. Notice how the copy of this report is smaller than the image. In tabloid articles the copy may consist of only a few short paragraphs written in a style intended to grab the reader's attention. For this reason the language is usually sensational and loaded.

Image

Since sensationalism appeals to the senses, most tabloids make use of images, usually of people's faces, as these attract the most attention. Images, especially on the front page of tabloids, are usually large in relation to the copy or other articles. Images are almost always 'anchored' by a caption.

Headline

The choice of words in a headline is essential to setting the tone of an article. The headlines are often the only things that are read. The word 'werewolf' attracts one's attention. As one could read further in the article, this mythological creature turns out to be 'a 43-year-old married builder from Southend'. A headline such as 'Builder seized in Southend' would not have drawn the reader's attention, though.

Subheading

Good subheadings also entice the reader to read on. The subheading in this text expands on the implications of the heading. 'He fights cops on all fours' intrigues the reader as it appeals to the senses and elaborates on the concept of 'werewolf'.

Activity 3.4

Study the sample written task in Chapter 5 on page 134, a tabloid article by a student.

1. Find examples in her work of the defining characteristics of tabloids, as presented here.
2. Compare her use of images, ears, copy, headlines and subheadings with the use of these devices in Text 3.3. How well has the student adhered to the structural conventions of tabloid newspaper writing?

In the introduction to this chapter on page 68 was a quote from Marshall McLuhan, who said, 'The medium is the message.' In other words, content (the message) is influenced by form (the medium). In the past decades many broadsheet newspapers with fair and balanced reporting have switched to a smaller, tabloid format because their readers often read the newspapers in public spaces such as trains or cafés. With this shift, many readers have become concerned that less space for print translates into less depth of coverage. Concerns about a more superficial coverage of news increase as more and more people are turning away from traditional paper newspapers and are reading the news online. In the next unit, you will explore the 'new' medium of the Internet and you will be asking yourself whether it is changing the message.

Figure 3.7 The Buggles predicted the end of radio in 1980 with their MTV hit 'Video killed the radio star'.

Unit 3.2 **The Internet**

In 1980 a new TV network called MTV was launched and the first video to be aired was the song 'Video killed the radio star' by The Buggles. The title of the song captured the fear of many people at this time. Decades later we can safely say that people still listen to the radio and DJs. Nevertheless, what people now listen to on the radio has changed thanks to visual media. Your parents and grandparents, for example, were probably more likely to have listened to a sports match or a play on the radio than you are today. Although the Internet has *changed* the way we communicate, it has not *killed off* radio, books, newspapers or TV – but might it do so in the future?

We live in a visual age, with screens all around us, and the need to become media literate has never been stronger. Especially on the World Wide Web, we have to be more critical than ever when assessing sources of information. Global society is interconnected and faces some very big questions about cultural values and norms.

Although it may not be possible to answer all the questions raised in this unit, by the end of it you will have gained a better understanding of how the Internet is redefining communication. You will be looking at the mechanics of one particular website – Last.fm – as an example of how most websites work.

Extended essay

EE

How the Internet has changed newspapers: a look at The Sun, The New York Times *and the* Hindustan Times *both on-and offline.*

Write an extended essay discussing the relationship between the Internet and traditional news media using a title similar to the one above. Every year the Bivings Group publishes a report on how newspapers are adopting more online applications for communicating with their readers. You could consult their reports (www.bivings.com) as part of your research.

Activity 3.5

As a class, discuss the following questions.
1 Can one medium 'kill' another? Will the Internet mean the end of newspapers, books and radio as we know them?
2 Is the Internet dumbing us down and making us lazier? Or is it empowering the masses by giving access to more information?
3 Is the Internet a trustworthy source of information? Is it as reliable as print?
4 What is the Internet doing to copyright laws? Is it eroding a cultural norm or is it encouraging us to redefine our economies in a positive way?
5 Are we using the Internet, or is the Internet using us?

(The questions in this activity provide good discussion material, which will help in preparing for the part 2 written tasks and further oral activities. There are no prescribed answers to the questions.)

A deconstructed web page

These days it is difficult to imagine what life would be like without digital communication. Human interaction has changed considerably following the appearance of websites like Facebook, Twitter and YouTube. On such sites, we, the users, are empowered to consume *and* produce the content at the same time; the content of many websites is generated by the people who use them.

The text in this unit, (Text 3.4) is no exception to this trend. Last.fm is an online music machine, playing the songs the site's users say they like and suggesting others they might like as well.

Personalisation

Many websites ask you to 'sign in' so that your web experience is personalised and your web history recorded. Last.fm suggests new music based on music previously listened to and liked on the website. Clicking on a heart icon records the fact that the user likes a particular song and prompts more suggestions from similar genres.

Text 3.4 Last.fm

Personalisation

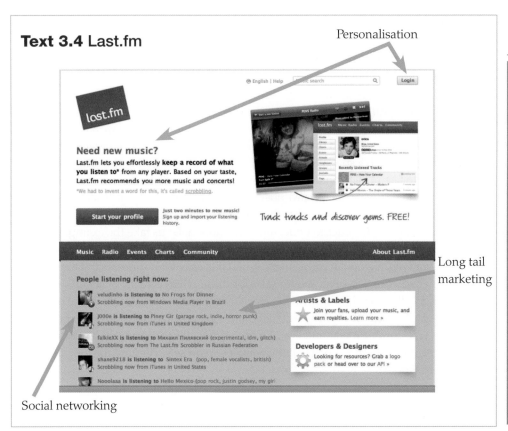

Social networking

Long tail marketing

Further resources

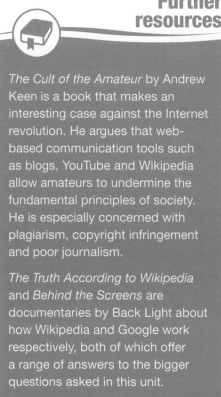

The Cult of the Amateur by Andrew Keen is a book that makes an interesting case against the Internet revolution. He argues that web-based communication tools such as blogs, YouTube and Wikipedia allow amateurs to undermine the fundamental principles of society. He is especially concerned with plagiarism, copyright infringement and poor journalism.

The Truth According to Wikipedia and *Behind the Screens* are documentaries by Back Light about how Wikipedia and Google work respectively, both of which offer a range of answers to the bigger questions asked in this unit.

Last.fm does not rely just on an individual's personal history on the site but on the histories of thousands of other listeners. Ian Ayres, a media analyst and professor of law, has popularised the term '**super crunching**' to describe this phenomenon of drawing on data about thousands of users. The super crunching of numbers in a split second is possible thanks to cleverly designed algorithms and intricate hardware. Information is fed into algorithms every time a user clicks on a Google search result, or 'hit', for example. Assume everyone clicks on the second hit in a list generated by a search for a particular term, then that hit will soon become the first hit. In a sense, the Internet is using us, the users, to make it smarter.

Last.fm works in a similar way. Essentially the Last.fm website outsources the research traditionally done by a few professional DJs to a large crowd of amateur listeners. We call this **crowdsourcing**. In order to understand how crowdsourcing works, think of a jar full of marbles. If you ask a large crowd of people to guess how many marbles are in the jar, you will see a natural clustering of guesses around the actual number. Last.fm operates in a similar way: the larger the crowd that is consulted, the more likely the suggestions will be on target.

Finally, you will notice that the website has read the Internet protocol address of this particular user and suggested music events that are taking place nearby. This is an example of how the Internet uses personalisation as a tool for marketing, which leads on to the next point.

Advertising

As your media literacy improves, ensure you take into account the business model of the website. Think about how Last.fm can claim to provide you with a *free* music channel. The site receives funding from advertisers who pay to have adverts included

'**Getting information off the Internet is like taking a drink from a fire hydrant.**'
Mitch Kapor (1950–)

Key terms

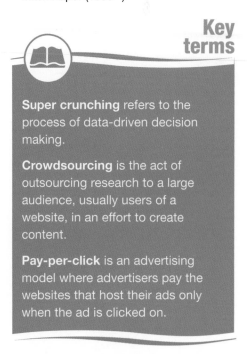

Super crunching refers to the process of data-driven decision making.

Crowdsourcing is the act of outsourcing research to a large audience, usually users of a website, in an effort to create content.

Pay-per-click is an advertising model where advertisers pay the websites that host their ads only when the ad is clicked on.

Key terms

Long tail marketing is selling a large range of products for which there is a small demand in small quantity instead of a small range of popular products in large quantity; the total number of people with various specialised interests is greater than the number of people with popular interests.

Virals are commercials that travel like viruses on the Internet through social networks. Friends voluntarily send friends these ads.

on it and commission on a **pay-per-click** basis. As you explore user profiles, artist pages and music events on the Last.fm website, you see listings of shows in your area. The venues that host these shows pay Last.fm once you click to learn about their event. This is a common form of Internet advertising.

Long tail marketing

As we communicate with friends, order books and listen to music online we are creating an interwoven web of people with similar behaviours. The Internet can bring together groups of people with unusual or specialised interests, from all over the world, who otherwise do not meet face to face at all but have all their contact entirely online. Before the Internet, it was difficult, and definitely not lucrative, for companies to target such small audiences.

Nowadays, websites open up what the Internet guru Chris Anderson aptly calls the **long tail market**. In order to understand this notion, let us take the example of music sales. Musicians who enjoy popular success, such as Madonna, U2 or Beyoncé, are at the head of the popular music market, and it is easy for businesses to target this mainstream audience. However, album sales for these artists actually make up the minority of all albums sold worldwide. It is in fact the smaller bands who make up the majority of music sales. The sub genres, alternative scenes, traditional tastes, 'straight edge', 'acid jazz', 'gothic metal' and even Bulgarian folk-dance music account for more sales between them than the better-known, mainstream acts. They are the long tail, as illustrated in Figure 3.8.

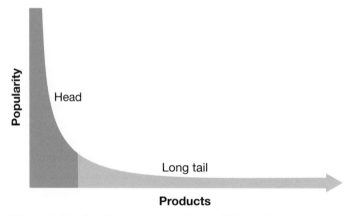

Figure 3.8 A visualisation of the 'long tail' in marketing.

Social networking

The Last.fm website offers users the possibility to 'shout' to friends that they are going to a particular concert. It allows users to reach out to other people with similar music tastes through its profile page, its events page and its artists page. Social networking has revolutionised the Web, because it has created a means for information to come to the user instead of the user having to seek it out. On websites such as Facebook and Twitter, users follow or subscribe to information posted by their friends. The Last.fm website makes use of similar tools, notifying users about a band or friend's activities.

Ads can travel by means of social networking, since short videos or images are easily shared on such platforms. Such ads are called **virals** – commercials that travel like viruses. Virals are sometimes personalised, as people provide a business with information for their friends so that the business in turn can create personalised, and often funny, ads. On Last.fm, it is possible to notify your friends that you have added a new favourite artist to your profile. This becomes a viral for that artist.

Activity 3.6

Look at some of the communication tools (1–6) on the Internet and explain how the terms (a–e) relate to them. More than one term may relate to each tool.

1	StumbleUpon.com	a	Super crunching
2	YouTube.com	b	Crowdsourcing
3	Facebook.com	c	Social networking
4	Wikipedia.org	d	Long tail marketing
5	Adwords.Google.com	e	Virals
6	Twitter.com		

Assessment: Part 2 written task 1

At least one of the written tasks in your portfolio has to reflect your understanding of part 2 of the course, and the assessment requirements and criteria on pages vii– viii apply to this as to all written tasks. Mass communication is a popular topic with students for a written task but you should be aware of some of the pitfalls associated with it.

Keep the following four points in mind when preparing and writing a part 1 or 2 written task 1 on language and mass communication.

1 *Make it plausible*

Good written tasks look and feel like texts that you would encounter in the real world. They seem genuine because the content is a good match for that particular type of text. A poem would be a bad choice for a written task on journalism, for example when was the last time you read a *poem* about good journalism? If you choose to write a news article, ask yourself what sort of newspaper it would appear in. If you write a speech, ask yourself who your target audience is.

Here are two ways to make your text as plausible as possible.

a For parts 1 and 2, it is especially important to focus on a real event, place or person. This helps your written task sound authentic. A letter to the editor in response to a real article, for example, will give you a focus for your writing and help it seem genuine.

b Step into someone else's shoes – imitating someone's style shows that you have researched your topic and proves you understand the relationship between text and context.

2 *Be knowledgeable*

Use the syllabus as a resource and draw on the theory you have covered on the course. There are terms and concepts that you can use in your written task and rationale that will demonstrate your understanding of the topic. The examiner will be reassured that you have done your research.

3 *Keep it relevant to Anglophone culture*

Students sometimes produce an excellent written task on a topic that relates to language and media studies but which has nothing to do with an Anglophone culture. You will be penalised heavily if your work does not relate to English. This is why it is helps to focus on an event, writer or theme from an Anglophone culture.

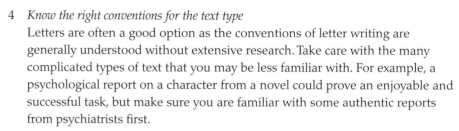

4 *Know the right conventions for the text type*
Letters are often a good option as the conventions of letter writing are generally understood without extensive research. Take care with the many complicated types of text that you may be less familiar with. For example, a psychological report on a character from a novel could prove an enjoyable and successful task, but make sure you are familiar with some authentic reports from psychiatrists first.

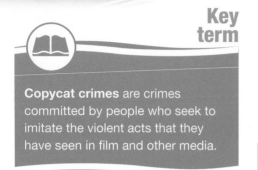

Key term

Copycat crimes are crimes committed by people who seek to imitate the violent acts that they have seen in film and other media.

Activity 3.7

1 Find examples of each of the four points in the sample student response in this unit on pages 84–86.
2 Re-read the sample written task in Chapter 1 on the use of English in Ireland (pages 23–25). Copy and complete the table below with examples from the sample task.
3 You could also use the table to check written tasks by students in your class before they submit their work.

Remember!	Examples
1 Make it plausible.	
2 Be knowledgeable.	
3 Keep it relevant to Anglophone culture.	
4 Know the right conventions for the text type.	

Figure 3.9 Michael Moore explores the correlation between violent acts and violent media in *Bowling for Columbine*.

The sample part 2 written task on pages 84–86 was inspired by research done in class on the correlation between committing violent behaviour and consuming violent media. The students had studied a brief summary of a scientific article on the subject entitled 'The influence of media violence on youth' by Craig A. Anderson and other psychologists. The students had also watched *Bowling for Columbine*, a documentary by Michael Moore about the shootings at Columbine High School in Colorado, USA, in 1999. It became evident that between these two sources there was a large gap in the amount of investigation and research. Whereas Michael Moore had interviewed a few teenagers at an arcade and made some cross-cultural comparisons, the scientists had carried out long-term tests with control groups. Michael Moore's conclusions were simple: consuming violent media does not inspire youths to commit copycat crimes. The scientists, on the other hand, found 'unequivocal evidence that media violence increases the likelihood of aggressive and violent behavior in both immediate and long-term contexts'.

Interestingly, the student did not elaborate in depth on the topic of media and violence. He chose instead to focus on sensationalism, bias and Michael Moore. He also chose to write a speech after studying the mechanics of speech writing. (You will learn more about speech writing in Chapter 4.)

"Do forgive me, sir, I've been seeing too much gratuitous violence on TV."

Figure 3.10 How does this cartoon imply that there is no correlation between violent acts and violent media? Does the cartoon make a fair argument?

Activity 3.8

Use this activity to become more confident with the written task criteria.

1   Before reading the examiner's comments, use the criteria to assess the sample written task.

2   Now read the examiner's comments and compare your assessment of the student's work with the examiner's. How does the examiner's assessment differ from yours?

	Your grade	**Examiner's grade**	**Explain any difference**
Criterion A			
Criterion B			
Criterion C			

Further resources

After a shooting incident at Columbine High School in Colorado in 1999, Michael Moore set out to find the answer to a very difficult question: *Why did these boys kill their classmates?* While his documentary, *Bowling for Columbine*, looks at a variety of issues, from gun laws to American history, much of the film focuses on violence and the effects of sensational media.

TOK

There is a lot of interesting debate about the correlation between violent acts and violent video games, television programmes and films. You may want to research the issues for your TOK presentation or essay. The sample written task in this unit presents two sources, by Michael Moore and Craig A. Anderson, which you could compare and contrast in your TOK assessment. You may want to focus on certainty in the relevant Areas of Knowledge (AOK), such as psychology and sociology (human sciences), and on language as a Way of Knowing (WOK).

Sample written task (SL)

Rationale

I was inspired to write this written task after watching a few extracts from Michael Moore's films, **Bowling for Columbine** and **Roger and Me**. We watched them in class in order to understand propaganda and media and violence, but we ended up talking about Michael Moore as a person. I thought it would be plausible for him to speak at his old university for the school of journalism.

I was particularly interested in propaganda, sensationalism and the correlation between media and violence. In the case of the latter, our class found some research on media and violence that proved Mr Moore's unscientific experiment wrong. Studies actually have proven that people who consume violent media are more likely to commit violent acts. Moore, however, just wants to create counter-propaganda, as I have him say in my written task. I also included in a reference to Moore's encounter with Phil Knight in **Roger and Me**, since this scene exemplifies how Moore is good at creating biased and sensational situations.

I studied speeches in class and learned about ethos, pathos and logos. I have Moore tell us why he thinks he has been invited (ethos), why the students may have to bend the rules of journalism (logos), and why they should care about good journalism (pathos). The text type lent itself well to my purpose because it allowed me to explore all of these things that were so relevant to the media and culture unit that we were studying in class. The text's target audience, a group of university graduates, eager for good advice and inspiration, suited its purpose.

All in all, I learned a lot about Michael Moore, propaganda and speech writing.

Written task

Figure 3.11 Michael Moore confronts Phil Knight in the film *Roger and Me*.

I have to admit, I'm a little jealous of all of you sitting here before me. Today you're going to walk away with something I never got from this university or any other; something that will be your ticket to a steady income, a fruitful social network and a brighter future, namely a college degree. George Bush once told me, on one of our rare encounters, that I needed to get a real job. I knew he was right. But I didn't have the qualifications to get one. You see, I'm actually very unemployable, because I don't have what you're getting: a college degree.

So you may wonder why I've been asked to stand before you today as a role model. Actually I'm kind of wondering the same thing. But I think I know a few reasons why, and I'll share them with you today.

I think I was invited here today because we share a common goal. We want tomorrow to be better than today. And what's more, we all want to be a part of the change that makes tomorrow better than today. Many of us believe in what Gandhi once said: 'Be the change you want to see in the world.'

Let me tell you about how I have tried to change the world through journalism. Now I know that may come as a surprise to many of you, that I use that word 'journalism'. Let's be honest, you've probably had professors who've told you not to watch my films because they're so-called 'propaganda' films. It's OK. I'm not offended. The professors are probably right as usual. Come to think of it, maybe that's why I dropped out of college. I was too stubborn to listen to them. But to come back to my point, I've always wanted to create journalism that's objective, balanced and not sensational. In fact I still uphold those values each and every time I make a new film.

The problem is: It's too tempting to cut corners. When, for example, I wanted to prove that there was no correlation between consuming violent media and committing violent acts, as I did in my film **Bowling for Columbine**, it was so much easier to interview a bunch of teenagers at a video arcade than to delve into the scientific research. And let's look at the result of that film. We got Wal-Mart to stop selling weapons and ammunition. Now I ask you: Did my ends justify my means? I would say they did.

Sometimes, as it turns out, we have to fight propaganda with propaganda. I'll give you another example. In my film **Roger and Me** I offered the CEO of Nike, Phil Knight, two tickets to Indonesia, a country where he was mass producing sneakers in sweatshops, but also a country he had never even been to. The look on his face when I showed up at his office with those two tickets was better than any documentary I could have done on the sweatshops in Indonesia. And when he refused the tickets, I challenged him to a 100-meter sprint, pushing him even further into a corner, and yes, increasing the level of sensation. Again, you may accuse me of propaganda and poor journalism, but look at where Nike is today. To their credit they have made an honest effort to clean up their practices and pay their workers fair wages.

I know what you're thinking: 'Mr Moore, this is all good for you because you're a media rock-star, but what's this supposed to mean for me as I enter the highly competitive media business and start out at the bottom?'

Well, let me finish by telling you a little anecdote about my first real job as the editor of **Mother Jones**, a liberal political magazine, and why I was fired after four months. It wasn't because I didn't have a college degree. It was because I fought for what I believed in. I refused to run a story on the Sandinistas in Nicaragua, and I insisted persistently on publishing a story about the laid-off workers of GM in my hometown of Flint, Michigan. I even went behind my boss's back and put the picture of a laid-off worker on the cover of the magazine. I was accused of being biased toward my hometown. Of course I was biased. But I hadn't taken my eye off the target of creating a better world.

I suppose my final point is this: There will be times in your careers when you look at your own work on the TV or in the newspapers and think: 'Did I create that piece of sensational, biased propaganda?' Just remember this, though. We are all learning on the job. We are all racing against deadlines, and we're all tempted to cut corners. But in the long-term, if you keep your eye on that ideal of improving the world through journalism, you will improve your own ability to create good journalism. You will find your voice. You will put into practice those lofty ideals that you learned here.

Thank you, University of Michigan School of Journalism, for inviting me here today. Again, I'm jealous of all of you for those hard-earned degrees. Now go and use them to make a difference.

Examiner's comments

The text is inspirational, as an inspirational speech should be, mostly because the guiding idea was so appropriate – that is, that journalists can make the world a better place. The text is also very plausible, as one could imagine Michael Moore giving such a speech in such a context. Nevertheless there are a few concerns, which will be elaborated on below, using the criteria for the task.

Criterion A: Rationale – 2 out of 2

The rationale provides insight into the learning experience on speech writing and propaganda. It explains the student's choice of texts, i.e. *Roger and Me* and *Bowling for Columbine*, and the focus on Michael Moore.

Criterion B: Task and content – 6 out of 8

The task is appropriate to the purpose that the student set out to accomplish. It is plausible, as it looks and feels like a Michael Moore speech to a crowd of graduating students of journalism. The student demonstrates a good understanding of the conventions of speech writing as he addresses ethos, pathos and logos in a balanced way.

The student's choice of content is good in some places and not suitable in other places. The example of Michael Moore challenging Phil Knight to a sprint in *Roger and Me* illustrated sensationalism very well. However, Moore is remarkably, and perhaps unrealistically, honest about poor investigative journalism in *Bowling for Columbine*. Since the student's coursework focused on the correlation between media and violence, it would have been more effective to see more understanding of this topic. Instead it is glossed over briefly in the task.

On a critical note, the anecdote about how Michael Moore placed a GM worker on the front page of *Mother Jones* is not inspirational. Rather it almost encourages the

tip

By now you will have noticed that the purpose of the written task 1 is not to produce a persuasive essay. It may be tempting to write a philosophical, discursive piece on one of the deeper questions asked in part 2, but remember that you are writing a creative piece. Step into someone's shoes, respond to a real-life event or interview someone. Keep it fun and real.

students of journalism to be biased. It is almost as if Moore says, 'Never mind those lofty values – break the rules of good journalism.' This is not consistent with Moore's message of changing the world through good journalism.

Finally, the student shows the effects of Moore's language. He explains that Nike changed their policies thanks to Moore's sensational form of journalism. Similarly he explains that Wal-Mart stopped selling weapons thanks to Moore's criticisms. These examples are consistent with Moore's message of changing the world through good journalism.

Criterion C: Organisation and development – 5 out of 5

The task is well organised and coherent. It has a guiding idea, or thesis: journalism can make the world a better place. Moore's examples help support this main idea. Furthermore, he includes the necessary structural indicators such as *my final point*, *Thank you* and *Again*. These words make it a coherent piece

Criterion D: Language – 3 out of 5

Although the task is appropriate to the purpose, the student writes in a register that is not always acceptable in such a situation. Phrases such as *you see* and *I know what you're thinking* make it too informal for the occasion. On the whole though, the text looks and feels like a speech because it uses many of the rhetorical devices that are characteristic of speeches. Moore states his purpose clearly and he uses humour.

Ideas for the part 2 written task 1

1   You have seen an imaginary speech that Michael Moore could have given to an audience. Imagine you are Bob Woodward, Naomi Klein, Ellen Goodman or any other famous journalist. Give a speech to a specific audience about good journalism. Be sure to create an appropriate topic and context that reflect an understanding of an Anglophone culture.

2   Look at some of the predictions made about the future of media and communication by people like Marshall McLuhan, Bill Gates or Clifford Stoll. Write one of these people a personal letter in which you explain why you think their predictions were right or wrong, based on cultural practices of today.

3   There are magazines where writers discuss the cultural ramifications of the Internet, such as Wired or .Net. Look for an article that you can write a response to in the form of a letter to the editor. More specifically, *Time* magazine ran a feature article that named 'You' its Person of the Year in 2006 for becoming so active on the Web. Try to apply some of the terminology that you have learned in this chapter in your response, such as *social networking, crowdsourcing* or *long-tail marketing*. Discuss how these devices are reshaping communication in the Anglophone world.

'The world is changing very fast.
Big will not beat small any more.
It will be the fast beating the slow.'
Rupert Murdoch (1931–)

Chapter 3 summary

We began this chapter by presenting two alternative views on the media. On the one hand, you have seen how public opinion is consciously shaped through linguistic tools such as emotive words, euphemisms and vague language. On the other, you have seen how people are taking ownership of distribution channels on the World Wide Web.

With regard to a conscious shaping of public opinion, you explored how the pressures of publishing newsworthy news can lead to sensationalism. You looked at two articles and studied how they use very different language to report on presidential campaigns.

You have also explored Marshall McLuhan's statement 'The medium is the message' by looking at how the content of a music website is shaped by technology. As media and modes of communication are constantly redefined through the Internet, you have read about new tools of communication. Social networking, data-driven decision making and long tail marketing are forcing us to become more media literate. Media literacy is not something new, however. As you will find out in the following chapter, media literacy includes identifying and understanding the language of persuasion, a practice that people have engaged in for years.

Chapter 4 The language of persuasion

Objectives
By the end of this chapter you will be able to
- identify propaganda techniques
- define the characteristics of rhetoric and powerful speech writing
- understand how an advertisement works
- plan and conduct a part 2 further oral activity.

Persuasive language comes into all kinds of text, from brochures to speeches. Have you ever purchased something you did not really need? Have you ever been so moved by a speech that you got goosebumps? Your response may have been the result of persuasive language.

In this chapter you will be looking at three important applications of persuasive language. In Unit 4.1 you will focus on propaganda, in Unit 4.2 on powerful speeches and the use of rhetoric, and in Unit 4.3 on a form of persuasion that makes its way into our lives every day – advertising. At the end of the chapter you will study a sample part 2 further oral activity which makes good use of persuasive techniques.

Imagine if persuasive language had a recorded history. We would start with Aristotle and the ancient Greeks, whose ideas Cicero brought to Rome a few hundred years later. We would have to include religious figures such as Thomas Aquinas and scientists such as Charles Darwin, not to mention rulers and leaders such as Abraham Lincoln and Winston Churchill.

As we fast forward to modern times, we cannot overlook Edward (Eddie) Bernays, also known as 'the father of public relations'. Although not a famous speaker, he may have done more to shape public opinion in America in the 20th century than any other person. He convinced Americans that eating sausages for breakfast was patriotic. He told them that Thomas Edison invented the light bulb. He helped overthrow the Guatemalan government in 1954 by staging a workers' riot, filming it and disseminating it across the USA. As the nephew of psychologist Sigmund Freud, Bernays understood that if you could tap into people's subconscious through the use of images and persuasive language, you could manipulate them.

An illustration of how Bernays changed the ideological landscape of America is his 'Torches of Freedom' campaign. Bernays told the press that the 1929 Easter Day parade in New York City would go down in history as a great day for women's emancipation. The press was told to look out for 'torches of freedom' in the parade. On a cue from Bernays, his secretary and her friends, as they marched in the parade past press photographers, lit cigarettes and smoked them in public.

Figure 4.1 Edward (Eddie) Bernays (1891–1995), known as 'the father of public relations'.

Further resources

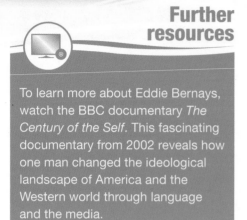

To learn more about Eddie Bernays, watch the BBC documentary *The Century of the Self*. This fascinating documentary from 2002 reveals how one man changed the ideological landscape of America and the Western world through language and the media.

Figure 4.2 The Lucky Strike ad for the 'Torches of Freedom' campaign.

Key term

Propaganda is the conscious effort to shape public opinion to conform to an ideological position.

Up until 1929 it had been illegal for women to smoke in public in the USA. After that moment, however, it became widely accepted. Lucky Strike, the tobacco company which had hired Bernays as a public relations consultant, saw its potential market double almost overnight. Lucky Strike ran ads with pictures of women holding cigarettes and slogans saying: *An ancient prejudice has been removed. It's toasted.* Audiences recognised the *It's toasted* phrase from previous Lucky Strike ads, a phrase which originally referred to the method used to produce Lucky Strike cigarettes. Now, however, *It's toasted* stood for women's rights and emancipation and, thanks to the ad campaign, women began to feel confident about smoking in public: they felt equal to men.

In 1954 Eddie Bernays helped overthrow the government of Guatemala with a camera and a newspaper, so how much more possible would it be to do something similar today, in the age of the Internet? If Bernays could change women's rights through an advertising campaign, could we do more today to change how women are portrayed in the media? Bernays's 'Torches of Freedom' campaign provides lessons in media literacy for us today. In Chapter 3 you saw that media literacy is about identifying biased language and sensationalism. In this chapter you will continue to develop your media literacy skill by looking at the language of persuasion. You will be exploring how language has been used in recent years to influence public opinion.

Unit 4.1 **Propaganda**

The successes of Eddie Bernays are lessons in the power of propaganda. Propaganda is the conscious effort to shape public opinion towards a certain ideological position. Bernays's ideological position was one of capitalism and consumerism. During the First and Second World Wars he used propaganda to fight fascism, and in peacetime he used the same techniques to promote products and entire industries. During the Cold War his public relations firm fought communism.

In this unit we will look at how the words of another man, George W. Bush, were used to shape US public opinion. Propaganda is successful when it is used on an uninformed public. In other words, people are easily persuaded because they do not have counter-arguments to the information they are being given. It is necessary to make an active effort to identify and understand the techniques involved in propaganda. Living in a digital age does not always make this easier. In fact it requires an even stronger effort to stay aware and critical of persuasive language.

Seven propaganda techniques

Persuasion involves propagating convincing ideas, and part of becoming media literate includes being able to identify and label the common techniques used in propaganda. You will be looking at George W. Bush's 2003 State of the Union address and seeing these propaganda techniques in use.

Text 4.1 The State of the Union address, George W. Bush, January 2003

On 11th September 2001, three hijacked planes were flown into the World Trade Center in New York and the Pentagon in Washington DC. A fourth hijacked plane crashed into a field. Declaring a 'war against terrorism', President George W. Bush vowed to bring al-Qaeda, the terrorist organisation behind these attacks, to justice. The USA and NATO invaded Afghanistan and overthrew the Taliban government which had protected al-Qaeda. In 2003 the war on terrorism was extended to Iraq, where there had been reports of weapons of mass destruction (WMDs), and in March 2003 the regime of Saddam Hussein in Iraq was overthrown. The following extract is on abridged extract from the State of the Union address by George W. Bush, given weeks before the invasion of Iraq.

Mr Speaker, Vice President Cheney, members of Congress, distinguished citizens and fellow citizens, every year, by law and by custom, we meet here to consider the state of the union. This year, we gather in this chamber deeply aware of decisive days that lie ahead.

You and I serve our country in a time of great consequence. During this session of Congress, we have the duty to reform domestic programs vital to our country, we have the opportunity to save millions of lives abroad from a terrible disease. We will work for a prosperity that is broadly shared, and we will answer every danger and every enemy that threatens the American people. In all these days of promise and days of reckoning, we can be confident.

In a whirlwind of change and hope and peril, our faith is sure, our resolve is firm, and our union is strong.[1]

This country has many challenges. We will not deny, we will not ignore, we will not pass along our problems to other Congresses, to other presidents, and other generations.[2] We will confront them with focus and clarity and courage.

There are days when our fellow citizens do not hear news about the war on terror.[3] There's never a day when I do not learn of another threat, or receive reports of operations in progress, or give an order in this global war against a scattered network of killers.[4] The war goes on, and we are winning.

We've got the terrorists[5] on the run. We're keeping them on the run. One by one the terrorists are learning the meaning of American justice.[6]

Our war against terror is a contest of will in which perseverance is power. In the ruins of two towers, at the western wall of the Pentagon, on a field in Pennsylvania, this nation made a pledge,[7] and we renew that pledge tonight: Whatever the duration of this struggle, and whatever the difficulties, we will not permit the triumph of violence in the affairs of men; free people will set the course of history.

Today, the gravest danger in the war on terror, the gravest danger facing America and the world, is outlaw regimes that seek and possess nuclear, chemical and biological weapons. These regimes could use such weapons for blackmail, terror, and mass murder. They could also give or sell those weapons to terrorist allies, who would use them without the least hesitation.

Figure 4.3 President George W. Bush delivering the State of the Union address in 2003.

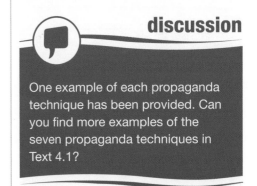

discussion

One example of each propaganda technique has been provided. Can you find more examples of the seven propaganda techniques in Text 4.1?

1 Assertion

When George W. Bush declares *our union is strong*, there is no indication as to how such an assertion can be measured. Making bold statements is a common propaganda technique. The audience is not invited to question the validity of such statements as they are delivered with confidence and enthusiasm.

2 False dilemma

When politicians present false dilemmas, they essentially claim that there are only two answers to one problem. The string of logic that George W. Bush presents is simple and binary: Americans can on the one hand bring the battle to the enemy, or on the other they can deny the problem exists, ignore it or pass it on to future

TOK

The word *propaganda* may have negative associations because it often makes use of invalid arguments, or **argumentation fallacies**. As you may know from your TOK lessons, these are invalid strings of logic. How are the seven propaganda techniques in George W. Bush's 2003 State of the Union address different from the argumentation fallacies that you are studying in TOK? Do you think that propaganda also utilises valid logic? Explore Text 4.1 and look for both valid and invalid arguments.

Key terms

Stereotyping is the act of presenting a person or group in a certain way, through simplified and biased media.

Argumentation fallacies are common but invalid syllogisms, or in other words, poor strings of logic.

congresses. In essence Americans are being presented with two extremes and told to choose between the lesser of two evils. There is really no 'choice' involved in such statements, and the dilemma created is actually a false one.

3 Plain folks

The president is separating himself from the *fellow citizens*, who do not know as much about the war as him. He is making use of the 'plain folks' argument, a propaganda technique that generalises about the average person and groups the public together as plain folks. It is not surprising that the president knows more about national threats as he has powerful intelligence and security organisations working for him. Plain folks have no access to his sources of information and cannot know as much. Just like all of these propaganda techniques, the plain folks argument relies on an information gap, with the public being relatively uninformed.

4 Name-calling and pinpointing the enemy

George W. Bush refers to terrorists as a *network of killers*. Pinpointing the enemy is a common tactic used during wartime to stir up anger and manufacture consent. It gives the audience a very clear sense of right and wrong when the issues involved might be a lot less clear-cut than that.

5 Simplification

Simplifying a complicated situation is a common propaganda technique and is similar to name-calling and pinpointing. Simplification results in the formation of stereotypical images which are often distortions of the truth and which can lead to opinions that are based on prejudice. Many different groups have been referred to as terrorists, for example, and not just the organisations behind the 9/11 attacks. In another example of simplification, the groups are likely to refer to themselves as freedom fighters, even though this term covers a wide range of aims and ideals.

6 Glittering generalities

Phrases such as *American justice* are glittering generalities. These are words connected to worthy abstract concepts, such as freedom, democracy and justice, that would be difficult if not impossible to be against.

7 Card stacking

George W. Bush presents the case for war with facts. The series of events of 9/11 are presented as a strong reason to go to war. This method of propaganda is also known as card stacking, which is the act of selectively including arguments that support your cause while ignoring the counter-arguments.

Activity 4.1

The First World War changed not only the physical borders of the world but also the mental state of many people around the world. Many men went to fight with great enthusiasm, optimism and patriotism. For these men there was much at stake: national pride, family honour and friendships. Many went to fight in the belief that they would be 'home by Christmas'. Trench warfare, being exposed to poisonous gases and suffering from shell shock, caused thousands of troops from around the world to lose their early sense of innocence and hope.

1 Look at the propaganda posters (Figures 4.4–4.7) and discuss how they reflected and instigated sentiments of enthusiasm, optimism and patriotism.
2 How are the propaganda techniques discussed above used in each poster? More than one technique might be used in each example.

Figure 4.4 How does this British poster from 1915 persuade men to go to war?

Figure 4.5 Compare this Australian poster from 1915 with Figure 4.4.

Figure 4.6 How does this Canadian poster present a false dilemma?

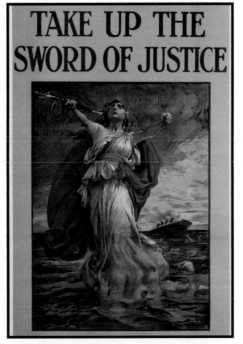

Figure 4.7 This British poster taps into the public outrage felt in 1915 after the RMS *Lusitania* was torpedoed. What propaganda techniques can you find in it?

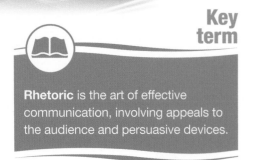

Key term

Rhetoric is the art of effective communication, involving appeals to the audience and persuasive devices.

Unit 4.2 **Rhetoric**

People who speak in public know how important it is to sound convincing. They want to move their listeners; they want to 'take them places', so to speak. How speakers achieve this effect on their audience is the study of **rhetoric**. Imagine persuasive speech is a car. A good driver will know what kind of fuel makes it go and how the engine works. In the same way, a good speaker has mastered the mechanics of rhetoric. In this unit you will be looking first at the ways a speaker appeals to the audience and then at nine rhetorical devices. The appeal is like the fuel and the rhetorical devices like the mechanics of a good, persuasive speech. You will study Barack Obama's victory speech from the 2008 presidential election as an example of rhetorical language.

Appeal

Text 4.2, like all speeches, contains three essential ingredients: ethos, pathos and logos. These are the terms used by the ancient Greeks to describe the different ways a speech appeals to an audience. These three qualities are the fuel of persuasive speeches. (As you read Text 4.2, do not worry about the numbers next to some of the passages for now – they will become clear when you study the next section on rhetorical devices.)

Ethos

Ethos refers to the trustworthiness of the speaker or writer. When speakers stand before an audience, they must ask themselves an important question: *What gives me the right to stand before you?* To answer it, they must establish credit with the audience and feel confident of their right to deliver the speech to that audience. In the case of Obama's victory speech, you will see that ethos runs through the opening lines and is at the heart of his message.

Pathos

Pathos is that part of a speech that appeals to our emotions. The word may remind you of other words, such as *pathetic, sympathetic* or *empathy*. Whenever speakers make you feel patriotic, afraid, joyful or guilty, they are appealing to your sense of emotion. There is no doubt that the audience of Obama's speech, as they stood listening to it in cold Chicago, felt a sense of elation run through their bodies. Obama included emotional language to evoke an emotional response.

Logos

Logos is the part of a speech that appeals to our sense of logic and all good speeches do this. Logical speech usually takes the form of an argument with several premises and a conclusion (in TOK you will learn to refer to such arguments as syllogisms). You may find examples of reasoning in a speech that carries a degree of validity and certainty.

Text 4.2 'This is your victory', Barack Obama, November 2008

Barack Obama was the first African American to become president of the USA. His victory speech, written with his speechwriter Jon Favreau, was delivered in his home city of Chicago in November 2008.

If there is anyone out there who still doubts that America is a place where all things are possible, who still wonders if the dream of our founders is alive in our time, who still questions the power of our democracy,[1] tonight is your answer.[2]

It's the answer[3] told by lines that stretched around schools and churches in numbers this nation has never seen, by people who waited three hours and four hours, many for the first time in their lives, because they believed that this time must be different, that their voices could be that difference.

It's the answer spoken by young and old, rich and poor, Democrat and Republican, black, white, Hispanic, Asian, Native American, gay, straight, disabled and not disabled. Americans who sent a message to the world that we have never been just a collection of individuals or a collection of red states and blue states.[4] We are, and always will be, the United States of America.

It's the answer that led those who've been told for so long by so many to be cynical and fearful and doubtful about what we can achieve to put their hands on the arc of history and bend it once more toward the hope of a better day.[5]

It's been a long time coming, but tonight, because of what we did on this date in this election at this defining moment change has come to America.

I was never the likeliest candidate for this office. We didn't start with much money or many endorsements. Our campaign was not hatched in the halls of Washington. It began in the backyards of Des Moines and the living rooms of Concord and the front porches of Charleston. It was built by working men and women who dug into what little savings they had to give $5 and $10 and $20[6] to the cause. It drew strength from the young people who rejected the myth of their generation's apathy who left their homes and their families for jobs that offered little pay and less sleep.

It drew strength from the not-so-young people who braved the bitter cold and scorching heat[7] to knock on doors of perfect strangers, and from the millions of Americans who volunteered and organized and proved that more than two centuries later a government of the people, by the people, and for the people[8] has not perished from the Earth. This is your victory.[9]

The road ahead will be long. Our climb will be steep. We may not get there in one year or even in one term, but America – I have never been more hopeful than I am tonight that we will get there. I promise you – we as a people will get there.

There will be setbacks and false starts. There are many who won't agree with every decision or policy I make as president, and we know that government can't solve every problem. But I will always be honest with you about the challenges we face. I will listen to you, especially when we disagree.

Figure 4.8 President Obama making his victory speech in Grant Park, Chicago, 2008.

Activity 4.2

In Chapter 3, you studied a sample written task in the form of a speech by Michael Moore (pages 84–86).

1 Read the student's speech in Chapter 3 again and look for examples of ethos, pathos and logos, the three qualities of appeal, in that speech.

2 Now study Text 4.2, President Obama's victory speech, and look for examples of the three qualities in this speech.

3 Compare and contrast the speech the student wrote as a written task with Obama's speech.

	Sample written task: a speech by Michael Moore	Text 4.2: Barack Obama's victory speech
Ethos		
Pathos		
Pathos		

Nine rhetorical devices

Rhetorical devices are the nuts and bolts of speech; the parts that make a speech work. Separately, each part of a speech is meaningless, but once put together they create a powerful effect on the listener. As you read President Obama's speech again, look at the examples of the nine rhetorical devices (these are labelled 1–9 in Text 4.2). However, this list isn't exhaustive, and these nine devices here represent just some of the many rhetorical devices used by speechwriters.

1 Parallelism

Parallelism is a stylistic device that you often hear in speeches but also one that is very useful for writing. Writing structures that are grammatically parallel helps your reader or listener understand your points better because they flow more smoothly. In the first sentence of Text 4.2, Obama uses three clauses, making the sentence very long, but the clauses are easy to follow because they all have the same structure: *If there is anyone out there* (1) *who still doubts* … (2) *who still wonders* … (3) *who still questions* … Obama's speeches are famous for their use of parallelisms, and there is more than one example in this victory speech.

2 Hypophora

A common technique is to start a speech with a hypophora, in which the speaker first asks a question and then answers it. In Obama's speech, the word *answer* is used regularly as an obvious signpost of the speaker's intention to give his audience answers. Note that here the questions were embedded in the first sentence and not asked as direct questions.

"Let me be vague."

Figure 4.9 Which rhetorical device is the speaker deliberately ignoring in this cartoon?

3 Repetition

Notice that the opening words of the second, third and fourth paragraphs are the same: *It's the answer*. Repetition, when used properly, can be very effective in creating a sense of structure and power. You may have been warned not to sound too repetitive in your written work. In speech writing, however, repeating small phrases can ingrain an idea in the minds of your audience.

4 Antithesis

Obama is famous for having said *There are no red states or blue states, there are only the United States of America*. This is an example of antithesis, a technique often used by speechwriters. In order to tell people what you believe in, it is useful and effective to tell them what you do *not* believe in.

5 Figurative speech

People like to think in metaphors. The image of bending the *arc of history* up towards hope is powerful. Figurative speech tends to work best when set off by concrete images, such as found here a few lines on from the *arc of history* with *the backyards of Des Moines and the living rooms of Concord and the front porches of Charleston*. (See Chapter 4, page 95)

6 Tricolon and polysyndeton

A tricolon is a sort of list of three, or a sentence in which there are three parts or clauses. The cumulative effect of three has a powerful effect on an audience. Here, the *backyards*, *living rooms* and *front porches* build up a strong picture of 'plain folks', and the three amounts of money underline the big achievement of modest donations by ordinary Americans. (Note too the parallelism of *the backyards*, *the living rooms* and *the front porches*.)

Furthermore, there is a peculiar kind of tricolon present in the *backyards* example. Obama uses the word *and* in between each and every item listed whereas usually in a list it is only necessary to use *and* before the last item. This technique is known as polysyndeton and is used to stress the importance of every item. We see it also in the example of *$5 and $10 and $20*. Can you see why he uses *and* twice?

7 Juxtaposition

When two things of opposite nature are mentioned together, readers and listeners tend to notice. Obama talks about 'the not-so-young people who braved the bitter cold and scorching heat to knock on doors of perfect strangers'. The juxtaposition of 'bitter cold' and 'scorching heat' stresses the extreme conditions in which people campaigned for Obama, convincing the audience of their dedication.

8 Allusion

The words *government of the people, by the people, and for the people* are lifted from the famous Gettysburg Address delivered by President Abraham Lincoln in 1863 (hence the *more than two centuries later* reference), and most Americans in the audience would know them. Allusion is when your speech echoes another speech or famous phrase. By using allusion, you not only associate yourself with the ideas of the original text but also create a bond with the audience by evoking shared knowledge.

9 Varied sentence length

Varying the length of your sentences is always a good way to strengthen any writing style, be it for speech writing or essays. In this paragraph of the speech, notice how long the first sentence is compared to the second sentence: *It drew strength from the not-so-young … has not perished from the Earth. This is your victory.*

tip

Notice that for each of the nine rhetorical devices, there is an explanation of the effects of the device on its audience. For example, repetition, it is stated, ingrains an idea in the minds of an audience. As you begin to analyse various types of texts, be careful to go beyond the process of identifying and labelling the stylistic devices. In all forms of assessment, you need to explain the effects of stylistic devices on their readers.

tip

As we discuss the characteristics of a good speech, notice where the spoken word and written word are different and where they are similar. Parallelism, hypophora and epithet are good in both speeches and essays. Repetition and polysyndeton are not recommended in essay writing. Be aware also that a public speech is very different from a conversation with a friend and make sure your writing does not sound too colloquial or informal.

Key terms

Brand is a product's identity and the feelings and values customers associate with it.

Marketing is the process of creating, developing, promoting and selling goods and services to customers, managing the customers' interest in and need for the product.

'When a thing is current, it creates currency.'
Marshall McLuhan (1911–80)

Further resources

The Merchants of Cool by the US Public Broadcasting Service (PBS) is an interesting documentary, showing how high school students are both the target group and the source of inspiration of big brands. It describes how large corporations hunt for cultural trends, capitalise on them and kill them in an endless cycle.

Confessions of an Ad Man by Rory Sutherland is an excellent talk on the Internet site TED.com about the value added to our lives through branding. Sutherland makes the case that as a society we should learn to appreciate intangible values more than material goods. His anecdotes are drawn from a wealth of experience in the field of advertising. Go to www.ted.com and follow the links to 'Talks' and Rory Sutherland.

Activity 4.3

1 Watch the full speech given by Barack Obama online. Can you find more examples of the rhetorical devices that you have studied in this unit?
2 Below are suggestions for speeches that you may want to research in your study of rhetorical devices. Can you find examples of the nine rhetorical devices in these speeches as well?
   • Queen Elizabeth I's speech to the troops at Tilbury, 1588.
   • Winston Churchill's 'Blood, toil, tears and sweat' speech, 1940.
   • Martin Luther King's 'I have a dream' speech, 1963.
   • President John F. Kennedy's 'Ich bin ein Berliner' speech, 1963.
   • Mahatma Gandhi's 'One world' speech, 1947.

At the beginning of this chapter you were asked whether you had ever got goosebumps from listening to a speech. The idea may sound silly, but good rhetoric can have a *physical* effect on audiences and prompt people to act. You have seen how Barack Obama and his speechwriter, Jon Favreau, made good use of these nine rhetorical devices to create a sense of hope, appealing to our sense of logos and emotion through the language in the speech.

In the following unit you will look at how similar devices used in advertising move us to buy products. Advertising, just as propaganda and rhetoric, demonstrates the power of persuasive language.

Unit 4.3 Advertising

If you have ever travelled to another country, you will know how interesting it can be to look at adverts on hoardings and on television. Even if you do not understand the language of the country you are visiting, these images often tell you a lot about the local culture. Advertisements contain more than persuasive speech: they offer a window on different cultural values.

Some of the world's largest corporations have made expensive mistakes by showing a lack of cultural sensitivity in their ads. In 2005 McDonald's ran an ad on Chinese television in which a desperate customer begged on his knees a McDonald's restaurant manager to accept an expired coupon. Chinese viewers found this more disgraceful than funny. Similarly, the mobile phone provider Orange had to change its *The future is bright. The future is Orange* slogan for their Irish market as in Ireland the colour orange is associated with the staunchly Protestant Orange Order and the ad was causing offence to Irish Catholics.

In Chapter 1, *culture* was defined as a common system of values (page 1). What people buy and what **brands** they feel loyal to reveal a lot about this system of values. For some people, a chain of coffee shops might just mean coffee, muffins and free Internet access. For other people, however, the same brand may represent much more than that, anything from warmth to environmental correctness, friendship to sophistication.

Such feelings are created through **marketing**. Marketing is the process of building value and meaning for customers around a brand. It could include placing brochures on sales counters to tell customers about your company's commitment to reducing carbon emissions, or setting up a group of fans on a social networking site. Marketing includes advertising. Advertising is the art of persuading an audience to buy into an idea or product. While marketing executives make sure brands permeate our daily lives, advertisers make sure brands are persuasive.

Activity 4.4

Advertising is not always a straightforward field of study. There are some fundamental questions that behavioural scientists have been researching for decades. In groups, discuss the following questions. Try to support your views with good arguments and examples.

1 How can the effectiveness of an ad be measured? When do we know whether an ad has been successful?

2 What are the effects of featuring scantily dressed men and women in advertisements? Do such images distract from the product or do they draw our attention to the product?

3 Are we simply creatures of imitation? In other words, do we all want to be like the people in the ads?

4 Can advertisements instigate social progress? Can they emancipate a group? If women are frequently pictured in top-level positions, will they begin to be treated as equals with men as far as employment opportunities are concerned?

5 Is culture for sale? Can the spaces around us, from basketball courts to hospital beds, be branded or sponsored?

> 'Advertisements contain the only truths to be relied on in a newspaper.'
> Mark Twain (1835–1910)

"I think the dosage needs adjusting. I'm not nearly as happy as the people in the ads."

Figure 4.10 How true is this cartoon? Do we all want to be like the people in the ads?

TOK

In the activity, the first question for discussion is a rather philosophical one: *How can the effectiveness of an ad be measured?* This is a great knowledge issue for TOK presentations as it points towards the differences between the exact sciences and the human sciences.

For a TOK presentation, you could compare Martin Lindstrom's methods with psychologists' research into advertising. Which comes closer to revealing the truth, the practice or the theory?

Key terms

Focus group, in marketing, is a group of people who are asked by a company to talk about their likes and dislikes concerning a product or ad.

Brand loyalty describes a consumer's allegiance to a product and their habit of buying it regularly.

Further resources

Buyology by Martin Lindstrom is an engaging and accessible book despite the serious scientific nature of its subject. Lindstrom has spent years researching consumers' brain activity, using MRI scans, while they view images of brands and ads. Lindstrom's guiding question is 'How can we measure the effectiveness of ads?' His results have sometimes been different from those of marketing and advertising experts.

discussion

1 How does Tata Motors use language and image to sell us this car?

2 How is this ad conventional in its structure and layout?

'Buyology'

Common sense may tell us that sales figures reflect good advertising, but this is misleading as in practice a wide variety of factors can influence sales. You might think that it would be possible to simply ask consumers through marketing **focus groups** what kinds of ads they like, but who can say they really *know* what they like? Consumers may only tell market researchers what they think the researchers want to hear, or what they want to say to conform to a certain idea they have of themselves. A more accurate picture might emerge if it were possible to simply to look inside the consumer's head.

Martin Lindstrom, a well-known marketing consultant, carried out some research in which he did look at people's brain activity, thus using hard science to demonstrate the effectiveness of images and language in advertising. He showed people images of brands, icons, logos and faces and measured their brain activity with an MRI scanner. The results of his research suggested that people are creatures of imitation. For example, Lindstrom took some anti-smoking ads which featured unhappy and unattractive people smoking, and showed them to people who smoked. The result was that the people who smoked began to crave cigarettes. Similarly, Lindstrom found that an ad highlighting the dangers of anorexia which portrayed a dangerously thin girl actually stimulated anorexic behaviour in anorexic girls. Furthermore, Lindstrom's research found that the parts of the brain that are stimulated during religious activity, such as prayer or worship, are the same as the those that were stimulated when the people saw pictures of their favourite brands. **Brand loyalty** appears to originate in the same part of the brain as religious devotion.

Advertising techniques

While advertising is not an exact science, it is possible to analyse the methods commonly used to sell a product, idea or value. In order to become media literate, we need to be able to identify the techniques used by advertisers in their efforts to persuade.

Problem and benefit

Many ads try to sell an image, brand or feeling. For example many car commercials show people looking 'tough', 'sophisticated' or 'in control' behind the wheel of a particular car. Some ads, however, actually try to sell you something you need, such as the one in Figure 4.11. This ad presents the Tata Nano as a fuel-efficient car, arguably something that appeals to one's pocket book and needs. The target audience, people in India who are in the market for buying a new car, may not have even considered fuel efficiency in their decision process. This ad may convince them of a need they were not yet aware of. Good advertising knows how to blur the line between needs and wants. Identifying a problem and offering a solution is an age-old advertising technique.

Bandwagon effect

In Activity 4.4, you were asked to discuss whether ads had the power to emancipate, or liberate, a group of people. Look at Figure 4.12. Can you see how this McDonald's ad is selling social progress? Whether you hate it or love it, McDonald's has revolutionised the way people eat by bringing the assembly line into restaurants. Figure 4.12 is best understood in the context of the 1950s, when families with young children were not usually welcome at restaurants. The ad shows families enjoying eating out and seems

Figure 4.11 This ad aims to convince potential customers of a need, even though they may not be aware of it.

'Advertisements may be evaluated scientifically; they cannot be created scientifically.'
Leo Bogart (1921–2005)

to be saying, 'Other families are eating out; you can too!' This technique is known as the **bandwagon effect**, referring to something that becomes popular quickly as people follow the example set by others.

Testimonials

Testimonials are statements from ordinary people, recommending a certain product. Similar to the 'plain folks' argument we looked at earlier in the unit on propaganda, the Tata Nano ad (Figure 4.11) makes use of an average man's story. He tells about a trip he made on a particular road for a particular purpose. Nothing extraordinary seems to be going on except for his fuel efficiency, which stresses the main point: You too as an ordinary person in India could enjoy high fuel efficiency.

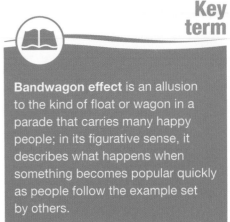

Key term

Bandwagon effect is an allusion to the kind of float or wagon in a parade that carries many happy people; in its figurative sense, it describes what happens when something becomes popular quickly as people follow the example set by others.

Celebrities

Figure 4.13 uses a slightly different, but similar technique to sell a product. Because David Beckham 'endorses' Motorola phones, people may be more likely to buy one. The premise for understanding endorsement is that people want to identify with the individuals they see in ads. *If David Beckham uses this phone, and you want to be like David Beckham, then you had better buy this phone.* This is the line of logic inherent in ads that involve celebrities.

Association

Association is the technique of linking products closely with certain values. It can be assumed that people value the way a phone feels in their hands from Figure 4.13. What's more, people value the attributes of snakeskin, as it is often associated with both expensive products, such as chic clothing and handbags, and the dangers of the wild. In order to achieve association in an ad, the placement of a product is very important. Notice that close proximity of the snake's head to the actual phone. Notice, in Figure 4.12, the close proximity of the happy family to the famous 'golden arches'. The positioning of images in these ads is not accidental or arbitrary. Instead, these ads are carefully constructed to appeal to the emotions of the audience. In the same way that pathos is important in rhetoric, an appeal to the emotions is an important part of the persuasive language of many ads.

Figure 4.12 An ad for McDonald's from the 1950s.

Figure 4.13 An ad from 2006, featuring the footballer David Beckham.

A deconstructed ad

Having looked at the persuasive techniques that make ads effective, you are now going to examine how ads are assembled. Many of the advertisements you have looked at in this chapter have common structural qualities. Becoming media literate also means being able to identify the structure of ads.

What structural elements define an ad? While different restrictions are placed on ads depending on where they are located (for example, on large hoardings, on websites or in magazines), most have the same four elements: image, slogan, copy and signature. We will look at how these are used in an ad for Marlboro cigarettes from the 1960s. The Marlboro cigarette ads are good examples of ads over the years and many have come to be seen as icons in the world of advertising.

Text 4.3 Marlboro cigarettes ad, 1968

Slogan   Image

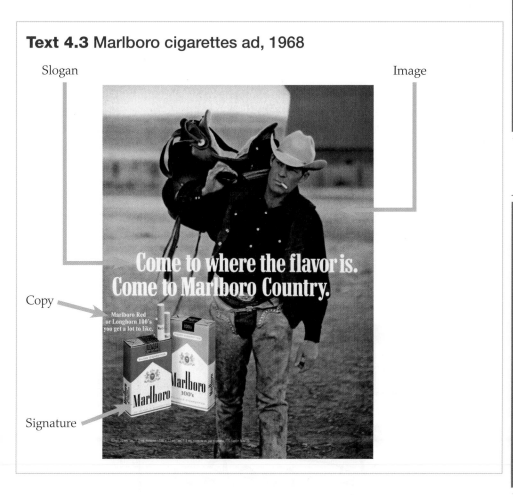

Copy

Signature

Higher level

As you collect a library of texts for your class, search for examples of ads that illustrate the advertising techniques discussed in this unit. You can create an activity for your class using a variety of ads in which you have to match the techniques you have learned about to the ads.

discussion

1   What does the Marlboro ad in Text 4.3 say about cultural values? Why might this ad work well in North America but not in the UK or other Anglophone countries?
2   This ad makes use of a technique that you have not come across yet: it creates a character. The Marlboro Man was once an icon. Why do you think he gained fame? Can you think of other ad campaigns that create a character?

Image

Advertisers rely heavily on the saying *An image is worth a thousand words*. The placement of an image in relation to the text is crucial as readers normally scan and digest an ad within a matter of seconds. You saw from Martin Lindstrom's research that people often want to imitate what they see in ads, so the image must engage the audience. Contrast is also an important factor to keep in mind when working with image. White letters on a red background, for example, work well.

Slogan

As the image is all-important in ads, the text is usually kept to a minimum and, as with a headline, the most prominent text is the slogan. The slogan here is *Come to where the flavor is. Come to Marlboro Country*. The slogan, or tagline, should be short, catchy and poignant, because the audience's attention span is usually brief and fleeting.

Copy

Ads sometimes offer a small story. Volkswagen, for example, is famous for its large, simple images of Volkswagen cars with a lot of small-print copy, or text, below. One of the most famous Volkswagen ads, 'Lemon', describes the rigorous safety controls through which the cars must pass before they are sold. The trend has been for increasingly smaller amounts of copy in ads but it still depends on the product: some products require more information to be given than others. The copy in Text 4.3 is *Marlboro Red or Longhorn 100's — you get a lot to like*. It gives some product information and aims to persuade people to buy the product.

Signature

Traditionally, ads show a product and the company name, though this is not always the case. You will have noticed that there is no image of the actual product in many of the ads in this unit. Occasionally not even the name of the company is given, although this is unusual. These days Internet addresses are used more and more as the signature for an ad.

Activity 4.5

Look at Figure 4.14. How does this cartoon prove that language can be used to manipulate people? Cigarette companies are no longer allowed to advertise in many countries. Do you think this is right and fair?

"That's a crazy idea but it might work."

Figure 4.14 The problem of advertising for tobacco companies.

Counter-advertising

The Marlboro Man and the ban on smoking ads brings us to an important part of our look at advertising: the potential harm that advertising can do. Should society protect itself from the harmful effects of advertisements? Can ads have too much influence over us?

For the last century, in all corners of the Anglophone world, there has been a trend towards the privatisation of public services and goods. Public basketball courts in the USA are often sponsored by soft drinks companies; schools award contracts to fast food companies to provide lunches. A homogeneous culture has arisen, with a few brands dominating areas such as supermarkets, coffee shops, mobile phones and personal music players: we are beginning to live 'branded' lives.

Efforts have been made to raise awareness of the adverse effects of corporate advertising and marketing. As well as the ban on smoking ads, there have also been anti-smoking ads. Some adverts deliberately flout the conventional rules of advertising to shock their audiences. Large corporations have used advertising and marketing to enhance their image as philanthropists and to accomplish good works. To finish this unit, you are going to look at four ways in which branded culture can be called into question: with anti-ads, philanthropic ads, culture jamming, and parody and pastiche.

Anti-ads

The car manufacturer Volvo has the slogan *There is more to life than a Volvo*, which startles the reader at first. Like all counter-advertising, this slogan draws our attention to the conventions of advertising. Then it breaks them. It essentially says, 'Your life and safety are more important to us than this advertising campaign.'

Another company who has been famous for breaking all the advertising rules is the clothing company Benetton (see Figure 4.15). Many of the Benetton ads do not even show the company's product. What is more, they sometimes have nothing to do with fashion but are there to raise awareness of political problems, as with this one, which depicts child labour in South America. As unconventional as this ad may seem, it does something that all good advertisers know is effective: it shocks. If an ad can make people stop and think, it is already being successful. Another Benetton ad carried a picture of a real prisoner on death row.

Philanthropic ads

Some companies have presented themselves as foundations or non-profit organisations in an effort to boost their image as philanthropists. The Dove toiletries brand, part of Unilever, goes to great lengths to convince people that it is more than a beauty product with its campaign aimed at raising self-esteem and encouraging women to feel confident about their bodies. By placing ordinary women of all ages, shapes and colours in their ads, they are making a counter-statement to that of the other beauty product companies that use unrealistic images of women's bodies. Figure 4.16, shows an ordinary, yet very happy, woman who happens to be flat-chested. In this ad Dove aims to make people aware of how other ads portray unrealistic appearances to promote their products.

Many companies have taken up a noble cause in a different way from Dove's approach. An organisation called PRODUCT (RED) has taken the effectiveness of advertising, marketing and branding and put it towards eradicating AIDS in Africa. The best way to explain the RED concept is through the organisation's own words, which you can read in Text 4.4. The RED concept is an excellent example of image management for large corporations. Consumers consume commercial products without feeling guilty, and the corporations contribute to a good cause.

Further resources

No Logo is a polemic against the dominant position of companies and the space that brands occupy both in our physical surroundings and in our minds. The author, Naomi Klein, focuses on the cultural implications of this corporate dominance, looking at how brands permeate our daily lives.

Extended essay

Compare and contrast the stereotypical roles that men and women are assigned in advertisements.

The Razr2 ad featuring David Beckham (Figure 4.13) and the Dove ad of the 'real' girl (Figure 4.16) raise the issue of how men and women are portrayed in the media. This complex topic is perfect for an extended essay. Is the Razr2 ad, for example, targeting young men who want to look like David Beckham, or is it appealing to women who would like their boyfriends to look like him? A lot of research has been done on this subject, which you can draw on for your extended essay. Make sure that you also demonstrate your media literacy skills. It is easy to get caught up in the psychology research and lose sight of what you are supposed to be writing about: the effects of language and images on an audience.

Figure 4.15 A Benetton ad raising awareness of problems in South America.

Figure 4.16 This Dove ad persuades people to feel confident about their bodies.

discussion

What do you think of the (RED) idea? Do you think the partner companies involved in the scheme are doing more to promote their product names or eradicate AIDS in Africa?

Text 4.4 The (RED) idea, PRODUCT (RED), 2010

(RED) is a simple idea that transforms our incredible collective power as consumers into a financial force to help others in need.

(RED) works with the world's most iconic brands – including American Express, Apple, Bugaboo, Converse, Dell, Emporio Armani, Gap, Hallmark, Nike, Penguin and Starbucks – to make unique (PRODUCT)^{RED} products, giving up to 50 percent of their profits to the Global Fund to invest in HIV and AIDS programs in Africa. Every dollar goes straight to people who need it, helping them stay alive so that they can go on taking care of their families and contributing to their communities.

Since its launch in 2006, (RED) has generated over $160 million for the Global Fund and over 5 million people have been impacted by HIV and AIDS programs supported by your (RED) purchases.

Buy (RED), save lives. It's as simple as that.

Further resources

Adbusters is both a magazine and a website which generates a lot of counter-advertising and culture jamming. Their media is very stimulating and engaging, as they make us more conscious of the effects of advertising techniques. Go to www.adbusters.org/.

Culture jamming

The counter-advertising techniques of anti-ads and philanthropic ads, as unconventional as they may seem, still make use of conventional channels of mass communication. What happens, however, when people take these communication channels into their own hands? The result is **culture jamming**. This term refers to the ways in which individuals distort the messages and advertisements of large corporations.

Culture jamming can be done in several ways. In mash-ups, individuals rearrange a company's graphic or iconic images to create new meaning, often defaming the company. Mash-ups can be done easily using the Internet and photo manipulation programs. Another culture-jamming method is graffiti, whereby individuals deface billboards in order to draw our attention to the wrongdoings of a company. Look at Figure 4.17 to see how two small lines added to the company's name in its logo completely change the original message.

Key term

Culture jamming refers to the distorting of messages and advertisements produced by large corporations.

Activity 4.6

In groups or as a class, discuss whether it is acceptable for individuals to mash-up or deface a company's advertisements. Give reasons for your views.

Parody and pastiche

When individuals take a well-known ad and change it to give it new meaning, they are in essence parodying the style of that ad. Parody is the art of mocking someone or something by imitating them or their style. Figure 4.18 is a mash-up ad from Adbusters parodying the 'Got Milk?' campaign that featured many celebrities. Where a famous person usually appears, we see a seemingly ordinary woman. The imitation is obvious so that people can contrast the parody with the original.

Similar to parody, pastiche is another way of drawing attention to a cultural value. It also makes use of imitation, but not by obviously parodying a particular text in a genre. Rather, it could be compared to any well-known example of that genre and could almost pass itself off as a genuine example. Figure 4.19, despite appearances, is not a real ad from the 1950s. It is a pastiche of ads from the 1950s, when cigarette and beverage companies made false claims about how healthy their products were and the benefits they would bring you if you used them. Because the claims in the pastiche cola ad are so preposterous, they make us think about the adverse effects of cola. Pastiche holds up a mirror in order to mock and question our cultural values.

Figure 4.17 Parody can change, for example, a company's name and give it new meaning.

Figure 4.18 This 'Why Milk?' ad parodies the well-known 'Got Milk?' campaign.

Figure 4.19 A pastiche of a 1950s ad to draw attention to the harmful effects of some soft drinks.

Part 2 – Language and mass communication

Further resources

Micah Wright is a parody and pastiche artist who is inspired by the kinds of images you saw earlier in the chapter in the First World War propaganda posters (Figures 4.4–4.7). Through his art he draws a parallel between the values that were prevalent during the world wars and those that are current today in modern conflicts. Visit his website at propagandaremix.com

Higher level

1 Research the advertising campaigns of Dove, Volvo and Benetton. How noble do you think these companies are in spreading awareness about self-esteem, safety and social injustices respectively? Are they instigating social progress?

2 Do some research on the (RED) campaign. Do you think it is effective? Give reasons for your answer.

Key terms

Negative ads are ads that carry an attack and are often used in political campaigns when opponents make attacks on each other, often using the ad hominem argument.

Ad hominem is a type of argument that attacks a person rather than their ideas, words or actions.

Assessment: Part 2 further oral activity

In Chapters 3 and 4 you have come across a number of discussion questions and may have found yourself in a heated classroom debate on the effects of advertising on culture or the social implications of the Internet. These are the perfect starting points for a further oral activity. An improvised discussion, however, is not in itself a further oral activity. You will have to plan and structure your activity carefully in order to reflect an understanding of classroom discussion and course material. Remember that further oral ctivities can take formats other than debates. Sketches, television shows, plays, interviews and presentations are all possible.

Before you read the sample further oral activity on pages 109–114, go back and remind yourself of the assessment criteria and requirements (page ix) for the task. To check you understand the criteria, try assessing the sample activity yourself before reading the teacher's comments.

The inspiration for the sample further oral activity came from a genre of advertisements that you have not yet explored but which appears more and more frequently during political campaigns. **Negative ads**, also sometimes referred to as 'mudslinging' or 'attack ads', are ads that attack political opponents directly by saying negative things about them. It is similar to and makes use of the **ad hominem** argument, which you will have studied in your TOK lessons as one of the many argumentation fallacies. This is an argument that attacks the person rather than the person's ideas, words or actions.

Figure 4.20, one of the more famous negative ads in British history, created quite a controversy in 1997 for portraying Tony Blair, then the respected Labour Party leader as well as a Christian, as a demon. The Conservative Party, which was behind the ad, would not say who had produced it. The poster became news in itself, with public debate on whether such a poster was acceptable or not.

In preparation for the further oral activity, the students studied the 1988 ad attacking the presidential candiate Michael Dukakis, a transcript of which is found in Text 4.5. The students also compared the context of the 1988 election with that of the 2008 presidential election, in which Barack Obama made use of the Internet and did not use any smear campaigns. The students did research on the effectiveness of negative ads for both the Republican and Democratic political parties in the USA.

Text 4.5 Michael Dukakis negative ad, National Security Political Action Committee, 1988

This text is a transcript of a televised ad from the 1988 US presidential election campaign between George H.W. Bush and Michael Dukakis. Although the ad shocked many people, it proved surprisingly effective and established a new threshold of what was acceptable in a smear campaign.

Bush and Dukakis on crime.

Bush supports the death penalty for first-degree murderers. Dukakis not only opposes the death penalty. He allowed first-degree murderers to have weekend passes from prison.

One was Willie Horton, who murdered a boy in a robbery, stabbing him 19 times.

Despite a life sentence, Horton received 10 weekend passes from prison. Horton fled, kidnapped a young couple, stabbing the man and repeatedly raping his girlfriend.

Weekend prison passes. Dukakis on crime.

The students' teacher took an active role in helping them prepare and participating in the final further oral activity. This is not only permissible but in some cases, such as an interview, recommended. After the students had chosen the topic, the teacher guided them towards the idea of a radio talk show. They were assigned roles and encouraged to listen to a talk show called *Weekend Edition* on National Public Radio (NPR). The students researched their roles of the two guests on the talk show. Before the activity, they also submitted the talk show host questions to the teacher. Both the students and the teacher occasionally moved away from the script, which prevented the oral activity from sounding overscripted.

Activity 4.7

In preparation for the further oral activity, research another negative ad and present it to the rest of the class.

1   Choose a negative ad to present. You could do some online research for ideas and material. For example, the ad known as 'Daisy' from the 1960s is a remarkable use of images associating Barry Goldwater with nuclear war. It cost him the US presidential election in 1964. In 1993 Canada's Progressive Conservatives ran ads against the candidate Jean Chrétien, mocking his facial condition known as Bell's palsy.

2   Comment on the techniques or devices used in the ad.

3   Comment on the context of the ad and discuss whether the ad's creator was justified in making the attack.

Figure 4.20 A negative ad attacking Tony Blair.

Sample further oral activity (HL)

The following is an edited transcript of the students' further oral activity.

The roles of the participants

Host (Scott Simon) – Teacher who co-ordinates the talk show.

Floyd Brown (FB) – Author and political consultant. In 1988, Brown was responsible for the 'Willie Horton' ad that was made by the NSPAC. He has had a very prolific career as a conservative media consultant. He has run various attack campaigns on Al Gore, Bill Clinton and Barack Obama.

David Plouffe (DP) – Campaign manager for Barack Obama in 2008.

Rick Farmer (RF) – Professor at University of Akron, who has researched the effects of negative ads.

The transcript

Host Today on *Weekend Edition* we'd like to revisit an issue that returns every election season: negative ads. Specifically on this 20-year anniversary, we will look back on a seminal[1] piece of negative advertising, the Willie Horton ad, which ran for two weeks during the Bush/Dukakis race in 1988. It changed the way we run presidential campaigns today.

With us today are several experts. David Plouffe, campaign manager for Barack Obama, Rick Farmer, professor in communications and political science at University of Akron, and Floyd Brown, who famously came up with the Willie Horton ad in 1988.

First of all, let's start by asking Mr Brown if he feels he deserves the fame. Mr Brown, do you feel that the Willie Horton ad indeed changed the way presidential campaigns are run?

FB Ha, ha, I would like to take credit for what you call this 'seminal'[1] work, but in fact there were others like Lee Atwater and Jim Pinkerton who were really responsible for finding this story of Dukakis and the furlough[2] programme in Massachusetts. I just made sure it was told to the world.

Host Yes, and I think that's at the heart of our matter here today. Do you think people need to hear these kinds of ads in the months leading up to the election?

FB Yes, most definitely. Would you trust national security to a governor who gave weekend passes to murderers? The public has the right to know this. I won't deny that the ad helped Bush Senior. But who is to blame here? I was just the messenger. If Dukakis wanted to stand a chance in the elections, he shouldn't have allowed for the furlough programme in Massachusetts in the first place. It's as simple as that.

Host Right, 'Don't shoot the messenger.' OK, I understand that line of thinking, but I'm curious if the others do too. What would you say, Mr Plouffe, Mr Farmer? Is Mr Brown simply the messenger of negative news?

DP Well, there are many different ways you can tell a message. You can simply say that Dukakis approved of this furlough programme. He did not approve of Willie Horton's actions. Or you can take Mr Brown's approach and make the message sensational. The ad uses the word *stabbing* twice. I do not deny that what Horton did was horrific. But what is the effect of telling it in the context of the campaign season? Horton's horrific deed becomes Dukakis's horrific deed through association. Mr Brown understood this 20 years ago all too well.

FB I would like to think Americans are smarter than that. This theory of association cannot be proven. If you want to know why it was so convincing, look at the numbers and facts. Bush Senior was indeed for the death penalty. The boy was stabbed 19 times; Horton received 10 of these passes and Dukakis signed for the furlough programme. These are the facts and they speak for themselves.

DP Actually his predecessor put the furtlough programme in effect. Dukakis did not change his predecessor's policies.

FB The ad states that he *allowed* the furlough programme. People can read that how they want.

DP Actually it's vague language. In the context of an attack ad, the audience is naturally going to assume that *allowed* means 'approved' or even 'signed into action' as you believed yourself.

[1] **seminal**   something that strongly influences later developments

[2] **furlough**   a temporary leave of absence from employment, military duty or prison sentence

Host So this brings us back to the main question, which I'd like to present Mr Farmer with. Is Mr Brown simply the messenger? Or is he, like Mr Plouffe would have us believe, a manipulator of public opinion?

RF Well, technically speaking, Mr Brown was not the messenger, because he here was not working for the Bush Senior campaign directly. He was working as a private agent. Like the Swift Boat Veterans for Truth people that we saw in 2004, who spoke out against Kerry. They worked independently from Bush Junior. What we see during the campaign season more and more are ads that are not officially approved by the candidates, but still actually benefit the candidates. They outsource the dirty work and mudslinging to people like Mr Brown, so that the candidate doesn't have to be held accountable for ad hominem cheap shots.

FB Now wait a minute. You're contradicting yourself. First, you say I acted as a lone agent, which was true, and then you accuse Bush Senior of having something to do with the Horton ad. Doesn't that sound a little hypocritical?

RF Wasn't it proven that Bush Senior knew of your plans before they went on the air? Didn't you receive money from his campaign manager?

FB I will not answer these kinds of accusations here. This went to court over 20 years ago.

Host I would also like to return to what you, Mr Farmer, touched on briefly. You said that candidates actually *benefit* from negative ads. Is that what you, Mr Plouffe, are discovering this election season in your efforts to elect Obama?

DP Well, no, actually, the opposite. We see that negative ads, like Hillary Clinton's '3 a.m.' ad, actually hurt the sender in the polls. They often backfire.

Host Can you explain to our listeners why Clinton's '3 a.m.' ad actually hurt her?

DP Sure. First of all, if you remember, the ad consisted almost entirely of images of children sleeping in bed at night. They are holding their teddy bears; they are cute and innocent as can be. The voiceover explains that the phone is ringing at the White House with something urgent. It asks us: *Who would you want to answer the phone?* The voiceover explains that Hillary's experience on national security is very great, implying that it is greater than Obama's. In the background you can hear military drums growing louder. Finally you see a concerned mother enter her child's room in panic.

Now, you have to consider the target audience is already Democrat. The ad is not successful first and foremost because Democrats are not supposed to sling mud at other Democrats in the Primaries. But secondly, Americans could see right through the ad. Hillary answers the phone with make-up and glasses, looking sophisticated and in charge. Her voice states clearly that she approves this message. But in fact there is no message other than fear, which is not one you want to approve. The voiceover says she has years of experience, but it does not tell us what kind of experience. There you have vague language again.

Another problem is that the question *Who would you want to answer the phone?* is rhetorical and loaded. The question many viewers hear is *Would you really want Obama answering the phone?*

RF I'd like to confirm what Mr Farmer has said. The reason why the ad did not work was because she so openly approved it. If there's anything we learned from Mr Brown's seminal work, it is that you have to outsource the mudslinging. Let someone else be the bad guy, while the politician reaps the benefits.

Host Mr Brown, how do you respond to that?

FB Well, I don't like the term *bad guy*. I preferred *messenger*. But gentlemen, we are all men of the media. We understand how the game is played today. Thanks to YouTube and the Internet in general, many little battles are being fought every day and these count for more than the expensive prime-time slots and radio ads. No one is outsourcing anything anymore. Everyone is spontaneously defending his or her favorite man by digging up dirt on the opponent. If anyone here knows that the playing field has moved to the Internet, it's you, Dave.

DP I do, and you do too. You're sending e-mails to 5 million people saying that Obama is soft on crime.

FB Because he is.

Host Mr Farmer, I'm listening to this discussion on who's responsible for negative ads. It seems that the candidates want to keep their hands clean. I would like to return to what you said about negative ads backfiring. Is that true? Do they actually hurt the sender more than the opponent?

RF Yes, they can. Like I said, we saw that after the '3 a.m.' ad that Hillary Clinton ran in the primaries. It wasn't even such an aggressive attack ad. But Hillary publicly approved it. And it came back to haunt her.

Mr Brown is right in saying that the Internet is a great feeding ground for attack ads, because no one knows what official material has been 'mashed-up' or what amateur material is false. And because they're so anonymous, they work. The audience walks away wondering *Could that be true? Is Hillary secretly a Republican? Is Obama soft on crime? Did Kerry throw away his medals or ribbons?* In fact the truth does not matter anymore. The debate has been opened up and muddled, and that is enough to influence voters.

Host That's an interesting point you raised about John Kerry. Can you clarify? You say that negative ads can backfire, but they can be effective if they 'muddle' the debate. Is this what happened with the Swift Boat Veterans for Truth campaign in 2004? Certainly those did not backfire?

RF Well, first of all, these veterans claimed responsibility for their own ad. But for those who do not remember the ad, I'll explain briefly how it set precedence in the genre of negative ads. Like most negative ads, it too relied on one or several basic images. The most effective Swift Vets' ad I remember had a camera scanning a row of some 50 Vietnam veterans between the ages of 50 [and] 60. The voiceover claimed, *These are the men who served under Kerry's command. Unlike Kerry, they kept their medals. Unlike Kerry, they did not question the actions of young American soldiers in Vietnam. Unlike Kerry, they continue to serve the country as teachers, farmers, community leaders and grandfathers.* I'm summarising here, but you see the point. They gloss over Kerry's history without much care or nuance. They make insinuations. And worst of all, *they* are his people! They were organised and could afford their own prime-time ads. They were community leaders, whatever that might be. In fact it turned out that none of these men were actually on Kerry's boat or served under his leadership. It was full of lies. But in the end that didn't matter. Like I said, the debate had been muddled and that was all that mattered.

Host Mr Brown, does it look like you have competition? Will the Swift Vets' ad top Horton's on the chart of most effective negative ads?

FB I don't see this as a competition, but we have to agree that the Swift Vets' campaign was a historical phenomenon. The term *Swift Boat* has even become a verb. If you are swiftboated, then someone has used something you can be proud of against you. It's paradoxical. But honestly, I find swiftboating disgraceful. These ads were orchestrated lies, which is why I took sides with many prominent Republicans in denouncing them. But like Mr Farmer has stated, once a seed of doubt has been planted in the voter's mind, the debate is already over. These ads really target swing voters.

Host How do attack ads or negative ads influence swaying voters? Are there a lot of undecided voters out there? And if so, what's the effect of these ads on them?

RF Well it's difficult to say how many swaying voters are out there today. But our research tells us that Republicans don't sway much. They are loyal to their base, no matter what an attack ad will tell them. The Democratic candidates know that their attack ads are not effective on these loyal Republican voters. Those who vote Democrat, on the other hand, *are* more influenced by negative ads. They sway. People like Mr Brown are familiar with our research. They know it works. And that is why you see more negative ads coming from the Republican side.

Host Is that true, Mr Brown? Are you familiar with the research on this subject? And do Republicans seem to have a kind of home-field advantage in the world of negative ads?

FB If we have an advantage, I've never been made aware of it. I do not take votes for granted. We work hard to win every single one out there.

Host Using every means possible?

FB If that means exposing our opponents for what they are — as in the case of Dukakis — then yes.

RF I would like to add that there is a side effect, though, for 'exposing the opponent'. Negative ads keep voters home, away from the voting booth, because, like I said, they know that they have been confused on the issues. And because they are questioning their understanding of the issues, they don't feel empowered to go out and vote. This usually works in the Republicans' favour.

This is why you always hear the Democratic candidates encouraging people to vote, without saying whom you should vote for. 'Just vote', they say, because they know that the more people who go to the booths the more likely they are to win.

Host Mr Plouffe, is this the message you are broadcasting these days, 'Just vote', in a hope that people will vote for Obama?

DP Yes, we are very aware of Mr Farmer's research. We are responsible for many vote stickers and signs. High voter turnout always means more votes for us. And he is right in saying that the negative ads benefit the Republican candidates but backfire on the Democratic ones. That is why we are focusing on a positive campaign. We want America to know who has the moral high ground.

FB I suppose that's you.

DP Well ... we're not spamming people with negative ads. Rather we're inviting ordinary people, with little spending power, to become part of our campaign by posting stories on our site. We had one high-ranking military man upload a video from Afghanistan, saying how patriotic it would be to vote for Obama. We asked for small donations and we made people excited about knocking on their neighbours' doors to talk about Obama. I think this will be the first true grassroots campaign to win in national history.

FB Grassroots? You book more prime-time TV than any other candidate ever has. ...

Reflective statements

Floyd Brown

My aim was to show how politics influences the media. I did this by focusing on the Willie Horton ad. I had to defend this ad that I supposedly made as a spin-doctor for Bush Senior in 1988. I talked about vague language in the ad. I also had the chance to talk about how mudslinging is being outsourced to anonymous individuals on the Internet. I thought that point was very relevant to our media studies as well. All in all I think we did a good job interacting and discussing the subject matter in depth.

Rick Farmer

My aim was to show how the media use language to persuade voters. Specifically I tried to achieve this aim by focusing on the Swift Boat Veterans for Truth campaign. I described the language of this ad in detail and told how it was used to manipulate voters. Furthermore I gave a lot of background information on the effectiveness of negative ads on Democratic and Republican audiences. I used some of my research to support David Ploufe's arguments on the '3 a.m.' ad. In this sense I interacted well with my classmates and answered the host's questions effectively.

David Ploufe

My aim was to show how language is used to manipulate voters. In the further oral activity I had the chance to talk about Hillary Clinton's '3 a.m.' ad in depth. In my analysis of this ad, I gave good reasons to account for why the ad backfired and hurt Clinton in the end. I explained how the ad appealed to the audience's sense of fear, using sensational images and frightening language. Furthermore I did a little research on David Ploufe and his involvement in the Obama campaign, which was so successful. I think I demonstrated my understanding of this subject matter quite well towards the end of the activity, where I talked about websites and small donations. Overall, I feel I did a good job participating in the activity and meeting the aims that we set.

tip

When working in groups it is important to give each other equal speaking time as the teacher can only assess what is heard during the activity. The teacher cannot assess students on the amount of work they have done during the preparation process: it is only the oral activity itself that counts for the marks.

Teacher's comments

Generally speaking the work is relevant to the learning outcomes of part 2. The students demonstrate how politics influences the media and how language is used to persuade. Their activity pertains to two relevant topics in part 2 as well: political campaigns and the direct manipulation of public opinion. What's more, this is the level of discussion you would expect to hear on National Public Radio. The following comments indicate how a teacher might have assessed these students' work. Here, only the transcript has been assessed.

Criterion A: Knowledge and understanding of text(s) and subject matter or extracts

Floyd Brown – 7 out of 10

The student plays his role very well. You can see that he researched the person, when he refers to the court case 20 years ago. He accuses Obama of being soft on crime, which sounds like a recurring theme for Floyd Brown. *Exposing the opponent for who they are* is another recurring argument, which works well when playing devil's advocate. This student is aware of the importance of the Willie Horton and Swift Boat Veterans' ad to the context of smear campaigns.

Rick Farmer – 9 out of 10

The student has researched the effectiveness of negative ads in relation to the two political parties. He shows good critical thinking. His ideas are highly relevant to the questions asked. His exploration of the Willie Horton ad, Hillary Clinton's '3 a.m.' ad and the Swift Boat Veterans' ad are all relevant in this context. He is particularly knowledgeable on the effects of negative ads. His points on voter turnout and candidate endorsement are particularly effective.

David Plouffe – 8 out of 10

This student has relevant answers to the host's questions, and he demonstrates critical thinking. He explores the Hillary Clinton example well and shows his understanding of the Obama campaign. In general he seems to understand the context of negative ads.

Criterion B: Understanding of how language is used

Floyd Brown – 7 out of 10

Whereas the other students were each responsible for explaining the language of one negative ad, Floyd Brown's comments on the use of language in all of the ads is not detailed. His analysis of the Willie Horton ad is good from the perspective of devil's advocate. He defends his use of vague language, while claiming to include facts and numbers. This is very clever, and it shows an appreciation of how language is used.

Rick Farmer – 8 out of 10

Rick Farmer analyses the Swift Boat Veterans' ad with clarity and insight. He shows appreciation for the use of camera angles and the statements made by the veterans. Furthermore, he understands the effects of this ad on its audience. His analysis of the effectiveness of the 'vote' sticker is enlightening.

David Plouffe – 9 out of 10

This student analyses the Hillary Clinton ad well, discussing the use of images and voiceover to create an effect on the audience. The student makes a convincing case that the ad is ineffective. Furthermore, he explores *why* negative ads backfire. This is very pertinent and relevant to the discussion on the use of language.

Criterion C: Organisation

Floyd Brown – 4 out of 5

Although the teacher plays a role in guiding the discussion, this student does well interacting with the other students. He does not take the discussion in new directions and answers his question with well-developed arguments. At the same time, he engages David Plouffe well. The only criticism is that his answers are often short and that he could have spent more time investigating the questions.

Rick Farmer – 5 out of 5

This student also has well-developed arguments. He answers the questions with good answers. He yields the floor to the host at the proper moments and interacts well with the other speakers.

David Plouffe – 5 out of 5

This student explains and integrates many examples well into his arguments. His presentation of the Hillary Clinton ad is an example of how well-developed ideas are coherently structured. The way this student interacts with the other students is very relevant and effective.

Criterion D: Language

Floyd Brown – 4 out of 5

This student uses language very effectively. His sharp interjections are appropriate to his role. The task is free from error and the exchange flows very freely.

Rick Farmer – 5 out of 5

This student has the difficult task of presenting his research in layman's terms. At the same time, his language is appropriate to the register of NPR. He uses some appropriate phrases, such as *the Internet is a great feeding ground* and *the debate had been muddled*. Well done.

David Plouffe – 5 out of 5

This student uses a good degree of accuracy in speaking. His register and style are effective and appropriate to the task. Phrases such as *Horton's horrific deed becomes Dukakis's horrific deed through association* are well worded.

Ideas for part 2 further oral activities

1   For a further oral activity you can create a conversation between two influential people, who may or may not have lived in the same time period. What if Naomi Klein had had a discussion with Eddie Bernays? What if media tycoon Rupert

Murdoch could talk with Marshall McLuhan? They could talk about how the media have changed over the years for better or worse. An oral activity like this gives you the opportunity to step into someone's shoes and demonstrate your understanding of his or her great ideas. Be sure to have these influential people discuss a particular text, be it a news report or an ad.

2   To prepare for this sort of part 2 oral activity it is a good idea to watch several documentaries. You could base an activity round an interview with a producer of one of these documentaries. Prepare a list of questions to be asked, and give it to your teacher or another student, then engage in a dialogue about the documentary.

3   A group of students could create a court scene in which culture jammers like Adbusters are being sued by a large corporation for mashing-up or manipulating one or several of their ads. Here you can present both sides of the discussion that you explored in Activity 4.6 on page 107.

Chapter 4 summary

In this unit you have looked further at media literacy by exploring the language of persuasion. You have discovered that propaganda can be a dangerous manifestation of persuasive language when a public is uninformed and uneducated. The work of Eddie Bernays and the lead-up to the war in Iraq both demonstrate the power of propaganda. Understanding how propaganda works necessitates learning to identify its techniques, such as glittering generalities, name-calling and false dilemmas.

You explored how appeal and rhetorical devices are used in speeches. Notions such as ethos, pathos and logos are fundamental to human interaction and persuasive communication. If you were moved by Barack Obama's victory speech, you were most likely affected by his use of rhetorical devices such as parallelisms, hypophora, repetition and antithesis.

You have established that advertisements are part of our cultural fabric, as they are woven into our daily lives and reflect our system of values. Ads use persuasive tools that are similar to those of rhetoric and propaganda, appealing to our emotions and convincing us to buy into ideas. You have explored how counter-advertising warns against an overly branded culture, by imitating, defacing or mashing-up ads, and how some philanthropic campaigns use the mechanics of branding to create a better, more egalitarian world.

Finally, you studied a sample further oral activity and saw how it can be an effective medium for demonstrating your understanding of mass communication and persuasive language. Specifically, the sample activity focused on one particular genre of ads, negative ads, and you saw how it demonstrated good research and critical thinking skills on the part of the students who performed it.

In part 3 of the coursebook you will continue to explore language and communication as cultural phenomena, but your attention will now be on artistic literacy. The shift from media literacy to artistic literacy leads to another definition of culture, which goes beyond the shared values of a society and looks at the texts and art that a society holds in high esteem. You will be asking what we, in the Anglophone world, consider 'literature' to be.

3 Literature: texts and contexts

Chapter 5 The context of interpretation

Objectives

By the end of this chapter you will be able to
- understand why we read literature
- use different approaches to study literature
- identify different traditions of literary criticism
- plan and write a part 3 or 4 written task.

'The answers you get from literature depend on the questions you pose.'

Margaret Atwood (1939–)

Consider the following points when selecting your part 3 texts.

- Because of the nature of the Paper 2 exam, ensure that your part 3 texts have at least one common theme.
- Plays often make a good choice because you could look at a number of different productions of the same play (at different times and for various audiences). Looking at different productions of a play will highlight the importance of context.
- Contentious literary texts also work well for part 3, because with them there is an obvious emphasis on the context of interpretation and the context of composition.

On page 1 you read that the term *culture* can have two different meanings. In Parts 1 and 2 of this coursebook you focused on the first definition: the values, goals, convictions and attitudes that people share in a society. You saw how these values were reflected through non-fictional communication, such as posters, speeches and ads. The second definition of culture refers to the fine arts and a society's appreciation of the various forms of art. In Parts 3 and 4 of the coursebook you are going to look at the art of fiction in all of its forms, including poems, plays, novels and short stories.

In Chapter 2 you saw that texts are neither written nor read in a vacuum. What is more, as readers people may interpret a text in different ways, and these interpretations may be different from the author's intention. Figure 2.2 on page 38 illustrated the point that every reader and writer is influenced by the context in which they read or write. These influencing factors are called the context of interpretation and the context of composition. In this chapter you will be focusing on the context of interpretation, the 'receiving end' in the process of communication. (You will look at the context of composition in the following chapter.)

Reading literature is often about searching for meaning and in this chapter you will first explore, in Unit 5.1, several approaches to literature which help us discover meaning. You will then look at some traditions of literary criticism, in Unit 5.2. At the end of the chapter you will be able to study a sample written task. When you read texts, whether as part of your IB course or in your wider course reading, your aim is to make educated and insightful interpretations of them. Practising with the exercises in this coursebook will help you think more critically when reading the literary texts required for part 3 of the English language and literature course and writing about them in both your written task and the Paper 2 exam.

Remember that at standard level (SL) you have to read **two** literary texts in part 3:
- one from the IB's list of prescribed literature in translation (the PLT list)
- the other chosen freely by your school, originally written in English.

At higher level (HL) you have to read **three** literary texts:
- one from the prescribed list of authors (PLA)
- one from the PLT list
- the third chosen freely by your school, possibly a work in translation.

Unit 5.1 **Approaching fiction**

For as long as people have been using language to communicate, they have been making up stories. Ask yourself what we are all actually doing when we make up stories. The poet Samuel Taylor Coleridge once said that fiction relies on the suspension of disbelief. In other words, in fiction, we create and accept scenarios that we know are not true, and we rarely question why this does not matter to us.

In this unit you will be exploring two main questions: *Why do we read literature?* and *How should we approach literature?*

Why do we read literature?

Until now we have talked about *fiction* in general without specifying what it is that makes some fiction works of *literature*. *Literature* is a term often used for texts that do something more than simply entertain. In literary works readers usually find deeper meaning and more carefully crafted stylistic devices than they would in more popular/commercial works of fiction. The following activity will engage you in the process of writing and reading fiction and lead to a discussion about literature and why we read it.

Key term

Suspension of disbelief is a phrase coined by Samuel Taylor Coleridge to explain how readers of fiction accept implausible stories in order to ascertain some truth about life.

'Literature is a luxury; fiction is a necessity.'
G.K. Chesterton (1874–1936)

Activity 5.1

Work in groups for this activity. Each student needs a pen and paper. At the top of your paper write the following sentence:

When Gregor Samsa awoke one morning from troubled dreams, he found himself changed into a monstrous cockroach in his bed.

Now each of you continues to write the story of Gregor Samsa. After five minutes of creative writing, give your story to the student sitting on your left. Read what the first student has written before continuing their story. Write the continuation for five minutes and then give your paper to the student on your left. Continue in this way for as long as you feel is necessary and then discuss the following questions as a class.

1   In what ways was the other students' writing different from yours? How would you describe the other students as writers? Find examples from their writing to support your statements.

2   Were there any examples of 'literary' writing? Why would you describe it as 'literary'?

3   Did you find this an interesting activity? Has it helped you understand why people read fiction and, more specifically, literature? Why?

You could repeat this activity, taking as your starting point the first line of one of the literary texts you are studying for part 3 of the course.

Before reading the rest of the passage about Gregor Samsa (Text 5.1), which is taken from *The Metamorphosis* by Franz Kafka, first consider the following four points, all of which are reasons why we read literature and all of which offer an insight into what constitutes literature.

'Life imitates art more than art imitates life.'
Oscar Wilde (1854–1900)

'All good books have one thing in common – they are truer than if they had really happened.'
Ernest Hemingway (1899–1961)

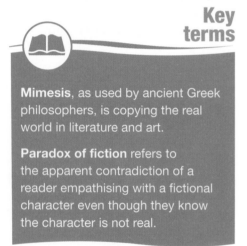

Key terms

Mimesis, as used by ancient Greek philosophers, is copying the real world in literature and art.

Paradox of fiction refers to the apparent contradiction of a reader empathising with a fictional character even though they know the character is not real.

Communication

As part of the activity about Gregor Samsa you will have already discussed some of the issues to do with literature. It would be unusual not to think about the fiction we write or read. If authors have an important message about the meaning of life which they wish to communicate, why do you think they do not simply come out and tell us about it? Why must they wrap it in layers of fiction for us to unravel? If you have ever listened to a talk by a literary author, or attended a reading by an author, you will know that they often want to prompt discussion about their book rather than provide simple answers to issues raised in their work. After all, this would only spoil the experience for most readers. Authors rarely set themselves up as the only experts on their book and do not usually attempt to tell others how to interpret it. Readers sometimes read more into a text than the author intended. The message that is communicated is therefore open to interpretation and different readers will take a different message from the same literary text. Authors tell a story they think needs to be told and readers often talk about what it really means.

Imitation

Literary authors may have a message about the deeper meaning of life. The ancient Greeks had a word to describe the imitation of real life in art and works of fiction: they called it **mimesis**. Have you ever identified with a fictional character? Faced with a decision to make, have you ever asked yourself what such and such a character from literature would do in the same situation? Fiction imitates real life in such a way that we can react to fiction with the same range of emotional responses we would feel in real life, and we can feel a strong emotional connection with a character in a book although we know that this character is not a real person. This phenomenon is called the **paradox of fiction**.

"I like novels where the protagonist is a thinly veiled version of me."

Figure 5.1 What reason does this cartoon give for reading fiction?

Education

If fiction imitates real life, then we can learn more about real life by reading fiction. As the paradox of fiction shows, empathising with people in fiction often gives us deeper insight into our own life experience as well as other people's. Studying literature and then discussing different interpretations of it are educational because this teaches us about human nature. By analysing a character in a novel, for example, you may be more able to understand why real people think and behave the way they do. We can have a better understanding of the world we live in through literature.

Catharsis

Do you sometimes come out of the cinema or theatre feeling 'emotionally drained'? The Greek philosopher Aristotle believed it was possible to purge or cleanse ourselves of our emotions through art. He called this process **catharsis**. You have seen that fiction can imitate reality and that that can help us have a better understanding of the real world. People also enjoy fiction, however, because they like *escaping from* reality in order to clear their heads of what is going on in their life. For example, while some people believe that watching violent films can prompt people to commit violent acts, others believe that escaping from reality through violent, fictional films can cure people of their violent tendencies through catharsis. In other words, literature can be seen as a medicine for the soul.

As you read Text 5.1, ask yourself why you might want to read the whole of the story. Can you relate the four reasons for reading literature you have looked at above to this story?

'Fiction's about what it is to be a human being.'
David Foster Wallace (1962–2008)

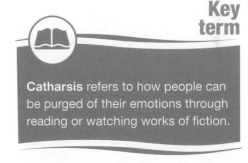

Key term

Catharsis refers to how people can be purged of their emotions through reading or watching works of fiction.

TOK

In exploring the question posed at the start of this section, *Why do we read literature?*, it may appear that you have only been given reasons why you *should* read literature. You have not been asked to explore any reasons not to read it, such as that fiction may rot your brain or be a waste of your time. To return to the ancient Greeks, Plato, for one, did not approve of the popular theatre of his time. He felt that emotions, often referred to as 'the language of art', get in the way of rational thinking. As you saw in the paragraph above about catharsis, Plato's student, Aristotle, had a different view – according to Aristotle, art can clear the mind and so be an aid to rational thinking. Who do you think was right? How can we tell whether literature or fiction is cathartic?

Text 5.1 *The Metamorphosis*, Franz Kafka, 1915

When Gregor Samsa awoke one morning from troubled dreams, he found himself changed into a monstrous cockroach in his bed. He lay on his tough, armoured back, and, raising his head a little, managed to see – sectioned off by little crescent-shaped ridges into segments – the expanse of his arched, brown belly, atop which the coverlet perched, forever on the point of slipping off entirely. His numerous legs, pathetically frail by contrast to the rest of him, waved feebly before his eyes.

'What's the matter with me?' he thought. It was no dream. There, quietly between the four familiar walls, was his room, a normal human room, if always a little on the small side. Over the table, on which an array of cloth samples was spread out – Samsa was a travelling salesman – hung the picture he had only recently clipped from a magazine, and set in an attractive gilt frame. It was a picture of a lady in a fur hat and stole, sitting bolt upright, holding in the direction of the onlooker a heavy fur muff into which she had thrust the whole of her forearm.

From there, Gregor's gaze directed itself towards the window, and the drab weather outside – raindrops could be heard plinking against the tin window-ledges – made him quite melancholy. 'What if I went back to sleep for a while, and forgot about all this nonsense?' he thought, but that proved quite

discussion

1 Despite the fact that the story of *The Metamorphosis* is so unrealistic, what do you think it tells us about real human behaviour? In what ways does Gregor Samsa act like someone you know or have met in your life?

2 Did you feel engrossed by the story? Would you want to continue reading this novella in order to clear your head and give your emotions a holiday? In other words, is it an invitation to escape from reality? Give examples from the text to illustrate your answer.

3 Do you think that Kafka wrote such a bizarre tale simply to instigate discussion, or to give us something to think and talk about? Do you think he was consciously trying to convey a deeper meaning to his readers?

impossible, because he was accustomed to sleeping on his right side, and in his present state he was unable to find that position. However vigorously he flung himself to his right, he kept rocking on to his back. He must have tried it a hundred times, closing his eyes so as not to have to watch his wriggling legs, and only stopped when he felt a slight ache in his side which he didn't recall having felt before.

'Oh, my Lord!' he thought. 'If only I didn't have to follow such an exhausting profession! On the road, day in, day out. The work is so much more strenuous than it would be in head office, and then there's the additional ordeal of travelling, worries about train connections, the irregular, bad meals, new people all the time, no continuity, no affection. Devil take it!' He felt a light itch at the top of his belly; slid a little closer to the bedpost, so as to be able to raise his head a little more effectively; found the itchy place, which was covered with a sprinkling of white dots the significance of which he was unable to interpret; assayed the place with one of his legs, but hurriedly withdrew it, because the touch caused him to shudder involuntarily.

He slid back to his previous position. 'All this getting up early,' he thought, 'is bound to take its effect. A man needs proper bed rest. There are some other travelling salesmen I could mention who live like harem women. Sometimes, for instance, when I return to the *pension* in the course of the morning, to make a note of that morning's orders, some of those gents are just sitting down to breakfast. I'd like to see what happened if I tried that out with my director some time; it would be the order of the boot just like that. That said, it might be just the thing for me. If I didn't have to exercise restraint for the sake of my parents, then I would have quit a long time ago; I would have gone up to the director and told him exactly what I thought of him. He would have fallen off his desk in surprise! That's a peculiar way he has of sitting anyway, up on his desk, and talking down to his staff from on high, making them step up to him very close because he's so hard of hearing. Well, I haven't quite given up hope; once I've got the money together to pay back what my parents owe him – it may take me another five or six years – then I'll do it, no question. Then we'll have the parting of the ways. But for the time being, I'd better look sharp, because my train leaves at five.'

How should we approach literature?

The Metamorphosis, like all works of fiction, can be approached from three different approaches.

1 The first approach is to focus on the reader and the reader's reaction or response to a text.

2 The second approach is to focus on the text itself: a kind of 'what you see is what you get' approach.

3 The third approach involves learning more about the context in which the author wrote the text.

Figure 5.2 illustrates the three different approaches to literature.

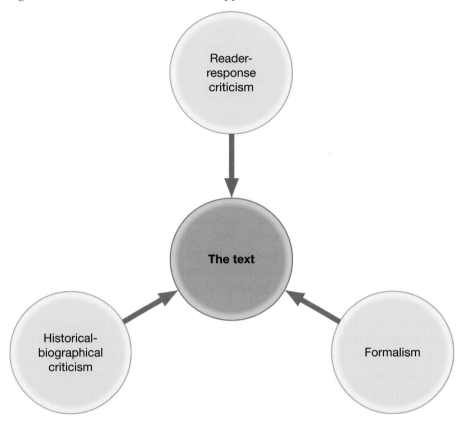

Figure 5.2 Three different ways to approach literature.

Reader-response criticism

When you looked at the reasons for reading literature, you focused on *you* as the reader and *your* reaction to Text 5.1. What a text means to you is bound to be influenced by your own context, i.e. your personal history, culture and surroundings. In the 1930s, an experiment with a group of students at Cambridge University stressed the importance of the role of the reader in interpreting literary texts. The Cambridge students were given some texts to read, from which the author's name and other context had been removed, and their various readings and 'misreadings' of the texts were then studied. These misreadings were explained because the students were free from any preconceived notions of the literature they were studying or ready-made analyses imposed on them by their teachers: each student was entitled to a personal response to the literature. This form of literary criticism has become known as reader-response criticism.

Formalism

Formalism is a very different approach from reader-response criticism. In Part 1 of this coursebook, you were told that you would be approaching texts like a detective approaching a crime scene or an anthropologist an unknown people. Formalism is a way of analysing a text that is free from any personal experience or feelings that might affect the way we interpret that text.

Formalists argue that a work of art is complete in itself, without the cultural baggage of the reader or the background of the author. This is the most common approach taken in secondary schools for analysing texts, as you will know from your work for the Paper 1 exam. Arguably the Formalist approach is good for exercising literacy and analytical skills. However, it may not always be the best approach for understanding an author's intention.

Further resources

Many students are quick to turn to online and printed study notes for secondary school students when they approach a text. Although useful, these resources must be used carefully and at the appropriate time. Always read the text first and consult a guide only after you have had a chance to discuss the text in class. However, published guides are especially helpful when it comes to understanding the context of composition, which you need to do when you are preparing for the Paper 2 exam.

'All meanings, we know, depend on the key of interpretation.'
George Eliot (Mary Anne Evans) (1819–80)

TOK

As you read literary texts for the IB course, you will most likely form an opinion about them. You may like them or dislike them, but how is that different from saying they are 'good' or 'bad' pieces of literature? The philosopher Immanuel Kant suggested we study art with 'disinterest'. By that he did not mean not liking a work. He meant it in the sense of becoming emotionally detached from a text when making aesthetic judgements. Is it possible to dislike a work but still appreciate its literary quality?

Figure 5.3 Franz Kafka (1883–1924).

discussion

1 How does the extra contextual information about Franz Kafka, including the letter to his father, change your understanding of *The Metamorphosis*? Make special reference in your answer to the themes of family, work, fear and being different.

2 Figure 5.4 is of some drawings done by Kafka. How do these drawings tell you more about who Kafka was? Are any of the ideas and emotions apparent in the drawings similar to those in *The Metamorphosis* and the letter to his father?

3 In the opening sentence to *The Metamorphosis* a lot of meaning hinges on the word *cockroach*. In German, Kafka originally wrote *Ungezeifer*, which means something more like 'vermin' or 'bug' with a connotation of 'unclean'. How does this change your perspective on the rest of the text?

Historical-biographical criticism

The third way to analyse texts is known as historical-biographical criticism. According to this approach, we must have an understanding of the historical and biographical background of a text if we are to understand its wider implications and significance.

The best way to understand the effectiveness of the historical-biographical method is to test it out. Text 5.2 is more about the life of Franz Kafka and his relationship with his father. Reading the text will give you more information in order to better understand *The Metamorphosis*.

Text 5.2 Letter to his father, Franz Kafka, 1919

Franz Kafka grew up in Prague, Czechoslovakia, at the end of the 19th and beginning of the 20th centuries. He belonged to the wealthy and influential German-speaking Jewish minority, a group that tended to be despised by both the working-class Czechs and the German elite of the Austro-Hungarian Empire. Kafka's father gave his children German names and registered them as Czech citizens in an attempt to integrate into Czech life, but Franz, rebelling against his father, showed a lot of interest in his Jewish roots, Judaism, Palestine and Zionism.

Kafka was withdrawn, though he showed affection for his younger sisters. His father did not understand why he chose to be vegetarian and interested in Yiddish theatre. In 1911 Kafka refused to comply with his father's wish for him to run his brother-in-law's factory. Instead he kept to his monotonous work by day at an insurance company and wrote fiction by night.

He was engaged more than once but never married for several reasons: he met someone else, feared becoming intimate with them or was not healthy enough to maintain the relationship. In 1919 his father particularly disapproved of his plan to marry a poor Jewish girl, which was why Kafka wrote the letter to him. Kafka died in 1924 of tuberculosis.

Dearest Father,

You asked me recently why I maintain that I am afraid of you. As usual, I was unable to think of any answer to your question, partly for the very reason that I am afraid of you, and partly because an explanation of the grounds for this fear would mean going into far more details than I could even approximately keep in mind while talking. And if I now try to give you an answer in writing, it will still be very incomplete, because, even in writing, this fear and its consequences hamper me in relation to you and because the magnitude of the subject goes far beyond the scope of my memory and power of reasoning. …

There is only one episode in the early years of which I have a direct memory. You may remember it, too. One night I kept on whimpering for water, not, I am certain, because I was thirsty, but probably partly to be annoying, partly to amuse myself. After several vigorous threats had failed to have any effect, you took me out of bed, carried me out onto the *pavlatche*,[1] and left me there alone for a while in my nightshirt, outside the shut door. I am not going to say that this was wrong – perhaps there was really no way of getting peace and quiet that night – but I mention it as typical of your methods of bringing up a child and their effect on me. I dare say I was quite obedient afterward at that period, but it did me inner harm. What was for me a matter of course, that senseless asking for water, and then the extraordinary terror of being carried outside were two things that I, my nature being what it was, could never properly connect with each other. Even years afterward I suffered from the tormenting fancy that the huge man, my father, the ultimate authority, would come almost for no reason at all and take me out of bed in the night and carry me out onto the *pavlatche*,[1] and that consequently I meant absolutely nothing as far as he was concerned.

That was only a small beginning, but this feeling of being nothing that often dominates me (a feeling that is in another respect, admittedly, also a noble and fruitful one) comes largely from your influence.

[1] **pavlatche**   a Czech word for the long balcony in the inner courtyard of old houses in Prague

Which approach is the best?

Now that you have looked at the three approaches to literature, you may have a favourite one. However, it is important to recognise that they all have their strengths and weaknesses.

Take for example *Huckleberry Finn*, a book by Mark Twain, which is banned in many schools in the southern states of the USA because of its racial slurs and stereotypes. Interestingly, the work did not cause much controversy in 1885, when it was published, because people in those states at that time understood its context. They knew that Mark Twain had deserted from the Confederate Army during the Civil War and that he was opposed to slavery. They consequently did not question his use of the word *nigger* for a black man, which today is considered offensive. Using the historical-biographical approach to a text such as *Huckleberry Finn* means that we can understand why that word was used at that time, whereas we would be shocked by it if our approach was based on reader-response criticism.

Choosing the most appropriate approach for a particular text is very important and you need to become familiar with which approach is suitable for which particular type of text. The table below gives an overview of the strengths and weaknesses of each approach.

Figure 5.4 Various drawings by Franz Kafka.

Approach	Strengths	Weaknesses
Reader-response criticism	Reader is entitled to individual, personal interpretation of text	Author's intentions are ignored
Formalism	Encourages critical analysis and close reading	Important contextual information is ignored
Historical-biographical criticism	Allows for greater contextual understanding	New and modern interpretations of old texts are discounted

Activity 5.2

Practise applying the three approaches to literary criticism to Text 5.3, an extract from *The Crucible* by Arthur Miller. After reading Text 5.3, say whether the following statements belong to (a) reader-response criticism, (b) Formalism or (c) historical-biographical criticism.

1   This scene has all of the classic elements of a courtroom scene from a John Grisham novel.
2   This is Arthur Miller's dramatisation of the Salem Witch Trials in Massachusetts in 1692–3.
3   At the heart of this passage is the dialogue between Hathorne and Corey, whose voices are only heard and faces not seen.

Further resources

To familiarise yourself with literary commentaries you will find it helpful to read book reviews. One excellent magazine of literary criticism is the *London Review of Books*, which has well-written articles about recently published books. Another excellent resource for book reviews is *The New York Times*, containing book reviews that have for decades set the standard for criticism of contemporary literature. In its online archive, you may be able to find a review of a book that you are reading as part of your IB course.

Figure 5.5 An illustration from 1876 of the Salem Witch Trials, which took place in Massachusetts in 1692–3.

Answers: Activity 5.2
1a; 2c; 3b; 4c; 5b; 6a

4   Through this play, Miller draws a parallel between the Salem Witch Trials and McCarthyism, which accused Americans of being communists in similar hearings in the 1950s.
5   The courtroom seems improvised, as *heavy beams jut out, boards of random widths make up the walls.*
6   This interrogation reminds me of arguing with my mother.

Text 5.3 *The Crucible*, Arthur Miller, 1953

Act III
The vestry room of the Salem meeting house, now serving as the anteroom of the General Court.

As the curtain rises, the room is empty, but for sunlight pouring through two high windows in the back wall. The room is solemn, even forbidding. Heavy beams jut out, boards of random widths make up the walls. At the right are two doors leading into the meeting house proper where the court is being held. At the left another door leads outside.

There is a plain bench at the left, and another at the right. In the center a rather long meeting table, with stools and a considerable armchair snugged up to it.

Through the partitioning wall at the right we hear a prosecutor's voice, Judge Hathorne's, asking a question; then a woman's voice, Martha Corey's, replying.

Hathorne's voice	Now, Martha Corey, there is abundant evidence in our hands to show that you have given yourself to the reading of fortunes. Do you deny it?
Martha Corey's voice	I am innocent to a witch. I know not what a witch is.
Hathorne's voice	How do you know, then, that you are not a witch?
Martha Corey's voice	If I were, I would know it.
Hathorne's voice	Why do you hurt these children?
Martha Corey's voice	I do not hurt them. I scorn it!
Giles' voice, *roaring*	I have evidence for the court!

Voices of townspeople rise in excitement.

Unit 5.2 **Traditions of literary criticism**

An underlying question which ran through the previous unit on approaching literature was *How subjective can we be in our interpretation of texts?* Reader-response criticism, for example, welcomes subjectivity in the interpretation of a text. Many critics understand that they are influenced by current ideologies and they embrace these in their analyses of literature. In other words, they subscribe to a particular tradition of literary criticism.

In this unit you will explore how one text can be looked at through three different lenses or ideological frameworks. Different ideological frameworks have allowed people to find new meaning in old texts, such as Shakespeare's plays. You may find that you will be inspired by the ideological frameworks presented in this unit to look for a new understanding of the texts that you are studying for part 3 of your IB Diploma course.

First, read Text 5.4 and make your own interpretation of the text. Be warned, however: the story seems simpler than it really is.

Text 5.4 *Sitting*, H.E. Francis, 1983

In the morning the man and woman were sitting on his front steps. They sat all day. They would not move. With metronomic regularity he peered at them through the pane in the front door. They did not leave at dark. He wondered when they ate or slept or did their duties. At dawn they were still there. They sat through sun and rain.

At first only the immediate neighbors called: Who are they? What are they doing there? He did not know. Then neighbors from farther down the street called. People who passed and saw the couple called. He never heard the man or woman talk. When he started getting calls from all over the city, from strangers and city fathers, professionals and clerks, garbage and utilities men, and the postman, who had to walk around them to deliver letters, he had to do something. He asked them to leave. They said nothing. They sat. They stared, indifferent. He said he would call the police. The police gave them a talking to, explained the limits of their rights, and took them away in the police car. In the morning they were back. The next time the police said they would put them in jail if the jails were not so full, though they would have to find a place for them somewhere, if he insisted. That is your problem, he said. No, it is really yours, the police told him, but they removed the pair.

When he looked out the next morning, the man and the woman were sitting on the steps. They sat there every day for years. Winters he expected them to die from the cold.

But he died.

He had no relatives, so the house went to the city.

The man and woman went on sitting there.

When the city threatened to remove the man and the woman, neighbors and citizens brought a suit against the city: after sitting there so long, the man and the woman deserved the house.

The neighbors and citizens won.

In the morning strange men and women were sitting on front steps all over the city.

discussion

1   Which characters do you sympathise with? As a reader, do you empathise with the man or woman, the owner of the house, the neighbours or the police? What is the effect of the characters not having names?

2   Comment on the use of language. H.E. Francis uses basic vocabulary, short sentences and no quotation marks. What is the effect of this use of language?

3   Read the last line again, *In the morning strange men and women were sitting on front steps all over the city*. What do you think it means? What is its message?

Psychoanalytical literary criticism

Psychoanalytical literary criticism is based on the ideas of Sigmund Freud and others, who considered stories in the same way as they thought of dreams – as expressions of the subconscious. According to psychoanalytical literary criticism, analysing stories reveals the internal conflicts of the author, and characters embody suppressed emotions. The settings of stories are full of symbols, representing our hidden fears and anxieties. Storylines reflect the battles between our animal urges (the Id) and our self-regulating habits (the Ego and the Super Ego).

A psychoanalytical literary criticism of *Sitting*

This story is about the fear of losing one's sense of security. The house represents a safe haven, like a mother's womb, which the strangers want to enter through the front door. The steps represent a dangerous threshold of private space, which the strangers are violating. The man, who reflects the author's fears, deals with these invaders by calling on another agent of security: the police. The state is like a mother, who, from her caring position, cannot

Key term

Gender bias is the tendency to favour one gender over the other, often manifested through language.

Extended essay

Write an extended essay that demonstrates understanding of a text or texts. Remember that you cannot base your extended essay on the literary texts that you are reading as part of your English language and literature course.

- You could apply all three traditions of literary criticism from this unit – psychoanalytical, social and feminist – to one or two literary texts.
- You could focus on one tradition of literary criticism and apply it to two or three examples of contemporary and more traditional fiction as a means of testing the strengths and weaknesses of this particular approach.
- You could look at how one text (such as a Shakespeare play) has been interpreted differently over the centuries.

Whichever approach you take, remember to include several supporting passages with in-depth analysis and informed interpretations.

physically harm or reprimand the sitters. The state's attempt to remove them is futile. Because the man cannot overcome his separation anxiety, he is left with no choice but to die. Once these territorial urges are removed from the neighbourhood, the neighbours are civilised towards the couple and express empathy for them by imitating their behaviour.

Social literary criticism and the Marxist approach

Social literary criticism looks at literary texts in an effort to understand how ruling majorities oppress suffering minorities. Social literary critics often study how characters in texts embody this oppression. For example, they would want to understand the tension between women and men, or rich and poor groups of people.

Marxist literary criticism is a branch of social literary criticism. More specifically, the Marxist approach views the history of society and the representation of this history in literature as a constant struggle between social classes. Karl Marx believed that the working class would eventually rise up to take political control and distribute wealth more evenly. Marxist literary critics seek to put literary texts into this context. For example, *Oliver Twist* by Charles Dickens is about an orphan who demands fundamental human rights, and *Wuthering Heights* by Emily Brontë is about how social class inhibits true love.

A Marxist literary criticism of *Sitting*

The main characters of this story are the man and woman. They are homeless because of an inept state that cannot house or imprison people properly. They need shelter because it is a basic human right. The man's house could be anyone's house. It is everyone's responsibility to help the couple. But the people of this anonymous society fail to acknowledge their social responsibility because they are too individualistic. The owner is not interested in finding a solution and only protects what is 'his'. After he dies, the state seizes his property, which is hypocritical. They take possessions from the people, but cannot provide services in return. This is why the people rise up and take action. In the end they realise that they must protect the rights of those who are less fortunate. They demonstrate by holding a 'sit-in'.

Feminist literary criticism

Feminist literary criticism is a tradition of analysing texts which aims for a clearer understanding of gender inequality. On one hand, feminist literary criticism, as a movement, seeks to promote the position of female authors in society. On the other, it addresses the portrayal of women in literature, in both contemporary fiction and older works. Furthermore, feminist literary critics raise awareness about **gender bias** in language and style.

A feminist literary criticism of *Sitting*

The story is about a man without a woman. He is lonely, frustrated and inhospitable. When he finds himself confronted by a couple sitting on his doorstep, he fails to show empathy or compassion because he lacks both a feminine side and a female presence. He is not the only one in this society who lacks compassion. The neighbours side with the man because they live in a male-dominated society that is preoccupied with guarding territorial rights. When the state steps in to seize the man's property, after he has died, the citizens of this society wake up and realise how aggressive this power-hungry state is. In an exemplary act of egalitarianism, both men and women demonstrate compassion for the couple and uphold their rights by a sit-in demonstration.

Which tradition is best?

As you saw with the three different analyses of *Sitting*, one single text can lend itself to multiple interpretations. This story happened to be versatile enough to allow for different interpretations and you may find that one approach works best for a particular text you are studying. A 'one size fits all' approach to literature is impossible as every book and every reader is different. You have looked at three major traditions – psychoanalytical, social and feminist literary criticism – but there are in fact many more ways to approach literature. It is important to be aware of the different perspectives that can be taken on literature in order to expand your own understanding of literary texts.

The following activity will allow you to further explore the psychoanalytical, social and feminist approaches to literary criticism.

Higher level

There are many more traditions of literary criticism that you can explore as a class. Working in pairs or individually, research one of the theories of literary criticism below and apply it to Text 5.5 or any other text that you are working on in class.

- archetypal literary criticism
- the Chicago School of literary criticism
- Russian Formalism
- the New Critics
- post-colonial literary criticism

Write a short analysis of the text using your chosen approach, like the ones on *Sitting* on pages 127–29.

Activity 5.3

The following quotations (1–5) are taken from Text 5.5, an extract from *The Handmaid's Tale* by Margret Atwood. Read Text 5.5, then look at phrases 1–5 below and indicate which tradition of literary criticism (a–c) offers the most suitable approach in each case, giving reasons for your choice. You may find that there is more than one tradition that is appropriate – there are no right or wrong answers to this exercise, only more informed or considered ones.

1 Such things are considered vanities.
2 For them, things are bad enough as it is.
3 that we will be touched again, in love or desire
4 I want to be held and told my name. I want to be valued, in ways that I am not.
5 I want to steal something.
   a Psychoanalytical literary criticism
   b Social literary criticism
   c Feminist literary criticism

Key term

Dystopian literature is a genre of fiction that offers a picture of an imagined world in which everything is bad and in which individuals are often oppressed by a ruling government.

Text 5.5 *The Handmaid's Tale*, Margaret Atwood, 1985

Margaret Atwood is an award-winning Canadian author of novels and poetry. Central to her novel *The Handmaid's Tale* is the role of women in society. *The Handmaid's Tale* is a **dystopian** novel, meaning it takes place in a fictional time and place where an oppressive government is trying to create a utopian, or perfect, society but has created the exact opposite. In this society, because people have been exposed to chemicals,

Figure 5.6 A scene from the 1990 film version of The *Handmaid's Tale*.

only a few women are fertile. The fertile women are trained to be concubines for the ruling military men and are named after the men who own them. The name of the main character, Offred, is derived from 'of Fred'. This dystopian state is also a theocracy, meaning it is run on fundamental religious principles.

This is what I do when I'm back in my room:
I take off my clothes and put on my nightgown.

I look for the pat of butter, in the toe of my right shoe, where I hid it after dinner. The cupboard was too warm, the butter is semi-liquid. Much of it has sunk into the paper napkin I wrapped it in. Now I'll have butter in my shoe. Not the first time, because whenever there is butter or even margarine, I save some in this way. I can get most of the butter off the shoe lining, with a washcloth or some toilet paper from the bathroom, tomorrow.

I rub the butter over my face, work it into the skin of my hands. There's no longer any hand lotion or face cream, not for us. Such things are considered vanities. We are containers, it's only the insides of our bodies that are important. The outside can become hard and wrinkled, for all they care, like the shell of a nut. This was a decree of the Wives, this absence of hand lotion. They don't want us to look attractive. For them, things are bad enough as it is.

The butter is a trick I learned at the Rachel and Leah Center. The Red Center, we called it, because there was so much red. My predecessor in this room, my friend with the freckles and the good laugh, must have done this too, this buttering. We all do it.

As long as we do this, butter our skin to keep it soft, we can believe that we will some day get out, that we will be touched again, in love or desire. We have ceremonies of our own, private ones.

The butter is greasy and it will go rancid and I will smell like an old cheese; but at least it's organic, as they used to say.

To such devices have we descended.

Buttered, I lie on my single bed, flat, like a piece of toast. I can't sleep. In the semi-dark I stare up at the blind plaster eye in the middle of the ceiling, which stares back down at me, even though it can't see. There's no breeze, my white curtains are like gauze bandages, hanging limp, glimmering in the aura cast by the searchlight that illuminates this house at night, or is there a moon?

I fold back the sheet, get carefully up, on silent bare feet, in my nightgown, go to the window, like a child, I want to see. The moon on the breast of the new-fallen snow. The sky is clear but hard to make out, because of the searchlight; but yes, in the obscured sky a moon does float, newly, a wishing moon, a sliver of ancient rock, a goddess, a wink. The moon is a stone and the sky is full of deadly hardware, but oh God, how beautiful anyway.

I want Luke here so badly. I want to be held and told my name. I want to be valued, in ways that I am not; I want to be more than valuable. I repeat my former name, remind myself of what I once could do, how others saw me.

I want to steal something.

Assessment: Part 3 or 4 written task 1

As you continue to add written tasks to your portfolio, you will have to write at least one about a literary text that you have read for your IB course. The way you approach a written task on a fiction text will be different from the way you approached your non-fiction tasks for parts 1 and 2. Nevertheless, the two basic principles of the written task 1, which you saw on page 21, still apply, namely that you:

• imitate a certain form of writing *and*

• demonstrate your understanding of the topics covered in class.

For a written task 1 on part 3 or 4 you will explore the literary texts you have read in several ways. You could focus on a fictional character, or a setting from a novel or a scene from a play, for example. To show your understanding of the texts, you can choose one of several different formats for your task. You may want to write a diary from a character's perspective, or add an additional scene that is in the spirit of the playwright's intentions. You may want to write a newspaper article that reports on a major event from your novel. While the possibilities are endless, be careful to select a type of text that is appropriate for your literary work (see pages 135–36 for part 3 written task 1 ideas).

The student who produced the sample written task in this chapter had read *The Tempest*, a play by William Shakespeare. Shakespeare's plays are a good choice for part 3 because they have been interpreted in so many ways through the centuries. *The Tempest* is particularly interesting because it is set on an island. Shakespeare does not tell us where this is, but it may be in the New World, perhaps in the Bahamas. In 1611 most Europeans did not know much about the indigenous people of the Caribbean and thought of them as 'monsters'. It is very likely that Caliban was portrayed this way in earlier performances of the play. In our post-colonial times, however, audiences have become used to more sympathetic portrayals of this character.

Similarly, directors have presented the main character, Prospero, differently over time. Prospero, the Duke of Milan, has been banished from Italy; he and his daughter, Miranda, arrive on Caliban's island. The character of Prospero can be played in many different ways: as a magician or a scientist, a coloniser or a refugee, a sympathetic father or a ruthless slave driver.

Text 5.6 is an extract from Act 1 Scene 2 of the play and is one of several that inspired the student to explore the relationship between Caliban and Miranda. Like her father Prospero, Miranda appears quite angry at Caliban in the following exchange.

discussion

1 How does the writing style shape the tone and the mood of the text?

2 Where do you see evidence that Offred lives in a dystopian and oppressive society?

3 Do you think that because this novel is written by a woman and is about an oppressed woman in a male-dominant society, feminist literary criticism is the best perspective to take on this work? Why might other traditions of literary criticism be equally suitable?

Figure 5.7 Julie Taymor's film version of *The Tempest* (2010) depicts Prospero as a woman called Prospera. How might this depiction change your interpretation of the play or even your understanding of the extract? How does the portrayal of Prospero and Caliban in this image reflect your understanding of them from the extract (Text 5.6)?

tip

Students often assume that they must choose a literary format for a part 3 or 4 written task, such as a missing chapter, a poem or a film adaptation. In fact, however, you are not limited to this sort of writing and could choose to produce a tabloid newspaper, for example, as you can see in the sample written task below. Bear in mind the following advice when preparing to write your written task 1.

- Remember that the written task 1 cannot be an essay.
- You have a free choice of format, as long as it is appropriate for the text you have studied.
- Whatever type of text you choose, be sure to be creative.

Text 5.6 *The Tempest* (Act 1, Scene 2), William Shakespeare, 1611

Caliban	I must eat my dinner.
	This island's mine by Sycorax my mother,
	Which thou tak'st from me. When thou cam'st first
	Thou strok'st me and made much of me; wouldst give me
	Water with berries in't, and teach me how

335

	To name the bigger light, and how the less,
	That burn by day and night. And then I loved thee
	And showed thee all the qualities o'th'isle,
	The fresh springs, brine-pits, barren place and fertile –
	Cursèd be I that did so! All the charms

340

	Of Sycorax – toads, beetles, bats – light on you!
	For I am all the subjects that you have,
	Which first was mine own king; and here you sty me
	In this hard rock, whiles you do keep from me
	The rest o'th'island.

Prospero	Thou most lying slave,

345

	Whom stripes may move, not kindness! I have used thee,
	Filth as thou art, with humane care, and lodged thee
	In mine own cell, till thou didst seek to violate
	The honour of my child.

Caliban	O ho, O ho! Would't had been done!

	Thou didst prevent me – I had peopled else

350

	This isle with Calibans.

Miranda	Abhorrèd slave,

	Which any print of goodness wilt not take,
	Being capable of all ill! I pitied thee,
	Took pains to make thee speak, taught thee each hour
	One thing or other. When thou didst not, savage,

355

	Know thine own meaning, but wouldst gabble like
	A thing most brutish, I endowed thy purposes
	With words that made them known. But thy vile race –
	Though thou didst learn – had that in't which good natures
	Could not abide to be with; therefore wast thou

360

	Deservedly confined into this rock,
	Who hadst deserved more than a prison.

Caliban	You taught me language, and my profit on't

	Is, I know how to curse. The red plague rid you
	For learning me your language!

365

Sample written task 1 (SL)

Rationale

The written task for **The Tempest** takes the form of a tabloid paper. Much of the play includes the retelling of sensational events that happen off-stage. Therefore the tabloid paper lent itself well to the content.

The title of my tabloid is 'Idle Island', which is relevant to the island in **The Tempest**. The word *idle* refers to how few people are on the island and how little news there is to go around. To make the masthead more like a tabloid I added the date of release, the price and the website. Beside the masthead is the *ear*, which refers to an important story concerning Ariel's release. There I included a common stylistic device of tabloid articles: I wanted to draw the reader's interest by asking a question, *Has their master–servant relation ended or will their paths cross once more?* It makes the reader want to turn the page to the story on Ariel.

My objective when writing the copy was to make it look attractive and sensational. I demonstrated this with the background in a dark colour and the headline in massive white letters. This is the perfect contrast to grab the reader's attention. The font size of the headline is big because *I DO* is the most sensational component. Furthermore the subheading offers depth on what the text on the page is about, which is Caliban's love confession. The wording of this subheading, *Wedding of the century*, also pays tribute to the conventional style of tabloids. I used exaggerations like this throughout my article to keep it sensational and thrilling, e.g. *shot down heartlessly, shocking confession* and *vicious and sinister*.

Tabloids need something sensational to sell, which is why I added Caliban's confession. We see that Caliban has potential throughout the play to become a civilised human being. He feels guilt and shows remorse after his plan to usurp Prospero fails. Since he shows this potential to change, it makes sense for him to fall in love with Miranda. It is very conceivable that he sees the errors of his ways and feels sorry for trying to rape Miranda. Miranda's response to his proposal is quite fitting, as she is seen in the play as being quite harsh to him. She is a very flat and naive character.

I considered all conventions when I made this tabloid and I would definitely buy this tabloid paper if I saw it in the store.

IDLE Island

Netherlands €2 France €2 Belgium €2

TUESDAY, MARCH 8, 2011

ARIEL FLIES FREE

Prospero finally frees the airy spirit Ariel. Has their master-servant relation ended or will their paths cross once more?

page 4

"I DO Love You"

Miranda looks surprised towards Caliban's "I do".

Caliban confesses love at wedding of the century

Savage Caliban confessed his love for Miranda yesterday night at Miranda and Ferdinand's wedding. What started out as an amazing ceremony with everyone from the Tempest invited, was unexpectedly interrupted when Caliban exclaimed, "I do love you! His timing came at the most crucial part when Ferdinand was just about to say "I do". Leaving the whole room silent including the priest. Miranda was overtaken by tremendous shock and demanded he'd leave immediately.

Caliban is infamous for his rape attempt on Miranda which nearly had him killed by the furious father Prospero. Back then Prospero assumed Caliban was merely barbaric and overwhelmed by lust and thus tried to force himself on virgin Miranda.

However now the truth has come to light that Caliban has harbored feelings towards the girl who in his earlier years was his teacher. If his feelings were love when he attempted the rape has yet to be disclosed.

All the people at the wedding were stunned at the shocking confession. None of them would have believed it if they hadn't experienced it for themselves. Prospero said. "I always thought he was truly vicious and sinister however he's truly wicked to destroy the most important day to Miranda." "Even if he claims he 'loves' her". He added with a face full of disgust and disbelief.

The distressed married couple were able to say a few words regarding the incident. Both husband and wife agreed that whatever happened wouldn't effect their future happiness. Their love is stronger than ever. To which Ferdinand said. " My love outshines that of the savage a billion times, not that any one can call what he feels love. He's simply irrational and has caused problems to the very end."

The unexpected love declaration by Caliban was shot down heartlessly by Miranda's "I don't".

Examiner's comments

Overall the student did an excellent job demonstrating her understanding of both the characters in *The Tempest* and the conventions of tabloid writing. The following comments indicate how an examiner might respond to the student's work.

Criterion A: Rationale – 1 out of 2

The student explains the purpose of her task well, describing how she adheres to the conventions of tabloid newspapers and explores the characterisation of Caliban and Miranda.

Unfortunately she has one point deducted for the rationale, which is too long. While the rationale should be 200–300 words, hers is over 400 words.

Criterion B: Task and content – 7 out of 8

The content of the written task is very appropriate to its form. As mentioned in the rationale, the tabloid lends itself well to a play in which many sensational events happen off-stage and are retold on-stage. We see this in lines such as *Back then Prospero assumed Caliban was merely barbaric and overwhelmed by lust and thus tried to force himself on virgin Miranda.* The rationale also offers good supporting arguments for creating the imagined wedding scene, where Caliban expresses feelings for Miranda. It makes sense for Miranda to heartlessly reject Caliban, as she is harsh towards him in the play. It also makes sense for Caliban to express his feelings for Miranda, as he develops into a more civilised human being over the course of the play. Therefore the student shows her understanding of the text.

Criterion C: Organisation – 3 out of 5

The task is very well organised, using the formatting of tabloid newspapers. The use of ears, mastheads, headlines and subheadings gives the task structure. The copy is a coherent piece of journalism which introduces the sensational story well, provides the reader with background information, embellishes the events and concludes strongly. The student has two points deducted for not meeting the minimum word count of 800.

Criterion D: Language – 4 out of 5

The student uses a style of language that is appropriate for tabloid newspapers. Words like *sinister*, *heartlessly* and *wicked* are effective in setting the tone of the text. Some sentences in the written task do not flow well, even though they are grammatically correct. For example, the sentence *If his feelings were love when he attempted the rape has yet to be disclosed* is slightly awkward. It would be better put as an active sentence, with *We* as the subject, such as: *We may never know if what happened was attempted rape or an expression of love.*

Ideas for parts 3 or 4 written task 1

1 A common and successful idea for a written task on a literary text is to write a letter from one character of a novel to another. This could be embedded in the middle of the novel, at a crucial part of the plot, or it could be part of an epilogue, where one character discloses sentiments that he or she has withheld from the reader or other characters throughout the text. Either way, be sure to give enough textual information for the examiner in your rationale.

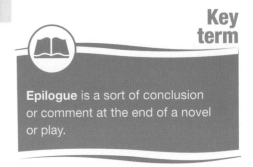

Key term

Epilogue is a sort of conclusion or comment at the end of a novel or play.

Is there a difference between the written task 1s that you write for parts 3 and 4? The simple answer to this question is no. There is no formal requirement that differentiates between these two tasks. The written task (or tasks) that you write for part 3 will simply be based on one of the works that you have read for that part. The same applies for part 4.

2   You may feel that part of the literary text is missing. Perhaps there is an event that happens off-stage or in the mind of a character that deserves more attention. Writing an extract from a novel can be an interesting challenge, as it involves a study of the author's writing style and an in-depth understanding of the plot. Try to imitate the author's 'voice' and report on your experiences doing this in your rationale.

3   Can you imagine a situation in which one character from your literary text makes a speech or has a monologue? For this idea, be sure to create a plausible setting in which they are able to voice a lot of the themes or sentiments of the text. In your rationale explain why the character says these things and whom to.

4   Another popular idea is to write a journal or diary entry for a particular character. This can be a tricky choice, however, and it is important to take into account what the character knows at each particular developmental stage of the plot. You can reflect how their awareness of events and their views change over the course of the text through multiple journal entries. Not every literary text lends itself well to this format.

Chapter 5 summary

This chapter has addressed some fundamental questions of approaching literature, focusing on the context of interpretation. You have explored four reasons for reading fiction: communication, education, imitation and catharsis. Many of these reasons focused on 'you', the reader, and your experiences when reading fiction. This approach related to reader-response criticism, one of the ways of approaching literature that you looked at, along with Formalism (the school of literary criticism that focuses on texts out of context) and historical-biographical criticism (which focuses on texts in their context of composition).

You have also seen how ideological frameworks, such as Marxism, feminism and Freudian psychoanalysis, influence the ways in which readers read fiction. Critics who adhere to these traditions of literary criticism approach texts with a set agenda, finding examples from literature to support their view of the world. You saw how such views can give people new insights into old texts. Because literary texts are so diverse, it helps to know about these different approaches to literature.

Finally, you saw how one student approached a written task on Shakespeare's *The Tempest*, choosing a modern tabloid newspaper as a medium to explore a 17th-century play, focusing on the sensational qualities of the text.

In the next chapter you will continue to look at literary texts and their context. The focus will turn now to the context of composition and the writer's experience.

Chapter 6 The context of composition

Objectives

By the end of this chapter you will be able to

- identify and discuss the characteristics of various types of novels
- appreciate the importance of literary movements in shaping the contexts in which texts are written
- plan and write a timed essay for your Paper 2 exam.

In the last chapter you looked at various different approaches to literature and traditions of literary criticism. You saw that there are different contexts in which texts can be interpreted. In this chapter you are going to turn your attention to the different contexts of composition and explore more about the context in which some sample texts were composed. You will look at different types of novel first, in Unit 6.1, then at literary movements in Unit 6.2. At the end of the chapter you will find a sample Paper 2 to study and will be able to see how the knowledge you gain in this chapter can be put into practice in your IB exam.

Reading novels, watching plays or viewing films often prompts the question *What was the writer thinking when writing this text?* This question is at the heart of the context of composition. It can be broken down into two subsidiary questions:

1 Which literary forms inspired the writer to shape the text in this particular way?

2 What experiences, topics or ideas inspired the writer to write?

The first question is one of **genre**. Prose, poetry and drama are easily identifiable categories, or genres, of literature. However, it should always be remembered that *not every* work of fiction will fit neatly into a literary category or subcategory. There is no reader's handbook to help identify literary genres, unlike the handbooks that exist to help identify species of birds or flowers, for example. In Unit 6.1 you will discover several different types, or genres, of novel and the qualities that define each of them. Learning to identify the characteristics of different kinds of novel will help put your part 3 texts into perspective.

The second question relates to the literary, social, political or historical **movements** that have influenced the writer, which you will pursue further in Unit 6.2. Writers do not write in a vacuum. They are influenced by their surroundings and the trends of their times. The German word *zeitgeist* has been adopted in English to capture all of these factors and describe 'the spirit of the times'.

For centuries, great writers have 'stood on the shoulders' of other writers who have gone before them. In other words, good writers build on traditions that others have started. Studying writers' texts in the context of different literary genres and movements will help you understand how they have built on traditions. It will also show you how their writing style and form have been influenced by this context.

Key terms

Genre describes a category of literature that can be defined by the structural and stylistic conventions that are frequently found in that category.

Movement, in a literary sense, is a collection of works which seek to address similar concerns or express similar ideas, or which come out of a certain period in history.

Unit 6.1 **Types of novel**

Most bookshops these days have prominent displays of fiction best-sellers, and the most popular best-sellers are usually novels. Novels have become part of the fabric of our literary culture. What exactly are they, and why do authors choose to write a certain type of novel in order to express their ideas?

Longer pieces of narrative writing have been around for nearly two thousand years. The art has evolved over time, from Ancient Greek sagas, Old French romances and medieval Italian tales. In 1719 Daniel Defoe wrote *Robinson Crusoe*, which tells the story of a man who learns to survive when he finds himself alone on an island in the Caribbean. Today, survival is still a popular theme in novels and has been treated in many best-sellers. In Defoe's time, however, describing the trials and tribulations of one character, and allowing readers to hear his thoughts and see his actions, were revolutionary ideas.

Novels are usually defined by several key characteristics, such as plot, setting and characterisation, which you will look at more closely in Chapter 7. For now the focus will be on some of the main *types* of novel and the labels that are often attached to them – for example, detective novels, social novels or science fiction novels.

First, let us consider the term *science fiction*. In the last chapter you read an extract from *The Handmaid's Tale* by Margaret Atwood (Text 5.5), which in 1987 won the Arthur C. Clarke Award, the UK's most prestigious award for science fiction writing. Atwood was surprised: she thought science fiction was a type of novel that included 'rockets and chemicals' or 'talking squids in outer space', as she told the *New Scientist* and the BBC. She explained that *The Handmaid's Tale* was a work of 'speculative fiction', a type of novel she believed had the ability to explore themes that 'realistic fiction' could not.

The question here is *Why did she choose a particular genre, whether that genre is termed science fiction or speculative fiction, to express her ideas?* For the answer, we have to look at the context of the novel. In the case of *The Handmaid's Tale*, several important events took place in the early 1980s that shaped the zeitgeist of our world. The Islamic Revolution changed Iran into a totalitarian theocracy; prominent feminists in the USA began to align themselves with the religious right, a group of people who wanted more Christianity in the US government; Presidents Jimmy Carter and Ronald Reagan used religious rhetoric openly and proudly; televised Evangelism or 'televangelism' became popular in the USA; chemical warfare and the Cold War were looming threats for many people in the world.

In the context of what was happening at the time, it makes sense that Atwood wanted to reflect these influences through science fiction or speculative fiction. What is more, after reading the novel, you can see that she is building on a tradition established by other writers, such as Mary Shelley, George Orwell and Aldous Huxley, called dystopian literature (see page 129).

Dystopian literature

The term *Utopia* was coined by Sir Thomas More in 1516 in his description of the perfect society. The Greek word *utopia* means 'no place', and it sounds like another Greek word, *eutopia*, meaning 'good place'. *Dystopian* is the opposite of *Utopian*. The roots of dystopian literature can be found in Jonathan's Swift's novel, *Gulliver's Travels*, of 1726, in which the character Lemuel Gulliver travels to many fictitious lands, seeing the good and bad qualities of various societies. As a genre, dystopian literature is concerned predominantly with the values of a society.

What makes a novel a dystopian novel? Look out for the following characteristics:
• The main character is an oppressed individual.
• The main character suffers at the hands of an oppressive state, often a totalitarian state.
• A major theme of the novel might be justice, freedom or happiness.

• The text has the purpose of warning its readers about certain trends in politics or society at the time it was written.

As you read the following extracts, Text 6.1, look for the four characteristics of dystopian literature in the list. Text 6.1 is 3 extracts from the novel *Fahrenheit 451* by Ray Bradbury, an author who is often associated with the genre of dystopian fiction.

Text 6.1 *Fahrenheit 451*, Ray Bradbury, 1953

This novel takes place in America at a time in the future. The main character, Guy Montag, is a 'fireman', which in this novel means a person who burns books. *Fahrenheit 451* refers to the temperature at which paper and therefore books spontaneously combust. After Montag meets his neighbour, a young intellectual, he begins to question why the state employs him to burn books. He begins to secretly collect books and eventually stays away from work to read them. At this point, he is visited by the chief of the fire department, Captain Beatty, who is speaking in the extract below, sitting at Montag's bedside.

Extract 1

'When did it all start, you ask, this job of ours, how did it come about, where, when? Well, I'd say it really got started around about a thing called the Civil War. Even though our rule-book claims it was founded earlier. The fact is we didn't get along well until photography came into its own. Then – motion pictures in the early twentieth century. Radio. Television. Things began to have *mass*.'

Montag sat in bed, not moving.

'And because they had mass, they became simpler,' said Beatty. 'Once, books appealed to a few people, here, there, everywhere. They could afford to be different. The world was roomy. But then the world got full of eyes and elbows and mouths. Double, triple, quadruple population. Films and radios, magazines, books levelled down to a sort of paste pudding norm, do you follow me?'

'I think so.

Extract 2

Yes, but what about firemen, then?' asked Montag.

'Ah.' Beatty leaned forward in the faint mist of smoke from his pipe. 'What more easily explained and natural? With school turning out more runners, jumpers, racers, thinkers, grabbers, snatchers, fliers, and swimmers instead of examiners, critics, knowers, and imaginative creators, the word "intellectual", of course, became the swear word it deserved to be. You always dread the unfamiliar. Surely you remember the boy in your own school class who was exceptionally "bright", did most of the reciting and answering while the others sat like so many leaden idols, hating him. And wasn't it this bright boy you selected for beatings and tortures after hours? Of course it was. We must all be alike. Not everyone born free and equal, as the Constitution says, but everyone *made* equal. Each man the image of every other; then all are happy, for there are no mountains to make them cower, to judge themselves against. So! A book is a loaded gun in the house next door. Burn it.

Extract 3

'You must understand that our civilization is so vast that we can't have our minorities upset and stirred. Ask yourself, what do we want in this country, above all? People want to be happy, isn't that right? Haven't you heard it all your life? I want to be happy, people say. Well, aren't they? … That's all we live for, isn't it? For pleasure, for titillation? And you must admit our culture provides plenty of these.'

discussion

1 What examples are there in Text 6.1 of the characteristics of dystopian literature?
2 How convincing do you find Beatty's case for censorship? Explain your answer with examples from the text.
3 How might the ideas of this novel reflect the zeitgeist of the 1950s?

tip

Several works of dystopian literature offer interesting insight into the topic of media that you explored in Part 2: Language and mass communication. You may want to explore more texts from this genre that relate to the media. Try, for example, *Nineteen Eighty-Four* by George Orwell, *Vernon God Little* by D.B.C. Pierre, or the screenplay *The Truman Show* by Andrew M. Niccol.

discussion

1. How well do you think the student has understood the novel? Where do you see evidence of good understanding? Is there evidence of poor understanding?
2. How does the student make a connection between the context in which the novel was written and the themes and structure of the novel?

Key terms

Anti-novel is a novel that ignores all of the structural conventions of regular novels such as plot, characterisation and consistent point of view.

Bildungsroman belongs to a tradition of novel writing about young individuals coming of age who learn a lifelong lesson through a transformational experience; the German word *Bildung* means 'development' or 'formation', and *roman* means 'novel'.

Gothic fiction is a mixture of horror and romance that came out of the Romantic movement of the 18th and 19th centuries.

Magic realism is a style of fiction with origins in South America. It creates a very realistic setting with a few highly unrealistic elements.

Social novel is a type of novel that stresses the importance of real social and economic circumstances on fictional characters in an attempt to persuade the reader towards an ideological position.

Fahrenheit 451: style and context

To prepare for your Paper 2 exam, you need practice at writing about how the context of a work is reflected through its content, style and structure. Look at the following response written by a student after reading *Fahrenheit 451*.

> Ray Bradbury was devoted to writing fiction when he wrote **Fahrenheit 451**. This may explain why the main topic of the novel is the importance of literature and books in society. After the Second World War, the memory of Nazis burning Jewish books was etched into the minds of millions, including Bradbury. Besides being concerned about the rights of minorities in America, his greater issue was with the state of education and literacy. Visual mass media was on the rise in America in the 1950s. Bradbury feared that with more screens projecting sensational images, people would forget to read and not want to be bothered with intellectual ideas, engaging in self-censorship.
>
> The above-mentioned ideas can be seen in the passage from **Fahrenheit 451**. Bradbury creates a scene with a lot of dialogue between Captain Beatty, who voices the opinion of the state and the masses, and Guy Montag, who, like the reader, questions the reasoning behind the state's ways. As we, the readers, eavesdrop, we hear the arguments for censorship.
>
> The novel is intriguing. It drops the reader in a strange setting and quickly explains how to navigate. Because the novel was originally written in instalments as a serial in both **Galaxy** and **Playboy** magazines, it had to be intriguing. It had to make the reader want to buy the next publication.

So far in this unit you have come across several types of fiction: science fiction, speculative fiction and dystopian literature, and have looked at these terms in relation to two novels: *The Handmaid's Tale* and *Fahrenheit 451*. Figure 6.1 shows how a Venn diagram can be used to show how the two novels, plus some others, can be identified with the genres and the relationship between then. The diagram allows for an overlap where some texts have characteristics of more than one genre.

There are, of course, many more genres than the three you have looked at so far in this unit. The following is a list of some of the other types of novel.

- **anti-novel**
- **Bildungsroman**
- crime / detective novel
- documentary novel
- fantasy novel
- **Gothic** novel
- historical novel
- horror novel
- **magic realism** novel
- psychological novel
- romance
- **social novel**
- speculative novel
- spy novel
- thriller

Activity 6.1

1. Construct a Venn diagram like Figure 6.1 (page 141) to show the genres the books you are reading as a class belong to. Although constructing a Venn diagram of your texts cannot be an exact science, this is a useful exercise to do as a class when you are discussing your part 3 or 4 texts, or even works you have read outside class.
2. Why do you think the authors chose these particular types of novel to express their ideas?

3 Choose some of the other genres in the list above and carry out some further research on these types of novel. Make more Venn diagrams using the genres you have found out about.

Historical fiction

Historical fiction brings history to life by placing us, the readers, in a specific historical time and place. We see and experience the ideas of the times through the characters in the novel, enduring the same hardships and living their lives vicariously. As with all fiction, we must suspend our disbelief and not question how true the events or the characters are although we are always conscious that they are inspired by true events and real people.

You are going to explore one novel of historical fiction to understand why its author chose to write this type of novel, and you will see how style and structure are influenced by the context in which the author wrote.

Text 6.2 *One Day in the Life of Ivan Denisovich*, Alexander Solzhenitsyn, 1962

While many in the West knew about the Soviet labour camps of the early 1950s, known as the gulags, it was not until *One Day in the Life of Ivan Denisovich* was published in 1962 that the world really understood the hardships endured by so many prisoners in the USSR under Stalin. Solzhenitsyn was serving in the Red Army in 1945 when he was arrested for making derogatory remarks about Stalin in private letters to a friend. He was eventually imprisoned and sent to a labour camp close to Kazakhstan, where he experienced the cold, hunger and ill treatment described in his novella.

When Stalin died in 1953, Solzhenitsyn was freed but exiled. In 1956 he was allowed to return to the USSR, where he taught in a secondary school. Solzhenitsyn submitted the manuscript of *One Day in the Life of Ivan Denisovich* in 1961 to the literary magazine *Novy Mir,* which had to seek approval from Krushchev and the government to publish the novella. As Stalin had by then fallen out of favour, the publication was approved. Solzhenitsyn won the Nobel Prize in 1970 but was not able to receive it until 1974, when he was deported from the USSR for being anti-Soviet.

No sense in getting your boots wet in the morning. Even if Shukhov had dashed back to his hut he wouldn't have found another pair to change into. During eight years' imprisonment he had known various systems for allocating footwear: there'd been times when he'd gone through the winter without valenki[1] at all, or leather boots either, and had had to make shift with bast sandals or a sort of galoshes made of scraps of motor tyres – 'Chetezes' they called them, after the Cheliabinsk tractor works. Now the footwear situation seemed better; in October Shukhov had received (thanks to Pavlo, whom he trailed to the store) a pair of ordinary, hard-wearing leather boots, big enough for a double thickness of foot-cloth. For a week he went about as though he'd been given a birthday present, kicking his new heels. Then in December the valenki arrived, and, oh, wasn't life wonderful?

But some devil in the book-keeper's office had whispered in the commandant's ear that valenki should be issued only to those who surrendered their boots. It was against the rules for a prisoner to possess two pairs of footwear at the same time. So Shukhov had to choose. Either he'd have to wear leather throughout the winter, or surrender the boots and wear valenki even in the thaw. He'd taken such good

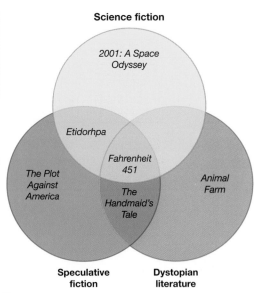

Science fiction

2001: A Space Odyssey

Etidorhpa

Fahrenheit 451

The Plot Against America

The Handmaid's Tale

Animal Farm

Speculative fiction

Dystopian literature

Figure 6.1 Venn diagrams can be useful when discussing genres and texts.

Figure 6.2 The Soviet writer Alexander Solzhenitsyn.

care of his new boots, softening the leather with grease! Ah, nothing had been so hard to part with in all his eight years in camps as that pair of boots! They were tossed into a common heap. Not a hope of finding your own pair in the spring.

[1] **valenki**   knee-length felt boots for winter wear

Activity 6.2

Before reading the sample response below, write your own response to Text 6.2, drawing connections between Solzhenitsyn's life and *One Day in the Life of Ivan Denisovich*. Write about 300–500 words. Remember that your writing must answer the following question: *How do the style and structure of the text reflect the context in which it was written?*

One Day in the Life of Ivan Denisovich: style and context

Look at the following response written by a student after reading *One Day in the Life of Ivan Denisovich*.

Key term

Free indirect speech is a kind of limited third-person narration that allows the reader to hear a character's thoughts (see page 183).

discussion

1 How does the student's response differ from your own?
2 What evidence does the student's response show of critical thinking and contextual understanding?

Alexander Solzhenitsyn wrote **One Day in the Life of Ivan Denisovich** as a work of historical fiction and most notably not as a memoir or autobiography. He may have done this for several reasons.

Under the circumstances, Solzhenitsyn was not certain how his personal history of the gulag would have been received. After being released from prison, he had every reason to fear imprisonment again for speaking out about the camps. Hiding behind fictional characters and speaking through the imaginary Ivan Denisovich Shukov was safer and therefore made sense from the author's perspective.

Besides this reason, though, there is an even greater reason why Solzhenitsyn wrote fiction instead of non-fiction. He wanted to be known as an artist, or novelist, instead of a former prisoner of the gulag. His writing style draws us into the mind of Shukov through the use of free indirect speech. We see examples of this when the narrator says, 'Then in December the valenki arrived, and, oh, wasn't life wonderful?' We feel the elation of the main character for such simple small things in prison life. Solzhenitsyn goes one step further to make us feel empathy for Shukov by writing in the second person: *Not a hope of finding your own pair in the spring.* This feels like an extreme let-down from the *kicking his new heels*.

Solzhenitsyn wrote a piece of historical fiction because it allowed him to bring the gulag to life. He describes everything, from shoes to disease, in such detail that we feel we are there, experiencing the hardships of this Soviet labour camp.

As you follow your IB Diploma course and prepare for the Paper 2 exam, you might find it useful to keep a record of the texts you read. You can use a table such as the one below to record in summary form what you have read. Not only is this a good exercise for analysing a text, it will also be a useful overview when you come to revise for your exam. (You may not be able to fill in the last row of the table just yet. You will be looking more at the mechanics of fiction and literary devices in Part 4 of this coursebook. Chapter 7 has more about point of view and narrative technique.)

	Text 1 (from PLA)	Text 2 (from PLT list)	Text 3 (free choice)
Title	*The Handmaid's Tale*	*One Day in the Life of Ivan Denisovich*	*Vernon God Little*
Author	Margaret Atwood	Alexander Solzhenitsyn	D.B.C. Pierre
Themes	Women in society, religion, totalitarian states	Totalitarian state (Stalinism), dignity, individualism versus socialism	Individual versus society, dignity, media and violence
Genre	Dystopian fiction / speculative fiction	Historical / memoir	Dystopian fiction / Bildungsroman
Defining characteristics of genre	Oppressed person, oppressive state, happiness and society	Influential period from someone's life, wisdom with benefit of hindsight	Coming of age, life-shaping decisions, journeys
Context (political, social, cultural, religious)	USA, religious right and feminism, Iran, Cold War	Stalinism, personal experience in Siberian labour camp	Columbine shootings, reality TV
Stylistic and structural devices that reflect context of composition	1st person, stream of consciousness, present tense	3rd person, free indirect speech, detailed description of physical labour	1st person, stream of consciousness, present tense

Activity 6.3

Find out more about the contexts of the texts that you are reading for part 3. Use the following questions to help you.

1 What inspired the author of the text you are reading?
2 Learn more about the characteristics that define the genre to which your text belongs. Why do you think the author chose that particular genre to express their ideas?
3 Comment on how any stylistic and structural devices reflect the context of composition.
4 As a class, fill in a table similar to the one above to act as a record of the texts you are reading.

Unit 6.2 **Literary movements**

Many literary works are closely associated with a particular historical or artistic movement. Movements often transcend the boundaries of one art form, and characteristics of a movement can sometimes continue beyond the time period usually given as the beginning and end of the movement. Romanticism, for example, was a movement that took hold in Europe in the second half of the 18th century, rooted in the idea that emotions and nature were true sources of knowledge. It gave rise to an explosion of visual arts, philosophical essays, music and literature. The effects and influence of Romanticism continue to this day. Even after the movement had been succeeded by the Victorian period, realism and the Industrial Revolution, there were

TOK

Romanticism was a philosophical and artistic movement that came about as a reaction to the neo-Classicism and Enlightenment of the 18th century and the beginnings of the Industrial Revolution. The main idea behind Romanticism was that emotions were a source of truth. Other sources of inspiration included nature, beauty and youth.

1 Read Text 6.3, a poem by William Wordsworth, and comment on how it reflects the ideas of Romanticism.
2 Comment in particular on the notion that *The child is father of the man*. Can a child know more or be wiser than an adult? What do you think Wordsworth means when he says a child can be *father of the man*? Discuss the relevance of the TOK terms (a) intuition and (b) wisdom in your answer.

Extended essay

EE

- *William Blake: laying the foundations of Romanticism.*
- *'Middlemarch': the epitome of realism in English literature.*
- *Understanding post-modernism through Paul Auster's 'New York Trilogy'.*

You may want to devote an extended essay to exploring a literary movement. Besides focusing on one or two of its key literary works in depth, you should have a broad understanding of many of the texts associated with this movement in order to comment on the contexts of composition and interpretation. You could structure your essay around questions such as: *To what extent did the authors of your works contribute to a particular movement? Were the ideas of the authors understood by the audiences of their times? Were they ahead of their times?*

Figure 6.3 In the 1984 film *A Passage to India* the Marabar Caves are an important but mysterious part of the story. The unsolved events in the Marabar Caves are what characterise the novel as a work of modernism.

still writers who were inspired by romanticism and continued in its tradition. One such writer is the poet Robert Frost.

Attempts at defining literary movements can, however, be as difficult as defining literary genres and types of novel. While some movements transcend art forms and time periods, others are very much confined to a particular art form or period. Some movements are sub-movements. We will explore one movement in this unit, modernism, and see how it inspired writers such as John Fowles and E.M. Forster.

Text 6.3 *My heart leaps up*, William Wordsworth, 1807

> My heart leaps up when I behold
>   A rainbow in the sky:
> So was it when my life began,
> So is it now I am a man,
> So be it when I shall grow old,
>   Or let me die!
> The child is father of the man,
>   And I could wish my days to be
> Bound each to each by natural piety.

Modernism

In 1924 a novel by E.M. Forster, *A Passage to India*, challenged readers to read novels differently. In the story several British colonists are taken on an expedition by local Indians into the mysterious Marabar Caves. A British woman is possibly assaulted by one of the local men but the reader never finds out the truth about what happened in the caves. Instead we see how the characters have to deal with the aftermath.

This, in essence, is a modernist novel. Modernism had begun much earlier than 1924, towards the end of the 19th century, when writers and intellectuals started reacting against the common ideas of the Victorian era. They believed that subjective experience was more valuable than objective reality. What really happened in the Marabar Caves in *A Passage to India* does not matter as much as the emotional consequences suffered by the characters of the novel.

Another characteristic of modernism is the rejection of the notions of natural order and authority. Hence, in *A Passage to India*, the attempts at persecuting the alleged perpetrator of the crime seem unjust and baseless. The two authorities of religion and the Raj (the British colonial rule in India) are questioned in the novel. Modernism especially took root after the atrocities of the First World War, which seemed senseless to so many. The world seemed to lack guiding principles and moral order.

Finally, modernism questions form. E.M. Forster challenges the readers of the novel by not allowing them to know as much as some of the book's characters. Not solving the mystery of the Marabar Caves breaks a widely accepted convention of storytelling. By drawing our attention to the novel's form, Forster is a modernist.

In summary, a modernist work can be identified by the following three characteristics:

- Subjective experience matters more than objective reality.
- The world lacks moral order or natural authorities.
- Form and convention are there to be broken.

Text 6.4 *The Collector*, John Fowles, 1963

John Fowles was the son of a veteran of the First World War. He was gifted in languages and athletics, which became apparent while he was at Bedford School during the years of the Second World War. He completed his navy officer training on Victory in Europe Day in 1945. In 1947, after two years of military service, he went to Oxford University to study French. In 1947 he wrote: *I … began to hate what I was becoming in life – a British Establishment young hopeful. I decided instead to become a sort of anarchist.* He was interested in Albert Camus, Jean-Paul Sartre and the ideas of **existentialism**. After leaving university he taught in Greece but he quarrelled with the school. He returned to England, got married and was teaching English as a foreign language when he wrote *The Collector*. The story is about a young man, Frederick Clegg, who kidnaps a young girl, Miranda Grey. The story is told twice, from the perspective of each of the characters. The extract below contains the very last lines of the novel. They are told by Frederick after Miranda has died of pneumonia.

The days passed, it is now three weeks since all that.

Of course I shall never have a guest again, although now Aunt Annie and Mabel have decided to stay Down Under, it would not be difficult.

Still as a matter of interest I have since been looking into the problems there would be with the girl in Woolworths. She lives in a village the other side of Lewes from here, in a house a quarter mile or so from the bus-stop. You have to go along a country-lane to get to it. As I say, it would be possible (if I hadn't learnt my lesson). She isn't as pretty as Miranda, of course, in fact she's only an ordinary common shop-girl, but that was my mistake before, aiming too high, I ought to have seen that I could never get what I wanted from someone like Miranda, with all her la-di-da ideas and clever tricks. I ought to have got someone who would respect me more. Someone ordinary I could teach.

She is in the box I made, under the appletrees. It took me three days to dig the hole. I thought I would go mad the night I did it (went down and got her in the box I made and outside). I don't think many could have done it. I did it scientific. I planned what had to be done and ignored my natural feelings. I couldn't stand the idea of having to look at her again, I once heard they go green and purple in patches, so I went in with a cheap blanket I bought in front of me and held it out till I was by the bed and then threw it over the deceased. I rolled it up and all the bedclothes into the box and soon had the lid screwed on. I got round the smell with fumigator and the fan.

The room's cleaned out now and good as new.

I shall put what she wrote and her hair up in the loft in the deed-box which will not be opened till my death, so I don't expect for forty or fifty years. I have not made up my mind about Marian (another M! I heard the supervisor call her name), this time it won't be love, it would just be for the interest of the thing and to compare them and also the other thing, which as I say I would like to go into in more detail and I could teach her how. And the clothes would fit. Of course I would make it clear from the start who's boss and what I expect.

But it is still just an idea. I only put the stove down there today because the room needs drying out anyway.

Figure 6.4 John Fowles (1926–2005). He once wrote, *I … began to hate what I was becoming in life … I decided instead to become a sort of anarchist.*

discussion

1 Find evidence of the three characteristics of modernism in Text 6.4.
2 How does the narrator draw you into his world?
3 What kind of person is the narrator? Give examples to illustrate your ideas.
4 How does Text 6.4 reflect John Fowles's interest in modernism and anarchy?

There are, of course, many literary movements, and not just that of modernism that you have looked at so far in this unit. The following is a list of some other literary movements.

- beat poetry
- Dadaism
- existentialism
- First World War poetry
- Harlem renaissance
- imagism
- lost generation writers
- metaphysical poetry
- modernism
- post-colonialism
- post-modernism
- realism
- Renaissance
- Romanticism
- surrealism
- Victorian literature

Activity 6.4

As you study the contexts in which your part 3 texts were written, you will want to learn more about the sources that inspired the authors. Albert Camus, Jean-Paul Sartre, the ideas of existentialism and the Theatre of the Absurd inspired John Fowles. Read Text 6.5, an extract from *The Stranger* by Albert Camus, to see how Fowles might have been inspired. Find out about existentialism and the Theatre of the Absurd in order to gain a deeper understanding of both Texts 6.4 and 6.5. Here are some questions to consider when comparing and contrasting the two texts:

1 How are the personal lives of the authors different? How are they similar? Can you see how their lives are reflected through their writing?
2 Both stories are told in the first person, or the 'I' form, from the perspective of the main characters (the murderers). How are Frederick Clegg and Meursault similar in their thoughts and actions? How are they different?
3 Read the short summaries of the main ideas of existentialism and the Theatre of the Absurd. Can you find evidence of these ideas in the two texts?

Existentialism

- A philosophy that focuses on the condition of the individual person: their thoughts, emotions, responsibilities and actions.
- Only an individual can give their life meaning.
- In order to give their life meaning, the individual must overcome existential obstacles such as fear, alienation, boredom and absurdity.

The Theatre of the Absurd

- A movement comprising plays written by playwrights who believed human existence has no meaning in a godless world.
- The mismatch between people's urge to give their lives meaning and the meaninglessness of life often results in absurd situations.

Figure 6.5 Albert Camus (1913–60), a source of inspiration for John Fowles.

Text 6.5 *The Stranger*, Albert Camus, 1942

Albert Camus came from a poor, pied noir family (of French origin) in Algeria. His father died in the First World War; his mother, of Spanish descent, was half deaf. Just years after joining the French Communist Party in 1935, Camus was kicked out for making anarchist claims. He spoke out about the inequalities between the Algerians and French in Algeria, which was a French colony until 1962. In 1940, after he saw some Nazis murder a French communist politician, Gabriel Péri, Camus joined the underground Resistance movement. Like Solzhenitsyn, Camus was also a winner of the Nobel Prize in Literature (1957).

Although Camus rejected the existentialist label, *The Stranger* is often seen as a work of existentialism. In it, the main character, Meursault, leads an ordinary life that begins to fall apart after his mother dies; he meets an old girlfriend and his neighbour beats an Algerian lover. Meursault becomes involved in his neighbour's affairs and finds himself being tailed by angry Arabs. In an act of what seems like random violence he shoots and kills an Arab. The following extract begins after he is imprisoned for murder.

Figure 6.6 How does this image from Luchino Visconti's film of *The Stranger* (*Lo Straniero*) depict the narrator, Meursault, from Text 6.5?

The next day a lawyer came to see me at the prison. He was short and stout, quite young, with his hair carefully greased back. In spite of the heat (I was in my shirt-sleeves), he was wearing a dark suit, a wing collar and a peculiar tie with broad black and white stripes. He put the briefcase which he had under his arm down on my bed, introduced himself, and told me that he'd studied my file. My case was tricky, but he was confident of success provided I had faith in him. I thanked him and he said, 'Let's get straight on with it.'

He sat down on the bed and explained that some investigations had been made into my private life. It had been discovered that my mother had died recently in a home. Enquiries had then been made in Marengo, and the magistrates had learned that I'd 'displayed a lack of emotion' on the day of mother's funeral. 'You will understand,' my lawyer said, that I feel rather embarrassed at having to ask you this. But it matters a great deal. And the prosecution will have a strong case if I can't find anything to reply.' He wanted me to help him. He asked me if I'd felt any grief that day. This question really surprised me and I thought how embarrassed I'd have been if I'd had to ask it.

I replied though that I'd rather got out of the habit of analyzing myself and that I found it difficult to answer his question. I probably loved mother quite a lot, but that didn't mean anything. To a certain extent all normal people sometimes wished their loved ones dead. Here the lawyer interrupted me, looking very flustered. He made me promise not to say that at the hearing, or in front of the examining magistrate. But I explained to him that by nature my physical needs often distorted my feelings. On the day of mother's funeral I was very tired and sleepy. So I wasn't fully aware of what was going on. The only thing I could say for certain was that I'd rather mother hadn't died. But my lawyer didn't seem pleased. He said, 'That's not enough.'

He thought for a moment. Then he asked me if he could say that I'd controlled my natural feelings that day. I said, 'No, because it's not true.' He looked at me in a peculiar way, as if he found me slightly disgusting. He told me almost spitefully that whatever happened the warden and staff of the home would be called as witnesses and that this 'could make things any unpleasant for me'. I pointed out to him that none of this had anything to do with my case, but he merely replied that obviously never had anything to do with the law.

Higher level

At higher level you are expected to have an even greater understanding of the contexts in which literary works are written. The following activity provides useful research into literary movements. You could divide the research work among all the higher level students in the class. You may also only want to focus on the literary movements that are relevant for your part 3 works.

To what degree are the movements of your part 3 works defined by (a) form, (b) philosophy and (c) time period?

An example answer may be: 'Poetry of the First World War is not necessarily defined by a particular philosophy, as there were poets both for and against the war. First World War poetry, however, is famous for its sonnets, a form explored by many poets both critical and supportive of the war. While war poetry is still written today, First World War poems are characteristic of their times, describing the horrors of trench warfare and the causes of these seemingly senseless deaths.'

You have seen how a literary text is shaped by the context of the writer – the context of composition. By now you will also have realised that research is the key to understanding the contexts in which the literary texts you are studying are written. Learning about a movement or a genre of novel writing will help shed light on the underlying ideas of a literary text. Research will help you read between the lines. As you read the Paper 2 sample responses below, you will notice that they demonstrate as much knowledge of the *context* of the literary texts as of the texts themselves.

Activity 6.5

To what movement or movements do your literary texts from Part 3 belong? Look back at the list of movements on page 146 to help you. How does a little research on a particular movement shed light on and give new meaning to the works you are reading?

Assessment: Paper 2

In Paper 2 you must demonstrate in an essay your understanding of the contexts in which your part 3 texts were written. The Paper 2 essay is a timed exam, which means you will be assessed on your ability to perform under a time constraint. Before you begin practising for the exam, make sure you are familiar with its requirements and grading criteria (see page V). Study the standard level and higher level sample student responses on pages 149–50 and 154–55 to give you an idea of what you are expected to do.

The sample exams in this unit, like the real exams, contain six questions from which the student has chosen one to answer on. It is a good idea to begin your preparation by writing an essay without any time pressure in answer to one of the sample exam questions, either in class or by yourself, and not under exam conditions. Try to focus on two main things:

• *what* you are going to write
• *how* you are going to write it.

Then, when you feel confident about the content, or what you want to say, and the conventions of essay writing, or how you are going to say it, you can begin writing some timed essays on previously unseen questions.

Sample exam Paper 2 (SL/HL)

*Answer **one** essay question only. You must base your answer on at least two of the Part 3 works you have studied. Answers which are **not** based on a discussion of at least two Part 3 works will **not** score high marks. Your answer should address the ways in which language, context and structure contribute to your reading of each work.*

1 How can we explain the continued interest in a particular work in different contexts and at different times?
2 What do you think of the assertion that the meaning of a text is fixed and does not change over time?
3 To what extent do male and female literary characters accurately reflect the role of men and women in society?
4 How can a literary text's style and structure reflect the context in which it was written?
5 How can political pressure or censorship shape the way literary texts are both written and read?
6 How do literary texts capture the spirit of the times and the values of a culture?

Sample student response (SL)

1 How can we explain the continued interest in a particular work in different contexts and at different times?

Some works are timeless. For example, Shakespeare's plays have been read by students and performed for audiences for centuries. Even though audiences have changed as social values have changed, the plays have always been relevant. Why is this? In *The Handmaid's Tale*, by Margaret Atwood, and *One Day in the Life of Ivan Denisovich* by Alexander Solzhenitsyn, we can see two reasons why literary works have received continued interest in different contexts and at different times by looking at their timeless themes and their literary devices.

The Handmaid's Tale and *One Day in the Life of Ivan Denisovich* similarly explore timeless themes, namely, the themes of oppression and dignity. The question at the heart of these novels is: 'How can you keep your dignity under extreme circumstances?' In the case of the character Offred, from *The Handmaid's Tale*, she is reduced to a fertility machine in a dystopian theocracy. Ivan Denisovich, or 'Shukov' as he is called, is reduced to a manual labourer in a camp near Kazakhstan, where temperatures are minus 40 degrees Celsius. For Offred, her dignity means being loved and found beautiful. She steals butter to keep her skin moist. For Shukhov dignity means refusing to lick his bowl or wear his hat at the dining table, which other prisoners do because of the hunger and cold.

Even though the Stalin labour camps and the Republic of Gilead are very remote for many readers, the novels are just as relevant today as when they were written. While Offred's situation sounds so unrealistic, readers know that religious oppression is a real threat. Atwood wrote the novel in 1985, just years after Iran became a theocracy and made women cover themselves in public, like the women of Gilead. Today, war is fought against the Taliban, who impose strict rules on the way women dress and are educated. While the Soviet labour camps have been dismantled, the world has learned about places like Abu Ghraib. People will always fear oppression and will therefore always be intrigued by works like *The Handmaid's Tale* and *One Day in the Life of Ivan Denisovich*.

There is another reason why these works will remain timeless. They are cleverly crafted. Margaret Atwood makes use of a **stream of consciousness** style, retelling flashbacks in the present tense, which keeps the reader engaged. She drops the reader in a very strange world, where people wear uniforms and have designated roles in society. It is up to the reader to piece together the logic of this strange setting. In a very clever structural device Atwood presents an epilogue to explain how Offred's narrative has come to us through the transcription of a dictaphone that Offred secretly kept. The transcription is presented as a historical document in a futuristic, still fundamentally religious society. Such devices show Atwood's technical skill as a writer in a genre of dystopian and speculative fiction, a genre most suitable for the themes of her novel.

Alexander Solzhenitsyn wrote a historical novel in the third-person limited perspective, a style and structure that reflected the context that he was writing in.

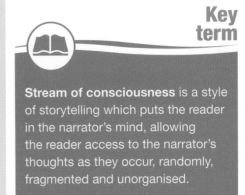

Key term

Stream of consciousness is a style of storytelling which puts the reader in the narrator's mind, allowing the reader access to the narrator's thoughts as they occur, randomly, fragmented and unorganised.

If he had written a memoir in the first person, blatantly presenting his personal story as fact, he would have run the risk of being imprisoned again. Instead he told the story as fiction and he distanced himself from the main character by writing in the third person. Nevertheless, readers are drawn into the everyday experiences of Shukov in the labour camp through Solzhenitsyn's use of free indirect speech. There are times when we read Shukov's thoughts, which are not written with quotation marks. He can become very excited about warm boots, a proper spoon or a morsel of bread.

All in all Solzhenitsyn and Atwood, like many great writers, have written timeless works by writing about timeless themes. Through their novels we see our fascination with themes of dignity and oppression. Furthermore, these authors have used stylistic devices and literary structures that suit the contexts of their works, be they speculative fiction or historical fiction. It is for these reasons that readers return to literary geniuses, like Shakespeare, again and again.

Examiner's comments

Generally speaking the student's work is well structured and relevant to the question. The following comments give a good indication of how an examiner would assess this sample student response.

Criterion A: Knowledge and understanding – 3 out of 5

The student puts his main ideas into the contexts of the reader and the writer, comparing the times in which they were written and the times in which they are read today. While the contexts of the composition are compared with the contexts of interpretation today, with parallels made between Iran and the Taliban, the gulag and Abu Ghraib, there is not much illustration of the effects of the works on readers then and now.

Criterion B: Response to the question – 4 out of 5

The student rewords the question a little to change the focus away from *explaining the continued interest in a work* to *explaining what makes a work timeless*. Nevertheless, the candidate understands the implications of the question. The argument that a work is timeless because of timeless themes is a basic but important one. Focusing on two common themes, oppression and dignity, is also relevant and insightful.

Criterion C: Understanding of the use and effects of stylistic features – 3 out of 5

There is clear evidence of critical thinking when the student makes a link between Solzhenitsyn's use of free indirect speech and his fear of imprisonment. When explaining the correlation between Atwood's style, the use of dystopian fiction and the historical context, the student is not as clear. It would have been nice to have an explanation of dystopian and historical fiction, along with examples of illustrations from the work.

Criterion D: Organisation and development– 5 out of 5

This essay is well structured. The student makes good comparisons of the works within most paragraphs. Once a guiding question is asked, such as *How can you keep your dignity under extreme circumstances?*, the answer is related to both novels immediately. The student integrates examples into the essay, referring to careful details of the novels, such as the butter incident in *The Handmaid's Tale* or how Shukov refuses to lick his bowl or wear his hat at dinner. The student makes use of linking words such as *nevertheless, while* and *even though*, which act as signposts for the reader. The opening idea about continued interest in Shakespeare returns in the conclusion as well, which gives the piece a sense of coherence.

Criterion E: Language – 4 out of 5

The student uses a good register that is characteristic of academic essays. The introduction is a good example of this, where the student writes a long but clear thesis statement. The student uses a wide range of vocabulary. The sentence structures follow parallel patterns. For example, the student starts one sentence with *While Offred's situation may sound unrealistic* and then another with *While the Soviet labour camps have been dismantled*. This creates a clear link between the ideas of these sentences. Well done.

How to structure an essay

In Chapter 2 you read about the PIE structural pattern that occurs throughout good paragraphs (see pages 60–61). PIE stands for Points, Illustrations and Explanations. We will take this method one step further here and ask *What kind of points belong in a literature essay, and where do we put them*?

A good essay is a well-structured essay. You may be bubbling with good ideas, but if they are not presented in a logical order for the reader, then they will be lost. The solution for this is a good outline. While you might think in a timed exam that there is no time to write an outline, writing one will actually *save* you time. If you simply write your ideas down as they come to you, you will find yourself backtracking, crossing lines out or squeezing lines in. Outlines help you think before you write.

What should your outline look like? There is no single outline to fit all essays. There is, however, a particular way of organising an essay that is commonly accepted as standard. Often referred to as the 'five-paragraph essay', this sort of essay has an introduction, usually three body paragraphs (but sometimes more), and a conclusion. The student's outline below is for the sample essay you read above, and the outline follows this five-paragraph structure. (Notice that the sample response has six paragraphs, not five, because of the four body paragraphs, not three).

Here are several key building blocks of essays.

Introduction

Attention grabber → Why are Shakespeare's plays timeless?
Factual information → Study of *The Handmaid's Tale* (HT) and *One Day in the Life of Ivan Denisovich* (ODLID)
Thesis → 2 reasons explain why works are timeless: 1 timeless themes, 2 good literary technique

Body paragraph 1

Point → Timeless themes – oppression and dignity. She = fertility machine. He = hard worker.
Illustration → She steals butter, he doesn't lick his bowl.
Explanation → Expression of beauty for her. Display of pride for him.

Body paragraph 2

Point → Novels' themes were relevant when written and relevant today.
Illustration → HT written 1985 during Islamic Revolution in Iran. Today – the Taliban.

ODLID about gulag in 1950s. Today – Abu Ghraib.
Explanation → People will always fear oppression.

Body paragraph 3
Point → HT cleverly crafted and therefore timeless.
Illustration → Stream of consciousness and clever epilogue.
Explanation → Style and structure suitable for dystopian literature.

Body paragraph 4
Point → ODLID cleverly crafted and therefore timeless.
Illustration → Not memoir: historical novel for a reason – risk of imprisonment.
Explanation → Free indirect speech puts author at safe distance from main character but draws reader in.

Conclusion
Summary → Timeless themes – oppression and dignity. Style and structure suit genre.
Put ideas into greater context and/or link to ideas from introduction → Reasons why we always return to writers such as Shakespeare.

Attention grabber

Try to capture your reader's attention immediately, by using a bold statement, a question, a quote or a brief anecdote in the first line of the introduction. (It is also important that you first write out the question that you are responding to at the top of the essay. This will help both you and the examiner.)

Factual information

In the opening paragraph state briefly what the essay will respond to. Just as in a letter to the editor you find the name of the article, the date of publication and author of the article the letter responds to, similarly in a literature essay you should give the title of the text or texts and author's name. This can be done in passing, as in the sample student response.

Thesis

A thesis statement captures the main idea and purpose of the essay. Half of the thesis is given to you in the Paper 2 exam question. The other half will be your answer to the question. Thesis statements are clear, succinct and persuasive. The sample student response suggests two reasons why literary works have received continued interest: timeless themes and strong literary devices. This thesis already provides a structure for the rest of the essay. Furthermore, notice how the sample student response mentions the titles of the works, the author's names and the thesis in one fluid statement. There is no weak or over-obvious wording such as *In this essay I will …* or *My essay is about question number …* Avoid the word *I* and make a strong statement.

Topic sentence (point)

Body paragraphs start with a topic sentence in which the first point is made. A topic sentence refers to one of the main ideas of the thesis statement. For this reason it is effective if the thesis statement consists of two or three components. The topic sentence serves as the guiding idea for a paragraph. Within the paragraph, there should be illustrations and explanations of the point that the topic sentence makes. Notice that the sample student response refers to the *timeless themes* idea of the thesis statement in the first topic sentence of the first body paragraph. This acts as a structural signpost for the reader.

Conclusion

The conclusion is often the most difficult bit to write because you need to keep the reader's interest without introducing any new ideas. Make a note of the following tips for concluding your essay:

- Try linking the conclusion to earlier ideas from the introduction. Notice how the sample student response starts with the Shakespeare question and answers it in the last line of the conclusion.
- Signposts are important for the examiner. Phrases like *To conclude, In summary* or *All in all* work well. If your sentences already sound conclusive and summative, you can skip them.
- Although you will need to summarise the main ideas, avoid simply repeating the points you have already made. For this reason it is important to use synonyms. The sample student response has the word *intrigued* in the body of the essay but the word *fascination* in the conclusion.
- Put your points into a wider context. The sample student response does this through the Shakespeare example.
- Do not apologise or sound weak. Avoid statements such as *We have examined only one of many positions on this subject.*

Activity 6.6

Read the HL sample student response on pages 154–55. Then using the five-paragraph essay structure, write the outline you think the student could have made before writing the essay.

Sample exam Paper 2 (SL/HL)

*Answer **one** essay question only. You must base your answer on at least two of the Part 3 works you have studied. Answers which are **not** based on a discussion of at least two Part 3 works will **not** score high marks. Your answer should address the ways in which language, context and structure contribute to your reading of each work.*

1 How do different forms of publishing affect the way literary texts are written and received?
2 How are changing family values reflected in literary texts?
3 How have certain philosophical movements influenced writers of literary texts?
4 How has one of the universal themes, for example love, murder, ambition or jealousy, been treated similarly or differently by writers in different cultures and in different times?
5 How have dominant and minority social groups been portrayed similarly and differently in literary texts through the ages?
6 How have literary texts been used over time as a form of social protest?

Sample student response (HL)

4 How has one of the universal themes, for example love, murder, ambition or jealousy, been treated similarly or differently by writers in different cultures and in different times?

One of the universal themes that we see in many literary works is murder. Three authors, William Shakespeare, Albert Camus and John Fowles, have treated this theme of murder both similarly and differently. By exploring *Macbeth*, *The Stranger* and *The Collector* we will see how each author used murder to comment on the meaning of life, how their ideas were influenced by their contexts, and how they used language to express these ideas.

While the storylines of all three works are different, they have one thing in common: someone dies. Since readers usually look for meaning behind such catastrophic events, we can assume that the characters of these works die for a reason. Why do the characters in these works die and what are we supposed to learn from their deaths? Macbeth kills Duncan, the King of Scotland, because he wants to become king himself, but his guilt comes back to haunt him and he is eventually killed too. There is an obvious moral lesson that ambition is dangerous and murder is not a shortcut to the top. The moral lesson is less obvious in *The Collector*, where Miranda, a posh, young, pacifistic girl, is abducted by an autistic, young madman, Frederick Clegg. She needlessly dies of pneumonia in his cellar. Nevertheless, there is a moral message that one can and should use violence to preserve one's life. *The Stranger*, however, offers a nearly impossible message to comprehend. When Meursault is asked in court why he killed an Arab on the beach, his only answer is 'because of the sun'. It is as if Camus is trying to say people are murdered for no reason at all. In this sense Camus is different from Shakespeare or Fowles, by telling us not to look for meaning behind the story of a murder.

In each story, *Macbeth*, *The Stranger* and *The Collector*, murder is treated differently because each author was inspired by different contexts. *Macbeth* is based on the history of King James I, who had just come to the throne in 1606 when Shakespeare presented his play. In reality, Banquo, who was James I's ancestor, helped Macbeth kill Duncan to become king. It would have created a political scandal and cost Shakespeare his head if he had presented it this way. Shakespeare presented Banquo as the rightful and just leader of Scotland. This flattered King James. People at that time believed it was a religious sin to kill a king. Kings were chosen by the hand of God. Shakespeare's moral lesson was not only 'murder is wrong', but 'murdering your king is wrong'. In order to understand the contexts of *The Stranger* and *The Collector*, we must also discuss the notion of God and religion. In a religious world, murder is obviously wrong and life naturally has meaning. Both characters, Meursault and Frederick Clegg, do not believe in religion and their murders are meaningless. The fact that they do not feel regret or remorse makes the reader feel rather uncomfortable. Instead these works seem to say, 'Murder happens. Accept it and move on.' Both Camus and Fowles were inspired by the ideas of Sartre, existentialism and the Theatre of the Absurd, a movement that explores the mismatch between people's attempts to create meaningful lives and the fact that life lacks meaning. Fowles's work is less absurd than Camus's in that Miranda seems to die for a reason: she is a victim of her own pacifism.

In the writing styles of all three authors, the focus is on portraying the thoughts of the murderer. In **Macbeth**, King Duncan is killed off-stage. We see Macbeth contemplating the murder, and he feels guilty about the murder. His speeches *Is this a dagger which I see before me …?* and *Will all great Neptune's ocean wash this blood / Clean from my hand?* are evidence of this. Just like Shakespeare, Camus and Fowles show us the thoughts of their perpetrators through first-person narration. In contrast, though, Meursault and Clegg are both surprisingly bland in how they describe their murders and indifferent about the aftermath of their murders. The language of both is simple and basic. Events are told to the reader as they unfold in a stream of consciousness and matter-of-fact tone. Only the immediate 'here and now' action seems to matter to the main character. This is a typical characteristic of existentialism.

The mind of a madman is something that intrigues all of us. We have seen how three authors approach this universal theme of murder differently. For a large part their contexts and sources of inspiration account for how they portray this theme differently. Interestingly the first-person perspective lends itself best to this subject matter. It is ironic that readers look for the meaning of life in the death of others.

Examiner's comments
The following comments give a good indication of how an examiner would assess this sample student response.

Criterion A: Knowledge and understanding – 5 out of 5
The student has done research on the contexts of the part 3 texts, as is seen in the references to King James and existentialism. The explanation of how kings and religion were perceived in Shakespeare's time is especially relevant. Similarly the student explains how Camus and Fowles were influenced by existentialism and the Theatre of the Absurd to different degrees. There is evidence of critical thinking, as the student sees similarities and differences between all three works with regards to theme.

Criterion B: Response to the question – 3 out of 5
The focus of the essay remains on the title question for the most part, but ignores the aspect of different cultures. Is there something typically French in the portrayal of Meursault, compared to Fowles's portrayal of the British Clegg? While this is a difficult question to answer, it remains part of the exam question and is expected of the student.

Criterion C: Understanding of the use and effects of stylistic features – 3 out of 5
The student identifies and compares the use of stylistic features very well. The tone of Meursault and Clegg is matter-of-fact, and the use of first-person, stream of consciousness narration is prevalent in the novels. However, what is the effect of these on the audience? Why did the authors choose these points of view for these stories about murder? These are questions that could receive more attention.

You will notice from the criteria that, as far as content is concerned, your essay must have three areas of focus: your understanding of the works in light of the question, the importance of context, and your understanding of stylistic devices. While criteria D (organisation) and E (language) must be apparent throughout the essay, the first three points can be tackled one by one in the essay. In fact, you will notice that both SL and HL sample responses are structured along the lines of the first three criteria. First they discuss common themes in relation to the question (Criterion B). Then they explain the significance of context (Criterion A). Finally they explore the effect of stylistic features (Criterion C). Following such a format will help keep your essay focused and effective.

Criterion D: Organisation and development – 4 out of 5

The essay follows a classic five-paragraph essay structure, with a thesis statement and topic sentences. The question *Why do the characters in these works die and what are we supposed to learn from their deaths?* is particularly effective. Such questions give paragraphs a lot of guidance and structure. Illustrations are integrated effectively as well, such as the quotations from *Macbeth* after a statement about the thoughts of the murderer. There could have been more examples like these for *The Collector* and *The Stranger*. The structure could have been a little more coherent with better use of linking words and clauses as well.

Criterion E: Language – 4 out of 5

The flow of the text is very good. While the essay is free of grammatical errors, the student could have taken risks with more difficult sentence structures. Many sentences are fragmented and choppy, needing to be connected to other ideas. With a few minor slip-ups, the register is for the most part academic and appropriate.

Ten ways to invigorate your writing

The higher level sample student response could have been written more effectively. While writing styles may vary from person to person, there are several characteristics of good writing that everyone should be aware of. Here are ten ways to invigorate your writing style. When used properly, they can change a score of 7 for Criterion C into a 10.

1 Avoid *One of …* and *The fact that …*

Sentences that begin with *One of the …* or *The fact that …* tend to be cumbersome for the reader. They are more characteristic of spoken language.

Instead of

> One of the universal themes that we see in many literary works is murder.
> The fact that they do not feel regret or remorse makes the reader feel rather uncomfortable.

use

> Murder is a universal theme found in many literary works.
> Their lack of regret or remorse makes the reader feel uncomfortable.

2 Avoid *There is* or *It is*

The verb *be* can often be replaced by stronger, more descriptive verbs. Similarly the impersonal subjects *there* and *it* can usually be replaced by stronger, more meaningful subjects.

Instead of

> There is an obvious moral lesson that ambition is dangerous.
> It is ironic that readers look for the meaning of life in the death of others.

use

> The moral lesson here is that ambition is dangerous.
> Ironically, readers look for the meaning of life in the death of others.

3 Avoid *obviously* and *naturally*

Nothing is obvious for the reader, so words such *obviously* or *naturally* are presumptuous. (Notice in the example above that the word *obvious* has been removed, making giving the statement more impact.)

Instead of

> In a religious world, murder is obviously wrong and life naturally has meaning.

use

> In a religious world, murder is wrong and life has meaning.

4 Avoid passive verbs

Avoid passive verb constructions. Active ones engage the reader more.

Instead of

> In each story, **Macbeth, The Stranger** and **The Collector**, murder is treated differently.

use

> Each story, **Macbeth, The Stranger** and **The Collector**, treats murder differently.

5 Avoid vague language

If you want to be persuasive in your essay, you will have to be clear. This is especially applicable to quantifiers, or words that indicate an amount.

Instead of

> For a large part their contexts and sources of inspiration account for how they portray this theme differently.

use

> Their contexts and sources of inspiration account for how they portray this theme differently.

6 Use the *-ing* form

Using subject–verb–object syntax can become very boring for the reader, when the subjects are always common countable nouns. Instead try creating noun phrases using gerunds (-*ing* forms).

Instead of

> It would have created a political scandal and cost Shakespeare his head if he had presented the play this way.

use

> Presenting the play this way would have created a political scandal and cost Shakespeare his head.

7 Use efficient noun phrases

This tip is similar to Tip 2 above and is about avoiding clumsy sentences with too many words.

Instead of

> Both Camus and Fowles were inspired by the ideas of Sartre, existentialism and the Theatre of the Absurd, a movement that explores the mismatch between people's attempts to create meaningful lives and the fact that life lacks meaning.

use

> Both Camus and Fowles were inspired by the ideas of Sartre, existentialism and the mismatch between people's attempts to create meaningful lives and the meaninglessness of life.

8 Use parallel structures

Readers and listeners like parallel constructions because they contain patterns that can be easily understood. The sentence below can be rewritten with a repeated -*ing* form.

Instead of

> We see Macbeth contemplating the murder, and he feels guilty about the murder.

use

> We see Macbeth contemplating the murder and feeling guilty about it.

9 Use varied sentence length

Keep your reader interested by varying the lengths of your sentences. Offset long sentences with short ones, and look for choppy, fragmented sentences that can be strung together.

Instead of

> The language of both is simple and basic. Events are told to the reader as they unfold in a stream of consciousness and matter-of-fact tone. Only the immediate 'here and now' actions seem to matter to the main character. This is a typical characteristic of existentialism.

use

> The reader learns of events as they unfold via a stream of consciousness, recounted simply and in a matter-of-fact tone, where only the immediate 'here and now' seems to matter to the main character. This is typical of existentialism.

10 Use linking words and clauses

You must indicate the relationships between your ideas as you present them to your reader. Look again at the list of linking words on page 67. Besides using linking words, also make good use of relative clauses, which are clauses like this one that use words such as *which* and *that* to link ideas together and make longer sentences. If you have a sentence starting with *This*, you can probably join it on to the sentence before.

Instead of

> Shakespeare presented Banquo as the rightful and just leader of Scotland. This flattered King James. People at that time believed it was a religious sin to kill a king. Kings were chosen by the hand of God.

use

> Instead, Shakespeare presented Banquo as the rightful and just leader of Scotland, which flattered King James. Furthermore, people at that time believed it was a sin to kill a king, as kings were chosen by God.

Chapter 6 summary

The focus in this chapter has been the context of composition, on gaining a greater understanding of literature by placing ourselves in the mind of the writer and learning about literary traditions. You began by looking closely at some examples of dystopian and historical fiction. You have also seen the importance of researching the contexts in which literary texts are written and examined the philosophical and artistic movements of modernism and existentialism in relation to an extract from a novel by John Fowles. Understanding the zeitgeist of a writer opens new windows on a literary text and allows you to read more deeply between the lines. Finally, as preparation for the Paper 2 exam, you have learnt about the five-paragraph essay structure and worked through ten tips to improve your writing style.

Chapter 6 brings to a close Part 3 of the coursebook. By now, you will be familiar with the contexts of interpretation and composition, and know how they can shape meaning in the literary texts you are studying. In the next chapter you will be finding out more about the mechanics of fiction. Before deciding how effective a certain writing style is for the purpose of a text, it is necessary to know more about the writing devices writers have at their disposal and how well they have chosen them in their texts.

tip

You may have noticed that the list is divided into two sets: Tips 1–5 start with *Avoid …* and Tips 6–10 with *Use …* Think of them as the dos and don'ts of writing. In pairs, check each other's essays in response to an exam question. Have you included all the dos and avoided all the don'ts? Make a checklist for reviewing each other's work.

You could also try working in groups of ten, with each student assigned one of the tips to watch out for. Pass your essays around and as a group screen them for all ten ways to invigorate your writing style.

Further resources

The Little, Brown Compact Handbook by Jane E. Aaron is an excellent, American guide on how to organise essays, invigorate writing style, use punctuation and cite sources. You will also find it useful long after you have finished your IB Diploma course!

Chapter 7 The mechanics of fiction

Objectives

By the end of this chapter you will be able to

- explain how plot, character and setting reflect the deeper meanings of a literary text
- discuss the conflicts and themes found in literary texts
- understand how narrative techniques enable writers to engage readers
- plan and write a written task 2, a critical response to a text, or texts (HL only).

In Chapters 5 and 6 you concentrated on the reasons for reading fiction and the importance of context in interpreting literary texts. In order to gain a deeper understanding of literature, you learnt to explore the contexts in which texts were written and received. The focus in Part 4 is again on gaining a deeper understanding of literary texts, but whereas in Part 3 you took a historical-biographical approach to texts, in Part 4 you will take a Formalist approach. In other words, through the close reading of texts you will be looking at the literary devices writers use to convey meaning.

To start you thinking about how writers engage readers, you will first read a literary text in the short Unit 7.1 and begin to question aspects of the writer's craft. Then in Unit 7.2 you will look more closely at the devices of plot, character and setting. These are important for your understanding of the deeper, more abstract notions contained in the text, such as theme and conflict, which you will look at in Unit 7.3. In Unit 7.4, you will explore narrative voice, or the different points of view, tenses and ways of narration and speech that can be used to tell stories. Finally, at the end of the chapter, you will have a chance to see two samples of work.

Throughout this part of the coursebook you will meet and become familiar with a bank of literary terms and concepts that you can use in the individual oral commentary. This exam, which will be covered more thoroughly in Chapter 8, tests your understanding of literary devices and your ability to analyse a passage of fiction. Before you begin, however, make sure you know exactly what you will be required to do in part 4 of the exam, the individual oral commentary, and how you will be assessed.

Unit 7.1 Engaging the reader

Have you ever read a novel that you just could not put down? What makes a novel a 'page-turner'? In Chapter 7 we discussed the idea that reading fiction involves the suspension of disbelief, meaning readers accept the situation the author presents to them without questioning the plausibility of a storyline. Having said this, the writer also has to give the reader a reason to engage further with the story.

In Chapter 5 you examined the question of why writers of literary texts use literary devices and explored their purpose of evoking a response from their readers. In this last part of the coursebook you will be exploring the craft of literature further and discovering more about the devices authors use to keep readers listening, viewing and reading. Remember that learning about literary devices, and how they are applied to literary texts, will help you answer one fundamental question: *How does the writer engage the reader?*

Start thinking about how writers engage readers by examining how various devices are employed at the start of the novel *Enduring Love* by Ian McEwan. Text 7.1, an extract of the opening paragraphs of the book, illustrates a number of literary concepts you will be meeting in this chapter. Read Text 7.1 and ask yourself how it manages to engage you.

Figure 7.1 A scene from the 2004 film of Ian McEwan's page-turner *Enduring Love*, (directed by Roger Michell).

Text 7.1 *Enduring Love*, Ian McEwan, 1997

The beginning is simple to mark. We were in sunlight under a turkey oak, partly protected from a strong, gusty wind. I was kneeling on the grass with a corkscrew in my hand, and Clarissa was passing me the bottle – a 1987 Daumas Gassac. This was the moment, this was the pinprick on the time map: I was stretching out my hand, and as the cool neck and the black foil touched my palm, we heard a man's shout. We turned to look across the field and saw the danger. Next thing, I was running towards it. The transformation was absolute: I don't recall dropping the corkscrew, or getting to my feet, or making a decision, or hearing the caution Clarissa called after me. What idiocy, to be racing into this story and its labyrinths, sprinting away from our happiness among the fresh spring grasses by the oak. There was the shout again, and a child's cry, enfeebled by the wind that roared in the tall trees along the hedgerows. I ran faster. And there, suddenly, from different points around the field, four other men were converging on the scene, running like me.

I see us from three hundred feet up, through the eyes of the buzzard we had watched earlier, soaring, circling and dipping in the tumult of currents: five men running silently towards the centre of a hundred-acre field. I approached from the south-east, with the wind at my back. About two hundred yards to my left two men ran side by side. They were farm labourers who had been repairing the fence along the field's southern edge where it skirts the road. The same distance beyond them was the motorist, John Logan, whose car was banked on the grass verge with its door, or doors, wide open. Knowing what I know now, it's odd to evoke the figure of Jed Parry directly ahead of me, emerging from a line of beeches on the far side of the field a quarter of a mile away, running into the wind. To the buzzard Parry and I were tiny forms, our white shirts brilliant against the green, rushing towards each other like lovers, innocent of the grief this entanglement would bring. The encounter that would unhinge us was minutes away, its enormity disguised from us not only by the barrier of time but by the colossus in the centre of the field that drew us in with the power of a terrible ratio that set fabulous magnitude against the puny human distress at its base.

What was Clarissa doing? She said she walked quickly towards the centre of... the event I am about to describe, the fall – she had almost caught us up and was well placed as an observer, unencumbered by participation, by the ropes

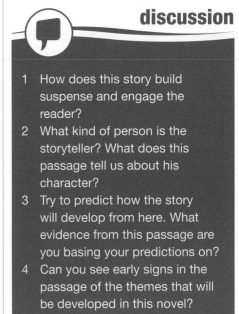

discussion

1 How does this story build suspense and engage the reader?
2 What kind of person is the storyteller? What does this passage tell us about his character?
3 Try to predict how the story will develop from here. What evidence from this passage are you basing your predictions on?
4 Can you see early signs in the passage of the themes that will be developed in this novel?

and the shouting, and by our fatal lack of co-operation. What I describe is shaped by what Clarissa saw too, by what we told each other in the time of obsessive re-examination that followed: the aftermath, an appropriate term for what happened in a field waiting for its early summer mowing. The aftermath, the second crop, the growth prompted by that first cut in May.

I'm holding back, delaying the information. I'm lingering in the prior moment because it was a time when other outcomes were still possible; the convergence of six figures in a flat green space has a comforting geometry from the buzzard's perspective, the knowable, limited plane of the snooker table. The initial conditions, the force and the direction of the force, define all the consequent pathways, all the angles of collision and return, and the glow of the overhead light bathes the field, the baize and all its moving bodies, in reassuring clarity. I think that while we were still converging, before we made contact, we were in a state of mathematical grace. I linger on our dispositions, the relative distances and the compass point – because as far as these occurrences were concerned, this was the last time I understood anything clearly at all.

What were we running towards? I don't think any of us would ever know fully. But superficially the answer was a balloon. Not the nominal space that encloses a cartoon character's speech or thought, or, by analogy, the kind that's driven by mere hot air. It was an enormous balloon filled with helium, that elemental gas forged from hydrogen in the nuclear furnace of the stars, first step along the way in the generation of multiplicity and variety of matter in the universe, including our selves and all our thoughts.

We were running towards a catastrophe, which itself was a kind of furnace in whose heat identities and fates would buckle into new shapes. At the base of the balloon was a basket in which there was a boy and, by the basket, clinging to a rope, was a man in need of help.

In Text 7.1 the writer draws you into the story and makes you want to read on by creating an atmosphere of **suspense**. As you read the opening lines from the novel, you have probably already used your first impressions to try to predict how the story will develop and what themes, or messages, may come out of it.

In your discussion about the extract from *Enduring Love*, before you could comment on abstract ideas such as suspense, theme and the personality of the storyteller, it was necessary to consider some basic questions about the story: *What is happening in the opening scene? Who are the people involved? And where does it take place?* These questions concern the concrete elements of fiction: plot, character and setting, which you will explore in the next unit.

Unit 7.2 Plot, character and setting

Has a friend ever asked you about a film you have recently seen? Your first response often includes a quick summary of the storyline or a brief description of the characters. You may have to describe the **setting** in order to give an impression of the story.

Plot, character and setting are the basic building blocks of fiction. From your reading of and discussion about Text 7.1 it should be becoming clear that writers do not decide upon the plot, characters and setting by chance. Every detail of a story is meaningful and placed there for a purpose in order to convey a deeper message.

Key terms

Suspense is the feeling of tension or anxiety felt by an audience as events develop and work towards their climax in a work of fiction.

Setting describes the backdrop against which the action of a story takes place. It can describe both the physical and the emotional landscape of a work.

Activity 7.1

Think of a film you have seen recently. Without giving away the name of the film or any of the actors in it, describe the storyline, the characters and the setting of the film.

1 Can the other students guess which film you are talking about? Can you guess which films they have seen?

2 Are you interested in watching any of the other films after hearing their descriptions? Why or why not?

3 Were your descriptions superficial compared with the literary discussions you have had before about novels or plays? In what ways?

As you think ahead and prepare for your individual oral commentary, it is important to know the difference between two key skills: summarising and interpretation. There is a continuum between these two. At one end you retell the superficial elements of a story (summarising); at the other you explain the deeper meaning of these (interpretation). The individual oral commentary requires you to maintain a balance between summarising and interpretation. Simply summarising will not show your understanding of the work, while offering interpretations without having established the basics of plot, character and setting will sound like hasty generalisations.

Plot

The simple definition of the word *plot* is the series of events and actions that occur in a story. A more complex definition includes the types of conflict that occur in a story. While these can be difficult to separate when discussing some stories, for the sake of clarity we will take the definition of *plot* to be the accumulation of dramatic events. (You will find out more about the element of conflict in Unit 7.3.)

Plot structure

As you read your part 3 and 4 texts, you will need to be able to identify the structural elements of plot. In 1863 the German novelist Gustav Freytag developed a simple visualisation of plot, known as Freytag's Pyramid. He identified five elements of plot structure: exposition, rising action, climax, falling action, and **denouement** or resolution. Although this model has its strengths and weaknesses, it serves as a good starting point for a discussion of plot and its structure. The following explanations relate the five aspects to the novel *Enduring Love*.

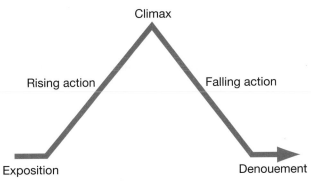

Figure 7.2 Freytag's Pyramid, showing the five component parts of plot structure.

Exposition

Text 7.1 is an excellent example of **exposition**. Exposition comes at the beginning of a story, where the reader learns key information about the characters, the setting and the plot. In the opening lines of Text 7.1 we learn that the main character has a girlfriend or wife, enjoys expensive wine and is somewhat scientific by nature. The setting is a grassy field in spring and the plot will have something to do with *a man's shout*, which triggers events and sets the story in motion.

Notice how the most significant word, *balloon*, is not mentioned until the final lines of the passage. The scream causes alarm, but the narrator delays information. When a character or narrator knows more than the reader, suspense is easily created.

Key terms

Denouement is the French word for 'unknotting', used to describe the resolution of a story's plot or complicated situation.

Exposition is the part of a story where the reader is provided with information about plot, character and setting.

Another key element to watch out for in the exposition is **foreshadowing**. Foreshadowing is where the narrator gives the reader clues about where the story is going. There are several examples of foreshadowing in Text 7.1, slight indications that this story will be about more than a hot-air balloon accident: *To the buzzard Parry and I were tiny forms, our white shirts brilliant against the green, rushing towards each other like lovers, innocent of the grief this entanglement would bring.* In fact the novel is about the narrator, Joe Rose, and this other man, Jed Parry. It is also about Joe's failing relationship with Clarissa, which we learn from the foreshadowing: *What idiocy, to be racing into this story and its labyrinths, sprinting away from our happiness among the fresh spring grasses by the oak.*

Rising action

The rising action of the plot is the part in which it develops and the characters come into a state of conflict. The action already heightens in this first scene from *Enduring Love*, as the main character stands up and runs towards the out-of-control balloon. Nevertheless, it is the aftermath of the event that creates the problem: after a man has fallen to his death, one of the potential rescuers, Jed Parry, falls in love with the narrator and potential rescuer, Joe. Jed suffers from de Clerambault's syndrome – a disorder that makes Jed think Joe loves him back. Jed stalks Joe, nearly driving Joe insane and straining his relationship with Clarissa, which is the rising action of *Enduring Love*.

Climax

The climax of the plot is the turning point in the story, where events have come to a head or the tension has reached its highest point. The illustration of Freytag's Pyramid in Figure 7.2 might make you think that the climax comes in the middle of a story. The climax, however, often comes shortly before the end. At the risk of giving away what happens at the climax of *Enduring Love*, events culminate after Joe has bought a gun, and Clarissa, who thought Jed was a figment of Joe's imagination, is finally confronted with Jed, who has broken into her flat armed with a knife.

Falling action

The falling action of the plot is often very brief, as readers discover the result of the climax. In *Enduring Love*, characters watch in horror as blood is spilled, an ambulance comes and tears are shed. The falling action does not always have to be brief and towards the very end of the story. Some unconventional stories, such as *Disgrace* by J.M. Coetzee (see Text 7.9 on pages 186–87), reach a climax very early on. The majority of the story is then about the characters dealing with the effects of the climax – so the falling action is the main part of the plot here. Remember that not all fiction follows the conventional structure implied by Freytag's Pyramid.

Denouement

This French word means an 'unknotting'. It suggests that the rising action and climax have become tied in a knot which has to be untied before the story can be resolved and end. Once the tension of a story has unravelled, we see the characters dealing with its effects. The novel *Enduring Love* ends with two appendices, which contain the denouement. In the first, containing a medical report on de Clerambault's syndrome, Joe and Clarissa are mentioned in passing as the victims of a patient, Jed. They have adopted a child and resolved the problems in their relationship. The second appendix is a letter from Jed to Joe, in which he explains that he will be admitted to a psychiatric hospital after years of treatment have failed to cure him of his love for Joe.

Activity 7.2

1 After reading your literary texts for parts 3 and 4, use a copy of the table below to analyse the stages of the plot in terms of the five parts of Freytag's Pyramid (see Figure 7.2). Think how the story evolves and mark the events of the story in the appropriate part of the table.

2 Your analysis may be different from how some of the other students group the events of the story. Discuss any differences in your tables.

3 Analysing the plots by completing a table will help you see the similarities and differences in structure between your texts. Bear in mind that some of the texts you read may not contain all five elements of Freytag's Pyramid, and there may be differences in the proportions of each stage.

	Part 3 texts			Part 4 texts		
	1	2	3 (HL)	4	5	6 (HL)
Exposition						
Rising action						
Climax						
Falling action						
Denouement						

Types of plot

Now that you are able to identify the elements of plot structure you will look at some of the types of plot that are popular with readers. Have you ever noticed that a lot of stories seem to be different variations of the same plot? For example: two people meet; they cannot be together; they overcome an obstacle that is keeping them apart; they are happy together. Simple outlines such as this strip stories of their intricacies and suggest there are only a few basic types of plot. Tolkien's *The Lord of the Rings* is one long quest, as are Homer's *Odyssey*, Stevenson's *Treasure Island* and Spielberg's *Raiders of the Lost Ark*. In all of these, someone is after something precious, be it treasure, an artefact or getting home. This sort of plot can therefore be called 'the quest'.

As you think about how stories engage readers, you have to ask what they have that appeals to human nature. People have always liked quests and always will. Similarly, love stories, comedies, tragedies or monster stories, if they are made relevant to a contemporary audience, will always strike a chord with readers. The key for writers is to avoid **cliché** when inventing new stories in classic genres. *Frankenstein*, *King Kong* and *Jaws* all brought something to the 'overcoming the monster' genre that was new at the time. Close imitations of them made today would not engage readers as successfully as the originals.

Ian McEwan engages readers of *Enduring Love* by creating a new rendition of the monster genre. People who suffer from de Clerambault's syndrome are considered odd and frightening. It is this fear which keeps many readers intrigued throughout the novel.

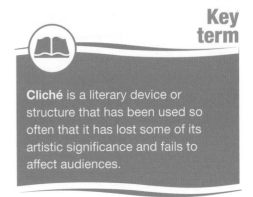

Key term

Cliché is a literary device or structure that has been used so often that it has lost some of its artistic significance and fails to affect audiences.

Activity 7.3

The journalist Christopher Booker argues that there are seven basic plots:

1 'Overcoming the monster' is a plot structure that involves a threatening predator: a person or thing that is abnormal and/or dangerous. Arguably *Enduring Love* falls into this category.
2 'Rags to riches' is a plot structure that focuses on the improvement of a character from a lower or deprived state of being to a more enlightened and wealthy position in society. *Pygmalion* fits this category.
3 'The quest' involves a call to a journey with a purpose, some thrilling ordeals and a triumphant end.
4 'The voyage and return' is different from 'the quest', as the main characters end up in a strange place and must find a way to get home.
5 'The comedy' is a classical term for works whose purpose is to make us laugh about the nature of life.
6 'The tragedy' is another classical term, to describe works that show how life can be sad and apparently unjust.
7 'Rebirth' is a kind of story where the main character goes through a change and discovers a truth by which to live a more fruitful life.

Decide which type of plot matches the texts you are reading for parts 3 and 4.

Figure 7.3 How true is this cartoon? Does the humour reflect our expectations of fiction?

Character

Writers of fiction most often engage readers through their portrayal of the characters involved. If they are depicted well, you can identify with fictitious characters and see life through their eyes. When studying the characters in your literary texts, ask yourself two questions: *What function do they serve in the story?* and *How does the author bring them to life?*

The function of characters

In every work of fiction there are characters who want either to move the action forward (the protagonists) or prevent an action from happening (the antagonists). Readers often feel empathy for a protagonist and want to see him or her achieve a goal. The antagonist, however, stands in the protagonist's way, which creates tension or conflict. As you will realise, in *Enduring Love* Joe Rose is the protagonist and Jed Parry is the antagonist, who stands in the way of Joe's relationship with Clarissa.

As you read your part 3 and 4 texts, you will also want to look out for characters who act as a foil. These are the characters whose qualities are in contrast to those of the main character. For example, in *Enduring Love*, Clarissa writes a dissertation on romanticism while Joe writes articles on science. Ironically, it is he who is emotionally caught up in the aftermath of the balloon accident while she remains very logical and detached. Authors often put two opposite characters in close proximity to each other in order to comment on people's behaviour, values and qualities.

Characterisation

When comparing and contrasting the characters in your literary texts, you will notice that some characters evolve more than others. While some characters are static or flat, others are more complex and rounded. How does a writer engage readers through characterisation and create rounded characters that we can believe in? Writers make use of several techniques to bring characters to life, through dialogue, actions and thoughts.

Dialogue

What people say in certain situations defines who they are. In the play *A Streetcar Named Desire* by Tennessee Williams, which we will look at more closely in the next unit (see Text 7.4), one character, Mitch, asks another, Blanche, what she does for a living:

Mitch	I bet you teach art or music? (*Blanche laughs delicately.*) Of course I could be wrong. You might teach arithmetic.
Blanche	Never arithmetic, sir; never arithmetic! (*With a laugh.*) I don't even know my multiplication tables! No, I have the misfortune of being an English instructor. I attempt to instil a bunch of bobby-soxers and drug-store Romeos with reverence for Hawthorne and Whitman and Poe!

Blanche's answer says a lot about who she is. She has the *misfortune* of being an English teacher. She is not ashamed of not even knowing her multiplication tables. She thinks of her students as *bobby-soxers and drug-store Romeos*. She does not just say she teaches her students about American writers; she says she *instils reverence* for them. Her speech in this dialogue is partly why audiences see her as melodramatic.

Key terms

Protagonist is the main character in a dramatic story who makes events and action move forward towards a particular goal.

Antagonist is the character of a dramatic story who stands in the way of the antagonists and tries to prevent them from achieving their goal.

Foil is a character whose qualities contrast with those of the main character, in order to expose them to the reader.

Melodrama refers to works of fiction that exaggerate plot or character and appeal to the audience's emotions.

Key terms

Soliloquy is a dramatic device in theatre where a character talks to himself or herself through a monologue addressed directly to the audience, expressing thoughts which the audience can hear and other characters cannot.

Atmosphere describes the mood of a story, created through both the tone of the narrator and the setting of the story.

Actions

What characters do in certain situations defines them. In Text 7.1 Joe Rose's instinctive response on hearing the cry for help is to race across the field towards the hot-air balloon: *I don't recall dropping the corkscrew, or getting to my feet, or making a decision, or hearing the caution Clarissa called after me.* This is contrasted with Clarissa's response: *She said she walked quickly towards the centre of… the event I am about to describe.* Readers empathise with the characters in fiction and find themselves asking what they would do in a similar situation, and writers engage those readers by answering that question.

Thoughts

Characters are brought to life when writers give us a window into their mind. In plays this is often done through **soliloquy**. In film it is often achieved with voiceover. In narrative prose it is possible to know the thoughts of the narrator or main character as the author can report them in the same way as they would report speech. (You will learn more about narration in Unit 7.4.) In Text 7.1 we establish quite quickly that Joe Rose is interested in science as he tells his story using words such as *compass*, *geometry* and *angles*. He speaks of the balloon as something *filled with helium, that elemental gas forged from hydrogen in the nuclear furnace of the stars.* Details such as these give a clue to the way the character thinks and reveals a lot about him.

Activity 7.4

1   In relation to one of the part 3 or 4 texts you are reading, explain which character is the protagonist, which is the antagonist and which the foil. How do the foils expose the flaws of the protagonists?
2   Using one of your texts, think about the author's use of characterisation. Make a few statements to describe one of the characters. Support your statements with examples of the character's dialogue, actions or thoughts.

Setting

Where a story takes place determines to a great extent what can plausibly happen and the context in which we interpret events. It is important to establish a broad understanding of setting so that you do not restrict yourself to discussing just the physical surroundings in a story. Setting includes the entire physical and emotional backdrop of where and when a story takes place. While setting can shape characters and mirror the ideas of their time, it can also make characters want to run away or feel lonely. Setting is the internal context of a story.

The following four concepts – mirror, mould, escape and alienation – all relate to setting. Think how you would use these tools when discussing the relationship between a story's setting, its characters and you, the reader, for your part 3 and 4 texts.

Mirror

The setting of a story usually reflects its **atmosphere**. Atmosphere describes the mood of a story. In a novel such as George Orwell's *Nineteen Eighty-Four*, for example, the mood is very dark, the atmosphere is one of fear, as characters live under the totalitarian regime of Big Brother. The setting acts as a mirror of the zeitgeist of the time in which the story occurs and lays down expectations for the reader.

Some of the most interesting stories are about characters who behave in stark contrast to the expectations produced by the setting. In *Enduring Love* (Text 7.1) for example, you do not expect someone to die on a sunny spring day when people are enjoying a glass of wine at a picnic under an oak tree.

Mould

Characters are often shaped by their setting. For example, in *Lord of the Flies*, a story about a group of boys who become stranded on a deserted island, some of the boys begin to act like savages, behaving according to the natural law of the survival of the fittest. In *Enduring Love* the balloon accident is part of the setting that shapes Joe Rose and makes him lose control of his life, leaving him wondering if he could have done anything different on that day that would have saved the man's life.

Escape

Sometimes, especially in works of fantasy, the setting allows us to escape our own reality. Writers engage readers by creating a setting that is different from our own world, such as in *The Wizard of Oz*, where Dorothy lands in a place of fairies and talking scarecrows. This story, however, is typical of many stories with escapist settings. The great and powerful wizard turns out to be a hoax. Escapist settings often end up reflecting and commenting on the reality of the reader.

Alienation

Many works of fiction use hostile settings in which characters are forced into exile, become refugees or feel homesick. Readers tend to be fascinated by these notions of alienation, as they appeal to our basic needs: shelter, warmth and love. Ian McEwan engages the readers of *Enduring Love* by creating a setting where Jed Parry, the stalker, causes Joe Rose to become alienated at work, in his relationship and at home.

Figure 7.4 Poverty in India: Mulk Raj Anand (1905–2004) was known for exposing the inequalities of the caste system in India through his novel *Untouchable*.

Activity 7.5

Read the following extract, Text 7.2, and comment on the four aspects of setting – mirror, mould, escape and alienation. How are all four concepts relevant to this text? Give examples from the extract to illustrate your answers.

Text 7.2 *Untouchable*, Mulk Raj Anand, 1935

The outcastes' colony was a group of mud-walled houses that clustered together in two rows, under the shadow both of the town and the cantonment, but outside their boundaries and separate from them. There lived the scavengers, the leather-workers, the washermen, the barbers, the water-carriers, the grass-cutters and other outcastes from Hindu society. A brook ran near the lane, once with crystal-clear water, now soiled by the dirt and filth of the public latrines situated about it, the odour of the hides and skins of dead carcasses left to dry on its banks, the dung of donkeys, sheep, horses, cows and buffaloes heaped up to be made into fuel cakes, and the biting, choking, pungent fumes that oozed from its sides. The absence of a drainage system had, through the rains of various seasons, made of the quarter a marsh which gave out the most offensive stink. And altogether the ramparts of human and animal refuse that lay on the outskirts of this little colony, and the ugliness, the squalor and the misery which lay within it, made it an 'uncongenial' place to live in.

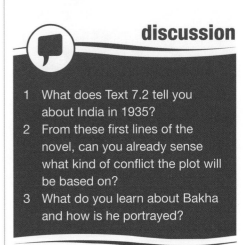

discussion

1   What does Text 7.2 tell you about India in 1935?
2   From these first lines of the novel, can you already sense what kind of conflict the plot will be based on?
3   What do you learn about Bakha and how is he portrayed?

Figure 7.5 Ernest Hemingway (1899–1961) was a prolific and adventurous author, who often set his stories in the countries where he had lived and travelled.

At least so thought Bakha, a young man of eighteen, strong and able-bodied, the son of Lakha, the Jemadar[1] of all the sweepers in the town and the cantonment, and officially in charge of the three rows of public latrines which lined the extremest end of the colony, by the brook-side. But then he had been working in the barracks of a British regiment for some years on a sort of probation with a remote uncle and had been caught by the glamour of the 'white man's' life. The Tommies had treated him as a human being and he had learnt to think of himself as superior to his fellow-outcastes. Otherwise, the rest of the outcastes, with the possible exception of Chota, the leather-worker's son, who oiled his hair profusely, and parted it like the Englishmen on one side, wore a pair of shorts at hockey and smoked cigarettes like them, and of Ram Charan, the washerman's son who aped Chota and Bakha in turn, were content with their lot.

[1] **Jemadar**   head or foreman

Plot, character and setting in practice

You have now been introduced to the basic building blocks of dramatic fiction: plot, character and setting. Arguably, without them, there cannot be a story. When these three devices are used effectively, readers are engaged and can unlock the deeper meaning of the text. You have seen how the concepts apply to Ian McEwan's novel *Enduring Love*. You are now going to examine how they are used in the opening lines of a short story by Ernest Hemingway, *Hills Like White Elephants*. As you read Text 7.3, ask yourself how you are engaged by the plot, the characters and the setting of the story.

discussion

1   Based on these first lines – the exposition of the story – what do we, as readers, know about the character, storyline and setting? Can you predict how the story will develop?

2   How does Hemingway bring his characters to life through dialogue and action? What can you say about the man, the woman and the waitress, based on this passage? Give evidence to support your statements.

3   The title of the story alludes to the setting. How do you think setting is important to understanding the meaning of the story? Refer to the aspects of setting (mirror, mould, escape and alienation) in your answer.

Text 7.3 *Hills Like White Elephants*, Ernest Hemingway, 1927

The hills across the valley of the Ebro were long and white. On this side there was no shade and no trees and the station was between two lines of rails in the sun. Close against the side of the station there was the warm shadow of the building and a curtain, made of strings of bamboo beads, hung across the open door into the bar, to keep out flies. The American and the girl with him sat at a table in the shade, outside the building. It was very hot and the express from Barcelona would come in forty minutes. It stopped at this junction for two minutes and went on to Madrid.

'What should we drink?' the girl asked. She had taken off her hat and put it on the table.

'It's pretty hot,' the man said.

'Let's drink beer.'

'Dos cervezas,' the man said into the curtain.

'Big ones?' a woman asked from the doorway.

'Yes. Two big ones.'

The woman brought two glasses of beer and two felt pads. She put the felt pads and the beer glasses on the table and looked at the man and the girl. The girl was looking off at the line of hills. They were white in the sun and the country was brown and dry.

'They look like white elephants,' she said.

'I've never seen one,' the man drank his beer.

'No, you wouldn't have.'

'I might have,' the man said. 'Just because you say I wouldn't have doesn't prove anything.'

The girl looked at the bead curtain. 'They've painted something on it,' she said. 'What does it say?'

'Anis del Toro. It's a drink.'

'Could we try it?'

The man called 'Listen' through the curtain. The woman came out from the bar.

'Four reales.'

'We want two Anis del Toro.'

'With water?'

'Do you want it with water?'

'I don't know,' the girl said. 'Is it good with water?'

'It's all right.'

'You want them with water?' asked the woman.

'Yes, with water.'

'It tastes like licorice,' the girl said and put the glass down.

'That's the way with everything.'

'Yes,' said the girl. 'Everything tastes of licorice. Especially all the things you've waited so long for, like absinthe.'

'Oh, cut it out.'

'You started it,' the girl said. 'I was being amused. I was having a fine time.'

'Well, let's try and have a fine time.'

'All right. I was trying. I said the mountains looked like white elephants. Wasn't that bright?'

'That was bright.'

'I wanted to try this new drink. That's all we do, isn't it – look at things and try new drinks?'

'I guess so.'

The girl looked across at the hills.

'They're lovely hills,' she said. 'They don't really look like white elephants. I just meant the coloring of their skin through the trees.'

'Should we have another drink?'

'All right.'

The warm wind blew the bead curtain against the table.

'The beer's nice and cool,' the man said.

'It's lovely,' the girl said.

…

Higher level

Higher level students have the opportunity to explore fiction through more classroom discussions and reading. You will want to make a collection of short stories that address the key points from part 4 of your course. A practical solution to collecting a good number of stories is to add an anthology to your course booklist.

Further resources

Perrine's Literature: Structure, Sound and Sense by Thomas R. Arp and Greg Johnson is both an anthology of fiction and a textbook on literature. It is very accessible, containing short stories that lend themselves well to classroom discussion.

The Riverside Anthology of Short Fiction by Dean Baldwin includes an excellent selection of stories and useful discussion questions.

Unit 7.3 **Conflict and theme**

In the previous unit we studied the basic building blocks of dramatic fiction – plot, character and setting – which relate to the physical elements of events, people and places. Once a writer has these physical structures in place, an abstract, meaningful story can unfold. But what makes a story meaningful?

By nature we, as readers, are intrigued by conflict. If you are a keen sports fan and have followed your team through a tournament, or if you have ever seen a crowd quickly forming round two people fighting, you will understand how fascinating human struggle can be. We look for a purpose in this struggle as we want life to have a deeper meaning. In fiction, there are many examples of themes that deal with human struggle, fictional representations of struggle caused by people's pride, lust, rage, ambition or inequality, for example. As we look for deeper meaning in the texts we read and these are themes that resonate with us all, they engage us as readers and keep us interested in turning the pages.

Conflict

Conflict is related to plot and plot structures that you looked at in the last unit. You saw how conflicts evolve in a text in a structured way (look back at Figure 7.2, Freytag's Pyramid, on page 163). The focus here will be on the nature of conflict in works of fiction. Conflicts in literary texts are rarely simple, but four basic types can be identified: the individual pitted against society, against another person, against circumstances and against him- or herself. You will explore these four strands of conflict in this unit. To begin the discussion, read the following extract from the play *A Streetcar Named Desire* by Tennessee Williams, Text 7.4, in which a conflict can be seen to play a key role.

Figure 7.6 A scene from the 1951 film of *A Streetcar Named Desire*, with Marlon Brando (Stanley) and Vivien Leigh (Blanche), depicting the violent conflict that takes place on the night of the poker game.

discussion

1   How many different conflicts are there in this extract from *A Streetcar Named Desire*? Describe the people or ideas that are in opposition.
2   What message does Tennessee Williams convey to his audience about the nature of men and women through this scene?

Text 7.4 *A Streetcar Named Desire*, **Tennessee Williams, 1947**

Mitch	What do you teach? What subject?
Blanche	Guess!
Mitch	I bet you teach art or music? (*Blanche laughs delicately.*) Of course I could be wrong. You might teach arithmetic.
Blanche	Never arithmetic, sir; never arithmetic! (*With a laugh.*) I don't even know my multiplication tables! No, I have the misfortune of being an English instructor. I attempt to instil a bunch of bobby-soxers and drug-store Romeos with reverence for Hawthorne and Whitman and Poe!
Mitch	I guess that some of them are more interested in other things.
Blanche	How very right you are! Their literary heritage is not what most of them treasure above all else! But they're sweet things! And in the spring, it's touching to notice them making their first discovery of love! As if nobody had ever known it before!

The bathroom door opens and Stella *comes out. Blanche continues talking to Mitch.*

Blanche	Oh! Have you finished? Wait – I'll turn on the radio.

She turns the knobs on the radio and it begins to play 'Wien, Wien, nur du allein.'
Blanche waltzes to the music with romantic gestures. Mitch is delighted and
moves in awkward imitation like a dancing bear. Stanley stalks fiercely through the
portières into the bedroom. He crosses to the small white radio and snatches it
off the table. With a shouted oath, he tosses the instrument out of the window.

Stella	Drunk – drunk – animal thing, you! (*She rushes through to the poker table.*) All of you – please go home! If any of you have one spark of decency in you –
Blanche	(*wildly*) Stella, watch out, he's –

Stanley charges after Stella.

Men	(*feebly*) Take it easy, Stanley. Easy fellow. – Let's all …
Stella	You lay your hands on me and I'll …

She backs out of sight. He advances and disappears. There is the sound of a
blow. Stella cries out. Blanche screams and runs into the kitchen. The men rush
forward and there is grappling and cursing. Something is overturned with a crash.

Blanche	(*shrilly*) My sister is going to have a baby!
Mitch	This is terrible.
Blanche	Lunacy, absolute lunacy!
Mitch	Get him in here, men.

Stanley is forced, pinioned by the two men, into the bedroom. He nearly throws
them off. Then all at once he subsides and is limp in their grasp. They speak
quietly and lovingly to him and he leans his face on one of their shoulders.

Stella	(*in a high, unnatural voice, out of sight*) I want to go away, I want to go away!
Mitch	Poker shouldn't be played in a house with women.

The individual versus society

Poker shouldn't be played in a house with women, Mitch so famously says in the last line of Text 7.4, commenting on the nature of the conflict. It is poker night in the Kowalski apartment and Stanley Kowalski's sister-in-law, Blanche, is also visiting. The sisters, Stella and Blanche, are getting ready to go out when the violence erupts. Are they simply at the wrong place at the wrong time?

Many literary texts present characters as victims of their time and place, allowing writers to comment on the unjust principles of contemporary society. The individual in conflict with society is a recurring theme that you may find at different levels in a single literary text. In Text 7.4 Mitch draws our attention to the dangers of a male-dominated setting. Stanley asks Blanche to turn off the radio several times before throwing it out of the window – possibly an act of territorial behaviour. Furthermore, to establish that he is in charge in this household, Stanley hits his wife, Stella, who is pregnant, when she tells the poker players to go home. Nevertheless she does not leave Stanley, as she threatens to. There are other conflicts in this play that suggest Williams is commenting on the suppression of women in the South of the USA in the second half of the 20th century.

One individual versus another

In many works of fiction one character is pitted against another. As you analyse the conflicts between characters in literary texts, remember that characters usually stand for something: they embody abstract ideas. In Text 7.4 Blanche represents romance; she is flirting with Mitch, talking about teaching literature, wearing a flowery dress which she has put on after her bath. When Stanley, her arch-enemy, comes home after a hard day's work, he is hot and sweaty so takes off his shirt. He is a coarse man who speaks English badly and likes playing poker. He stands for masculinity. Stella is caught in the middle of this conflict, as she is loyal to both her sister Blanche and her husband Stanley. She represents the prize for whoever will triumph in this conflict between romance and machismo.

The individual versus circumstances

Some works of fiction revolve around circumstances that are out of everyone's control. There may be war, a natural disaster or unexplainable aliens. Readers will wonder what they themselves would do in such adverse circumstances. As you read your literary texts for parts 3 and 4, ask yourself to what degree the characters are responsible for the conditions and circumstances that they are up against. In *A Streetcar Named Desire* the audience learns more about Blanche as the play progresses – she goes from being a sad widow after her husband's suicide to the victim of her own promiscuity.

The individual versus himself

It is often said that people are their own worst enemy, an idea that is found in many fictional works. It could be said of Blanche, whose past catches up with her and allows Stanley to discover she is living a lie. Stanley is also a character who suffers from his own violent ways, as he beats his wife, Stella, who is pregnant, and risks harming the baby. As you read your literary texts, ask yourself which characters are self-destructive, or which qualities do the most harm to the characters with those qualities. The writer may be commenting on the characters' harmful ways in incidents of conflict.

Activity 7.6

What types of conflict can you find in your part 3 and part 4 literary texts? You may find that there are different conflicts within each work. You may also find conflicts that do not fit nicely into these categories. Nevertheless, discussing the various types of conflicts in your literary texts is useful for gaining a deeper understanding of them.

Theme

The theme is the underlying message of a literary text. Theme is behind the difficult but important question that you should always try to answer when you read fiction: *What is the text about?* Uncovering the themes of literary texts requires the same practice and skill as you brought to non-fiction texts in part 1 of the coursebook. While there are no shortcuts to understanding literary texts, writers often leave clues in the form of symbols and motifs as to what the text is about. One of the most obvious clues can often be the title of the text itself.

Symbols

You have seen that characters can represent abstract ideas. Similarly, the physical objects mentioned in a text can often stand for abstract ideas. Good reading requires you to question the symbolic meaning of every object that appears in a literary text, as authors do not include them accidentally. In Text 7.4 Blanche turns on the radio and hears the song 'Wien, Wien, nur du allein' ('Vienna, Vienna, you and only you'). Of all the music on the radio in New Orleans in 1947, why did Williams choose this song? The song makes Blanche dream of a faraway, romantic place and love. This dream is contrasted with the reality in which she lives, where men are brutes and she has not been faithful to her husband. The title of the song gives a clue to the deeper meaning of the text.

Motifs

Motifs are recurring symbols, structures or stylistic devices that comment on a deeper literary theme. Take, for example, the role of bathing in *A Streetcar Named Desire*. In many works of fiction washing stands for the cleansing of sins or crimes. Prior to the scene in Text 7.4 Blanche is heard having a bath while Stella and Stanley argue. No matter how long she bathes, Blanche cannot cleanse herself of her past. Shortly after Stanley hits Stella, his male friends throw him in the shower to make him cool down and, it might be said, cleanse him of his sins. When a symbol such as water appears more than once in a work, it can be considered to be a motif.

The title

When analysing literary texts, students sometimes forget to mention the obvious: the title of the work. The title functions as a guiding light through a story, which is why the writer will have chosen it carefully. The literal meaning of the title *A Streetcar Named Desire* refers to a tram route: to get to Stella's home in the French Quarter of New Orleans, Blanche has to take a tram, or streetcar, and the tram route was known as Desire as it went along Desire Street. The title's metaphorical meaning is that she is someone who is constantly carried away by her desires – she is driven by desire.

Don't forget to refer to the title of the work when giving your individual oral commentary. The title often alludes to a theme by referring to symbols or motifs found in the text.

Figure 7.7 How does this illustration of *The Tell-Tale Heart* convey the mood of the story?

Activity 7.7

Exploring the themes and conflicts in texts has provided part of the answer to the question we asked at the start of this chapter on page 160: *How does the writer engage the reader?* A good literary text is meaningful and has multiple layers for readers to explore, with symbols and motifs to make us look below the surface of the writing, and intriguing conflicts that reflect human nature.

To test your understanding of theme and conflict, you are going to apply the terms and concepts you have met so far in this unit to Text 7.5, the opening lines from a short story by Edgar Allan Poe. *The Tell-Tale Heart* is considered a seminal piece of horror fiction. Read Text 7.5 and ask yourself how Poe engages his readers.

- Is there a conflict in the text?
- What symbols can you find?
- How does the writer create fear in his readers?
- Look for a theme that comments on human nature.

discussion

1. There seems to be an absence of conflict in the story of *The Tell-Tale Heart*, as the killer *loved* his victim. Nevertheless, without a conflict there would be no story and no killing. Where, then, do you detect a conflict? Refer to the types of conflict you have studied in this unit.
2. The old man's eye is an important symbol in this short story. What does it stand for?
3. What clue does the title offer about the message of the story?

Text 7.5 *The Tell-Tale Heart*, Edgar Allan Poe, 1843

True!—Nervous—very, very dreadfully nervous I had been and am; but why *will* you say that I am mad? The disease had sharpened my senses—not destroyed— not dulled them. Above all was the sense of hearing acute. I heard all things in the heaven and in the earth. I heard many things in hell. How, then am I mad? Hearken! and observe how healthily—how calmly, I can tell you the whole story.

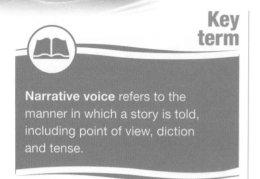

It is impossible to say how first the idea entered my brain, but, once conceived, it haunted me day and night. Object there was none. Passion there was none. I loved the old man. He had never wronged me. He had never given me insult. For his gold I had no desire. I think it was his eye! Yes, it was this! One of his eyes resembled that of a vulture—a pale blue eye with a film over it. Whenever it fell upon me, my blood ran cold; and so by degrees—very gradually—I made up my mind to take the life of the old man, and thus rid myself of the eye for ever.

Now this is the point. You fancy me mad. Madmen know nothing. But you should have seen *me*. You should have seen how wisely I proceeded—with what caution—with what foresight—with what dissimulation I went to work! I was never kinder to the old man than during the whole week before I killed him.

'I go straight from thinking about my narrator to being him.'
S.E. Hinton (1948–)

Unit 7.4 **Narrative voice**

The author Salman Rushdie, whose novel *The Satanic Verses* was condemned as a blasphemy against Islam in 1989, claimed that it was not he who spoke out against Islam but his characters. Writers of fiction speak to their readers through an art form, through a **narrative voice**. The narrative voice is the manner in which a story is told. It offers a perspective on a story.

How a story is told is often more important than *what* is told. Have you ever read a story even though you already knew the ending? What made it worth reading all the same? How a writer uses the following four devices helps to determine how engaged the readers feel:

- point of view
- narration
- speech
- tense.

author → narrator → reader

Figure 7.8 Authors make use of narrators and narrative voice to speak to their readers.

Point of view

On first sitting down to write a story, authors face an important choice. When determining how to tell the story, inevitably they have to decide who will tell it. Whose point of view will the reader be given? Who tells the story has a big influence on the reader's interpretation and experience of the events. The options are limited to the viewpoints of the following people:

1 the narrator of the story
2 the reader of the story
3 someone outside the story and looking in.

In the first, the narrator, the story is written in the first person – *I*. In the second, the reader, it is written in the second person – *you*. In the third, the story is written in the third person – *he, she* or *they*. You will look at the possibilities created by all three of these options and the effects each can have on the reader.

The first person

There is no better way to get into a narrator's head than to listen to him or her tell their own story. Not only is this engaging for the reader but it also poses an interesting question: do you believe the narrator's account of the story? Because narrators speak from experience, we tend to believe them. Sometimes, however, we should be wary as the author may have provided us with an **unreliable narrator**.

The first-person point of view is able to keep readers engaged as they second-guess the reliability of the narrator. This was the case with the narrator of Text 7.1, when Joe Rose in *Enduring Love* even questions himself: *as far as these occurrences were concerned, this was the last time I understood anything clearly at all*. In Text 7.5 the narrator of *The Tell-Tale Heart* seems to be defensive about his sanity and speaks as though we (the readers) are accusing him of being insane and therefore unreliable.

Key term

Unreliable narrator refers to fiction in which the reader is forced to question the storyteller's account of events.

Activity 7.8

Compare and contrast Joe Rose, the narrator in Text 7.1, with the narrator in Text 7.5. Complete a table like the one below, giving reasons these narrators might be reliable or unreliable.

	Joe Rose in Text 7.1	Narrator in Text 7.5
Reliable		
Unreliable		

'A narrative is like a room on whose walls a number of false doors have been painted; while within the narrative, we have many apparent choices of exit, but when the author leads us to one particular door, we know it is the right one because it opens.'
John Updike (1932–2009)

While the first-person point of view lends itself well to the horror and crime genres (taking the reader right into the criminal mind), it is also much used in fiction about young people coming of age (Bildungsroman). Because these narrators are young and still learning about how the world works, we, the readers, can sometimes understand the situations they face better than they can. We see this in popular modern works of fiction such as *The Catcher in the Rye* by J.D. Salinger, *The Curious Incident of the Dog in the Night-time* by Mark Haddon and *Extremely Loud and Incredibly Close* by Jonathan Safran Foer.

Often the first-person point of view allows us to get into the mind of the narrator by making use of a stream of consciousness (see page 149). As you saw in the extract from Margaret Atwood's *The Handmaid's Tale*, Text 5.5, on pages 129–30, in this style the narrator describes events as they unfold. Sentences and style are fragmented and not always sequential because the character's life, like real life, is full of interruptions and flashbacks. We see the stream of consciousness style also in Text 7.1, as Joe Rose fails to add structure to his ideas:

There was the shout again, and a child's cry, enfeebled by the wind that roared in the tall trees along the hedgerows. I ran faster. And there, suddenly, from different points around the field, four other men were converging on the scene, running like me.

Notice the word *again*, which shows the narrator is aware of his repetitiveness. Starting a sentence with *and* also adds to the randomness of his storytelling. Other novels that use the stream of consciousness style to greater degrees include *A Portrait of the Artist as a Young Man* by James Joyce, *Mrs Dalloway* by Virginia Woolf and *Surfacing* by Margaret Atwood.

The first-person point of view does not always include the random thoughts of the protagonist. Sometimes it is not the narrator's own thoughts that we hear but a

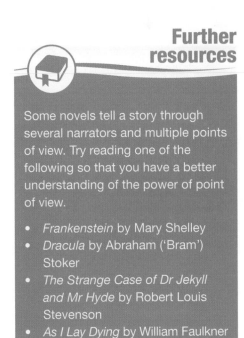

Further resources

Some novels tell a story through several narrators and multiple points of view. Try reading one of the following so that you have a better understanding of the power of point of view.

- *Frankenstein* by Mary Shelley
- *Dracula* by Abraham ('Bram') Stoker
- *The Strange Case of Dr Jekyll and Mr Hyde* by Robert Louis Stevenson
- *As I Lay Dying* by William Faulkner
- *The Collector* by John Fowles

discussion

1 Are there different types of *you*? In Text 7.6 is the reader really the protagonist, or is the protagonist anyone and no one in particular?
2 What is the effect of using the second person?

Key terms

Frame narrator is a storyteller who is not the protagonist of a story but a peripheral character who reveals someone else's story to us.

Omniscient narration offers an all-knowing perspective, giving the reader access to all characters, places and events of a story.

Limited narration offers the reader insight into the thoughts, actions and events of one character.

Objective narration includes storytelling that is not biased towards an ideological position or character.

Fly-on-the-wall narration is an extreme variant of objective narration, where the reader sees and hears of events, as a camera would record them, with nothing removed.

Subjective narration includes storytelling that is biased towards an ideological position or character.

narration of someone else's story. This device is called a **frame narrator**, as the narrator's story acts as a thin frame around the story of the protagonist or main character. We see peripheral characters telling a story in *Wuthering Heights* by Emily Brontë, *The Great Gatsby* by F. Scott Fitzgerald and *One Flew Over the Cuckoo's Nest* by Ken Kesey.

To sum up, first-person point of view creates several possibilities for storytelling. It can:
- call into question the reliability of the storyteller (unreliable narrator)
- give the audience a window into the narrator's mind (stream of consciousness)
- give the audience a vantage point from which the protagonist can be observed (frame narrator).

The second person

The second-person point of view is rarely used in literature as it lends itself better to instructional texts. You often see it in recipe books, for example (*You will need …*), or coursebooks like this one. In fiction the second-person point of view turns the reader into a protagonist. *Bright Lights, Big City* by Jay McInerney (Text 7.6) is a rare example of a successful work of literary fiction that uses the second-person point of view. This device allows the reader to feel that they are in control of the novel.

Text 7.6 *Bright Lights, Big City*, Jay McInerney, 1984

… How did you get here? It was your friend, Tad Allagash, who powered you in here. You started out on the Upper East Side with champagne and unlimited prospects, strictly observing the Allagash rule of perpetual motion: one drink per stop. Tad's mission in life is to have more fun than anyone else in New York City, and this involves a lot of moving around, since there is always the likelihood that where you aren't is more fun than where you are.

The third person

The third-person point of view does not use *I* or *you*, but rather *he, she* or *they*. When discussing works of fiction, there are several variables to consider: how **omniscient** or all-knowing is the narrator? Is the narrator a kind of god, who observes the characters, setting and action, knowing everything about how everyone thinks and what the future holds for them? Alternatively, is the narration a **limited narration**, where the storyteller follows just one character, the protagonist? With limited narration, important events in the story may happen off-scene, so that the protagonist and therefore the reader are at first unaware of them, thus allowing for an element of surprise later on. Detective stories rely on this limitation, so that readers have to unravel the mystery at the same time as the protagonist detective, who pieces the plot together as he learns of the evidence.

When commenting on third-person literary texts you will want to consider how biased, or subjective, the narrator is. Is the storyteller partial to a certain ideology or person, or is the narrator objective? The objectivity of the narrator varies from text to text and to different degrees. On one extreme, there is **objective narration**, where the reader observes characters' actions like a camera (this device is also known as **fly-on-the-wall narration**). On the other extreme, there is **subjective narration**, where readers are subjected to a biased account of events that are partial to one character.

Figure 7.9 illustrates third-person stories in a grid to show the various combinations of narration. There are two axes: the omniscient–limited axis and the objective–subjective axis.

Figure 7.9 diagram:

	Omniscient	
Subjective	a	b
	d	c
	Limited	

(with Objective on the right side)

Figure 7.9 Third-person narration can range from omniscient to limited, and from subjective to objective.

Activity 7.9

1 Read the following four short extracts from the story of Cinderella. Match each extract (1–4) to the quadrant in Figure 7.9 it corresponds to (a–d).
2 Explain how each extract gives a slightly different perspective on the events of the story.
3 As a class activity, draw a diagram like the one in Figure 7.9 on the board and discuss where you would place your part 3 and 4 literary texts in the grid. Plot them as single points in a quadrant. Support your answers with examples from the texts.

1 **Oh, how she wished she could go to the ball! She had suffered enough at the hands of her evil stepmother. Why couldn't she be granted this one freedom, this one right? She had seen the invitation too. All single women in the entire kingdom were invited, including her. Surely if anyone deserved a ticket to the royal palace it was Cinderella! She never contradicted Stepmother's orders but obediently – diligently – carried them out. There they went, walking across her freshly mopped floor, with grins that tore into her heart like knives. But she kept a straight face. That was, until the door slammed shut, leaving her alone to wallow in her despair.**

2 **All of the women of the house were busy preparing for the ball, all of them, that is, except for Cinderella, who had neither a gown nor the time to go. Although she had laboured away in quiet obedience, her list of chores was longer than her aching body could handle. Even if she could get away – a thought that would never cross her mind – she could not be seen at the palace in those rags.**

3 **Cinderella was mopping the last step of the marble stairs when she saw the frill of an evening gown go by. Looking up she saw her stepsisters standing before her. No words were exchanged, only looks. The slamming of the door reverberated in the hall. She paused, then once more lowered her head and continued with her cleaning. A single tear fell into the bucket of water.**

discussion

1 What effects do the examples of third-person points of view in the Activity have on you, the reader?
2 Is there any single third-person point of view that lends itself best to telling this story?

4   **Upstairs the stepsisters were busy preparing for the ball, putting on their gowns and beads, while at the bottom of the stairs, Cinderella continued to mop. The stepmother gave one last look into the hall mirror before calling to her daughters. The carriage waited outside. At the other end of the village, the prince was welcoming the first guests.**

Narration

Narration is slightly different from point of view. While point of view refers to who is telling the story, narration deals with the person the story is told to. There is one essential question to understanding narration: *Who is the narrator talking to?* Ask yourself this question as you read Text 7.7, the opening lines of the radio play *A Hitchhiker's Guide to the Galaxy* by Douglas Adams. Do you think the narrator is talking to you? There are three possible answers to the question asked above: *Who is the narrator talking to?* We will explore direct narration, frame narration and indirect narration.

Text 7.7 *The Hitchhiker's Guide to the Galaxy*, Douglas Adams, 1978

The narrator   This is the story of *The Hitch-Hiker's Guide To The Galaxy*, perhaps the most remarkable, certainly the most successful book ever to come out of the great publishing corporations of Ursa Minor – more popular than the *Celestial Homecare Omnibus*, better selling than 53 *More Things To Do In Zero Gravity*, and more controversial than Oolon Colluphid's trilogy of philosophical blockbusters: *Where God Went Wrong*, *Some More Of God's Greatest Mistakes* and *Who Is This God Person Anyway?*

   And in many of the more relaxed civilizations on the outer Eastern rim of the galaxy, the Hitch-Hiker's Guide has already supplanted the great Encyclopedia Galactica as the standard repository of all knowledge and wisdom, because although it has many omissions, contains much that is apocryphal, or at least wildly inaccurate, it scores over the older, more pedestrian work in two important ways. First, it is slightly cheaper, and second it has the words 'DON'T PANIC' inscribed in large, friendly letters on the cover.

   To tell the story of the book, it's best to tell the story of some of the minds behind it. A human from the planet Earth was one of them, though as our story opens he no more knows his destiny than a tea leaf knows the history of the East India Company. His name is Arthur Dent, he is a six foot tall ape descendant, and someone is trying to drive a bypass through his home.

Prosser   Come off it, Mr Dent, you can't win, you know! There's no point in lying down in the path of progress.

Arthur   I've gone off the idea of progress. It's overrated.

Prosser   But you must realize that you can't lie in front of the bulldozers indefinitely.

Arthur   I'm game, we'll see who rusts first.

Prosser   I'm afraid you're going to have to accept it. This bypass has got to be built, and it is going to be built! Nothing you can say or do …

Figure 7.10 Characters from the TV series of *A Hitchhiker's Guide to the Galaxy*, 1978. The original radio series went on to be adapted for film, television, video games, comic books and a series of novels.

Arthur	Why's it got to be built?
Prosser	What do you mean, why's it got to be built? It is a bypass, you've got to build bypasses.
Arthur	Didn't anyone consider the alternatives?
Prosser	There aren't any alternatives. Look, you were quite entitled to make any suggestions or protests at the appropriate time.
Arthur	Appropriate time? The first I knew about it was when a workman arrived at the door yesterday. I asked him if he'd come to clean the windows and he said he'd come to demolish the house. He didn't tell me straight away, of course. No, first he wiped a couple of windows and charged me a fiver. Then he told me.

Direct narration

If the narrator is directing the story towards you, then it is direct narration. The narrator is conscious of the act of storytelling. In Text 7.1 on pages 161–62 there are indications that the narrator, Joe Rose, is conscious of telling us his story: *I'm holding back, delaying the information. I'm lingering in the prior moment.* In Text 7.7 the narrator also indicates that he is consciously and deliberately telling us a story when he says: *To tell the story of the book, it's best to tell the story of some of the minds behind it.* In extreme cases, as for example in the novel *The Name of the Rose* by Umberto Eco, you even read comments such as *the book you hold in your hands.* This creates a kind of internal context or frame around the story.

Douglas Adams's radio play (Text 7.7) has an internal context as the target audience is spoken to directly by the narrator in the introduction. Strangely, we Earthlings might not even be part of the narrator's intended audience as he needs to explain that humans are from Earth (*A human from the planet Earth*) and refers to them as *ape descendant[s]* with an understanding of inter-galactic literature. Douglas Adams uses this narrative technique to create humour.

Frame narration

What if a story is directed from one character to another character? Or what if the narrator tells us a story about someone else? In both cases we are dealing with frame narration, which involves at least two layers of storytelling. We often see this in Gothic literature, such as in the novels *Wuthering Heights* by Emily Brontë or *Frankenstein* by Mary Shelley. In these cases, the reader 'listens' as a story within the story is told to the narrator. Both the narrator and the reader come away a little wiser.

Notice in Text 7.7 how there is a jump from narration to dramatic dialogue. Arguably this too forms a frame around the story. Like a voiceover in a film, the narrator's account anchors the story, which takes off into dramatic dialogue and action.

Indirect narration

Whereas in direct narration and frame narration the reader is being told a story, in indirect narration the reader is a witness to the story and is as if watching it happen from the outside. There is no one to retell, interpret or explain the events to the reader as they unfold. Hemingway's story *Hills Like White Elephants* (Text 7.3) is a good example of indirect narration, which characteristically relies heavily on dialogue. In fact most dramatic narration is indirect narration, which can also be seen in the second half of Text 7.7 in the dialogue between Arthur Dent and Prosser.

Although drama is mainly indirect narration, the only time we see direct narration in drama is in an **aside**. This is when a character turns to the audience and talks to them directly, telling them his or her thoughts. Asides are very common in

discussion

1 Look at the use of the word *more* in these lines: *More popular than* The Celestial Homecare Omnibus, *better selling than* 53 More Things To Do In Zero Gravity, *and more controversial than Oolon Colluphid's trilogy of philosophical blockbusters.* Does the use of *more* imply that we are supposed to know about some literary work called 'Fifty-two Things To Do In Zero Gravity'? Are we supposed to know about the Celestial Homecare Omnibus or Oolon Colluphid's trilogy? Where does this word *more* place you in relation to the target audience?

2 Does the description of Arthur Dent as a *six foot tall ape descendant* function similarly to the word *more* in implying a target audience? How?

3 How can you tell that this is the language of a radio play and not a screenplay? In the dialogue, where does the verbal language help the listener to create visual images? How does language point to action?

Key term

Aside is a dramatic device where a character turns and speaks directly to the audience, relating private thoughts that other characters on the stage cannot hear.

HL

Take an extract from a text you are reading and decide where it would go in a the table below. Choose a different box from the table and rewrite the extract using this new form of narration and point of view. In pairs, compare and contrast your work. How does a change in narration and point of view change the reader's experience of the literary text?

	First-person narration	Third-person omniscient narration	Third-person limited narration
Direct narration			
Indirect narration			

Shakespeare's plays. The other characters on stage cannot hear the aside so do not know as much as the audience.

Indirect narration can be used in the first-person and the third-person point of view. When the narration is in the third person, it is usually more objective and would be placed therefore towards the right in Figure 7.9. When it is in the first person, it can be a stream of consciousness, as the thoughts are not organised or packaged neatly into a story for the reader. As readers, we eavesdrop on the narrator's thoughts.

Speech

As well as point of view and narration, authors use the speech of their narrators as a structural device in their writing. There are three kinds of speech in narrative writing: direct speech, reported speech and free indirect speech.

Direct speech

Authors can make their characters speak for themselves. Quotation marks show when characters speak directly to other characters, or when they quote other characters. Direct or quoted speech is often found in indirect narration, where the narrator shows us the story rather than tells it. Text 7.3 on pages 170–71, the extract from *Hills Like White Elephants*, consists almost exclusively of direct speech with no added commentary. The dialogue is punctuated by quotation marks and none of it is summarised for the reader:

> The man called 'Listen' through the curtain. The woman came out from the bar.
> 'Four reales.'
> 'We want two Anis del Toro.'
> 'With water?'
> 'Do you want it with water?'
> 'I don't know,' the girl said. 'Is it good with water?'
> 'It's all right.'
> 'You want them with water?' asked the woman.
> 'Yes, with water.'

Reported speech

The opposite of direct speech is reported speech. In reported speech narrators summarise events and conversations for us, without the use of quotation marks. The effect of reported speech is that the reader becomes dependent on the narrator, which is often the case in direct narration, where we are spoken to directly by the narrator. The extract from *Hills Like White Elephants* above would look like this in reported speech:

> The man called the waitress, who came out from behind the bar. She asked him for four reales to pay for the drinks they had had. Instead he ordered two Anis del Toro drinks. The waitress asked them if they wanted the drinks with water. The man asked the girl whether she wanted hers with water. The girl wasn't sure if she wanted hers with water so she asked the man for his opinion. He said it tasted all right with water. The waitress asked them again if they wanted the drinks with water. The girl said she did.

Free indirect speech

In the third-person limited point of view, narrators have a way of showing us the thoughts of the protagonist without quotation marks or other obvious indicators such as *he thought*. The 19th-century French writer Gustav Flaubert was famous for using free indirect speech in his novel *Madame Bovary*. You also came across it in Text 6.2 on pages 141–42, the extract from *One Day in the Life of Ivan Denisovich*, where the protagonist had to part with his boots. Notice the use of exclamation marks and the second person *you*:

> **He'd taken such good care of his new boots, softening the leather with grease! Ah, nothing had been so hard to part with in all his eight years in camps as that pair of boots! They were tossed into a common heap. Not a hope of finding your own pair in the spring.**

In this extract, it is as though we hear the thoughts of Shukov in the first person, even though the point of view is really the third person (*He'd taken such good care; his eight years in camps*). This style is a good way to allow readers to empathise with the protagonist while observing the events from what seems an objective point of view.

Activity 7.10

Compare and contrast Text 6.2 (the extract from *One Day in the Life of Ivan Denisovich* on pages 141–42) with Text 7.8 (the extract from *Changes,* below). Comment on the use of free indirect speech in the two texts through the use of several linguistic devices.

	Text 6.2	Text 7.8
Quotation marks around thoughts		
Rhetorical questions		
Ungrammatical sentences characteristic of stream of consciousness		
Use of *he* to depict third-person point of view		

Text 7.8 *Changes*, Ama Ata Aidoo, 1991

He had always loved Esi. And what was wrong with that?
  'It's not safe to show a woman you love her … not too much anyway,' some male voice was telling him … 'Showing a woman you love her is like asking her to walk over you. How much of your love for how heavy her kicks.' And were they wrong? Look at Esi. Two solid years of courtship, six years of marriage. And what had he got out of it? Little. Nothing. No affection. Not even plain warmth. Nothing except one little daughter! Esi had never stated it categorically that she didn't want any more children. … He wanted other children, at least one more … a boy if possible. But even one more girl would have been welcome.

Tense

Just as the number of points of view is limited, there are only three tenses that an author can choose from: the past, the present or the future. For practical reasons, writers rarely tell a story in the future tense.

Past tense

Most stories are told in the past tense, as it is rich with possibilities. Specifically it allows for two key opportunities: **hindsight wisdom** and **flashbacks**. Often in cases of first-person point of view and direct narration, the narrator looks back to an event

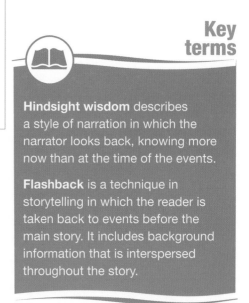

Key terms

Hindsight wisdom describes a style of narration in which the narrator looks back, knowing more now than at the time of the events.

Flashback is a technique in storytelling in which the reader is taken back to events before the main story. It includes background information that is interspersed throughout the story.

from a much wiser vantage point. They tell us their story so we too can learn what they learned from their experiences. We see this in Text 7.1, with Joe Rose's foreshadowing of his conflict with Jed Parry:

> **Knowing what I know now, it's odd to evoke the figure of Jed Parry directly ahead of me, emerging from a line of beeches on the far side of the field a quarter of a mile away, running into the wind. To the buzzard Parry and I were tiny forms, our white shirts brilliant against the green, rushing towards each other like lovers, innocent of the grief this entanglement would bring.**

Flashbacks take the reader back to events that happened before the main story. They serve as interjections of background information that help us understand the relevance of the main storyline. In Text 6.1 on page 139, taken from *Fahrenheit 451*, there was a brief flashback when Captain Beatty explained the history about burning the books to Montag and consequently the reader:

> **'Yes, but what about firemen, then?' asked Montag.**

> **'Ah.' Beatty leaned forward in the faint mist of smoke from his pipe. 'What more easily explained and natural? With schools turning out more runners, jumpers, racers, thinkers, grabbers, snatchers, fliers, and swimmers instead of examiners, critics, knowers, and imaginative creators, the word "intellectual", of course became the swear word it deserved to be.'**

The flashbacks allow the reader to gradually understand the strange internal context of the story.

There is another form of past tense that cannot go unmentioned: the **historical present**. Have you ever heard someone retell a story about the past using the present tense? This special use of the present to recount events that have already taken place is called the historical present. (It's often used in telling jokes: *A man goes into a bar and asks …*) The technique allows the reader to experience events as the protagonist confronts them, which can be very engaging and exciting. Figure 7.11 illustrates the use

"We are in the bears' house. Goldilocks has just eaten a bowl of porridge. Papa Bear enters."

Figure 7.11 How does the humour of this cartoon illustrate the importance of narrative tense and point of view?

of the present and present perfect tenses to draw the reader into the thrilling story of Goldilocks and the Three Bears.

Present tense

In Text 5.5 on pages 129–30, the extract from *The Handmaid's Tale*, there was an interesting piece of narration:

> **This is what I do when I'm back in my room:**
> **I take off my clothes and put on my nightgown.**
> **I look for the pat of butter, in the toe of my right shoe, where I hid it after dinner.**

The entire novel is written in the present tense, which, like the historical present, has the effect of engaging the reader. The difference between the historical present and the regular present tense is the narrator's understanding of the situation. In fiction written in the present tense the narrator knows as little as the reader about the situations that present themselves. Unlike with fiction in the past tense, the narrator does not have the wisdom of hindsight.

As you comment on your part 4 texts in your individual oral commentary, you will have to talk about the structural and stylistic devices that shape the narrative voice, so it helps to have a good understanding of them. You may find it helpful to commit the table in the activity to memory. Practise spotting the narrative devices before your exam by talking about the literary texts you are reading for part 4. How does the writer engage you? How does the writer tell the story?

Activity 7.11

1 Use one term from each column of the table below to describe the narrative voice of a part 3 or part 4 text. Look at several passages from each work before coming to any conclusions. You could work in groups to do this, with each group focusing on one column of the table.

Point of view	Narration	Speech	Tense
First person	Direct	Direct	Past
Second person	Frame	Reported	Historical past
Third person – limited – omniscient – subjective – objective	Indirect	Free indirect	Present

2 Remind yourself of one of the questions you came across in Chapter 6 and which you had to answer for part 3: *How do the style and structure of the text reflect the context in which it was written?* Now answer the following question: *How do the narrative techniques of your part 3 texts reflect the contexts in which they were written?* Write a paragraph about a literary text, its narrative technique and the context in which it was written like the sample student response on page 188.

Unit 7.5 **Revision**

You have been introduced to a lot of different terms in this chapter, which you will need to revise and practise applying. As much of this chapter is relevant to your part 3 texts you will want to go back and look at these again, applying the theoretical framework you have met in this chapter. Remember that one of the aims of part 3 is to comment on how literary devices reflect the contexts in which literary texts are written. In this final unit you are commenting on how the use of stylistic features reflect the context in which the work was written.

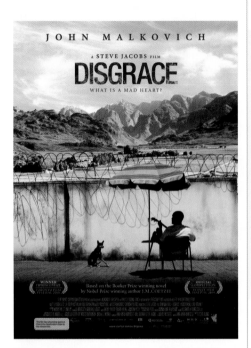

Figure 7.12 An image from the 2009 film, *Disgrace*, starring John Malkovich.

discussion

1 How is the setting – a concrete storage dam full of algae – important in determining the mood of the scene?

2 What kind of person is Petrus? How is the characterisation of Petrus created through dialogue in this passage?

3 What symbols can you find in the passage? What might the pipe stand for?

4 What kinds of conflict can you see in this passage? Use the terminology from this chapter (for example the individual versus society, one individual versus another, the individual versus circumstances, and the individual versus him- or herself).

5 How is a narrative voice established in this passage? Comment on the use of point of view, narration, speech and tense.

Text 7.9 *Disgrace*, J.M. Coetzee, 1999

John Maxwell Coetzee grew up in an English-speaking family of Afrikaner descent in Cape Town, South Africa, during apartheid.

When Coetzee was eight years old his father lost his job after he objected to apartheid laws. After secondary school and undergraduate studies in Cape Town, Coetzee worked and studied in the UK and the USA. In 1989 his son was killed in a car accident at the age of 23. At the same time as writing novels, Coetzee has taught English literature in the USA, South Africa and Australia. He has won the UK Booker Prize for fiction twice and the Nobel Prize in Literature in 2003.

Disgrace takes place after the ending of the official system of apartheid in South Africa. It is about David Lurie, a white man, who is a university professor of literature. After seducing one of his students he is dismissed from his university post and goes to the countryside to his daughter Lucy's farm, which is part run by Petrus, a black man. Some men carry out a vicious attack on the farm, and Lucy and David are assaulted and hurt while the farmhouse is ransacked. In the following scene David suspects Petrus of knowing about the attack beforehand.

Petrus has a vision of the future in which people like Lucy have no place. But that need not make an enemy of Petrus. Country life has always been a matter of neighbours scheming against each other, wishing on each other pests, poor crops, financial ruin, yet in a crisis ready to lend a hand.

The worst, the darkest reading would be that Petrus engaged three strange men to teach Lucy a lesson, paying them off with the loot. But he cannot believe that, it would be too simple. The real truth, he suspects, is something far more – he casts around for the word – *anthropological*, something it would take months to get to the bottom of, months of patient, unhurried conversation with dozens of people, and the offices of an interpreter.

On the other hand, he does believe that Petrus knew something was in the offing; he does believe Petrus could have warned Lucy. That is why he will not let go of the subject. That is why he continues to nag Petrus.

Petrus has emptied the concrete storage dam and is cleaning it of algae. It is an unpleasant job. Nevertheless, he offers to help. With his feet crammed into Lucy's rubber boots, he climbs into the dam, stepping carefully on the slick bottom. For a while he and Petrus work in concert, scraping, scrubbing, shovelling out the mud. Then he breaks off.

'Do you know, Petrus,' he says, 'I find it hard to believe the men who came here were strangers. I find it hard to believe they arrived out of nowhere, and did what they did, and disappeared afterwards like ghosts, and I find it hard to believe that the reason they picked on us was simply that we were the first white folk they met that day. What do you think? Am I wrong?'

Petrus smokes a pipe, an old-fashioned pipe with a hooked stem and a little silver cap over the bowl. Now he straightens up, takes the pipe from the pocket of his overalls, opens the cap, tamps down the tobacco in the bowl, sucks at the pipe unlit. He stares reflectively over the dam wall, over the hills, over open country. His expression is perfectly tranquil.

'The police must find them,' he says at last. 'The police must find them and put them in jail. That is the job of the police.'

'But the police are not going to find them without help. Those men knew about the forestry station. I am convinced they knew about Lucy. How could they have known if they were complete strangers to the district?'

Petrus chooses not to take this as a question. He puts the pipe away in his pocket, exchanges spade for broom.

6 Judging from this passage, how do you think Coetzee is commenting on post-apartheid South Africa?

Disgrace: style and context

In the following sample response you can see how a student has commented on *Disgrace* and related the literary devices of the text to the context in which it was written.

tip

The discussion questions on Text 7.9 consider the use of the literary devices that you have read about in this chapter. These five devices (plot, character, setting, conflict and theme, and narrative voice) can act as lenses through which you look at your individual oral commentary passage. You could use these devices as a kind of template for preparing your oral exam.

Disgrace by J.M. Coetzee came out in 1999, five years after the end of apartheid in South Africa. The story is told in the third-person limited point of view, and makes use of a lot of free indirect speech, which we see in the opening lines of this passage: *Petrus has a vision of the future in which people like Lucy have no place. But that need not make an enemy of Petrus.* These are the thoughts of David, though not indicated as such through quotation marks or signs like *he thought.* This style lends itself well to observing David Lurie, the protagonist, as it allows the reader to judge him from a safe distance and understand how his mind works at the same time. The novel is about how white people, like David, deal with the aftermath of apartheid. We need to be able to get into his head to understand the themes. The aftermath of apartheid, which includes rape, usurpation and theft, confronts David unexpectedly. Coetzee's use of the present tense allows the reader to experience the atrocities of David's life and South African life as they happen, randomly and yet rooted in racial conflict. You could argue that he uses the narrative voice of post-apartheid South Africa.

On an autobiographical level there are many parallels between David Lurie and Coetzee. Both are college professors of English literature. Both are divorced and both have gone through a traumatic event concerning a child. David's daughter is assaulted, while he is helplessly locked in the bathroom. Lurie's daughter refuses her father's compassion and suppresses his search for retribution. Coetzee lost his son in a car crash. Both have had to learn to let go of a loved one. Furthermore, Coetzee has always sought livelihood outside his country of birth. Lurie also has difficulty rooting himself in South Africa. He is on the move a lot, like Coetzee. You could argue that the context of the writer is reflected in the plot of this story.

discussion

How has the student demonstrated a connection between the context in which *Disgrace* was written and the literary devices employed by the author?

Activity 7.12

Go back to a text that you read for part 3 and write a response, like the one that the student has written here on *Disgrace*, about how the literary devices of the text reflect the context in which it was written.

Assessment: Written task 2 (HL only)

At higher level you will be required to write one or more responses for written task 2. These tasks are distinctly different from written task 1, in that they are not creative writing assignments. Rather, this form of assessment invites you to articulate a critical response to a text or texts. Your response will answer one of six prescribed questions in

Part 4 – Literature: critical study

tip

Any time you are faced with a question, be it on timed exam papers or written task critical responses, you will want to 'unpack' the multiple layers of the question. By 'unpack' we mean to say that several words in the question may imply and entail more concepts than those you see at a surface level. For example, see how the student has 'unpacked' question 5 in preparation for the written task critical response (Figure 7.13). The student has used the question to make a spider diagram that pertains to the text *Maus*. You too can practise unpacking one of the questions in relation to a text, either fiction or non-fiction, that you are reading for your coursework.

light of the text, or texts, that you have studied. You can find the six prescribed questions in the introduction of this coursebook on page x. Alternatively you can consult the IB Language A: language and literature syllabus for further reference and detail.

Your critical response will take the form of a formal essay, with an introduction, well-developed arguments in body paragraphs and a conclusion. You will also need to cite your sources and include a bibliography for any references that you make. Furthermore, a formal outline of your response is required, which you will fill in using an official IB cover sheet. As you will see from the examiner's comments later, you are assessed for 8 out of the 20 marks on your ability to answer the question. Therefore it is in your interest to understand the implications of the question thoroughly (see 'tip' box and Figure 7.13).

How does *Maus* adhere to the rules of graphic novel writing? Think of mature themes and frame narrator.

Maus breaks the rules of comic books by creating the anti-hero, voiceover and the use of images and words.

Are there 'rules' to writing graphic novels? Has *Maus* defined them?

How does the text conform to, or deviate from, the conventions of a particular genre, and for what purpose?

What distinguishes the graphic novel genre from the comic book genre?

Of all forms of literature, why did Spiegelman write a graphic novel? Purpose: to visualise the Auschwitz experience? To symbolise the Nazi/Jew cat/mouse analogy?

Figure 7.13 This spider diagram shows how the student from the sample response below explored the implications of the question in relation to *Maus* by Art Spiegelman (Figure 7.14), as a means of preparing for the written task critical response.

The student response that follows was inspired by a study of *Maus* by Art Spiegelman. In order to provide the examiner with a frame of reference, the student has included several images from *Maus* (see Figure 7.14). While including primary or secondary sources is not necessary or required for written tasks, this student includes images to support the points that they make in the critical response.

Sample written task 2 (HL only)

Written task: How *Maus* adheres to and breaks comic book conventions

- The prescribed question that has been chosen is *How does the text conform to, or deviate from, the conventions of a particular genre, and for what purpose?*
- The title of the text for analysis: *Maus* by Art Spiegelman.
- The part of the course to which the task refers: part 4: literature - critical study.
- Three of four points that explain the focus of the task:
  - Explore the genre of graphic novel.
  - Explain how Spiegelman adheres to and breaks the conventions of graphic novel.
  - Explain why Spiegelman chose this genre to express his ideas.

What do you think of when you hear the term 'comic book'? Do you think super heroes, flashy illustrations and implausible storylines? Most likely you do not think of the Holocaust, strained family relationships or identity struggles. Nevertheless, Art Spiegelman chose to write about these themes using the comic book convention in **Maus: A Survivor's Tale**, published in instalments between 1972 and 1991. Because Spiegelman explores such complex themes, many debate whether or not **Maus** should be considered a comic at all. Arguably, it should be considered a 'graphic novel'. In **Maus**, Spiegelman conforms to and deviates from the conventions of comic books in order to give his audience a new look at the themes as well as fresh perspective on the comic book genre.

Before we explore Spiegelman's purpose in writing **Maus**, and try to understand why he chose to write a comic book (or graphic novel) it is important to define these terms. While the term 'comic book' has a connotation of super heroes, serialisation and cheap entertainment, its use of style and structure does not have to be limited to these contexts. Extensive illustrations have accompanied literary texts for centuries. William Blake's **Marriage of Heaven and Hell** from the late eighteenth century and the Bayeux Tapestry from the eleventh century are examples of densely illustrated narratives.

However, what makes both comic books and graphic novels different from these historical works is how they explore an inter dependency of image and word. Comics and graphic novels can show what they do not tell and tell what they do not show. The dramatisation of action, the use of thought bubbles and the use of different angles or perspectives create possibilities in both comic books and graphic novels that cannot be explored in theatre, film or prose fiction. The only difference between the comic book and graphic novel genre, in fact, is their choice of subject mater. Graphic novels tend to address more complex themes. One could argue that there is a continuum of themes that range from lighter, entertaining material to more complex and literary material. Such a continuum blurs the border between the comic book and graphic novel genre, making it difficult to classify them neatly.

Spiegelman uses a range of comic book devices to tell the story of his father, constantly exploring layers of narration and symbolism. As you can see from Illustration 1, the story is told through a frame narrator, Vladek, Spiegelman's father, to 'Artie', who is at the same time the illustrator and author. **Maus** is about Spiegelman's search for identity and understanding of his father. We, the readers, overhear this series of interviews. The portrayal of Vladek on the stationary bicycle and Artie smoking shows a juxtaposition of character that words alone can hardly capture. The frame narration continues into further frames in Illustration 1 and the rest of the comic book through the use of the 'voiceover', which we see at the top or bottom of the frames. These are commentaries from the present looking back on events from the past. The comic book genre lends itself well to this layering of comments over depictions of flashbacks. It allows for a mixture of indirect and direct narration, reported and direct speech. Spiegelman explores these possibilities of the comic book genre to their fullest.

As if these layers of narration were not complex enough, Spiegelman explores yet another narrative device. Illustration 2 shows Artie's hypothetical comic book, titled **Prisoner on the Hell Planet: A Case History**. This text-within-a-text is a motif that

Figure 7.14 Illustration 1 (an illustration from *Maus* by Art Spiegelman)

runs throughout **Maus**, in which stereotypical comic book devices, such as flashy headings and funny caricatures, are offset with a serious and grave theme: Artie's' struggle to deal with his mother's suicide. The reader understands that Artie, the artist, writes **Prisoner on the Hell Planet** as a means of personal therapy. His mother, who survived the Nazi camps like his father, suffered from depression. Similarly to Artie, she deals with her grief by writing a diary. Although she wanted Artie to read her diary, he never gets to see it because his father has burnt it.

Of all the literary genres Spiegelman could have written he decided to write a comic book for several reasons. The reader comes to realise that Spiegelman has written **Maus**, like Artie wrote **Prisoner on the Hell Planet**, in order to understand his parents' and his own grief better. The comic book genre gives Spiegelman a wealth of narrative layers to explore his multiple identities of artist, journalist, Jew and son. Furthermore, the comic book tradition of depicting characters, such as Donald Duck and the Hulk, allows Spiegelman to portray the Nazis as cats, the Jews as mice and the Poles as pigs in a very plausible way. This _extended metaphor_ that constantly compares the round-up of the Jews to a cat-and-mouse game is what gives this comic book the literary depth of a graphic novel. Furthermore, Spiegelman's drawings act as literary symbols. In Illustration 1 the stationary bicycle symbolises the race that goes nowhere and the depiction of the tram foreshadows the Jews' deportation to Auschwitz on the train. Such rich imagery is what separates this graphic novel from light and entertaining comic books.

To conclude, one can see that Spiegelman has taken the possibilities of the comic book genre to new literary levels in **Maus**. It is no wonder that his masterpiece won the Pulitzer Prize in 1992. He gave the world new insight into an old theme, the Holocaust, and helped define a new literary genre, the graphic novel.

Bibliography

Leventhal, Robert S 'Art Spiegelman's MAUS'. _Institute for Advanced Technology in the Humanities_. Web. 18 Dec. 2010. www2.iath.virginia.edu/holocaust/spiegelman. html. Spiegelman, Art. Maus: a Survivor's Tale. New York: Pantheon, 2008. Print.

Figure 7.15 Illustration 2 (a text within a text: the hypothetical comic book in _Maus_).

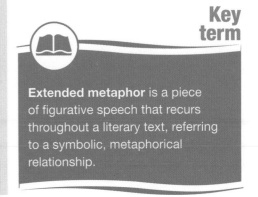

Key term

Extended metaphor is a piece of figurative speech that recurs throughout a literary text, referring to a symbolic, metaphorical relationship.

Examiner's comments

The student has written a relevant and insightful response to the question. Much care is taken to define the graphic novel and comic book genres. Generally speaking, this is the kind of written task 2 that is expected of students. The following marks and comments could be expected from an IB examiner for this written task.

Criterion A: outline – 2 out of 2

The student fulfils the requirement of the outline, as it is clearly reflects the main points of the response.

Criterion B: Response to the question – 7 out of 8

While there are many points to make about this literary work, the student stays on topic very well by exploring *Maus* in relation to the graphic novel genre. The examples

Further resources

You may want to read some of the following graphic novels:

- *A Contract with God and Other Tenement Stories* by Will Eisner
- *Ghost World* by Daniel Clowes
- *Maus* by Art Spiegelman
- *Persepolis* by Marjane Satrapi (originally in French)
- *Watchmen* by Alan Moore and Dave Gibbons

of stylistic and structural devices are relevant to the prescribed question and the thesis of this critical response. The prescribed question about genre proves particularly challenging in relation to this text, as a clear distinction must be made between 'comic book' and 'graphic novel'. The student explains this distinction well using it as a guiding idea in the response. The inclusion of two illustrations further increases the effectiveness of the student's references.

Criterion C: Organisation and argument – 5 out of 5

The student has structured the essay well with linking words and signposts, such as 'before we explore' and 'to conclude'. There seems to be a logical development of ideas, starting with the definition of the terms 'comic book' and 'graphic novel', followed by an explanation of how Spiegelman employs comic book devices and concluding with reasons why Spiegelman chose this particular genre. The argument that Spiegelman uses multiple layers of narration to explore his multiple identities is a strong one. The final body paragraph includes another convincing argument on symbolism and extended metaphor. The critical response is effectively developed.

Criterion D: Language and style – 4 out of 5

The student's ideas are clearly presented with an appropriate register and an effective choice of words. Furthermore the use of grammar is accurate and includes many parallel structures. Generally speaking the style of this critical response is mature and reflective.

Chapter 7 summary

This chapter began with the simple question: *How does the writer engage the reader?* You will now know more about the literary devices writers use when they construct stories that capture our interest. You looked first at the basic building blocks of fiction – plot, character and setting – which represent the foundation of storytelling. You also looked at the common types and structures of plot (see Figure 7.2, Freytag's Pyramid, on page 163). You discovered that the notion of setting goes beyond the geographical location of a text, and includes the emotional backdrop and its effect on the characters of a story. Characters play certain roles in a story and come to life through techniques such as dialogue, action and the expression of thought.

Building on these foundations of storytelling, abstract themes and intangible conflicts can also come to life. Conflict, in all of its varieties, acts as a driving force behind fiction and engages readers. Understanding the conflict in a story is often linked to understanding its underlying themes. You saw how devices such as symbols, motifs and the title help guide readers towards these underlying messages.

Not only did you explore *what* goes into stories, you also found out *how* they are told, looking at the various structural and stylistic devices that create narrative voice. The point of view from which a story is told, the way it is directed towards the reader, the tense in which it is told and the way in which events are reported or dialogue is constructed all help to create the narrative voice.

Looking at a wide variety of texts will help you gain a better understanding of the mechanics of literature. In the next chapter you will be asking the question *What makes English poetic?*

Chapter 8 What makes English poetic?

Objectives

By the end of this chapter you will be able to
- identify the different structural devices that make English poetic
- identify different stylistic devices such as imagery and figurative language
- plan and perform an individual oral commentary.

Before answering the question in the title of this chapter, there is a more fundamental question that we should ask and answer: *What is poetry?* Throughout this coursebook you have used broad definitions of terms such as *text*, *culture* and *persuasive language*. The definition of *poetry* will be no different. Perhaps you are someone who thinks of poetry as a form of writing for serious literature lovers, interested in Shakespearian sonnets or the Metaphysical Poets, for example, but poetry is really much broader than that.

Poetry is all around us, in advertisements, on T-shirts, in brochures and slogans. The slogan used by the electronics company Philips is *Sense and simplicity* (Figure 8.1); people wear T-shirts bearing messages such as *Green is the new Red* (Figure 8.2); and greetings cards exchanged at traditional holidays send wishes such as *May your home light up with the joy of Deepavali* (Figure 8.3). These are all examples of how poetry and poetic devices are used in everyday life. Understanding how poetic devices work makes us aware of how language is used as a tool to appeal to our senses.

The guiding question for this chapter asks *What makes English poetic?* You will explore two approaches to answering it, focusing on how literary devices appeal to our aural sense (Unit 8.1) and visual sense (Unit 8.2). Together, this theoretical framework on poetic devices and the mechanics of fiction that you explored in Chapter 7 are essential for the understanding you need when you approach the individual oral commentary part of your IB Diploma exam. This chapter will provide you with plenty of texts to analyse but you should also practise analysing passages of poetry and other literary texts that you are reading for part 4.

> **'Poetry is the rhythmical creation of beauty in words.'**
> Edgar Allan Poe (1809–49)

PHILIPS
sense and simplicity

Figure 8.1 This Philips slogan relies on the poetic device known as alliteration (see page 195) – the 's' sound is heard four times.

Figure 8.2 This T-shirt relies on a poetic device known as metonymy (see page 207) – the colours stand for ideologies.

May your home light up... with the joy of Deepavali

HAPPY DEEPAVALI

Figure 8.3 This greetings card makes use of figurative language (see page 202) – an abstract idea (joy) *does* something, such as lighting up your home.

Further resources

A Glossary of Literary Terms by M.H. Abrams is an excellent resource for any student of literature. Each entry reads like a fascinating story with illustrations that are full of insight.

'Poetry: the best words in the best order.'
Samuel Taylor Coleridge (1772–1834)

Unit 8.1 **Sound and structure**

To answer the question *What makes English poetic?* we need to explore the English language at different levels. In order to understand English, you will have to look at it in detail, just as a biologist needs to look at the smallest details of an organism under a microscope. The process starts by looking at the letters in words, and then we can 'zoom out' bit by bit to other levels: syllables, sentences and, eventually, whole poems.

After studying the devices of poetry, you will begin to identify and appreciate style and form more readily. This awareness should enhance rather than hinder your enjoyment of poetic language. You may read a poem and recognise in it examples of alliteration, rhyming schemes and patterns of syllables, but try not to let these distract you from the purpose of poetry, which is to appeal to your senses and convey a sentiment.

One way poetry appeals to our senses is through sound. Listening to poems being read out loud is an excellent way to experience poetry. Read the first poem of this chapter, Text 8.1, without studying its form or devices and ask yourself the simple question *How do I experience this poem?*

Text 8.1 *Bright star*, John Keats, 1819

```
1        Bright star, would I were stedfast as thou art –
              Not in lone splendour hung aloft the night
         And watching with eternal lids apart
              Like nature's patient, sleepless eremite,¹
5        The moving waters at their priestlike task
              Of pure ablution² round earth's human shores,
```

Or gazing on the new soft-fallen mask
      Of snow upon the mountains and the moors –
No – yet still stedfast, still unchangeable,
10   Pillow'd upon my fair love's ripening breast,
To feel forever its soft fall and swell,
      Awake for ever in a sweet unrest,
Still, still to hear her tender-taken breath,
And so live ever – or else swoon to death

¹ **eremite**   a hermit or recluse, someone living in isolation and devoting
themselves to their religious beliefs

² **ablution**   washing, here with the sense of a sacred ritual

discussion

1 How do you experience this poem after your first reading of it?
2 How do you experience this poem after your second reading of it?
3 Listen to the poem being read out loud. How does the sound of the poem affect your senses?
4 What sentiments do you think Keats is conveying to the reader through this poem?

Alliteration and onomatopoeia

The smallest unit of the English language is the individual phoneme, represented in writing as a letter (for example *t* for a 't' sound) or letters (for example *ch, sh, th* for 'ch', 'sh' and 'th' sounds). The effect of having the same sound repeated at the beginning of two or more words is pleasing. When the repeated sound is that of a consonant, it is called **alliteration**. It is found in several lines of Keats's poem 'Bright star', such as the repetition of the 'm' sound in line 8, *Of snow upon the mountains and the moors*.

As you read line 6, *Of pure ablution round earth's human shores*, you may notice that the long 'u' sound in *pure, ablution* and *human* is repeated. The repetition of the same vowel sound is known as **assonance**. In line 8 a 'z' sound is heard at the end of two words, *mountains* and *moors*, and in line 3 there is repetition of a 't' sound (heard three times) in *watching with eternal lids apart*. The repetition of consonants in the middle of words is known as **consonance**. Writers use alliteration, assonance and consonance for the purpose of creating an aesthetic effect on the reader or listener. You could say that the effect of Keats's poem is like listening to a lullaby or a beautiful song.

There is yet another way in which poets appeal to our sense of sound on the level of individual letters. Some words sound like the things that they represent. We call this phenomenon **onomatopoeia**. Words like *gurgle, snarled* and *rattled* are examples of onomatopoeia. You could argue that even a word like *swell* (line 11) is an example of this. Some words have a greater onomatopoeic effect than others.

Syllables and feet

Language has a natural **rhythm**, which is created by stressing or not stressing the syllables of words. Rappers are very conscious of where stresses naturally fall in words, as their use of language has to fit in with a beat. In the first line of the poem 'Bright star', Text 8.1, the words (or syllables) in italics are naturally stressed: *Bright star*, would *I* were *sted*fast *as* thou *art*. Knowing where the stress should lie is not always easy when you look at a poem on a page, but reading it aloud may help you understand which words are stressed and so appreciate the rhythm.

Ask yourself which sounds most natural:

1 Bright star

2 Bright star

3 Bright star

Key terms

Alliteration is the repetition of a consonant at the beginning of two or more words or stressed syllables.

Assonance is the repetition of a vowel sound in the middle of two or more words, such as the 'ow' sound in *loud mouth*.

Consonance is the repetition of a consonant sound in the middle or at the end of words, such as the 'l' sound in *fall and swell*.

Onomatopoeia refers to the use of words that sound like what they name or describe.

Rhythm in poetry is created through patterns of stressed and unstressed syllables.

The answer is number 3 – they are both stressed syllables. Furthermore, we see that they are the first two syllables of a line that consists of ten syllables in total. These first two syllables have a natural tendency to go together and comprise what we call a **metric foot**. A foot can consist of one or more words and can begin or end in the middle of a word. Feet are the patterns of stressed and unstressed syllables that make poetry sound rhythmical. When the foot consists of two stressed syllables, as in the first line of 'Bright star', it is called a spondee. It is useful to be familiar with these terms to be able to identify and talk about these patterns of syllables as you analyse poems for part 4 of your IB Diploma. Figure 8.4 provides an overview of the five kinds of feet often used by poets.

Name	Pattern	Examples
iamb	unstressed, *stressed*	would *I*
trochee	*stressed*, unstressed	*pil*low'd
spondee	*stressed, stressed*	*Still, still*
anapest	unstressed, unstressed *stressed*	(rip)ening *breast*
dactyl	*stressed*, unstressed, unstressed	*er*emite

Figure 8.4 The five sorts of feet used in poetry.

Activity 8.1

1 Look again at Text 8.1, the poem 'Bright star', and indicate the stressed and the unstressed syllables. To do this, write out the poem with double spacing between the lines and use a ◡ symbol above the unstressed syllables and a / symbol above the stressed symbols.

2 Compare answers as a class. Do you notice any patterns?

Key terms

Metric foot is a group of stressed and/or unstressed syllables that form the basic unit of rhythm in a poem.

Scansion is the process of finding patterns of unstressed and stressed syllables in lines of poetry.

Verse is a line of poetry.

Enjambement in poetry is the style of continuing a sentence from one line to the next without a pause.

Metre is the rhythmic structure of a verse of poetry.

Verse and metre

Analysing the poem 'Bright star' for its rhythmic pattterns of stressed and unstressed syllables has introduced you to the process known as **scansion**. You have looked at poetic language at the level of letter and syllable. Now your view will widen to include the lines of poetry, also known as **verses**. The term *verse* should not be confused with *sentence*, as sentences are always grammatical structures. In fact many verses of poetry neither begin at the beginning of a sentence nor end at the end of a sentence. When a sentence carries on at the end of one verse into the next without a pause at the end of the line, it is called **enjambement** (or enjambment). The following example is from the poem 'i carry your heart with me' by E.E. Cummings (the lower-case letters are deliberate – this writer is renowned for avoiding capital letters).

i carry your heart with me (i carry it in
my heart) i am never without it (anywhere
i go you go,my dear;and whatever is done
by only me is your doing,my darling)

If poets experiment with syntax so that verses are not necessarily sentences, what then is the organising principle of verses? The answer is **metre**, the rhythmic structure of poetic verse. After clustering syllables into feet, you need to see if there are patterns of feet. In the first line of 'Bright star', Text 8.1, there are five iambs in the verse (although the first is, as you have seen, a spondee). Notice how words can be split across different feet, as in the case of the word *stedfast*.

1	2	3	4	5
Bright star	would *I*	were *sted*	fast *as*	thou *art*

A pattern of five iambs is called an *iambic pentameter* (the prefix *penta-* is from the Greek word for five). We often see patterns of three, four or five metric feet in a verse (see Figure 8.5).

Number of feet	Name of metre	Examples (all iambic)
5	Pentameter	| Of snow | upon | the moun | tains and | the moors |
4	Tetrameter	| Amaz | ing Grace | how sweet | the sound |
3	trimeter	| That saves | a wretch | like me |
2	dimeter	| be gone | be gone |

Figure 8.5 Rhythmic metres in verse.

Activity 8.2

Match the verses of poetry (1–5) to the metres (a–e). Look back at Figures 8.4 and 8.5 for reference.

1 Tyger! Tyger! burning bright   *(William Blake)*
2 And miles to go before I sleep   *(Robert Frost)*
3 There was an old man with a beard   *(Edward Lear)*
4 If I should die think only this of me   *(Rupert Brooke)*
5 I love the jocund dance   *(William Blake)*

a iambic pentameter
b iambic tetrameter
c iambic trimeter
d trochaic tetrameter
e anapaestic trimester

Rhyme and stanza

What is a poem? People often think of poetry as rhyming verse, perhaps because we tend to remember poems that rhyme, but not all poetry has to rhyme. In fact, many poems do not. Look at these opening lines from the poem 'Out, out' by Robert Frost.

The buzz-saw snarled and rattled in the yard
And made dust and dropped stove-length sticks of wood,
Sweet-scented stuff when the breeze drew across it.
And from there those that lifted eyes could count
Five mountain ranges one behind the other
Under the sunset far into Vermont.

The final words of the lines (*yard, wood, it, count, other, Vermont*) do not rhyme. There are two types of poem that do not rhyme, **free verse** and **blank verse**. While free

Key terms

Free verse describes poetry that has neither rhyme nor consistent metre.

Blank verse describes poetry that has a consistent metre but no rhyming scheme.

Answers: Activity 8.2
1d, 2b, 3e, 4a, 5c

%!s(MISSING)

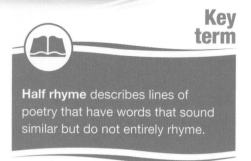

Key term

Half rhyme describes lines of poetry that have words that sound similar but do not entirely rhyme.

verse has no metre or pattern of syllables, blank verse does have metre. The example above from Frost's 'Out, out' does not rhyme but you will notice that each line has ten syllables. It is therefore pentameter with blank verse.

You may have noticed that the words *count* and *Vermont* almost rhyme. English poetry is full of such **half rhymes**, which poets employ to create a certain effect. Arguably Frost uses half rhyme here to chime in the beginning of a story – a story, nevertheless, which will be full of imperfections.

Look back at Text 8.1 and notice that it rhymes. Through rhyme, John Keats creates a mood that is pensive, soft and sweet. We can establish that he uses iambic pentameter throughout the poem. There is also a rhyming pattern from verse to verse. If we code the rhymes at the end of the verses with letters, a clear pattern emerges:

Bright star, would I were stedfast as thou art –	a
Not in lone splendour hung aloft the night	b
And watching with eternal lids apart	a
Like nature's patient, sleepless eremite,	b
The moving waters at their priestlike task	c
Of pure ablution round earth's human shores,	d
Or gazing on the new soft-fallen mask	c
Of snow upon the mountains and the moors –	d
No – yet still stedfast, still unchangeable,	e
Pillow'd upon my fair love's ripening breast,	f
To feel forever its soft fall and swell,	e
Awake for ever in a sweet unrest,	f
Still, still to hear her tender-taken breath,	g
And so live ever – or else swoon to death	g

Thanks to the rhyming scheme, we begin to see clusters of verses. In 'Bright star', there are three verse clusters that follow a similar pattern: abab, cdcd and efef. Clusters such as these are called stanzas, and stanzas are to poetry what paragraphs are to prose – they each usually contain a single idea. We use a series of Latin-based words to refer to stanzas, depending on the number of verses (lines) they contain:

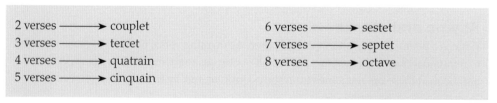

2 verses ⟶ couplet
3 verses ⟶ tercet
4 verses ⟶ quatrain
5 verses ⟶ cinquain
6 verses ⟶ sestet
7 verses ⟶ septet
8 verses ⟶ octave

Even-numbered stanzas are the most common. Poets cluster verses into stanzas for the same reason that novelists use paragraphs: to separate ideas. In Keats's poem 'Bright star', we can follow the evolution of his ideas by analysing the progression of the stanzas:

- The first stanza – a quatrain – expresses the narrator's (arguably the poet's) desire to be as unchanging and as alert as a star. He starts to explain what he means by this by saying he does not want the loneliness of a star, or the isolation of a hermit.
- The second quatrain continues with the narrator's explanation of what he does not want. This quatrain extends the image of the isolation and separateness of the star.

He refers again to religion, to the tide washing the shore and the purity of snow in isolated places.

- In the third quatrain the narrator explains why he wants to be like a star – to be unchanging in the sense of never leaving the woman he loves. We now understand why he has rejected the isolation and asceticism of the religious hermit because cutting himself off from the world would be incompatible with being in love. He wants to capture for ever the moment of sleeping beside his mistress and feeling her breathing.
- In the two last lines – the final couplet – he clarifies further where he always wants to be. He wants to always be with the woman he loves, hearing her breathing. If he cannot always be with her, he says he would rather die.

Figure 8.6 Elizabeth Barrett Browning (1806–61) was an English poet who achieved great success with her poems in both the UK and the USA, and beyond.

Activity 8.3

1 Read Text 8.2, a poem by Elizabeth Barret Browning. On a copy of the poem, write a letter at the end of each verse to indicate the rhyming scheme.
2 What kinds of stanzas does the poet use?
3 What is the main idea in each stanza?
4 Comment on the metre of the poem. What patterns do you see in the verses?
5 Comment on the use of enjambement. Why do you think the poet used this device?

Text 8.2 *How do I love thee?*, Elizabeth Barrett Browning, 1850

1   How do I love thee? Let me count the ways.
       I love thee to the depth and breadth and height
       My soul can reach, when feeling out of sight
       For the ends of being and ideal grace.
5   I love thee to the level of every day's
       Most quiet need, by sun and candle-light.
       I love thee freely, as men strive for right.
       I love thee purely, as they turn from praise.
       I love thee with the passion put to use
10   In my old griefs, and with my childhood's faith.
       I love thee with a love I seemed to lose
       With my lost saints. I love thee with the breath,
       Smiles, tears, of all my life; and, if God choose,
       I shall but love thee better after death.

Types of poem

In Chapter 1, which concentrated on analysing non-fiction, you learned that text types are defined by their audience and purpose. Traditionally, poetry abides by this rule as well, but what is the purpose of poetry? Why do certain ideas lend themselves well to the type of text we call a poem?

Sometimes people want to express their deeper feelings, especially on occasions marking important events in people's lives, such as when a baby is born, when two people get married, or when someone important to them dies. Poetry is a text type

Figure 8.7 People do not normally talk to each other in verse, even the sort of not very good verse found in greetings cards.

Key terms

Ballad is a form of rhyming verse, usually following a pattern of abcb, that tells a narrative and can be set to music.

Sonnet is a fourteen-line poem in iambic pentameter, containing three quatrains and a heroic couplet.

Heroic couplet is two lines of rhyming verse, usually at the end of a sonnet, which tend to be 'closed' (there is no enjambement between the lines) and self-contained.

tip

You may be given a sonnet to comment on in your individual oral commentary. If you have to talk about a poem, be sure to explain why you think the author chose that particular form and look for examples of the form reflecting the content of the poem. Remember that writers may choose the sonnet form in order to:

- continue in an established English tradition
- express love and passion
- sound rhythmic and musical
- show balance and structural harmony.

which focuses quickly on the essence of what someone feels and wants to express, without the need for lots of context or a logical sequencing of events such as you would find in a story. When people communicate for everyday purposes, they do not have the time to craft their words into exquisite phrases – everyday speech is more ordinary. In poems, however, the language is more obviously crafted and the message is therefore more deeply felt. Poetry is also a traditional form of text, having evolved from oral storytelling in the days when few people could read and the printing press (which allowed books to be printed) had not yet been invented. For example, the type of poem known as a **ballad** came about in medieval times as a form for singing short tales and stories. The form and tradition have evolved, shaping the roots of jazz, folk and rock music today.

The texts discussed so far in this chapter, 'Bright star' and 'How do I love thee?', are examples of another type of poem known as the **sonnet**. The sonnet came to England from the Italian *sonetto*, a traditional short song to a lover. There are different types of sonnet. The Italian, or Petrarchan, sonnet is most often used for expressing love. Elizabeth Barrett Browning's poem 'How do I love thee?', Text 8.2, is an example of an Italian sonnet. The English, or Shakespearian, sonnet is more versatile. Poems from the First World War are of this type, where soldiers used the sonnet both to call men to arms and to describe the horrors of the battlefield. Its use of iambic pentameter and three quatrains of the pattern abab, cdcd, efef, followed by a **heroic couplet** (gg), is one of the most common forms of poetry in the English language. Keats's poem 'Bright star', Text 8.1, is an example of an English sonnet.

If you are studying poetry for part 4 of your course, you need to be sure of the sorts of poem you are dealing with. Ask yourself why a particular form is effective for expressing certain ideas. Figure 8.8 provides a guide to understanding some of the common types of poetry found in English.

In order to understand the relationship between form and meaning, it is important to see how a poet uses a certain type of poem to express a certain sentiment. To end this unit you are going to look at a well-known poem by the Welsh poet Dylan Thomas. As you read the poem out loud, ask yourself how the metre, verse and rhyming scheme all contribute to the sentiments that the poet is expressing.

Genre	Sub genre	Purpose	Metre	Form
Lyrical poetry (song-like)	English sonnet	Expression of deep sentiment	Iambic pentameter	*abab, cdcd, efef, gg*
	Italian sonnet	Expression of love	Iambic pentameter	*abba, cddc, efgefg*
	Ode	Glorify an event or person	Free verse, though often iambic	*abab, cdecde*
	Villanelle	Usually pastoral (depicting a rural theme)	Often iambic pentameter	*a^{1}ba^2, aba^1, aba^2, aba^1, aba^2, aba^{1}a^2*
	Limerick	Humour	Anapaestic trimeter (a) and dimeter (b)	*aabba*
Narrative poetry (story-telling)	Ballad	Diverse	Iambic tetrameter (a,c) and trimeter (b)	*abcd*
	Epic	To tell long stories about heroes and great achievements	Free verse, and blank verse	

Figure 8.8 An overview of the more common types of English poem.

Text 8.3 *Do not go gentle into that good night*, Dylan Thomas, 1953

1   Do not go gentle into that good night,
       Old age should burn and rave at close of day;
       Rage, rage against the dying of the light.

       Though wise men at their end know dark is right,
5   Because their words had forked no lightning they
       Do not go gentle into that good night.

       Good men, the last wave by, crying how bright
       Their frail deeds might have danced in a green bay,
       Rage, rage against the dying of the light.

10   Wild men who caught and sang the sun in flight,
       And learn, too late, they grieved it on its way,
       Do not go gentle into that good night.

       Grave men, near death, who see with blinding sight
       Blind eyes could blaze like meteors and be gay,
15   Rage, rage against the dying of the light.

       And you, my father, there on the sad height,
       Curse, bless, me now with your fierce tears, I pray.
       Do not go gentle into that good night.
       Rage, rage against the dying of the light.

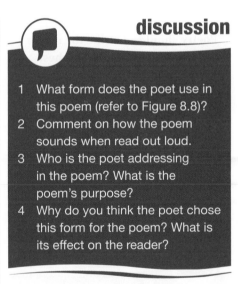

discussion

1 What form does the poet use in this poem (refer to Figure 8.8)?
2 Comment on how the poem sounds when read out loud.
3 Who is the poet addressing in the poem? What is the poem's purpose?
4 Why do you think the poet chose this form for the poem? What is its effect on the reader?

tip

When you are discussing the form of a poem during your individual oral commentary, go through the five levels of sound you have covered in this chapter:

1 Letter *(Is there alliteration or onomatopoeia?)*
2 Syllable *(What kind of metrical feet?)*
3 Metre *(How many feet in a line?)*
4 Rhyme *(Which lines rhyme? Is there a pattern? Can you find the stanzas?)*
5 Type of poem *(What type of poem is it? Why did the writer choose this type?)*

'Poetry should ... strike the reader as a wording of his own highest thoughts, and appear almost a remembrance.'
John Keats (1795–1821)

As you prepare for your individual oral commentary you will want to practise talking about the relationship between the form and meaning of your part 4 works. Read the following transcription of a teacher talking informally in class about the relationship between form and meaning in Dylan Thomas's poem 'Do not go gentle into that good night'.

'Do not go gentle into that good night': form and meaning

The poem is highly structured. Every syllable, foot and verse classifies it as a villanelle (see Figure 8.8). Villanelles are usually pastoral poems, meaning they offer a light and simple view of rural life. They follow a very strict rhyming scheme, which makes them sound like a folk song, with a lot of repetition. You see two lines come back again and again: *Do not go gentle into that good night* (we'll call that A1), and *Rage, rage against the dying of the light* (which we'll call A2). The other verses – we'll call them 'b' verses – all end with the 'ay' sound. That means there are only two sounds at the end of each line and a lot of repetition. This is why people see it as a simple and light form of poetry. So it's rather ironic that Thomas is using this form of all forms of poetry to speak to his dying father. It's as though he is saying, 'Come on, Dad, give it one last hurrah!'

Now, if we look at the syllables, you will see that the poem uses iambic pentameter, which is the standard metre for a villanelle. This rhythm is what makes the poem bounce along like a song, which is in contrast to the sombre mood of the content. He's talking about the regrets of dying men – wise men, good men, wild men and grave men – who all missed out on something in their lives. That's not the kind of theme you would expect to sound 'bouncy' or light. Thomas also throws in a few spondees to contrast that bounciness: *Rage, rage* is one we hear a lot. There are also the spondees with *men*: *wise men, good men, wild men* and *grave men*. These are all tough- and rough-sounding against the rhythm of the villanelle.

The last two lines really reveal the poem's message. Thomas is encouraging his father to be strong and shake a fist in the face of death. With this light-sounding poem, it's as if he dismisses the power of death. He's saying, 'Come on, Dad, we're stronger than this. Show me you can fight it.'

Unit 8.2 **Imagery and figurative language**

Key terms

Imagery is the use of descriptive language to evoke sensory experience.

Figurative language is language that is not intended to be taken literally but uses references to one thing to express ideas about something else.

In the last unit, you saw how sound and structure act as keys to help unlock the meaning of poetry and that by studying the form of a poem you can open up new ways of understanding the content. As you continue to uncover the deeper meaning of poems, you will need more of these keys. Since poetry appeals to the senses, in this unit you will be exploring the use of **imagery** to evoke sensory experiences. Imagery, in literature, is descriptive language that can conjure up sights, sounds, smells, feelings and tastes. Notice the difference here from the last unit, which was about the different sounds we hear, in the phonemes, syllables, words and verses, when a poem is read out loud. When we refer to sounds in this unit we mean the auditory impressions that a poem can evoke. Because poetry has the ability to stir our senses in this way, it can transport us to another world.

Not only does poetry appeal to our senses, it can also help us to look at the world differently. For example, poets often compare inanimate objects with animate ones. You saw how the poet John Keats addressed a poem to a star, an inanimate object, in his poem 'Bright star' (Text 8.1) even though the poem was all about the woman he loved. Poetry often challenges our understanding of the way the world works through the use of **figurative language**. In this unit you will meet several types of figurative language that poets regularly use.

The best way to explore these dimensions of poetry is to start by looking at a poem that paints a picture in the mind. As you read Text 8.4, the poem 'Aedh wishes for the Cloths of Heaven' by William Butler Yeats, ask yourself how it appeals to your senses and invites you to look at the world differently.

Text 8.4 *Aedh wishes for the Cloths of Heaven*, William Butler Yeats, 1899

> Had I the heavens' embroidered cloths,
> 2   Enwrought with golden and silver light,
>   The blue and the dim and the dark cloths
> 4   Of night and light and the half-light,
>   I would spread the cloths under your feet:
> 6   But I, being poor, have only my dreams;
>   I have spread my dreams under your feet;
> 8   Tread softly because you tread on my dreams.

Activity 8.4

1 Using coloured pens or pencils, draw what you see in your mind's eye when you read this poem. (It does not matter if you don't think you can draw – try and depict the image the poem conjures up for you.)

2 Compare your work with that of other students in your class and discuss the differences between them.

Imagery

When you read Text 8.4, did you imagine a blue and silver embroidered cloth? Did you see an image of shining stars? Some readers even 'see' a poor poet. These are experiences that readers have when reading the poem 'Aedh wishes for the Cloths of Heaven'. The picture you see in your mind is evoked by the imagery, in phrases such as *Enwrought with golden and silver light, The blue and the dim and the dark cloths / Of night and light and the half-light… I have spread my dreams under your feet.*

Although these examples appeal more to our sense of sight, imagery, in its poetic sense, refers to poetry's ability to create an experience for the reader by appealing to all of the senses: sight, sound, touch, taste and smell. Perhaps this poem reminded you of a time you walked barefoot on a textured surface. Perhaps you felt the softness of dark, crushed velvet when reading this poem. Memories of our experiences can easily be triggered by imagery.

Poets use imagery for the sake of making abstract ideas concrete. As you read Text 8.5, a poem by Grace Nichols, ask yourself how the concrete scene that is sketched by the poet is really about the abstract concept of beauty.

discussion

1 Name three qualities that you liked about this poem.

2 Name three aspects that you did not like or did not understand about this poem.

3 Think of three questions you would ask the poet if you could speak to him.

You could ask the same questions about any poem you read. They are useful questions to start off a discussion!

Further resources

Poetry.org is a very good website for anyone interested in poetry, with background information on poets and a glossary of poetic devices. (www.poetry.org)

The Poetry Archive website claims to be a 'treasure-trove of English-language poets reading their own work'. Not only are many great, modern poems made available, but you also get a sense of how they should be read. There is also a glossary of literary terms. (www.poetryarchive.org)

The Poetry Foundation is an American organisation for poetry and has a website and also publishes a magazine, called *Poetry*. The website has items on contemporary poets, links to blogs and lesson materials. (www.poetryfoundation.org)

Figure 8.9 Grace Nichols (1950–) is a prolific Guyanese poet who now lives in the UK.

Text 8.5 *Beauty*, Grace Nichols, 1984

```
     Beauty
2    is a fat black woman
     walking the fields
4    pressing a breezed
     hibiscus to her cheek
6    while the sun lights up
     her feet

8    Beauty
     is a fat black woman
10   riding the waves
     drifting in happy oblivion
12   while the sea turns back
     to hug her shape
```

Activity 8.5

Read the poem 'Beauty' (Text 8.5) again and choose words from the poem that appeal to each of the senses. Organise the words in columns in a table, like the one below. One word may fit into more than one category. Examples have been included.

Sight	Sound	Taste	Touch	Smell
fat	sea			sea

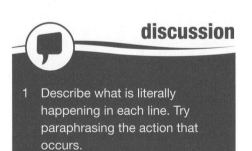

discussion

1 Describe what is literally happening in each line. Try paraphrasing the action that occurs.
2 What do you say to the claim that this is a poem about love?
3 Comment on the rhyming scheme of the poem. How is it like the sea?

Simile and metaphor

Poets often use imagery to compare two things. To introduce the idea of figurative language, re-read the final stanza of Yeats's poem 'Aedh wishes for the Cloths of Heaven' (Text 8.4):

> I would spread the cloths under your feet:
> But I, being poor, have only my dreams;
> I have spread my dreams under your feet;
> Tread softly because you tread on my dreams.

The poem evokes the old-fashioned, romantic image of a gentleman throwing his cloak down on the ground so that a lady can walk without soiling her shoes or hem of her dress. The poet is suggesting that Aedh would throw down the finest, most beautiful embroidered material if he could. Even though Yeats does not say it directly, he implies that Aedh's dreams *are* beautiful pieces of material. This sort of comparison is a metaphor (see page 49).

Metaphor is closely related to simile. Whereas a simile makes a direct comparison using the words 'like' or 'as', a metaphor is less obvious and often involves the verb 'be'. Metaphor compares things by substituting a literal term for a figurative term. Check you understand the difference between simile and metaphor with the examples below.

Simile

When the evening is spread out against the sky
Like a patient etherised upon a table
'The love song of J. Alfred Prufrock', T.S. Eliot

Metaphor

This flea is you and I, and this
Our marriage bed, and marriage temple is
'The flea', John Donne

As you analyse similes and metaphors in poetry, you must ask yourself whether the literal and figurative terms are *named* or *implied*. In 'The love song of J. Alfred Prufrock', the poet uses a simile, where the literal terms, *the evening* and *the sky*, and the figurative terms, *a patient* and *a table*, are named and compared explicitly. In 'The flea', the poet uses a metaphor, where both the literal term, *you and I*, and the figurative term, *This flea*, are named and linked with the use of the verb *be*.

Unlike similes, metaphors compare two things implicitly. In Text 8.4 Yeats *implies* that Aedh's dreams are like a cloak or an embroidered cloth by saying that he spreads his dreams under her feet. In some metaphors the literal term is not named at all – it is only implied and not mentioned explicitly – but the figurative terms, in contrast, are named. This is often seen in riddles, such as the one by Sylvia Plath in her poem 'Metaphors' (Text 8.6). As you read Text 8.6, ask yourself who 'I' is.

'Poetry provides the one permissible way of saying one thing and meaning another.'
Robert Frost (1874–1963)

Text 8.6 *Metaphors*, Sylvia Plath, 1959

    I'm a riddle in nine syllables,
2   An elephant, a ponderous house,
    A melon strolling on two tendrils.
4   O red fruit, ivory, fine timbers!
    The loaf's big with its yeasty rising.
6   Money's new-minted in this fat purse.
    I'm a means, a stage, a cow in calf.
8   I've eaten a bag of green apples,
    Boarded the train there's no getting off.

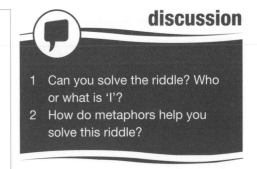
discussion
1 Can you solve the riddle? Who or what is 'I'?
2 How do metaphors help you solve this riddle?

Poets use simile and metaphor to make us look at the world differently. You are likely to come across similes and metaphors in your part 4 texts and be able to identify what the writers are comparing, literally and figuratively. Figure 8.10 gives an overview of simile and the four kinds of metaphor you have read about in this section. (In case you are still racking your brains over the riddle in Text 8.6, the answer can be found in Figure 8.10!)

		Poet	Literal term	Figurative term
Similes (like, as, seems, etc.)			*named*	*named*
		Eliot	evening	patient
			the sky	a table
Metaphors (is, are, etc.)	*Form 1*		*named*	*named*
		Donne	you and I	flea
	Form 2		*named*	*implied*
		Yeats	dreams	cloth (spread)
	Form 3		*implied*	*named*
		Plath	pregnancy (I)	melon
	Form 4		*implied*	*implied*
		Plath	baby (its)	bread (loaf, yeast)

Figure 8.10 An overview of simile and the four forms of metaphor.

Activity 8.6

For the extracts below state:
1 whether they are similes or metaphors
2 what the literal and figurative terms are
3 what is named and/or what is implied.

1 Bright star, would I were stedfast as thou art –
  Not in lone splendour hung aloft the night
  And watching with eternal lids apart
  Like nature's patient, sleepless eremite

2 I love thee freely, as men strive for right.
  I love thee purely, as they turn from praise.

3 Grave men, near death, who see with blinding sight
  Blind eyes could blaze like meteors and be gay

4 I have spread my dreams under your feet;
  Tread softly because you tread on my dreams.

5 Beauty / is a fat black woman / walking the fields

Personification, apostrophe, metonymy and synecdoche

As you look for figurative language in poetry, you are likely to come across **personification**. Personification is a type of metaphor where human qualities are given to an animal, object or concept. In Text 8.5, the poem 'Beauty', the sea is said to *hug* a woman. Because water and waves cannot literally hug a woman, we look for human attributes in the sea. Perhaps the sea accepts the *fat black woman* unconditionally and completely, as a friend would.

In Keats's poem 'Bright Star' (Text 8.1), you saw how a star can be personified. The star is given human qualities such as steadfastness and loneliness. It can look down on earth with open eyelids and stare at the snowy mountains. The star, however, is not only personified: Keats is addressing it, as though it were a living thing. This act of addressing an inanimate object, or someone dead or absent, is called **apostrophe**. Apostrophe allows the reader to listen to the poet's deeper thoughts. Apostrophe is often found in odes (poems that are devoted to someone or something great).

Another form of figurative language is **metonymy**. Metonymy is the use of a word that is commonly associated with the word that is actually meant. There was an example of metonymy at the beginning of this chapter, with the T-shirt that read *Green is the new Red* (Figure 8.2). The colour green is closely associated with environmentalism, and red is closely associated with socialism. The statement refers to a concept shared by environmentalism and socialism – revolution. Similarly, in the riddle poem 'Metaphors' (Text 8.6), the word *loaf* is used to imply bread, which in turn implies a baby. In this case another similar device, **synecdoche**, is used. Synecdoche is the reference to a whole idea through one of its parts. Yeast, for example, is part of bread. When the poet refers to *yeasty rising* she is implying that the baby is like bread being baked in the oven.

In poetry, personification, apostrophe, metonymy and synecdoche help create a world where inanimate things can talk or be talked to, and where nothing has to be mentioned directly by its name. We expect to find figurative language in poetry. In fact, figurative language is what distinguishes poetry from the evening news (Figure 8.12).

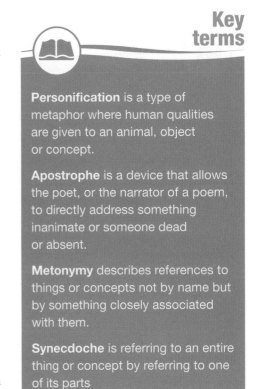

Key terms

Personification is a type of metaphor where human qualities are given to an animal, object or concept.

Apostrophe is a device that allows the poet, or the narrator of a poem, to directly address something inanimate or someone dead or absent.

Metonymy describes references to things or concepts not by name but by something closely associated with them.

Synecdoche is referring to an entire thing or concept by referring to one of its parts

Activity 8.7

Find examples of personification, apostrophe, metonymy and synecdoche in the following lines from poems you have read in this chapter. There may be more than one in each line.

1 And watching with eternal lids apart
2 I love thee to the depth and breadth and height / My soul can reach, when feeling out of sight
3 Old age should burn and rave at close of day
4 while the sea turns back / to hug her shape
5 O red fruit, ivory, fine timbers!

Revision

In the course of analysing Texts 8.1–8.6, you may have seen examples of devices that you have learned about in earlier parts of this course. For example, you may have noticed the use of symbolism (see page 201 in Unit 7.2) in Dylan Thomas's poem 'Do not go gentle into that good night' (Text 8.3), where night stood for death and light for life. You may have seen irony (see Text 2.5, pages 49–50) in this poem as well, as the light tone of the villanelle form did not match the seriousness of the subject matter.

"Here as on a darkling plain swept with confused alarms of struggle and flight, where ignorant armies clash by night, Matthew Arnold, Fox News, Channel Five."

Figure 8.11 What kinds of poetic devices are used in this news broadcast?

Higher level

At higher level you read one more literary text than at standard level. There are many activities that you can do to increase your understanding of this extra text and demonstrate your understanding of the coursework.

1 Imagine you have the opportunity of asking the author of your text ten questions about it. In groups, think of ten questions. Then, as a class, decide which ten questions will be the top ten. Narrow your class list down to the top five questions, followed by three and then one. Can you answer this question without speaking to the author? Why was this last one the most important?

2 Working individually or in groups, take a poem that you are working on and find the most important word in it. Write this word in the middle of a large sheet of paper. Around it, write a ring of words that you feel are of secondary importance. Then write a second ring of words that you feel are next in importance. Explain to your class why you selected these words for each ring.

3 Each HL student pretends to be a character from a novel or play that you have read for part 4. The HL students prepare their roles carefully before the lesson. At the lesson, the SL students ask any question they like of them. Although the SL students have not read the text, they must find out as much as they can about it by asking good questions.

'How do I love thee?' (Text 8.2, page 199), as you may have noticed, is a rhetorical question (see page 48 in Unit 2.4).

You will also understand that ideas from part 1 on tone and mood (pages 43–46 in Unit 2.3) are relevant to fiction in general and poetry in particular. Terms like *diction*, *denotation* and *connotation* apply also to poetry, as poets create an atmosphere and instigate a response through carefully chosen words.

The theory from this chapter, added to that from previous units of this coursebook, will give you an even greater insight into what you have studied earlier in the course. After your study of figurative language in this chapter, for example, you will be better equipped to understand Martin Luther King's 'I have a dream' speech (Text 2.2, pages 41–42). There may also be poetic language to explore in non-fiction, both in the examples used in this coursebook and in your wider reading.

You will by now have accumulated the tools you need to engage in close reading and text analysis, both for non-fiction and fiction texts. Before you tackle the final assessment of a literary text, you may want to look back over the previous chapters in this coursebook to review and consolidate what you have learned.

Text 8.7 *Father and child*, Gwen Harwood

Extract 1 *Barn Owl*

5   Let him dream of a child
       obedient, angel-mild – …

16   master of life and death,
       a wisp-haired judge whose law
       would punish beak and claw.

28   … I saw
       those eyes that did not see
       mirror my cruelty

39   I leaned my head upon
       my father's arm, and wept,
       owl blind in early sun
       for what I had begun.

Extract 2 *Nightfall*

5   Father and child, we stand
       in time's long-promised land.

35   … Old king
       your marvelous journey's done.
       Your night and day are one

40   … grown to learn
       what sorrows, in the end,
       no words, no tears can mend.

Activity 8.8

Read the five statements (1–5) below that a student made about the extracts from the poem 'Father and child' by Gwen Harwood (Text 8.7). The statements relate to many of the ideas that have been discussed in Chapter 2 on close reading. Match the statements with the illustrations (a–e) taken from the poem.

1 The narrator establishes a childlike tone through the use of diction.
2 The poem is about a girl coming of age and feeling remorse for killing a barn owl.
3 Harwood uses symbolism to comment on greater themes.
4 The final stanza relies on allusion, a stylistic device that unlocks a new level of meaning for the reader.
5 The poet uses metaphor to imply that the father is dying.

a The reference to King Lear (*Old king*) invites the reader to see the reconciliation between father and daughter.
b In the first line, the phrase *let him* sounds mischievous. The reader hears the voice of a daughter who wants to defy her father.
c One who experiences no difference between *night and day* has died. Similarly, life is often compared with a journey – in the father's case, a journey which is *done*.
d Seeing and blindness represent life and death, as the girl lives on and the father and owl die.
e She begins to understand the consequences of her actions in lines 6–8: *I saw / those eyes that did not see / mirror my cruelty.*

Assessment: The individual oral commentary

By this point in your IB Diploma course you will have the theoretical tools to approach the individual oral commentary. You have studied literary devices and applied them to texts throughout this coursebook. This oral exam asks you apply them to your part 4 texts. At first you may not feel confident about speaking for 10–15 minutes on a 40-line extract (for which you only have 20 minutes to prepare).

Performing under this sort of exam pressure can be a daunting prospect. Yet you can put these factors into perspective:

- You have probably had many classroom discussions on the part 4 texts, amounting to much more preparation time than the 20 minutes allowed in the exam.
- The passage should not be a complete surprise to you. You are likely to have a good idea about where in the text the extract might be selected from.
- If your class has discussed a poem for 30 minutes, you will find it quite easy to comment on the poem for least 10 minutes by yourself.
- Remember that although you cannot take notes into the exam, you can annotate the text quite heavily in the 20 minutes allowed.

Make a plan for yourself, using the Big 5 method (see page 35), the mechanics of fiction (see Chapter 7) or the different levels of poetic devices, including structure, sound and figurative language (pages 202–09). For certain types of text, you may simply want to go through it from beginning to end, commenting on each line as you go (this method tends to work best with poetry).

TOK

One of the fundamental questions in TOK and language arts is *What makes something art?* Similarly our guiding question for this chapter has been *What makes English poetic?* Although you have covered several literary devices to help you answer the question, you may still not have found a satisfactory answer. Just because a poem contains imagery, metre and alliteration, it does not necessarily mean that it is poetic! Furthermore, what one reader may consider poetic may not be poetic for another.

Select one text from this chapter and explain why you think it could be considered as art. Bear in mind the following three criteria often used to distinguish art from kitsch, or 'pulp'. (You can also apply these criteria to the texts you are studying for part 4.)

1 Art is created with intention.
2 Art has intrinsic quality (i.e. it is not good just because someone says it is good).
3 Art creates a response from its audiences.

Answers: Activity 8.8
1 b, 2 e, 3 d, 4 a, 5 c

However you prefer to prepare, always do the following:
- Re-read the requirements for the individual oral commentary (page viii).
- Make sure you know what the grading criteria are (pages viii–ix).
- Look at the sample student responses on pages 211–13 and 215–17.

Annotated extract

Nadsat – fictive language, dystopian setting: Slavic (communist) jargon of youth

A Clockwork Orange, Anthony Burgess, 1962

Purpose of Deltoid's visit – warning

Figurative speech, Alex – poetic + creative

Inward thoughts, enjoys negative attention

Hates idea of prison, want to avoid getting caught

Dystopian society only interested in rooting out the bad not encouraging the good – rationalising his behaviour

1   'Nobody's got anything on me, sir,' I said. 'I've been out of the rookers of the millicents for a long time now.'
    'That's just what worries me,' sighed P. R. Deltoid. 'A bit too long of a time to be healthy. You're about due now by my reckoning. That's why I'm warning you,
5   little Alex, to keep your handsome young proboscis out of the dirt, yes. Do I make myself clear?'
    'As an unmuddied lake, sir,' I said. 'Clear as an azure sky of deepest summer. You can rely on me, sir.' And I gave him a nice zooby smile.
    But when he'd ookadeeted and I was making this very strong pot of chai,
10 I grinned to myself over this veshch that P. R. Deltoid and his droogs worried about. All right, I do bad, what with crasting and tolchocks and carves with the britva and the old in-out-in-out, and if I get loveted, well, too bad for me, O my little brothers, and you can't run a country with every chelloveck comporting himself in my manner of the night. So if I get loveted and it's three months in this mesto and
15 another six in that, and then, as P. R. Deltoid so kindly warns, next time, in spite of the great tenderness of my summers, brothers, it's the great unearthly zoo itself, well, I say: 'Fair, but a pity, my lords, because I just cannot bear to be shut in. My endeavour shall be, in such future as stretches out its snowy and lilywhite arms to me before the nosh overtakes or the blood spatters its final chorus in twisted metal
20 and smashed glass on the highroad, to not get loveted again.' Which is fair speeching. But, brothers, this biting of their toe-nails over what is the cause of badness is what turns me into a fine laughing malchick. They don't go into what is the cause of goodness, so why of the other shop? If lewdies are good that's because they like it, and I wouldn't ever interfere with their pleasures, and so of the other
25 shop. And I was patronizing the other shop. More, badness is of the self, the one, the you or me on our oddy knockies, and that self is made by old Bog or God and is his great pride and radosty. But the not-self cannot have the bad, meaning they of the government and the judges and the schools cannot allow the bad because they cannot allow the self. And is not our modern history, my brothers, the story of
30 brave malenky selves fighting these big machines? I am serious with you, brothers, over this. But what I do I do because I like to do.

Direct speech

Direct narration – persuades us to understand

Deny free will = deny people the right to be bad

Conflict – individual versus society, 1 individual versus another

Guiding questions:
- *How does this passage give us insight into the deeper themes of the novel?*
- *What is the significance of the language used by Alex?*

Individual oral commentary transcript (SL)

I have a passage from *A Clockwork Orange*, which is by Anthony Burgess. It's from the part of the book after Alex has been sneaking around at night and doing evil things, like harassing people and rape. It's the next morning and he's skipping school. He's just slept in and now he gets a visit from P. R. Deltoid, who is the school counsellor or some kind of person who is trying to stop Alex from getting into trouble. You could say he's the antagonist because he's trying to stop Alex, the protagonist, from doing what he loves most: violence and crime. His name also sounds like some kind of medicine, which I think is symbolic. Deltoid stands for help. You see this early on in the passage *I'm warning you, little Alex, to keep your handsome young proboscis out of the dirt, yes.* It's right there in line 5. A proboscis is like a long protruding thing, like a stinger on a bee or a nose. It's an interesting choice of words because you could say Alex stings with his stinger. It's part of the nature versus nurture theme.

I'm going to talk about themes now and after that I'll comment on how a lot of the literary devices support these themes. I'll talk about various aspects, like point of view, narration, figurative speech and Nadsat, the language of the novel.

But first the major themes of this novel: I think Burgess is trying to say something deep and profound about human nature, and how we are all a little evil by nature. We can't really help it. Alex is trying to explain to the reader that he can't help being evil by nature. He says this in lines 25–27: *More, badness is of the self, the one, the you or me on our oddy knockies, and that self is made by old Bog or God and is his great pride and radosty.* He's saying that God makes everyone a little evil.

Human nature and how it's evil is one theme. Another is the notion of free will. Alex, in this passage, is arguing that he has a right to be evil. He's trying to convince us that it's acceptable to be violent and rape women. The *old in–out* is one particular reference to rape, which, you could argue, is a euphemism. It implies he has a right to do these things. He says that here, just before that last line I mentioned: *They don't go into what is the cause of goodness, so why of the other shop? If lewdies are good that's because they like it, and I wouldn't ever interfere with their pleasures, and so of the other shop.* As you know, he gets caught and the state tries to kill his free will to prevent him from committing acts of violence. All in all free will is a recurring theme in this book.

Another recurring theme of this novel is incarceration. He talks a lot in this passage about getting locked up and how he would hate for that to happen to him. He says, *I just cannot bear to be shut in.* He's like a wild animal that can't be

The individual oral commentary, the final assessment of this unit, is not the final assessment of your IB English language and literature course. The final assessment will be Papers 1 and 2. Although your teacher decides when you do your commentary, make sure you thoroughly revise your part 4 texts beforehand. Look back again at Chapters 7 and 8 to remind yourself of the key points. Your teacher may set you at least one mock individual oral commentary before taking the final exam. Listening to a recording of your mock exam can be very useful preparation for the real thing.

Your teacher will compile a selection of extracts from your part 4 texts. Although you are not allowed to know which passage you will be given to talk about in your individual oral commentary, you are allowed to know which extracts have been chosen by the teacher for the compilation. You can even suggest extracts for the compilation. As a useful class exercise, each student chooses an extract they consider significant to the text and prepares a presentation on it in class. Listen carefully to the other students' presentations, as one of their extracts may turn out to be yours in the real exam.

tamed. And he knows it. He calls the prison the *great unearthly zoo*, which is really poetic almost.

To shift from themes to narrative voice now, I'd like to talk about how Alex is really poetic when he describes things. I think this ties in with Burgess's themes of taming a wild beast and killing free will. When Deltoid talks to him at the beginning and asks him if he has been clear, Alex responds by saying, *As an unmuddied lake. As clear as an azure sky of deepest summer, sir.* I like that *sir* on the end, because Alex always has this tone of showing respect for others, when in fact he's not being respectful at all. It's a use of irony, actually.

Next there is a description of how he wants to avoid getting caught, *Fair, but a pity, my lords, because I just cannot bear to be shut in. My endeavour shall be, in such future as stretches out its snowy and lilywhite arms to me before the nosh overtakes or the blood spatters its final chorus in twisted metal and smashed glass on the highroad, to not get loveted again.* We see personification here. The future opens up its *snowy and lilywhite arms*. That's figurative language. And there's also a lot of imagery here with *blood spattering its final chorus in twisted metal and smashed glass on the highroad*. It sounds like a car crash. It's very visual and really gruesome.

I think Burgess has Alex use creative language because he wants to show us Alex's creative side. His creative side is part of his evil side. He loves Beethoven and is careful about how he dresses. After they beat the evilness out of him in that treatment he goes through, he's also allergic to Beethoven. It makes him throw up when he hears it. I think Burgess is trying to say something like evilness and creativity go hand-in-hand.

Oh and I also want to talk about Nadsat, this strange language that Alex is speaking in the book. We see these weird words here, like *rookers of the millicents* which means the 'hands of the police'. There are more words, like *tolchoks, britva* and *droogs*. Burgess actually made up a language for this novel. The idea is that this book takes place sometime in the future, when communism has taken over the world and people like Alex find Slavic languages cool. So they use it in their English. I think Burgess did this to show us what it would be like to live a world where the police try to 'fix' people by killing their free will. It's a communist idea. He's warning us against communism.

The title, by the way, **A Clockwork Orange**, is also about 'fixing' people. Clockwork refers to how people can be wound up like a clock under certain treatment so that they do what the state wants them to do and behave like the state wants them to behave. *Orange* is like the word *orangutan*, which is Malay for 'man of the forest'. You could say the title really means something like 'A tamed man'.

Getting back to the way Alex talks, I wanted to say a few things about narrative voice. Burgess has Alex tell his story to us directly. It's first-person point of view, and it's what you call direct narration. He's always using these phrases like *oh my brothers* which are supposed to make us feel sympathetic towards him. He's actually talking to the reader, telling the reader his life story. But there's also dialogue, which we see here in this passage too. He talks to us and he also shows us some action and dialogue. I think Burgess had Alex tell the story so that we could get into the mind of a madman and feel some empathy for him. He also shows us a lot of action to make the story come to life and feel real.

Finally I would like to talk about what kind of novel this is. It's dystopian. Dystopian novels are always concerned with some kind of oppressive state. In this passage that's P. R. Deltoid, who is warning Alex. Alex is also thinking about this oppressive state and talking to us about it in the last lines of the passage: *the judges and the schools cannot allow the bad because they cannot allow the self. And is not our modern history, my brothers, the story of brave malenky selves fighting these big machines?* The conflict in lots of dystopian novels, including this one, is the individual versus society. Just the fact that Deltoid is paying Alex a visit is a kind of conflict situation in itself, part of this individual versus society conflict.

We talked about the Bildungsroman genre in class, which **A Clockwork Orange** belongs to. It's about a young boy coming of age. Alex is only 15 years old. That's also why Burgess wanted to show us Alex's thoughts. He wants to show us what it means to grow up and outgrow these violent tendencies (that's what happens at the end of the book). In this passage Alex is thinking about Deltoid's warning and about what it would be like to go to jail. He's pretty stubborn in his thinking and a little hypocritical too. On the one hand he says, Oh, if I get caught, so be it. On the other hand he says, I would hate to go to prison – the *unearthly zoo*. He's going through growing pains, you could say. It's Alex versus Alex. That's the other kind of conflict situation that we're looking at here: one individual versus himself. He's struggling to understand himself.

So to conclude, this passage is a good example of some of the bigger themes of the book. It comments on nature versus nurture, free will and incarceration. Anthony Burgess comments on all of these things through Alex, a 15-year-old, violent boy. We get to see and hear his thoughts as Alex talks directly to us and tells us his story. He tells us what it's like to be him. It's a typical dystopian novel and Bildungsroman, because we see what it's like for him to come of age in this creepy society where the school counsellor pays him a visit, even though he hasn't been caught making trouble … yet. In fact you could say this passage is foreshadowing, because he talks about what it would be like for him to go to jail. And then he actually goes to jail.

Teacher's comments

Although the student's register is quite informal in his response, he demonstrates a good understanding of literary devices in relation to the text.

Criterion A: Knowledge and understanding of the text or extract – 8 out of 10

The student puts the passage into the perspective of the whole novel, without summarising the novel too much or digressing from the main topics. The student explores the author's intentions by discussing the extract in relation to several themes. Nevertheless some statements are not made relevant to the passage, for example he explains the title's meaning, 'a tamed man', but he does not show how Alex acts as a 'tamed man' in the extract.

Criterion B: Understanding of the use and effects of literary features – 6 out of 10

The student shows that he has understood the coursework, by referring to genre, theme, narrative voice and other stylistic devices. Applying them to this work demonstrates critical thinking. For example, he finds two types of conflict in the passage, identifies imagery and explores the characteristics of the dystopian novel. Although he states and illustrates his arguments well, his focus on the effects of the literary devices on the reader is often implicit.

Criterion C: Organisation – 3 out of 5

The student uses signposts, such as 'I'm going to talk about ...', which really help clarify the structure of the commentary. For the most part, the student sticks to his outline quite well. Nevertheless, we hear the student interrupt himself by saying, 'Oh, I would also like to talk about ...'. Many important ideas are presented as side notes, such as 'by the way' or 'getting back to this point'. The student also introduces the idea of foreshadowing in the last lines, which should be used to summarise earlier ideas. These inconsistencies have prevented the student from scoring a higher mark for this criterion. Finally, the student integrates examples into their narrative very well. The student has a clear intention of discussing certain extracts from the passage and using them to illustrate points on narrative voice, genre and theme.

Criterion C: Language – 3 out of 5

While the language flows freely, with few hesitations, the student does not consistently use an academic register that is appropriate to the exam situation. The use of vocabulary and idiom is somewhat varied. but limited to simple words such as *get* and *like*. Phrases used such as 'Finally I would like to talk about what kind of novel this is. It's dystopian,' are neither convincing nor academic. Instead the student should say, 'Finally I will talk about the dystopian literature, and how this work falls into that genre.' Other statements like 'P. R. Deltoid, who is the school counsellor or some kind of person who is trying to stop Alex from getting into trouble' contain imprecise language that suggests the student does not know the text very well.

Annotated extract

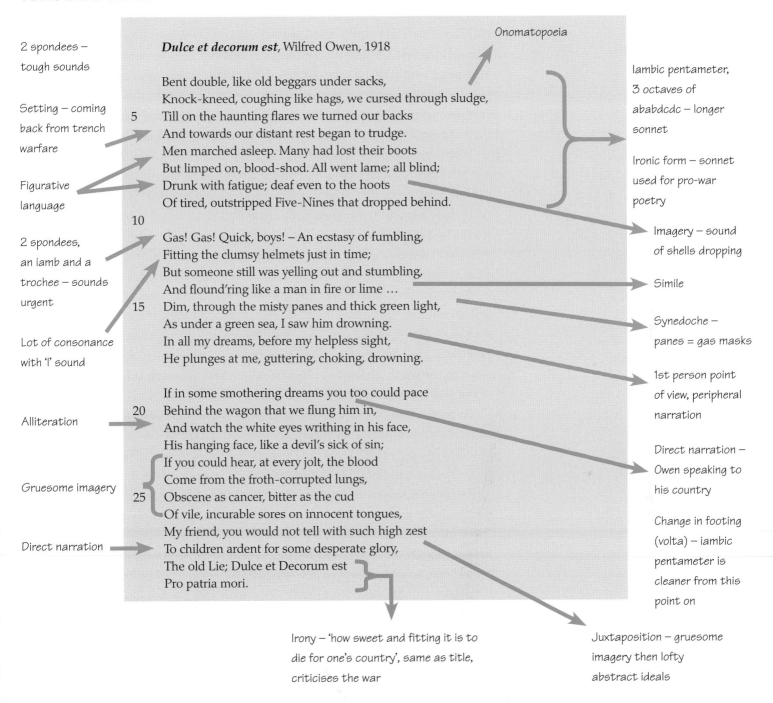

2 spondees – tough sounds

Setting – coming back from trench warfare

Figurative language

2 spondees, an iamb and a trochee – sounds urgent

Lot of consonance with 'l' sound

Alliteration

Gruesome imagery

Direct narration

Onomatopoeia

Iambic pentameter, 3 octaves of ababdcdc – longer sonnet

Ironic form – sonnet used for pro-war poetry

Imagery – sound of shells dropping

Simile

Synedoche – panes = gas masks

1st person point of view, peripheral narration

Direct narration – Owen speaking to his country

Change in footing (volta) – iambic pentameter is cleaner from this point on

Irony – 'how sweet and fitting it is to die for one's country', same as title, criticises the war

Juxtaposition – gruesome imagery then lofty abstract ideals

Dulce et decorum est, Wilfred Owen, 1918

Bent double, like old beggars under sacks,
Knock-kneed, coughing like hags, we cursed through sludge,
5 Till on the haunting flares we turned our backs
And towards our distant rest began to trudge.
Men marched asleep. Many had lost their boots
But limped on, blood-shod. All went lame; all blind;
Drunk with fatigue; deaf even to the hoots
Of tired, outstripped Five-Nines that dropped behind.
10
Gas! Gas! Quick, boys! – An ecstasy of fumbling,
Fitting the clumsy helmets just in time;
But someone still was yelling out and stumbling,
And flound'ring like a man in fire or lime …
15 Dim, through the misty panes and thick green light,
As under a green sea, I saw him drowning.
In all my dreams, before my helpless sight,
He plunges at me, guttering, choking, drowning.

If in some smothering dreams you too could pace
20 Behind the wagon that we flung him in,
And watch the white eyes writhing in his face,
His hanging face, like a devil's sick of sin;
If you could hear, at every jolt, the blood
Come from the froth-corrupted lungs,
25 Obscene as cancer, bitter as the cud
Of vile, incurable sores on innocent tongues,
My friend, you would not tell with such high zest
To children ardent for some desperate glory,
The old Lie; Dulce et Decorum est
Pro patria mori.

Individual oral commentary transcription (HL)

I've been presented with **_Dulce et decorum est_**, a poem by Wilfred Owen. The poem was written in 1918, towards the end of the First World War, from the battlefield. We can assume the poet is the narrator, because it is written from Owen's perspective. He was a captain in the British Army, fighting in Belgium against the Germans, and most likely witnessed the event that he recounts in this narrative poem.

It tells the story of a group of dejected soldiers retreating from the front lines. They are attacked by gas: a kind of invisible enemy. One soldier cannot get his gas mask on in time and dies a gruesome death, right there before Owen's eyes. The title and the last line of the poem, *Dulce et decorum est pro patria mori*, means 'How sweet and fitting it is to die for one's country.' It was used to recruit men to go to war. The death of this soldier, however, is anything but sweet and fitting. Therefore we can say that Owen is criticising pro-war propaganda by using irony. He wants to show the world how people really die on the front lines.

In this individual oral commentary I'm going to talk about how Owen criticises the war in his poem through irony. And I'm going to focus on the structure, the sound of the poem and some other poetic devices, such as imagery and figurative language. All of these express the writer's message and purpose: to criticise war propaganda.

To start off, we have to look at the kinds of sounds this poem makes. The poem opens with the line *Bent double, like old beggars under sacks*. This is not the most pleasant line of poetry. The 'b' sound, which is not the smoothest sound in English, is repeated three times in the first line. The 'l' sound too. Owen is using alliteration and consonance here, which is usually pleasant to the ears, if used with softer sounds. Here it sounds harsh and rough. We see alliteration throughout the poem. *And watch the white eyes writhing in his face* is another example of alliteration, which sounds really gross. Not only the image that it creates, but I mean the effect of the 'w' and 'eye' sounds when put so closely together.

On a sound level there is something else that Owen does very well: he uses a lot of onomatopoeia. Words like *sludge*, *gargling* and *guttering* are just a few of the examples of words that sound like the actions they represent. They are also really grotesque sounds. They add to the imagery of the poem, which I'll talk about later.

As far as syllables and metric feet are concerned, the poem is also full of harsh sounds. There are lots of spondees, like *Bent double* and *Gas! Gas! Quick, boys!* There are also some trochees, like *fumbling*, *stumbling* and *drowning*. These sounds are not very aesthetically pleasing. There're not as aesthetically pleasing as iambic pentameter, which we also find in this poem. You see mostly iambic pentameter in the last stanza, after Owen has finished describing the attack. I think Owen uses spondees and irregular feet, in contrast to iambic pentameter, to show the reader – no, to let the reader *hear* – what war sounds like.

The form of this poem is very interesting. The poem is a sonnet of 28 lines, or actually it's like two sonnets of 14 lines. Sonnets are usually 14 lines long, but in this one there are no heroic couplets. Maybe because there is nothing heroic about dying in war. I think this is what Owen is trying to say. Anyways this goes to illustrate the point I want to make here which is this: on the surface Owen uses a classical, formal, English structure: the sonnet. This was used by a lot of pro-war poets as well. Under the surface of the poem, however, we see a lot of distortion. The iambic pentameter doesn't feel right. There are no heroic couplets. Some lines have 11 syllables. All in all, it's not perfect. This is exactly what Owen is trying to say through the form of the poem: war is not perfect. All of those war poets who wrote perfect sonnets to get you to come to war are lying. I think this is what he is trying to say.

Now I'm going to talk about imagery. Just like the structure and sound of the poem, the imagery also shows us that war is ugly. Like I said earlier, the poem is full of sounds. You can hear the bombshells dropping in line 7, where it says *hoots*. You can hear how their boots go through the mud in lines 2 and 4 with *sludge* and *trudge*. And finally you can hear someone shout *Gas! Gas!* These sounds make it come to life. It's almost as if you're there.

Not only are there lots of sounds in this poem, there are also lots and lots of things to see. Actually Owen packs it so full of images that you almost see two things in every phrase. For example they *cursed through sludge*, and someone *was yelling out and stumbling*. This one is one of my favourites: *He plunges at me, guttering, choking, drowning*. There's a lot to see and hear in the poem. And it's all very gruesome and grotesque. Actually, it makes me understand why soldiers suffered from shell shock or post-traumatic war syndrome. In fact Owen also suffers from this at night, in his dreams, he says it right here, *In all my dreams, before my helpless sight*.

Getting back to what I said in the introduction, you see here that Owen is a character in this story. He talks about *we* in line 2. And in line 14 he says, *I saw him drowning*. He turns to the reader and speaks to him directly, as well. So it's direct narration. In lines 17, 21 and 25 he talks to you. Basically in this last stanza he's saying, Look, if you had to walk behind this cart that we threw this dead soldier into and you had to watch him die, you would not say it's so great to die for your country. This is the narrative voice of the poem.

Finally, there are a few more devices I want to talk about. I want to talk about figurative language. Owen uses a lot of metaphors in the poem to illustrate his point. The men were *drunk with fatigue*, and *marched asleep*. Those metaphors compare an implied tiredness with drunkenness and sleep. Like I said earlier, he also sees the man *drowning* in line 14. The choking sound of dying from gas is caused by the lungs filling up with fluid. It must have sounded like someone drowning. The gas also makes the man fumble around like he is on fire. This is a simile, which paints a picture of what it must have been like. So he uses metaphors and similes to tell us how horrific it was there.

He also uses synecdoche to describe what's literally going on. We know these soldiers are retreating from the front lines, because he talks about their backs turned to the flares. This is very sad because retreating is not the most patriotic thing. It's not something you think of when you hear *Dulce et decorum est pro patria mori*. There's more synecdoche in line 13 with the *misty pane* and the *thick green light*. We know that Owen has his gas mask on and he's watching the man die from the gas, because the *pane* and *green* indicate this.

So, to conclude: this poem is about the horrors of war. And it criticises all of those who glorify war. It does this by contrasting horrific imagery and ugly sounds with the beautiful phrase in Latin *Dulce et decorum est pro patria mori*. There's a big juxtaposition between these two, which is very symbolic of the entire poem. Owen conveys his criticism of an ugly war through this poem that is full of paradoxes.

Activity 8.9

1   Read the student sample responses for the individual oral commentary at standard and higher level.
2   Compare and contrast the two commentaries. How are they similar and different? Why do you think this is?
3   For each commentary, write the outline you think the student would have written before they gave their presentation. Use headings, bullet points and concise wording in your outlines.

tip

In individual oral commentaries students often forget to state the obvious. This sample student's response, however, includes important, basic information – that the soldiers are retreating and under attack – which allows her to make deeper interpretations. Although your teacher may be conducting the exam, pretend that he or she knows nothing of the extract. Such an approach will help you to include everything that needs to be said.

Teacher's comments

This is an excellent response to the poem. The student has used this poem to show that she understands poetry and poetic devices.

Criterion A: Knowledge and understanding of the text or extract - 9

The student has an excellent understanding of the poem and poetry in general. The student places this text in the context of First World War poetry, commenting on pro-war propaganda and the reasons for shell shock. What's more, the student understands what is literally going on in the poem, pointing out that the soldiers are retreating, that they are attacked with gas and bombs are dropping. The student's points are consistently supported with relevant examples, which are well integrated.

Criterion B: Understanding of the use and effects of literary features – 10 out of 10

Not only can the student identify the poetic devices in the poem, but she can also explain why the poet uses them. For example, the student talks about the use of an imperfect sonnet as a kind of protest against perfect, pro-war sonnets and explains that the effects of the literary devices are on the reader, sometimes speaking on a personal level. The student uses terms like 'distortion', 'gross' and 'gruesome' to describe how the images and sounds of the poem make her feel and applies terms such as synecdoche and iambic pentameter in a very relevant and clear way, explaining *why* Owen may have used them.

Criterion B: Organisation – 5 out of 5

The student has a clear outline in her mind and knows the order in which she wants to discuss her points. This is signalled to the teacher by using key literary terms followed by illustrations throughout her commentary. The student's illustrations are well integrated into the theoretical framework that is presented. The structure of her commentary is also very effective, because it looks at the different levels of sound and structure in the poem. As the student goes through each level, her main point – that Owen is criticising war propaganda – becomes clearer and more supported.

Criterion C: Language – 4 out of 5

The student's register and vocabulary are very good and she uses the proper literary terms to explain her points, such as metaphor and synecdoche. The student is consistently accurate in her use of grammar, and at times uses structures that are complex and challenging. Sentences such as *Just like the structure and sound of the poem, the imagery also shows us that war is ugly* are fluid and academic. These sentences are offset by the occasional fragmented sentence, which is acceptable in an oral presentation with little preparation.

Frequently asked questions The individual oral commentary

What if I don't talk for long enough?

You will lose points for criteria A and C, knowledge and understanding, and organisation. If this happens, you will probably demonstrate only superficial awareness of the subject matter (Criterion A) and you will not have organised your commentary effectively (Criterion B). You should not be marked down for Criterion C.

What if my mind goes completely blank?

If you stop, the recording will continue. Although your teacher is not allowed to help you by asking questions or instigating discussion, in extreme circumstances they can give small prompts and encouragement. If you find yourself panicking, then stop, take a deep breath (there is time for this) and read out part or all of the extract so that you become accustomed to hearing your own voice. You might also find that you spot things in the passage that are worth elaborating on.

What if I am interrupted?

No matter what happens, the recording will continue for the full duration of the commentary and will not be paused or switched off until the time is up. The recording continues even if someone walks into the exam room. If you are interrupted, simply stop, collect your thoughts, then continue. This will not affect how you are assessed.

What is my teacher's role?

In the first 10 minutes your teacher is not allowed to interrupt your commentary. Your teacher is there to listen, take notes and assess. After the first 10 minutes you and your teacher may engage in a discussion, in which he or she asks you to clarify any points made earlier in your commentary. Your teacher is not allowed to steer your commentary in any direction, influence your response or introduce you to any new ideas.

Is it fair to grade SL and HL students according to the same criteria?

You may be surprised to learn that SL and HL students are assessed according to the same criteria for the internal assessment. In fact the descriptors for the external assessment are not too dissimilar between SL and HL for that matter. Where then do examiners differentiate? The grade boundaries are different for SL and HL students and they are slightly different for each exam session, depending on the results. For example, while 11 out of 30 marks for an individual oral commentary might earn an SL student 4 out of 7, an HL student would receive a 3 out of 7. In short the expectations are higher at HL.

When do I find out my grade?

Your teacher decides whether to tell you the number of marks you have been awarded for your presentation. Even if you know your marks, however, you will not find out the grade boundaries until much later. You won't know your final grade for the individual oral commentary, on a scale of 1–7, until after your course grade has been awarded.

What happens to the recording?

Although your teacher marks your response according to the criteria, your recording may still be sent for moderation by the International Baccalaureate. You teacher will send the commentaries with the highest and lowest scores plus a selection of other commentaries that are randomly requested. The IB moderator may increase or decrease the marks your teacher awarded you. (Occasionally, the moderator may ask for all the commentaries from your class to be sent if it looks from the sample as though the teacher has been too harsh or too lenient.)

Chapter 8 summary

This chapter has introduced you to many of the tools you will need to analyse poetry. By looking at the various poetic devices that rely on sound, you have learned that you are meant to hear poetry as well as read it. Devices such as alliteration and onomatopoeia reflect the mood of a poem. Through scansion, you have seen how the syllables of words form metric feet. Poets select their words carefully, as stressed and unstressed syllables create a rhythm for the audience. Rhyme and rhyming patterns also affect the reader. Writers often use these devices to build on traditions of certain types of poetry, such as sonnets or villanelles.

Besides looking at the structure of poetry you have also looked at figurative language. Poets evoke sense perception to engage the reader, and sight, sound, taste, touch and smell are all part of the concrete imagery that poets use to convey abstract ideas. Furthermore, poets express their ideas by making comparisons, both literally and figuratively, naming some things and implying others. Simile, metaphor and personification are a few of the poetic devices that encourage readers to look at the world differently.

Finally you saw what close reading and text analysis look like in practice in the two sample responses for the individual oral commentary. The sample responses demonstrated a good understanding of the deeper meaning of the texts and their literary devices.

The aim of this whole coursebook has been to help you understand how both fiction and non-fiction texts work, presenting you with the tools to deconstruct a great variety of texts, from advertisements to poems. Providing you with better media literacy skills and encouraging your appreciation of literature are two major objectives of the IB Diploma course in English language and literature. This coursebook will have given you the theoretical framework you need to be successful in your exam.

Finally, it is worth mentioning here that this coursebook has always had a bigger aim than just preparing you for your exam. While it has focused on the various parts of the IB Diploma, close reading and textual analysis, there has been a greater purpose underlying all of the activities and discussions: to equip you with better skills for the world of communication. In the future you will be faced with hundreds of examples of written texts, with hundreds of messages and images – books, poems and websites, for example, from authors, advertisers, poets, politicians and more. What you have learned in this course will help you identify their purpose, understand their target audience and appreciate the devices they use, so that you have a better understanding of the world.

Glossary

Accent describes the way in which someone pronounces a language.

Ad hominem is a type of argument that attacks a person rather than their ideas, words or actions.

Alliteration is the repetition of a consonant at the beginning of two or more words or stressed syllables.

Analogy is the process of comparing two things or ideas.

Anecdote is a story or biographical incident that usually contains a small life lesson or moral message.

Anglophone world refers to the places in the world where English is spoken.

Antagonist is the character of a dramatic story who stands in the way of the protagonists and tries to prevent them from achieving their goal.

Anti-novel is a novel that ignores all of the structural conventions of regular novels such as plot, characterisation and consistent point of view.

Apostrophe is a device that allows the poet, or the narrator of a poem, to directly addresses something inanimate or someone dead or absent.

Argumentation fallacies are common but invalid syllogisms, or in other words, poor strings of logic.

Aside is a dramatic device where a character turns and speaks directly to the audience, relating private thoughts that other characters on the stage cannot hear.

Assonance is the repetition of a vowel sound in the middle of two or more words, such as the 'ow' sound in _loud mouth_.

Atmosphere describes the mood of a story, created through both the tone of the narrator and the setting of the story.

Audience is defined as the group of listeners or readers for whom a text or message is intended.

Ballad is a form of rhyming verse, usually following a pattern of abcb, that tells a narrative and can be set to music.

Bandwagon effect is an allusion to the kind of float or wagon in a parade that carries many happy people; in its figurative sense, it describes what happens when something becomes popular quickly as people follow the example set by others.

Bias is the skewed presentation of a story from a particular ideological position.

Bildungsroman belongs to a tradition of novel writing about young individuals coming of age who learn a lifelong lesson through a transformational experience; the German word Bildung means 'development' or 'formation', and roman means 'novel'.

Bilingualism is the phenomenon of people using two or more languages regularly.

Blank verse describes poetry that has a consistent metre but no rhyming scheme.

Brand is a product's identity and the feelings and values customers associate with it.

Brand loyalty describes a consumer's allegiance to a product and their habit of buying it regularly.

Broadsheet is a newspaper that is larger than a tabloid; the format is often associated with in-depth reporting and a balanced presentation of opinions.

Catharsis refers to how people can be purged of their emotions through reading or watching works of fiction.

Censorship is the intentional removal of information that the censor, be it a government or media agent, deems harmful, sensitive or controversial.

Cliché is a literary device or structure that has been used so often that it has lost some of its artistic significance and fails to affect audiences.

Close reading refers to the practice of analysing and interpreting texts.

Code-switching can be done by speakers who speak two dialects of a language or two entirely different languages, switching from one to the other depending on whom they are talking to or what they wish to accomplish.

Colloquialisms are linguistic features that are associated with informal situations.

Consonance is the repetition of a consonant sound in the middle or at the end of words, such as the 'l' sound in _fall_ and _swell_.

Content refers to what happens in a text, in terms of the action, events, people and places.

Context refers to the circumstances that surround the writing and the reading of a text. Trying to understand why a text was written (the purpose) and whom it was written for (the audience) are good starting points for understanding context.

Context of composition refers to the factors that influence a writer when creating a text, such as time, place and personal experience.

Context of interpretation refers to the factors that can influence a reader of a text, such as time, place and personal experience.

Convergence, in linguistics, describes what happens when people come together and accommodate for each other through their use of language.

Glossary

Copycat crimes are crimes committed by people who seek to imitate the violent acts that they have seen in films and other media.

Crowdsourcing is the act of outsourcing research to a large audience, usually users of a website, in an effort to create content.

Cultural bias is not being objective, but judging something from another culture with reference to what is usual in your own culture.

Culture can have two different meanings:

1 It describes the values, goals, convictions and attitudes that people share in a society. Parts 1 and 2 of the IB English language and literature course are particularly interested in this aspect of culture.

2 It refers to the fine arts and a society's appreciation of the arts. Parts 3 and 4 of the course are particularly concerned with this, through a study of literature.

Culture jamming refers to the distorting of messages and advertisements produced by large corporations.

Deductive reasoning refers to an argument that comes to a specific conclusion by drawing on general rules.

Denotation refers to what a word stands for in its most literal sense. Connotation refers to the aura of emotional meaning that we associate with a word.

Denouement is the French word for 'unknotting', used to describe the resolution of a story's plot or complicated situation.

Dialect is a variety of language that is unique in pronunciation, grammar and vocabulary.

Diction is the choice of vocabulary that a writer uses in order to create a tone.

Divergence is the process of cultures splitting off from each other, developing their use of language separately, with less – or even no – contact.

Double entendre is a stylistic device that relies on the secondary meaning of a phrase or word.

Dystopian literature is a genre of fiction that offers a picture of an imagined world in which everything is bad and in which individuals are often oppressed by a ruling government.

Emotive language is language that both reflects the emotional tone of the writer and instigates an emotional response from the reader. It is also known as loaded language.

Enjambement in poetry is the style of continuing a sentence from one line to the next without a pause.

Epilogue is a sort of conclusion or comment at the end of a novel or play.

Euphemisms are words or phrases that are substituted for more direct words or phrases in an attempt to make things easier to accept or less embarrassing.

Existentialism is the philosophy that individuals are responsible for defining their own existence and giving their life meaning. Existential literary works often include troubled protagonists who question the meaning of life.

Exposition is the part of a story where the reader is provided with information about plot, character and setting.

Extended metaphor is a piece of figurative speech that recurs throughout a literary text, referring to a symbolic, metaphorical relationship.

Figurative language is language that is not intended to be taken literally but uses references to one thing to express ideas about something else.

Flashback is a technique in storytelling in which the reader is taken back to events before the main story. It includes background information that is interspersed throughout the story.

Fly-on-the-wall narration is an extreme variant of objective narration, where the reader sees and hears of events, as a camera would record them, with nothing removed.

Focus group, in marketing, is a group of people who are asked by a company to talk about their likes and dislikes concerning a product or ad.

Foil is a character whose qualities contrast with those of the main character, in order to expose them to the reader.

Foreshadowing is a literary device in which hints are given of events to come, so that the reader can predict (or often fear) what might happen in the story.

Frame narrator is a storyteller who is not the protagonist of a story but a peripheral character who reveals someone else's story to us.

Free indirect speech is a kind of limited third-person narration that allows the reader to hear a character's thoughts.

Free verse describes poetry that has neither rhyme nor consistent metre.

Gender bias is the tendency to favour one gender over the other, often manifested through language.

Genre describes a category of literature that can be defined by the structural and stylistic conventions that are frequently found in that category.

Global village describes how members of a social group can be spread around the world, but be interconnected through various media.

Gothic fiction is a mixture of horror and romance that came out of the Romantic movement of the 18th and 19th centuries.

Half rhyme describes lines of poetry that have words that sound similar but do not entirely rhyme.

Heroic couplet is two lines of rhyming verse, usually at the end of a sonnet, which tend to be 'closed' (there is no enjambement between the lines) and self-contained.

Hindsight wisdom describes a style of narration in which the narrator looks back, knowing more now than at the time of the events.

Historical present tense is the use of the present tense to tell a story that happened in the past.

Idiolect is a person's unique use of vocabulary, grammar and pronunciation. It both distinguishes an individual from a group and identifies an individual with a group.

Imagery is the use of descriptive language to evoke sensory experience.

Inductive reasoning refers to an argument that comes to a general conclusion by drawing on specific cases.

Instrumental motivation explains how people often learn languages in order to accomplish something.

Integrative motivation refers to learning a language in order to become an integrated member of a particular society.

Jargon is the vocabulary and manner of speech that define and reflect a particular profession that are difficult for others to understand.

Language is a system of communication that is mutually intelligible among all members of a society.

Language borrowing describes the act of importing words into one language from another culture's language.

Language currency refers to the value of a language. Many people find English valuable, both financially and intellectually, as it helps them find a better job or acquire more knowledge. It has a high language currency.

Language death occurs when the last native speakers of a language have died and no new generations speak their ancestors' language fluently.

Language planning is a term for the efforts made to prevent language death.

Limited narration offers the reader insight into the thoughts, actions and events of one character.

Lingua franca is a language spoken by people who do not share a native language.

Linguistic determinism is the concept that language determines what we are able to think.

Linguistic imperialism is the dominance of one language over others. Many people see English as a threat to other languages.

Loanwords are the words that one culture borrows and incorporates from another language.

Long tail marketing is selling a large range of products for which there is a small demand in small quantity instead of a small range of popular products in large quantity; the total number of people with various specialised interests is greater than the number of people with popular interests.

Magic realism is a style of fiction with origins in South America. It creates a very realistic setting with a few highly unrealistic elements.

Manufactured consent is a term coined by the political scientist and linguist Noam Chomsky. It describes the phenomenon that a small ruling elite can shape public opinion in their favour by controlling the media.

Marketing is the process of creating, developing, promoting and selling goods and services to customers, managing the customers' interest in and need for the product.

Media literacy is the skill of analysing various texts in relation to the media in which they are published.

Melodrama refers to works of fiction that exaggerate plot or character and appeal to the audience's emotions.

Metaphor is the use of language to make a comparison between two things or ideas by applying a word or phrase to something that does not *literally* mean that.

Metonymy describes references to things or concepts not by name but by something closely associated with them.

Metre is the rhythmic structure of a verse of poetry.

Metric foot is a group of stressed and/or unstressed syllables that form the basic unit of rhythm in a poem.

Mimesis, as used by ancient Greek philosophers, is copying the real world in literature and art.

Mood refers to the atmosphere that is created for an audience through the tone of a text.

Movement, in a literary sense, is a collection of works which seek to address similar concerns or express similar ideas, or which come out of a certain period in history.

Narrative voice refers to the manner in which a story is told, including point of view, diction and tense.

Negative ads are ads that carry an attack and are often used in political campaigns when opponents make attacks on each other, often using the ad hominem argument.

Objective narration includes storytelling that is not biased towards an ideological position or character.

Omniscient narration offers an all-knowing perspective, giving the reader access to all characters, places and events of a story.

Onomatopoeia refers to the use of words that sound like what they name or describe.

Paradox of fiction refers to the apparent contradiction of a reader empathising with a fictional character even though they know the character is not real.

Pay-per-click is an advertising model where advertisers pay the websites that host their ads only when the ad is clicked on.

Personification is a type of metaphor where human qualities are given to an animal, object or concept.

Glossary

Pidgins are improvised languages, stripped of grammar, that are invented in order for people to communicate with each other. Creoles are complete languages that have been adapted and developed from pidgins.

Premises are statements or propositions that arguments rely on to come to conclusions.

Primary sources, in the context of studying English, are stories, plays, films and so on in English, which reveal the English language being used by people but without the aim of analysing how they are using it.

Propaganda is the conscious effort to shape public opinion to conform to an ideological position.

Protagonist is the main character in a dramatic story who makes events and action move forward towards a particular goal.

Public opinion is the collection of opinions and beliefs held by the adult population of a nation.

Purpose describes the writer's intentions in writing a text, be they to entertain, enlighten, persuade, inform, evaluate, define, instruct or explain. Writers and speakers want to instigate a response from their audience.

Register is the level of formality or informality expressed through one's use of language.

Rhetoric is the art of effective communication, involving appeals to the audience and persuasive devices.

Rhythm in poetry is created through patterns of stressed and unstressed syllables.

Sapir–Whorf hypothesis suggests that people of different cultures think and behave differently because their languages dictate how they think and behave.

Sarcasm is a form of verbal irony that includes humour and criticism. Rhetorical questions are questions that do not require answering because the situation already implies an obvious answer.

Scansion is the process of finding patterns of unstressed and stressed syllables in lines of poetry.

Secondary sources are texts about texts. They comment on how people use language.

Sensationalism refers to a style of writing that is exaggerated, emotive or controversial.

Setting describes the backdrop against which the action of a story takes place. It can describe both the physical and the emotional landscape of a work.

Social novel is a type of novel that stresses the importance of real social and economic circumstances on fictional characters in an attempt to persuade the reader towards an ideological position.

Soliloquy is a dramatic device in theatre where a character talks to himself or herself through a monologue addressed directly to the audience, expressing thoughts which the audience can hear and other characters cannot.

Sonnet is a fourteen-line poem in iambic pentameter, containing three quatrains and a heroic couplet.

Speech act is a broad term that refers to any situation in which spoken language is used.

Stereotyping is the act of presenting a person or group in a certain way, through simplified and biased media.

Stream of consciousness is a style of storytelling which puts the reader in the narrator's mind, allowing the reader access to the narrator's thoughts as they occur, randomly, fragmented and unorganised.

Stylistic devices are techniques that writers and speakers employ to instigate a response from their audiences.

Subjective narration includes storytelling that is biased towards an ideological position or character.

Super crunching refers to the process of data-driven decision making.

Suspense is the feeling of tension or anxiety felt by an audience as events develop and work towards their climax in a work of fiction.

Suspension of disbelief is a phrase coined by Samuel Taylor Coleridge to explain how readers of fiction accept implausible stories in order to ascertain some truth about life.

Synecdoche is referring to an entire thing or concept by referring to one of its parts.

Tabloid in its literal sense refers to a newspaper that is smaller than a broadsheet; it is also used to refer to sensational or biased newspapers.

Text is any written work or transcribed piece of speech. For the sake of our studies, we will think of texts as clues that lead to a better understanding of one of the many Anglophone cultures, and these clues can range from e-mails to poems and from advertisements and posters to books.

Theme contains the deeper message or main idea of a text.

Tone refers to the language used by a speaker or writer to instigate an emotional effect on the listener or reader.

Unreliable narrator refers to fiction in which the reader is forced to question the storyteller's account of events.

Verbal irony is a stylistic device in which the surface meaning and underlying meaning are not the same.

Vernacular is the opposite of a lingua franca. It is language that is characteristic of a region.

Verse is a line of poetry.

Virals are commercials that travel like viruses on the Internet through social networks. Friends voluntarily send friends these ads.

Index

Index

Index

Acknowledgements
Texts

The authors and publishers acknowledge the following sources of copyright material and are grateful for the permissions granted. While every effort has been made, it has not always been possible to identify the sources of all the material used, or to trace all copyright holders. If any omissions are brought to our notice, we will be happy to include the appropriate acknowledgements on reprinting.

p. 4 from www.24x7people.com/call-centre-training; p. 7 used by permission of CosmoGIRL! Holland; p. 10 from *Pygmalion* by George Bernard Shaw, by permission of The Society of Authors on behalf of the Bernard Shaw Estate; p. 12 from "Politics and the English Language" by George Orwell, copyright © 1946 by Sonia Brownell Orwell, renewed 1974 by Sonia Orwell, reprinted from his volume "Shooting an Elephant and other Essays" by permission of Bill Hamilton as the Literary Executor of the Estate of the late Sonia Brownell Orwell and Secker & Warburg Ltd, and Houghton Mifflin Harcourt Publishing Company; p. 15 'Coffin for Head of State' by Fela Kuti, used by permission of FKO Music, Paris; p. 20 '2 mothers in an hdb playground' by Arthur Yap, used with permission; p. 22 © An Coimisinéir Teanga, 2008; p. 38 from *The Whole Art of Dining* by J. Rey, 1921 from The British Library, shelfmark 07942.d.50; p. 41 'I have a dream' speech reprinted by arrangement with The Heirs to the Estate of Martin Luther King Jr., c/o Writers House as agent for the proprietor New York, NY, copyright 1963 Dr. Martin Luther King Jr., copyright renewed 1991 Coretta Scott King; p. 46 from *The Niger and the West Sudan; the West African's Note Book* by A.J.N. Tremayne, 1910, from the British Library, shelfmark 010097.h.16; p. 49 'Half-caste', John Agard, from *Alternative Anthem: Selected Poems with Live DVD* (Bloodaxe Books, 2009); p. 52 from *Letters from Robben Island* by Ahmed Kathrada, 1999, used by permission of Michigan State University Press; p. 57 from *Martha Stewart's Homekeeping Handbook*, copyright © 2006 by Martha Stewart Living Omnimedia Inc., 11 West 42nd Street, New York NY 10036, used by permission of Clarkson Potter Publishers, an imprint of Crown Publishing Group, a division of Random House Inc.; p. 58 from a 2002 FEMA 'Preparation Makes Sense' poster by permission of the US Department of Homeland Security; p. 61 'Family's fifth generation in care of state' by Caroline Overington, The Australian, February 20, 2009; p. 62 from *Rabbit Proof Fence* by Doris Pilkington, copyright © 1996 Doris Pilkington, reprinted by permission of Miramax Books c/o Hyperion, all rights reserved; p. 63 from *Undaunted Courage* by Stephen Ambrose, copyright © 1996 Ambrose-Tubbs Inc., all rights reserved, reprinted with the permission of Simon & Schuster Inc.; p. 64 screenshot adapted from www.lewisandclarktrail.com; p. 74 'Inside Bitama's Camp' from the New Vision, October 2010, by permission; p. 75 from The Washington Post © 1972, The Washington Post, all rights reserved, used by permission and protected by the Copyright Laws of the United States, the printing, copying, redistribution, or retransmission of the Material without express permission is prohibited; p. 76 *The Sun* cover, 1987, copyright NI Syndication; p. 79 screenshot used by permission of Last.fm Limited; p. 106 from www.joinred.com; p. 121 from 'Metamorphosis' from *Metamorphosis and Other Stories* by Franz Kafka translated by Michael Hofmann (Penguin Books 2007), translation © Michael Hofmann, 2007, reproduced by permission of Penguin Books Ltd and Penguin, a division of Penguin Group (USA) Inc.; p. 124 from *Letter to his Father* by Franz Kafka, translated by Ernst Kaiser and Eithne Wilkins, copyright 1953, 1954, 1966 by Schocken Books, used by permission of Schocken Books, a division of Random House Inc.; p. 126 from Act III of *The Crucible* by Arthur Miller copyright © Arthur Miller 1952, 1953, 1954 copyright renewed © Arthur miller 1980, 1981, 1982, all rights reserved, by permission of Wylie Agency and Viking Penguin, a division of Penguin Group (USA) Inc.; p. 127 'Sitting' by H.E. Francis; p. 129 from *The Handmaid's Tale* by Margaret Atwood, published by Vintage, reprinted by permission of The Random House Group Ltd and copyright © 1985 by O.W. Toad Ltd, first cloth edition published in Canada by McClelland & Stewart 1985, trade paperback edition first published in 1999, used with permission of the author and the publisher; p. 134 Esther Hayward; p. 139 from *Fahrenheit 451* by Ray Bradbury, reprinted with the permission of Don Congdon Associates Inc., © 1953, renewed 1981 by Ray Bradbury; p. 141 from *One Day in the Life of* Ivan Denisovich by Aleksandr Isaevich Solzhenitsyn, published by Gollancz, a division of The Orion Publishing Group, London, English translation © 1992 by Farrar, Straus & Giroux, LLC and William Collins Sons & Co. Ltd, reprinted by permission; p. 145 from *The Collector* by John Fowles, copyright © John Fowles, permission from Sheil Land Associates; p. 146 from *The Stranger* by Albert Camus translated by Stuart Gilbert, copyright 1946 and renewed 1974 by Alfred A. Knopf, a division of Random House Inc., used by permission of Alfred A. Knopf, a division of Random House Inc.; p. 161 from *Enduring Love* by Ian McEwan published by Vintage, reprinted by permission of The Random House Group Ltd; p. 169 from *Untouchable* by Mulk Raj Anand, published by Penguin Books Ltd; p. 170 from 'Hills Like White Elephants' contained within *The First Forty-Nine Stories* by Ernest Hemingway, published by Jonathan Cape, reprinted with permission of the Random House Group, and from *The Complete Short Stories of Ernest Hemingway* by Ernest Hemingway, copyright © 1927 by Charles Scribner's Sons, copyright renewed © 1995 by Ernest Hemingway, all rights reserved, reprinted with the permission of Scribner, a division of Simon & Schuster Inc.; p. 172 from 'A Streetcar Named Desire' by Tennessee Williams, copyright © 1947 by The University of the South, reprinted by permission of Georges Borchardt Inc. for the Estate of Tennessee Williams, all rights reserved, and New Directions Publishing Corp.; p. 180

edgements

…he *Hitchhiker's Guide to the Galaxy (Radio Scripts)* by Douglas Adams, published by Pan Macmillan, London © Douglas Adams, 2005; p. 186 from *Disgrace* by J.M. Coetzee, published by Harvill & Secker, copyright by J.M. Coetzee 1999, all rights reserved, used with permission from David Higham Associates and the Peter Lampack Agency Inc.; p. 190–191 from *The Complete Maus* (Penguin Books, 2003) and from *Maus I: A Survivor's Tale/My Father Bleeds History* by Art Spielgelman, copyright © Art Spiegelman, 1973, 1980, 1981, 1982, 1983, 1984, 1985, 1986, 1989, 1990, 1991, reproduced by permission of Penguin Books Ltd and Pantheon Books, a division of Random House, Inc.; p. 196 the excerpt from 'i carry your heart with me (i carry it in' is reprinted from *Complete Poems 1904-1962* by E.E. Cummings, edited by George J. Firmage, by permission of W.W. Norton & Company, copyright © 1991 by the Trustees for the E.E. Cummings Trust and George J. Firmage; p. 201 'Do not go gentle into that good night' by Dylan Thomas from *The Poems*, copyright © 1952 by Dylan Thomas published by Orion, by permission of David Higham Associates and New Directions Publishing Corp.; p. 204 'Beauty' © Grace Nichols 1984, reproduced from *The Fat Black Woman's Poems* by Grace Nichols by kind permission of Virago Press, an imprint of Little, Brown Book Group; p. 205 'Metaphors' from *Crossing the Water* by Sylvia Plath, published by Faber and Faber Ltd, copyright © 1960 by Ted Hughes, reprinted by permission of HarperCollins Publishers; p. 208 excerpts from 'Father and Child' from *Selected Poems* by Gwen Harwood (Penguin Books Australia, 2001); p. 210 from *A Clockwork Orange* by Anthony Burgess, published by William Heinemann, reprinted by permission of The Random House Group Ltd, copyright © 1962, 1986, renewed 1990 by Anthony Burgess, used by permission of W.W. Norton & Company Inc.

Photographs

p. 3*l* Bettmann/Corbis; p. 3*r* Sdbphoto Shipping/Alamy; p. 6 Amit Bhargava/Corbis News/Corbis; p. 8*l* B.O'Kane/Alamy; p. 8*c* Steven May/ lamy; p. 8*r* Tony Gentile/Corbis Wire/Corbis; p. 10 AF archive/ Alamy; p. 12 © J.B. Handelsman/The New Yorker Collection/ www.cartoonbank.com; p. 13 © CSU Archv/Everett/ Rex Features; p. 14*t* The Print Collector/ Alamy; p. 14*b* Time & Life Pictures/Getty Images; p. 15 Ian Dickson/Redferns/Getty Images; p. 20 By kind permission of Jenny Yap; p. 22 Peter Titmuss/Alamy; p. 36 © Liza Donnelly/The New Yorker Collection/www.cartoonbank.com; p. 39 James Jacques Joseph Tissot (1836–1902), *In the Conservatory (The Rivals)*, c.1875–8 (oil on canvas). Private Collection/ Photo © Christie's Images/The Bridgeman Art Library; p. 41*t* © Bruce Eric Kaplan/The New Yorker Collection/www.cartoonbank.com; p. 41*b* Francis Miller/Time & Life Pictures/Getty Images; p. 46 H.R. Bowers/Bettmann/Corbis; p. 47 © Harry Bliss/The New Yorker Collection/www.cartoonbank.com; p. 50 Denis Jones/Evening Standard/ Rex Features; p. 51 Casablanca/Warner Bros/ he Kobal Collection; p. 52 Iván Franco/Corbis Wire/ Corbis; p. 54 © Henry Martin/The New Yorker Collection/www.cartoonbank.com; p. 64 Alamy; Alamy; p. 68 Wag The Dog/New Line/Tribeca/The Kobal Collection; p. 69 Dennis Van Tine/Corbis News/Corbis; p. 71 Felipe Trueba/Corbis Wire/ Corbis; p. 72 © Mike Twohy/The New Yorker Collection/www.cartoonbank.com; p. 73 Tom Tomorrow/www.thismodernworld.com; p. 75 Bettmann/Corbis; p. 78 Fin Costello/ Redferns/Getty Images; p. 82 c.U.A./Everett/ Rex Features; p. 83 © J.B. Handelsman/The New Yorker Collection/www.cartoonbank.com. p. 84 Roger And Me/Warner Bros/The Kobal Collection; p. 89 Bettmann/Corbis; pp. 90, 93*tl*, 102*l*, 102*r*, 103, 106*l*, 106*r* The Advertising Archives; p. 91 Brooks Kraft/Corbis News/Corbis; p. 93*tr* H.J.Weston (1874–1938), *We took the hill, come and help us keep it*, 1918. nla.pic-an14155917, Poster Z92, Poster drawer 193/ National Library of Australia; p. 93*bl* *It's Men We Want*, 1914–1918, creator unknown, Archives of Ontario War Poster Collection reference C 233-2-4-0-200/I0016180/The Archives of Ontario, Canada; p. 93*br* Swim Ink 2, LLC/Corbis; p. 95 Chris McGrath/ Getty Images; p. 96 © David Sipress/The New Yorker Collection/ www.cartoonbank.com; p. 99 © Barbara Smaller/The New Yorker Collection/www.cartoonbank.com; p. 101 By permission of Tata Motors; p. 104 Morris/www.CartoonStock.com; p. 107*t* Copyright © Stefano Cagnoni/ reportdigital.co.uk; p. 107*bl* Adbusters Media Foundation; p. 107*br* /R J White/TheCityDesk.net; p. 109 The Conservative Party Archive/Getty Images; p. 120 © William Haefeli/The New Yorker Collection/ www.cartoonbank.com; p. 124 Pictorial Press Ltd/Alamy; p. 125 Archiv Klaus Wagenbac/AKG London; p. 126 Bettmann/Corbis; p. 130 The Handmaid's Tale, The/Cinecom/Bioskop/Cinetudes/The Kobal Collection; p. 131 The Tempest, (2010)/Touchstone Pictures/The Kobal Collection; p. 134 i love images/Cultura/ Getty Images; p. 142 Keystone/Corbis Wire/Corbis; p. 144 Passage To India, A/Columbia/Bray, Ken/ The Kobal Collection; p. 145 Ulf Andersen/Getty Images; p. 146 Bettmann/Corbis; p. 147 The Stranger, (1967)/Lo Straniero/De Laurentiis/Master/Marianne/Casbah/The Kobal Collection; p. 160 Archives du 7e Art/DR/ Photo12 Picture Library; p. 166 © Roz Chast/The New Yorker Collection/ www.cartoonbank.com; p. 169 Friedrich Stark/Alamy; p. 170 Bettmann/Corbis; p. 172 Photo12/ Alamy; p. 175 Edgar Allan Poe, *Tales of Mystery and the Imagination*, London, 1923. Illustrated by Harry Clarke, shelf mark 256d 347 frontispiece/The Bodleian Library, University of Oxford; p. 180 TV series of *The Hitchhiker's Guide to the Galaxy*, by Douglas Adams, David Dixon as Ford Prefect, Simon Jones as Arthur Dent and Joe Melia as Mr Prosser, photo Dom Smith/Copyright © BBC Photo Library; p. 184 © Mick Stevens/The New Yorker Collection/www.cartoonbank.com; p. 186 Disgrace/Fortissimo Films/ The Kobal Collection; p. 193 By permission of Philips; p. 194*l* CafePress.co.uk; p. 194*r* Art Directors & Trip/Alamy; p. 199 Classic Image/ Alamy; p. 200 © Henry Martin/The New Yorker Collection/www.cartoonbank.com; p. 204 Stuart Clarke/Rex Features; p. 207 © J.B. Handelsman/The New Yorker Collection/www.cartoonbank